NELSON · GCSE MATHS

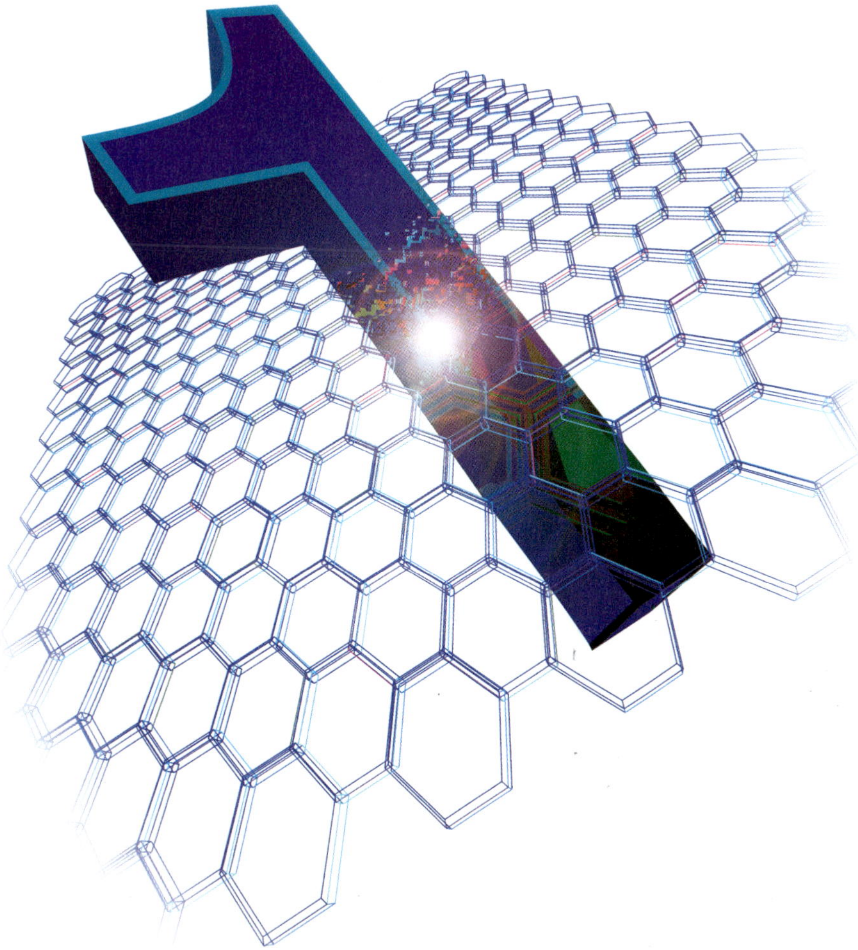

HIGHER 1

BARBARA BALL · DEREK BALL – SERIES EDITORS
CHRISTINE ATKINSON · WENDY FISHER · MARGARET POSTON
JEREMY RICHARDSON · ADRIAN SMITH

Thomas Nelson & Sons Ltd
Nelson House
Mayfield Road
Walton-on-Thames
Surrey KT12 5PL
United Kingdom

I(T)P® Thomas Nelson is an International Thomson Company
I(T)P® is used under licence

First published by Thomas Nelson & Sons Ltd 1999
ISBN 0-17-431485-X
9 8 7 6 5 4 3 2 1
03 02 01 00 99

Printed in China by L Rex Printing Co. Ltd

Acquisition: Jean Carnall
Editorial: Jenny Lawson, First Class Publishing
Production: Liz Carr
Design: Sharon Rudd
Cover design: R&B Creative Services

The authors and publishers are grateful to the following schools involved in trials of material from this series:

Worle School, Avon; Holte School, Birmingham; The Woodrush School, Birmingham; Hayle Community College, Cornwall; Ash Green School, Coventry; Stainburn School, Cumbria; The Deanes School, Essex; Cirencester Kingshill School, Glos; Pontllanfraith High School, Gwent; The Hayling School, Hants; Swakeleys School, Hillingdon; Crown Hills Community College, Leicester; Hampstead School, London; St Martin's in the Fields High School, London; Kenton School, Newcastle upon Tyne; Walbottle High School, Newcastle upon Tyne; Belfast Royal Academy, Northern Ireland; The Bluecoat School, Nottingham; Bretton Woods School, Peterborough; Eccles C of E School, Salford; Our Lady of Mount Carmel High, Salford; Ludlow C of E School, Salop; St Richard Gwyn R.C. High School, South Glam; Headlands School, Wilts.

Some of the revision questions on pages 263–276 have been reproduced from past examination papers, as cited in the text. Copyright in these questions is held by the examination boards, and the publishers would like to thank the Midland Examining Group (MEG), Northern Examinations and Assessment Board (NEAB), Northern Ireland Council for the Curriculum, Examinations and Assessment (CCEA), Southern Examining Group (SEG) and Edexcel (formerly University of London Examinations and Assessment Council, ULEAC) for permission to reproduce this material. The answers supplied to these questions are, however, the responsibility of the authors.

While every effort has been made to trace copyright holders, if any acknowlegements have been inadvertently omitted, the publishers will be pleased to make the necessary arrangements at the earliest opportunity.

CONTENTS

CHAPTER 1

Numbers and Algebra

This chapter is about:

- multiples, factors and primes
- mental methods of calculating
- decimals
- estimating and rounding
- calculating with fractions
- equivalence between fractions, decimals and percentages
- powers and indices
- trial and improvement
- standard form.

Multiples, factors and primes

Every positive whole number – except 1 – can be written as the product of prime factors. It is sensible to make the definition that 1 is *not* a prime number, because then it can be proved that every number can be written as the product of prime factors in *exactly one way* (apart from the order of factors). This is called the *Fundamental Theorem of Arithmetic*.
For prime numbers, there is only *one* number in the product.

$6 = 2 \times 3$ $\quad$ $100 = 2 \times 2 \times 5 \times 5$

$18 = 2 \times 3 \times 3$ $\quad$ $121 = 11 \times 11$

$23 = 23$ $\quad$ $1001 = 7 \times 11 \times 13$

$91 = 7 \times 13$

DISCUSSION POINT

Think of several multiples of 9. Find the sum of the digits for each of these multiples.

What do you notice? Does it always happen? Can you explain it?

This can be used to test whether a number is a multiple of 9. Which of these numbers are multiples of 9?

234 345 477 491 5235 8487

DISCUSSION POINT

What test can you find for multiples of 3?

What test can you find for multiples of 6?

How do you recognise a multiple of 5? A multiple of 25?

How do you recognise a multiple of 4? A multiple of 12?

What test can you find for multiples of 11?

EXERCISE 1

1 (a) List the prime numbers between 1 and 100.

(b) List the prime numbers between 160 and 170.

(c) One of these numbers is prime. Which one?

993 995 997 999 1001

> Index notation can be used when writing numbers as the product of prime factors.
> $72 = 2 \times 2 \times 2 \times 3 \times 3 = 2^3 \times 3^2$

2 (a) Express each of these numbers as the product of prime factors. Use index notation where appropriate.

(i) 20 (ii) 40 (iii) 60 (iv) 81 (v) 105 (vi) 238

(b) Find *all* the factors of each of these numbers.

(i) 81 (ii) 105 (iii) 238

> In Questions 2 and 3, your answers to part (a) might help you in part (b).

3 (a) Write each of these numbers as the product of prime factors.

(i) 35 (ii) 280 (iii) 231 (iv) 1386

(v) 96 (vi) 1344 (vii) 273 (viii) 105105

(b) Calculate these.

(i) $280 \div 35$ (ii) $1386 \div 231$ (iii) $1344 \div 96$ (iv) $105105 \div 273$

4 (a) List the first six multiples of 17.

(b) List six multiples of 43, starting at 860.

5 Each of these lists is part of the list of the multiples of a number. Some of the digits have been replaced by stars.

List A	List B	List C	List D
18	345	238	425
**	***	***	***
**	***	***	***
**	***	***	***
42	***	***	***
**	***	273	***
**	363	...	***
...	...	...	5**

Copy each list and complete them by replacing the stars in each list.

6 Each of these lists is part of the list of the multiples of a number.
Some of the digits have been replaced by stars.

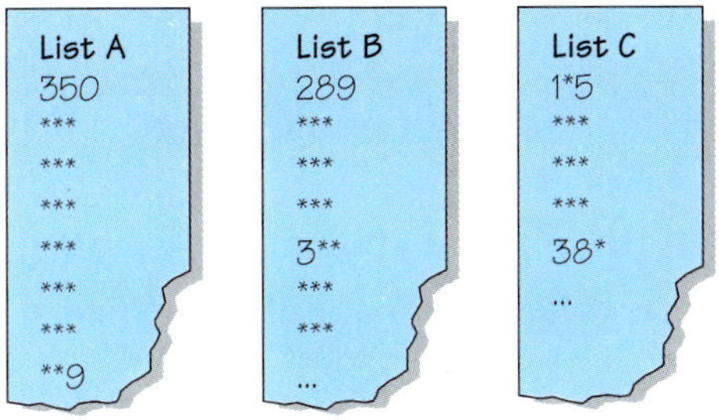

Copy each list, and complete them by replacing the stars in each list.

7 This list is part of the list of multiples of a number.

Copy the list, and complete it by replacing the stars.
There is more than one possible answer – find them all.

8 (a) Find 2^6, 2^7, 2^8, 2^9 and 2^{10}. (b) What is the last digit of 2^{157}?

9 (a) Find 5^6, 5^7, 5^8 and 5^9. (b) What are the last three digits of 5^{342}?

10 What is the last digit of

(a) 6^{89}? (b) 4^{4358}? (c) 9^{99}? (d) 3^{483}? (e) 7^{77}? (f) 8^{88}?

11 Write 6 and 16 as the product of prime factors.
Hence, find the smallest number which has both 6 and 16 as factors.

12 Answer Question 11 for these.

(a) 8 and 18 (b) 21 and 35 (c) 84 and 147
(d) 12, 18 and 30 (e) 21, 45 and 75

13 Write 24 and 80 as the product of prime factors.
Hence, find the largest number which is a factor of *both* 24 and 80.

14 Answer Question 13 for each of these.

(a) 56 and 84 (b) 147 and 343 (c) 30, 42 and 70
(d) 405, 567 and 729

15 (a) Find *all* the factors of each of these square numbers: 16, 25, 36.
(b) Square numbers always have an odd number of factors.
Explain why.

16 What numbers of factors are possible for a *cube* number?

17 (a) Write 66 as the product of prime factors.
Find *all* the factors of 66.

(b) Write 406 as the product of prime factors.
Find *all* the factors of 406.

(c) Give a reason why 66 and 406 have the same number of factors.

(d) Find a number, greater than a million, which has the same number of factors as 406.

18 (a) Write 60 as the product of prime factors.
Find *all* the factors of 60.

(b) Find a number, greater than a million, which has the same number of factors as 60.

19 Find the smallest number with exactly

(a) 7 factors (b) 8 factors

20 Find the smallest number with exactly

(a) 17 factors (b) 18 factors

COURSEWORK OPPORTUNITY

How many factors?

Questions 15 to 20 in Exercise 1 were about this.

How many factors do different types of numbers have?

- Square numbers always have an odd number of factors.
  Which square numbers have 1 factor?
  Which have 3 factors?
  Which 5? ...
- How many factors can a cube number have?
  What about a fourth power? ...
- Which numbers have a square number of factors?
- Which numbers have a prime number of factors?
- Which number less than 1000 has the most factors?
  Which number less than a million?

You can answer these questions or pose and answer your own questions about numbers of factors.

Explain your findings and justify them wherever you can.

Decimals without a calculator

DISCUSSION POINT

How would you work these out, *without* a calculator?

4×0.2	$0.4 \div 0.04$	$8 \div 0.5$
0.4×0.03	900×0.6	$0.03 \div 0.02$
$40 \div 0.8$	$0.03 \div 0.6$	0.6^2

EXERCISE 2

1 Work out these.

(a) 30×0.5 (b) 60×0.3 (c) 84×0.25 (d) 28×0.4

(e) 880×0.2 (f) 18×0.8 (g) 0.6×50 (h) 0.32×5

(i) 0.55×4 (j) 0.3×37 (k) 0.7×28 (l) 0.75×380

2 Work out these.

(a) $0.6 \div 2$ (b) $0.48 \div 4$ (c) $0.35 \div 7$ (d) $0.7 \div 4$

(e) $0.5 \div 8$ (f) $0.14 \div 40$ (g) $6 \div 0.5$ (h) $8 \div 0.25$

(i) $14 \div 0.2$ (j) $27 \div 0.3$ (k) $22 \div 0.4$ (l) $45 \div 0.6$

3 Work out these.

(a) 0.2×0.3 (b) 0.4×0.7 (c) 0.8^2 (d) 0.5×0.6

(e) 0.12×0.6 (f) 0.55×0.4 (g) 1.3×0.2 (h) 2.5×0.8

(i) 3.5×0.3 (j) 3.8×1.5 (k) 0.3^3 (l) $0.4 \times 0.6 \times 1.2$

4 Work out these.

(a) $0.6 \div 0.5$ (b) $0.3 \div 0.6$ (c) $0.4 \div 0.8$ (d) $0.7 \div 0.4$

(e) $0.35 \div 0.7$ (f) $\sqrt{0.64}$ (g) $\sqrt{0.81}$ (h) $\sqrt{1.44}$

(i) $3.6 \div 0.9$ (j) $5.6 \div 0.14$ (k) $81 \div 0.27$ (l) $14.4 \div 0.16$

5 Work out these.

(a) 0.3×0.02 (b) 0.06×0.04 (c) 0.007×0.01 (d) 0.04^2

(e) 0.006^3 (f) 14×0.004 (g) 500×0.006 (h) 144×0.004

(i) 52.4×0.02 (j) 13.5×0.0008 (k) 0.00036×450 (l) $0.03 \times 0.05 \times 0.07$

6 Work out these.

(a) $500 \div 0.05$ (b) $60 \div 0.003$ (c) $0.006 \div 0.003$

(d) $0.0012 \div 0.0048$ (e) $144 \div 0.009$ (f) $\sqrt{0.0049}$

(g) $\sqrt{0.0169}$ (h) $\sqrt{0.000289}$ (i) $1001 \div 0.013$

(j) $100.1 \div 0.0011$ (k) $1212 \div 101$ (l) $121.2 \div 0.000101$

Estimation, rounding and use of a calculator

DISCUSSION POINT

How would you estimate each of these, *without* a calculator?

$\frac{7.9 \times 6.11}{(3.9)^2}$ $\frac{8.88 + 3.43}{6.06 - 3.89}$ $\frac{438}{1.7 + 2.4}$ $\sqrt{\left(4.89 + \frac{25.87}{2.03} - \frac{57.8}{29.11}\right)}$

Use a calculator to work out each of the above calculations, correct to 3 significant figures.

EXERCISE 3

d.p. means decimal places

1 Give an approximation for each of these numbers, correct to the level of accuracy shown.

(a) 5.2621 (1 d.p.) (b) 21.455 (1 d.p.) (c) 3.452 (2 d.p.)

(d) 3.256 (2 d.p.) (e) 100.229 (2 d.p.) (f) 7.998 (1 d.p.)

s.f. means significant figures

2 Give an approximation for each of these numbers, correct to the level of accuracy shown.

(a) 0.005678 (3 s.f.) (b) 3657000 (3 s.f.) (c) 24.683 (3 s.f.)

(d) 9483000 (2 s.f.) (e) 475.62 (3 s.f.) (f) 902 (2 s.f.)

3 (a) Calculate 3000 ÷ 2999, correct to 3 d.p.

(b) Calculate 2999 ÷ 3000, correct to 3 s.f.

4 Estimate an answer for each of these, *without* using a calculator.

(a) $\frac{8.32 + 3.86}{4.11}$ (b) $\frac{12.33 + 20.65}{0.297}$ (c) $2.41 + 9.84 \times 0.627$

(d) $8.91^2 - 23.2$ (e) $7.11^2 + 50.88$ (f) $\sqrt{(4.92^2 + 3.07^2)}$

(g) $\frac{7.92^2 - 47.46}{5.59}$ (h) $(15.74 - 9.69)^2$ (i) $\frac{7.64 \times 5.11}{5.97 - 3.49}$

(j) $\frac{20.91}{15.54 - 8.58}$ (k) $\frac{11.37 - 3.89}{17.83 - 15.35}$ (l) $113.92 - 7.96^2$

(m) $\frac{3.48^2}{5.51^2 - 2.53^2}$ (n) $\left(\frac{103.6}{105.3} + \frac{14.15}{3.53}\right)^2$ (o) $\left(\frac{1}{1.97} + \frac{1}{4.04}\right)^2$

5 Use a calculator to work out each of the calculations in Question 4, correct to 3 s.f.

6 (a) *Without* using a calculator, estimate the value of $\frac{38.4 + \sqrt{2.24}}{(16.9 - 7.06)^2}$

(b) Use a calculator to obtain a more accurate value for the expression given in part (a).

(c) Why would it probably *not* be sensible to give you answer to part (b) correct to 5 s.f.?

Calculating with fractions

DISCUSSION POINT

Discuss these statements to make sure you understand them.

$\frac{12}{18} = \frac{2}{3}$ $\quad 1\frac{3}{5} = \frac{8}{5}$ $\quad \frac{1}{2} + \frac{1}{4} = \frac{3}{4}$ $\quad 1\frac{2}{3} + 2\frac{4}{5} = 4\frac{7}{15}$ $\quad \frac{4}{5} - \frac{1}{3} = \frac{7}{15}$

$\frac{12a^2b}{18b^2c} = \frac{2a^2}{3bc}$ $\quad \frac{a}{2} + \frac{a}{4} = \frac{3a}{4}$ $\quad \frac{1}{a} + \frac{2}{b} = \frac{b+2a}{ab}$ $\quad \frac{4}{a} - \frac{1}{ab} = \frac{4b-1}{ab}$

EXERCISE 4

1 Calculate these.

(a) $\frac{1}{6} + \frac{3}{16}$ (b) $\frac{7}{15} - \frac{4}{25}$ (c) $\frac{11}{12} + \frac{5}{18}$ (d) $4\frac{2}{3} + 5\frac{3}{4}$

(e) $\frac{8}{21} - \frac{3}{35}$ (f) $5\frac{1}{2} - 3\frac{1}{3}$ (g) $6\frac{1}{4} - 2\frac{2}{5}$ (h) $\frac{1}{6} + \frac{7}{12} - \frac{1}{18}$

(i) $\frac{4}{21} - \frac{7}{25} + \frac{13}{35}$ (j) $\frac{1}{3} + \frac{1}{7} + \frac{3}{5}$ (k) $\frac{2}{3} + \frac{2}{9} - \frac{1}{12}$ (l) $1\frac{1}{6} + \frac{5}{18} - \frac{7}{12}$

$\frac{2}{5} = \frac{1}{4} + \frac{1}{10} + \frac{1}{20}$
The three new fractions all have one as the numerator, and none have the same denominator as the first fraction, $\frac{2}{5}$.

2 Write these fractions as the sum of two or more fractions, which each have one as the numerator and which all have different denominators.

(a) $\frac{3}{5}$ (b) $\frac{2}{3}$ (c) $\frac{3}{7}$ (d) $\frac{4}{11}$ (e) $\frac{6}{11}$

3 Write each of these fractions in their simplest form.

(a) $\frac{44}{121}$ (b) $\frac{56}{72}$ (c) $\frac{114}{252}$ (d) $\frac{6ab}{2a}$ (e) $\frac{4b^2}{16bc}$

4 Rewrite each of these expressions as one fraction.

(a) $\frac{a}{4} + \frac{a-5}{3}$ (b) $\frac{a-5}{10} + \frac{a+5}{5}$ (c) $\frac{a-2}{2} + \frac{a+10}{9}$

(d) $\frac{a+3}{5} - \frac{a}{4}$ (e) $\frac{4(a+2)}{5} - \frac{5a}{3}$ (f) $\frac{3a-5b}{4} + \frac{2a-b}{3} + \frac{a+b}{12}$

5 Rewrite each of these expressions as one fraction.

(a) $\frac{1}{a} - \frac{1}{b}$ (b) $\frac{3}{a} + \frac{2}{b}$ (c) $\frac{4}{a} - \frac{2}{ab}$

(d) $\frac{8}{a} - 5$ (e) $\frac{a}{4} - \frac{4}{a}$ (f) $\frac{a}{b} + \frac{b}{a}$

If the denominator is added to both the numerator and denominator of one third, the fraction is doubled in size.
$\frac{1}{3} \rightarrow \frac{1+3}{3+3} = \frac{4}{6}$
$= \frac{2}{3}$

6 (a) Find a fraction which is tripled when the denominator is added to the numerator and denominator.

(b) Find a fraction which is quadrupled when the denominator is added to the numerator and denominator.

(c) Find a fraction which is multiplied by 8 when the denominator is added to the numerator and denominator.

(d) Find a fraction which is multiplied by n when the denominator is added to the numerator and denominator.

DISCUSSION POINT

Discuss these statements to make sure that you understand them.

$\frac{1}{2} \times \frac{1}{4} = \frac{1}{8}$ $\quad \frac{2}{3} \times \frac{4}{5} = \frac{8}{15}$ $\quad \frac{3}{4} \times \frac{4}{5} = \frac{3}{5}$ $\quad \frac{2}{3} \times \frac{3}{8} = \frac{1}{4}$

$1\frac{1}{5} \times \frac{1}{2} = \frac{3}{5}$ $\quad \frac{1}{3} \div \frac{1}{2} = \frac{2}{3}$ $\quad \frac{2}{5} \div \frac{3}{4} = \frac{8}{15}$ $\quad \frac{2}{3} \div \frac{5}{6} = \frac{4}{5}$

$\frac{ab}{c} \times \frac{bc}{d} = \frac{ab^2}{d}$ $\quad 1\frac{1}{3} \times 2\frac{1}{4} = 3$ $\quad \frac{a}{3} \times \frac{b}{4} = \frac{ab}{12}$ $\quad \frac{a}{b} \times \frac{b}{c} = \frac{a}{c}$

$\frac{3}{4} \div \frac{3}{5} = 1\frac{1}{4}$ $\quad 1\frac{1}{2} \div 1\frac{1}{3} = 1\frac{1}{8}$ $\quad \frac{a}{b} \div \frac{c}{d} = \frac{ad}{bc}$ $\quad \frac{b}{d} \div \frac{b}{a} = \frac{a}{d}$

$\frac{ab^2}{c} \div \frac{bc^3}{d} = \frac{abd}{c^4}$

EXERCISE 5

1 Calculate these.

(a) $\frac{1}{2} \times \frac{1}{3}$ (b) $\frac{3}{4} \times \frac{4}{7}$ (c) $\frac{4}{5} \times \frac{5}{8}$ (d) $1\frac{1}{2} \times \frac{2}{3}$

(e) $2\frac{2}{3} \times 1\frac{3}{4}$ (f) $\frac{1}{4} \div \frac{1}{2}$ (g) $\frac{1}{5} \div \frac{1}{3}$ (h) $\frac{2}{3} \div \frac{3}{4}$

(i) $\frac{3}{4} \div \frac{5}{8}$ (j) $4\frac{1}{2} \div 3\frac{1}{3}$ (k) $6\frac{1}{4} \div 1\frac{7}{8}$ (l) $\frac{1}{6} \times \frac{3}{8} \times \frac{4}{5}$

(m) $\frac{3}{4} \times \frac{8}{9} \div \frac{2}{3}$ (n) $1\frac{1}{2} \times 1\frac{1}{4} \div 1\frac{1}{3}$

2 Simplify these.

(a) $\frac{a}{4} \times \frac{b}{2}$ (b) $\frac{b}{c} \times \frac{c}{a}$ (c) $\frac{a}{c} \times \frac{c}{a}$ (d) $\frac{a}{4} \div \frac{a}{2}$

(e) $\frac{b}{3} \div \frac{b}{6}$ (f) $\frac{ab}{c} \div \frac{bc}{d}$ (g) $\frac{a}{b} \times \frac{b}{c} \div \frac{c}{d}$

3 Calculate these.

(a) $\frac{1}{2} \div \frac{3}{7}$ (b) $\frac{2}{27} \div \frac{1}{9}$ (c) $\frac{1}{2} \times \frac{3}{7} \div \frac{1}{5}$ (d) $\frac{3}{5} \div \frac{1}{3}$

(e) $\frac{4}{35} \div \frac{2}{7}$ (f) $\frac{4}{21} \div \frac{1}{9}$

4 For the fractions $\frac{1}{3}$ and $\frac{1}{4}$, $\frac{1}{3} - \frac{1}{4} = \frac{1}{3} \times \frac{1}{4}$

(a) Find other pairs of fractions, A and B, for which $A - B = AB$.

(b) State a generalisation and prove it.

Making and justifying a generalisation

5 (a) Calculate $(1\frac{1}{2})^2$, $(2\frac{1}{2})^2$ and $(3\frac{1}{2})^2$.

(b) Find a general pattern.

(c) Find 6.5^2, 85^2 and 125^2.

Equivalence of decimals, fractions and percentages

DISCUSSION POINT

These are all number lines from 0 to 1.

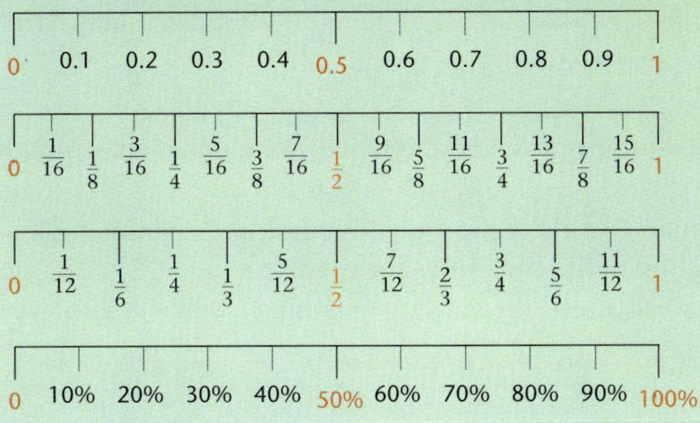

These scales are marked in decimals, fractions (sixteenths and twelfths) and percentages.

Check that you can convert a number from one scale to the equivalent on another scale.

Fraction		Decimal		Percentage
$\frac{5}{8}$	=	0.625	=	62.5%
	=	0.25	=	
	=		=	75%
$\frac{11}{16}$	=		=	
	=		=	$33\frac{1}{3}$ %

EXERCISE 6

1 Convert these to decimals.

(a) $\frac{7}{8}$ (b) 5% (c) 30% (d) $12\frac{1}{2}$% (e) $\frac{4}{5}$ (f) $\frac{7}{12}$

2 Convert these to percentages.

(a) $\frac{1}{2}$ (b) $\frac{3}{5}$ (c) 0.2 (d) 0.07 (e) 0.42 (f) 1.1

3 Convert these to fractions, in their simplest form.

(a) 12% (b) 0.55 (c) 1.4 (d) $37\frac{1}{2}$% (e) $6\frac{2}{3}$% (f) 0.4375

4 What *fraction* of an hour is

(a) 10 mins? (b) 48 mins? (c) $7\frac{1}{2}$ mins? (d) 40 mins?
(e) 70 mins? (f) 160 mins?

5 Write all your answers to Question 4 as *decimals* of an hour.

6 Convert each of these fractions to percentages. Then, rewrite the fractions in a list in order of size, starting with the smallest.

$\frac{5}{11}$ $\frac{6}{11}$ $\frac{7}{11}$ $\frac{5}{12}$ $\frac{1}{2}$ $\frac{7}{12}$ $\frac{6}{13}$ $\frac{7}{13}$ $\frac{8}{13}$ $\frac{3}{7}$ $\frac{4}{7}$ $\frac{7}{15}$ $\frac{8}{15}$ $\frac{9}{15}$ $\frac{7}{16}$ $\frac{9}{16}$

Some of the answers in Exercise 6 were decimals which never ended.

$\frac{1}{3} = 0.333...$ $\frac{5}{12} = 0.41666...$ $\frac{4}{11} = 0.363636...$

Decimals like these are called **recurring decimals** because the pattern of repeating digits continues for ever.

0.333... can be written $0.\dot{3}$ 0.833... can be written $0.8\dot{3}$

0.363636... can be written $0.\dot{3}\dot{6}$

Exercise 7

For Question 1, use the dot notation shown above.

1 Find the recurring decimals for these fractions.

(a) $\frac{2}{3}$ (b) $\frac{1}{6}$ (c) $\frac{4}{9}$ (d) $\frac{7}{11}$ (e) $\frac{7}{12}$

2 Find the decimal form of each of these fractions.

$\frac{1}{2}$ $-\frac{2}{5}$ $\frac{3}{4}$ $\frac{5}{16}$ $-\frac{3}{16}$

Place each fraction on a number line starting at –1 and finishing at 1 with 0.2 divisions

3 Repeat Question 2 for these fractions and number lines

(a) Start the number line at 1 and finish at 3 with 0.2 divisions and show these fractions.

$2\frac{1}{3}$ $2\frac{3}{5}$ $1\frac{4}{7}$ $2\frac{2}{9}$

(b) Start the number line at 7 and finish at 9 with 0.2 divisions and show these fractions.

$\frac{21}{3}$ $\frac{25}{3}$ $\frac{26}{3}$ $7\frac{1}{3}$ $8\frac{2}{3}$

(c) Start the number line at 0.2 and finish at 0.3 with 0.01 divisions and show these fractions.

$\frac{2}{9}$ $\frac{3}{11}$ $\frac{4}{15}$ $\frac{5}{17}$ $\frac{7}{27}$

4 (a) Express these fractions as recurring decimals.

$\frac{1}{7}$ $\frac{2}{7}$ $\frac{3}{7}$ $\frac{4}{7}$ $\frac{5}{7}$ $\frac{6}{7}$

(b) Explain how you can use this diagram to summarise your answers to part (a).

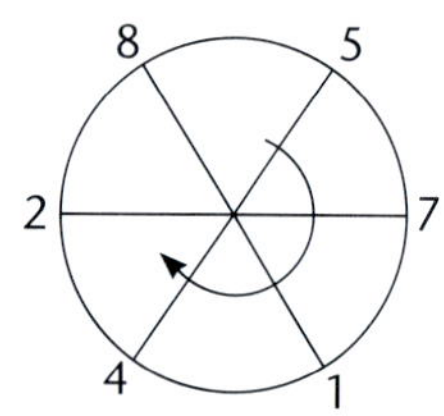

5 (a) Write the fractions $\frac{1}{13}, \frac{2}{13}, \frac{3}{13}, \ldots, \frac{12}{13}$ as recurring decimals.

(b) Summarise your results using diagrams similar to the diagram in Question 4(b).

Powers and indices

DISCUSSION POINT

Make sure you understand why $a^5 \times a^7 = a^{12}$.

What is $b^3 \times b^4$? What is $c^6 \times c^{11}$? What is $a^m \times a^n$? What is $3a^4 \times 4a^3$?

Make sure you understand why $b^5 \div b^2 = b^3$

What is $c^6 \div c^4$? What is $a^{11} \div a^5$? What is $12c^7 \div 3c^5$?

What is $b^m \div b^n$? What is $b^6 \div b^6$? What is $b^5 \div b^9$?

What meaning can be given to these expressions? a^{-3}, b^0, 4^{-2}, 13^0, 5^{-3}

EXERCISE 8

1 Evaluate each of these.

(a) 2^5 (b) 3^4 (c) 13^2 (d) 5^3 (e) 10^4 (f) $2^6 \times 5^6$

2 Simplify these expressions.

(a) $3a^2 \times 2a^2$ (b) $3b^4 \times 4b^5$ (c) $6b^2 \times 5b^9$ (d) $7c^6 \times 8c$

(e) $2a^3 \times 3a^4 \times 4a^5$ (f) $15c^8 \times 8$

3 Simplify these expressions.

(a) $3a^2 \times 4b^2$ (b) $7b^3 \times 8c^5$ (c) $4a^2b^3 \times 6a^3b^4$ (d) $5a^5 \times 6ab^5$

(e) $3a^2b \times 4b^2c$ (f) $3a^3b \times 4b^3c \times 5c^3a$

4 Evaluate these.

(a) $4^9 \div 4^7$ (b) $3^8 \div 3^5$ (c) $2^{22} \div 2^{12}$ (d) $2^4 \div 4^2$

(e) $4^4 \div 2^2$ (f) $3^6 \div 6^3$

5 Write each of these as whole numbers or decimals.

(a) 2^{-3} (b) 5^{-2} (c) 17^0 (d) 10^{-3}

(e) $(0.5)^4$ (f) $(0.2)^3$ (g) 2×5^{-3} (h) $5^2 \times 2^{-5}$

6 Simplify these expressions.

(a) $a^6 \div a^3$ (b) $b^{11} \div b^9$ (c) $c^6 \div c^6$ (d) $8a^5 \div 4a^4$

(e) $36b^3 \div 9b^3$ (f) $100c^{10} \div 4c$

7 Simplify these expressions.

(a) $a^2b^3 \div b^2$ (b) $a^4 \div a^7$ (c) $b^7 \div b^{13}$ (d) $b^5c^2 \div b^2c^5$

(e) $a^3b^4 \div a^4b^3$ (f) $6a^2bc \div 12ab^2c^3$

The **reciprocal** of n is $\frac{1}{n}$

8 Find the reciprocal of each of these numbers.

(a) 4 (b) 5 (c) 8 (d) $\frac{1}{3}$

(e) 0.5 (f) 0.4 (g) $1\frac{3}{7}$ (h) $(0.25)^3$

Write each of your answers either as a whole number or as a decimal.

9 What is the reciprocal of the reciprocal of 17.3?

10 Find the reciprocal of these expressions.

(a) a^2 (b) b^5 (c) c^{-2} (d) $\frac{a}{b}$

(e) $\frac{b^2}{c^3}$ (f) $\frac{ab^2}{c^3}$ (g) $(a^2b)^{-2}$ (h) $(a^2b^3c^{-5})^{-1}$

Trial and improvement

Spreadsheet

EXERCISE 9

1 Follow this method to find an approximation for the number $\sqrt{3}$.

Choose a number which is approximately equal to $\sqrt{3}$.

Calculate a second number by dividing 3 by your first number.

Find the mean of the first and second numbers, and then divide 3 by this mean. The result of this is your next approximation to $\sqrt{3}$.

Continue the process by finding the mean of the second and third numbers, then the third and fourth, and so on. Stop when your last two approximations are equal, when corrected to 4 d.p.

2 Find an approximation for $\sqrt{5}$ correct to 4 d.p., using the method in Question 1.

Use trial and error for Questions 3 onwards.

3 The area of a rectangle is 23 cm² and the length is 1 cm longer than the width. Find values for the length and the width, correct to 3 s.f.

4 The area of a rectangle is 54 cm² and the length is 2 cm longer than the width. Find values for the length and the width, correct to 3 s.f.

5 The area of a triangle is 12 cm² and the length of the base is 3 cm longer than the height. Find values for the base and the height, correct to 3 s.f.

6 The volume of a cuboid is 38cm^3 and the height is 1cm less than the width, which is 1 cm less than the length. Find values for the length, width and the height, correct to 3 s.f.

7 The circumference of a circle is 1 m longer than its diameter. Find the radius and the area of the circle, correct to 2 s.f.

Standard form

A number written in **standard form** is of the form $a \times 10^n$ where $1 \le a < 10$ and n is an integer.

These numbers have been converted to standard form.

$23000 = 2.3 \times 10^4$ $\quad$ $6347800 = 6.3478 \times 10^6$

$0.00002345 = 2.345 \times 10^{-5}$ $\quad$ $0.1382 = 1.382 \times 10^{-1}$

Exercise 10

1 Copy and complete this table.

Number	Standard form
2734	2.734×10^3
423.5	
	6.84×10^5
23000000	
0.00456	
	3.2×10^{-2}
Five million	
A millionth	
	9.9×10^{-1}
10	

2 Write each of these numbers in standard form.

(a) 682.45

(b) 0.0068245

(c) 68.2

(d) 68245

(e) 0.056789 to 2 s.f.

(f) 0.000000000781256 to 3 s.f.

Exercise 11

1 Calculate these.

(a) $(3.4 \times 10^4) \times (5.7 \times 10^6)$

(b) $(3.4 \times 10^7) \div (1.5 \times 10^3)$

(c) $(6.28 \times 10^{-4}) \times (1.32 \times 10^9)$

(d) $(6.53 \times 10^{-4}) \times (9.403 \times 10^{-5})$

(e) $(3.67 \times 10^4) \div (8.241 \times 10^{13})$

(f) $(6.02 \times 10^{-11}) \times (2.789 \times 10^5)$

(g) $(2.6 \times 10^{-3}) \div (1.3 \times 10^{11})$

(h) $(5.6 \times 10^{-4}) \div (3.46 \times 10^{-19})$

(i) $(7.52 \times 10^7) + (4.6 \times 10^4)$

(j) $(7.52 \times 10^7) - (4.6 \times 10^4)$

(k) $(7.4 \times 10^{-3}) \div (8.32 \times 10^{-12})$

(l) $(4.65 \times 10^5) \div (8.421 \times 10^{-2})$

2 This table shows the average distance of each planet, measured as a fraction of the Earth's distance from the Sun.

The average distance of the Earth from the Sun is 1.495979×10^8 km.

Find the *actual* distances of the planets from the Sun, in standard form.

Planet	Average distance from Sun
Mercury	0.387
Venus	0.723
Earth	1.000
Mars	1.524
Jupiter	5.203
Saturn	9.540
Uranus	19.18
Neptune	30.07
Pluto	39.44

3 The speed of light is 300000 km per second.
Using the data in Question 3, calculate how long it takes light from the Sun to reach

(**a**) Earth

(**b**) Mars

MeV means million electron volts.
1MeV ≅ 1.8×10^{-27}g

4 (**a**) The mass-equivalent of the sub-atomic particle muon is 106MeV.
Find the mass of a muon in grams, in standard form.

(**b**) The mass-equivalent of a lambda is 1116MeV.
Find the mass of a lambda in grams, in standard form.

(**c**) The mass-equivalent of a positive kaon is 8.89×10^{-25}g.
Find its mass in MeV.

1 dalton = 10^{-27}kg

5 (**a**) An atom of oxygen has a mass of 15.9994 dalton.
Find the mass of an atom of oxygen in kilograms in standard form and correct to 2 s.f.

(**b**) Find the mass in kilograms, correct to 2 s.f., of an atom of calcium which is given as 40.08 dalton.

6 Calculate the values of $a + b$, $a + c$, $a + d$, $b + c$, $b + d$ and $c + d$, where
$a = 3.4 \times 10^{17}$ $b = 2.3 \times 10^5$ $c = 6.8 \times 10^6$ $d = 7.83 \times 10^8$
Comment on your answers.

7 When the positive numbers e and f are expressed in standard form, $e = x \times 10^4$ and $f = y \times 10^5$.

(**a**) If $e + f = t \times 10^p$, in standard form, what are the possible values of p?

(**b**) If $f - e = u \times 10^q$, in standard form, what are the possible values of q?

(**c**) If $ef = v \times 10^r$, in standard form, what are the possible values of r?

(**d**) If $e \div f = w \times 10^s$, in standard form, what are the possible values of s?

CHAPTER SUMMARY

Prime factors are factors which are prime numbers. All positive whole numbers greater than 1 can be written as the product of prime factors in *exactly one way* (apart from the order of factors).

$30 = 2 \times 3 \times 5$ $\qquad$ $48 = 2^4 \times 3$

Estimation

Making an estimate of the answer to a calculation is a way of checking that your answer is correct.

	Roughly	Using a calculator
4.15×9.89	$4 \times 10 = 40$	41.0 to 3 s.f.
$\frac{4.96^2 + 3.11^2}{16.89}$	$\frac{25 + 9}{17} = 2$	2.03 to 3 s.f.

Calculating with decimals and fractions

You need to be able to calculate answers, *without* the help of a calculator.

Powers and indices

$a^m \times a^n = a^{m+n}$	$3a^4 \times 4a^5 = 12a^9$
$a^m \div a^n = a^{m-n}$	$15b^7 \div 5b^2 = 3b^5$
$a^0 = 1$	$37^0 = 1$
$a^{-m} = \frac{1}{a^m}$	$(0.25)^{-1} = \frac{1}{0.25} = 4$

The **reciprocal** of n is $\frac{1}{n}$.

Number	Reciprocal
3	$\frac{1}{3}$
$\frac{2}{5}$	2.5
$\frac{a}{b}$	$\frac{b}{a}$

Standard form

$8.3 \times 10^5 = 830000$ $\qquad$ $4.72 \times 10^{-4} = 0.000472$

CHAPTER 2

GEOMETRICAL PATTERNS

This chapter is about:

- quadrilaterals
- polygons
- symmetry
- translation, reflection, rotation and enlargement.

Fitting shapes together

The word *tessellation* comes from Latin, *tesselare*: to cover with a mosaic.

The simplest mosaics or tessellations which use mathematical shapes, have been known for over 2000 years.

Equilateral triangles

Squares

EXERCISE 1

Do not use a protractor for this exercise. All the questions can be answered by using the fact that angles round a point add to 360°.

1 Here is a tessellation of a shape. The shape has all its angles and all its sides equal.

(**a**) What is the size of one of the equal angles?

(**b**) What is the name of the shape? Make sure your name is as specific as possible.

2 What exactly is a *regular* pentagon?

3 Each of these designs is made using just one shape.

A

B

C

D

E
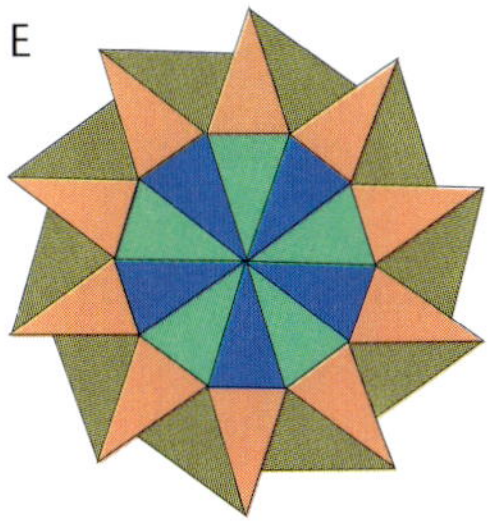
F

For each design, find all the angles in the shape.

4 Each of these designs is made using two different shapes. In each design, one of the shapes is either a square or an equilateral triangle or a regular hexagon.

A
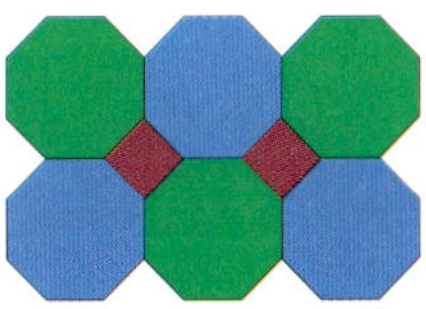
B
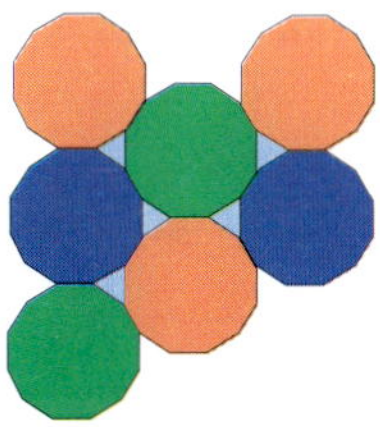
C

D
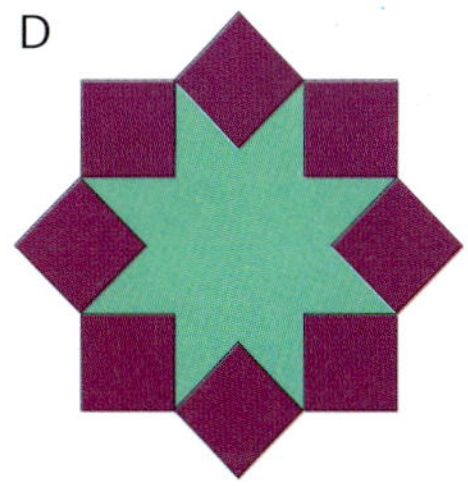

For each design, find all the angles in each of the two shapes.

Quadrilaterals and their properties

▶ Resource Sheet D: *Special quadrilaterals*

EXERCISE 2

1 A rectangle has two lines of symmetry and rotational symmetry of order 2.

This diagram shows the lines of symmetry of a rectangle.

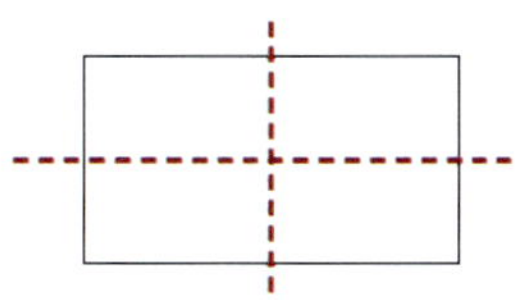

Describe the symmetry of each of these shapes as clearly as you can.

(a) Square **(b)** Rhombus **(c)** Parallelogram
(d) Kite **(e)** Trapezium **(f)** Isosceles trapezium

2 Here is a rectangle and its diagonals.

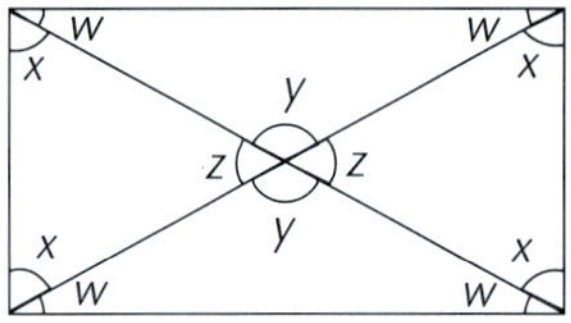

Letters have been used to show which angles are equal.

> *It may be helpful to draw the diagonals on a copy of Resource Sheet D: Special quadrilaterals.*

Draw sketches of these shapes and their diagonals, using letters to show which angles are equal.

(a) Square **(b)** Rhombus **(c)** Parallelogram

(d) Kite **(e)** Trapezium **(f)** Isosceles trapezium

3 The diagonals of a square are always the same length. They always cross each other at right angles, and they always cross at their mid-points. Copy and complete this table about the diagonals of various quadrilaterals.

	Diagonals always		
	same length	**cross at right angles**	**cross at mid-points**
Square	YES	YES	YES
Rectangle			
Rhombus			
Parallelogram			
Kite			
Trapezium			
Isosceles trapezium			

4 Find x and y for each of these shapes.

A

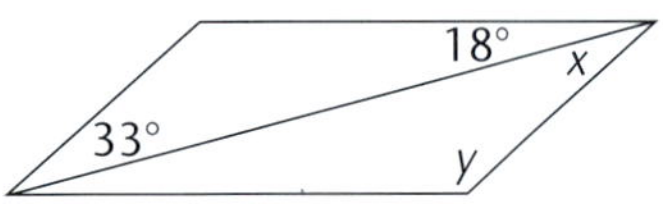

Parallelogram

B

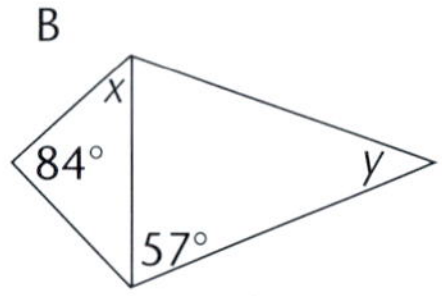

Kite

C

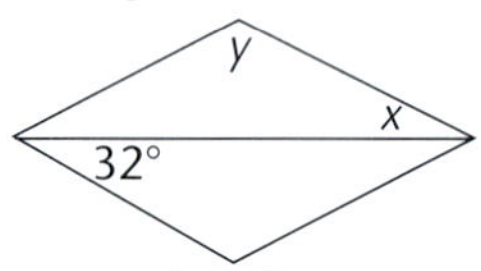

Rhombus

D

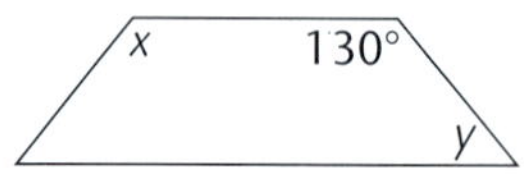

Isosceles trapezium

5 Find the size of the two unmarked angles in this kite.

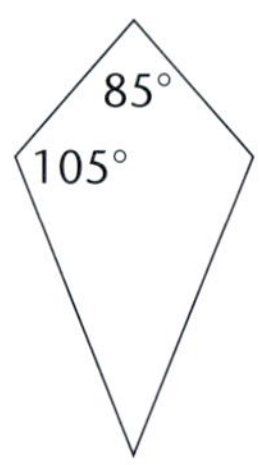

6 ABCD is a rectangle. $\angle BCA = 65°$.

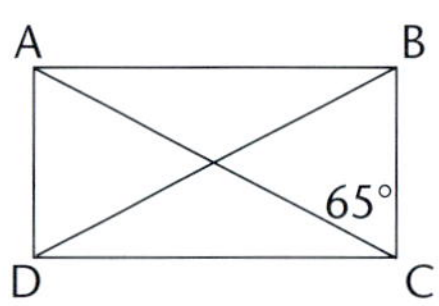

Draw a rough sketch of the diagram and fill in the sizes of the other angles.

7 PQRS is a rhombus. ∠QPR = 30°.

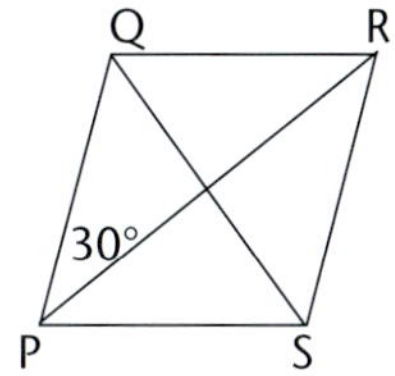

Draw a rough sketch of the diagram and fill in the sizes of the other angles.

8 ABCD is a rhombus. ∠BAC = 37°.
Draw a sketch and find the four angles of the rhombus.

9 ABCD is a parallelogram. Find x, y and z.

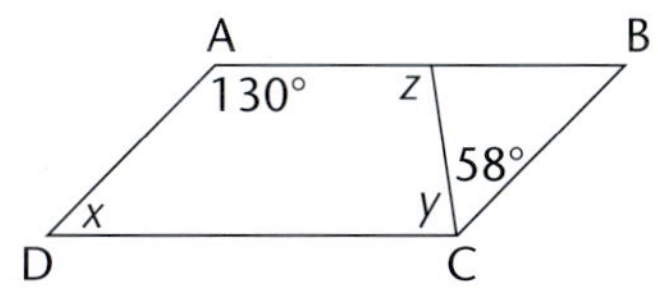

10 ABCD is an isosceles trapezium. ∠BAD is three times the size of ∠ADC.

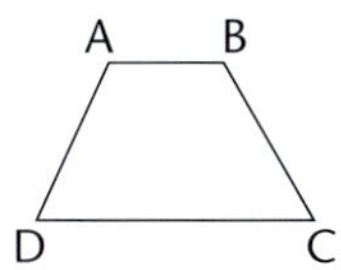

Find the angles of the trapezium.

11 Which of these shapes are possible?

A: A kite with its diagonals the same length

B: A trapezium with one right angle

C: A trapezium with two right angles

D: A kite with one right angle

E: A kite with two right angles

F: A rhombus which can be dissected into two equilateral triangles

G: A rectangle whose diagonals divide it into two equilateral and two isosceles triangles

H: A rectangle whose diagonals divide it into four acute-angled triangles

I: A parallelogram whose diagonals divide it into two isosceles and two scalene triangles

Where something is possible, draw a sketch to show how.
Where something is *not* possible, explain why.

Regular polygons

The Ancient Greeks knew much about polygons (flat shapes with straight edges) and polyhedra (3D shapes with polygonal faces). We know this from the 'Collections' of the fourth-century AD Greek writer, Pappus.

One of his comments refers to how well bees organise their honeycomb into a hexagonal mosaic. All the angles and all the sides are identical, i.e. the hexagons are **regular**. No space is wasted.

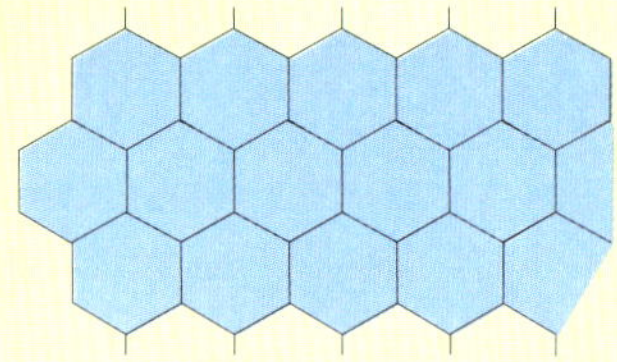

The tessellation of regular hexagons shows that each angle of the hexagon is 120°.

Another way of finding the angle of a regular hexagon is to divide it into equilateral triangles.

Regular hexagon

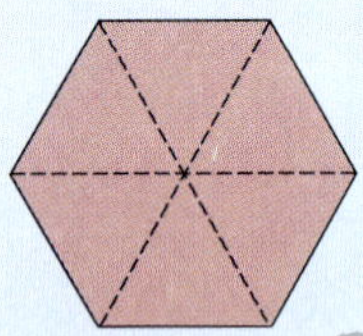

EXERCISE 3

Regular pentagon

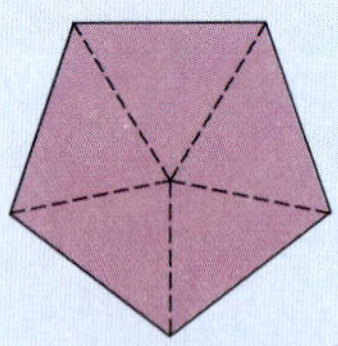

1 Prove that each angle of a regular pentagon is 108°.

2 Find the size of each angle of these regular polygons.

(**a**) Octagon (8 sides) (**b**) Nonagon (9 sides) (**c**) Decagon (10 sides)
(**d**) Dodecagon (12 sides) (**e**) Heptagon (7 sides)

Making and justifying generalisations

3 (**a**) Find and prove a formula for each angle of a regular polygon with n sides.

(**b**) Check that your formula gives the correct answer when $n = 3$, $n = 4$ and $n = 5$.

4 (**a**) When two regular pentagons are placed edge to edge how large is the angle u of the gap?

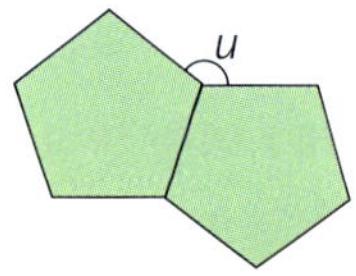

Why will a third pentagon fit in this gap?
How large is the remaining gap?

(**b**) When two regular octagons are placed edge to edge how large is the angle v of the gap?

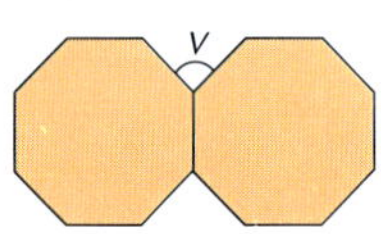

What regular shape would fill this gap?

Making and justifying generalisations

5 Explain why there are only *three* regular tessellations.

In a **regular tessellation**, the tile used is a regular polygon and all the tiles are identical.

DISCUSSION POINT

Here are two *semi*-regular tessellations.

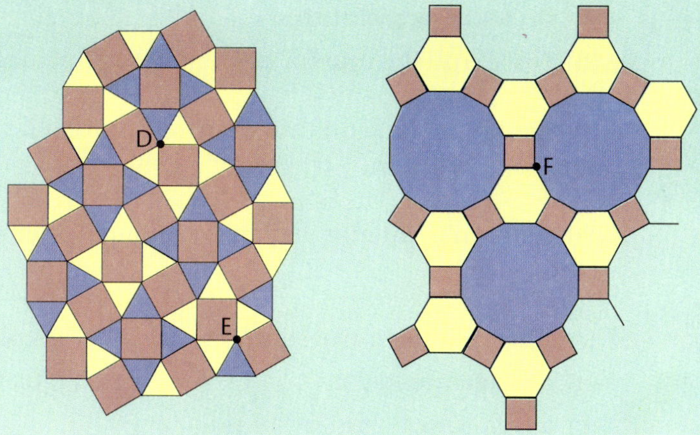

Explain why the shapes fit precisely at D, E and F.
What do you think a *semi*-regular tessellation is?

The sum of the angles of a polygon

An interior angle of a polygon is an angle at the vertex of the polygon and inside it.
An **exterior** angle of a polygon is an angle formed outside the polygon at a vertex when one of the sides is extended.

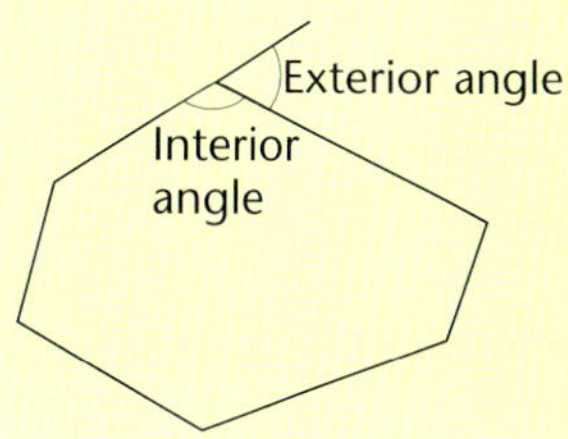

DISCUSSION POINT

Can any quadrilateral be cut into two triangles?

If you know that the sum of the angles of any triangle is 180°, what can you deduce about the sum of the interior angles of any quadrilateral?

EXERCISE 4

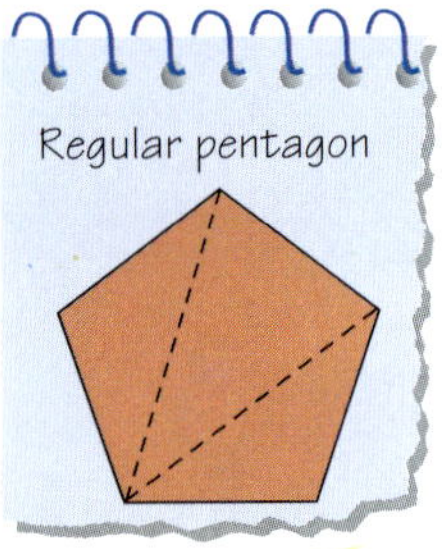

Making and justifying generalisations

1 (a) 'Any pentagon can be split into three triangles
Do you agree with this?

(b) Prove that the interior angle sum for a pentagon is 540°.

2 By dividing a hexagon into triangles, prove a result for the interior angle sum for a hexagon.

3 Prove that the interior angle sum for a polygon with n sides is $(180n - 360)°$.

4 Use the formula in Question 3 to find the size of each angle of

(a) a regular pentagon (b) a regular hexagon

(c) a regular polygon with n sides

5 Show that the formula you obtained in Question 4 part (c) is the same as the formula obtained in Question 3 part (a) in Exercise 3.

6 One of the shapes used in each of these three designs is a hexagon, but *not* a regular one. The other shapes are squares or equilateral triangles.

A

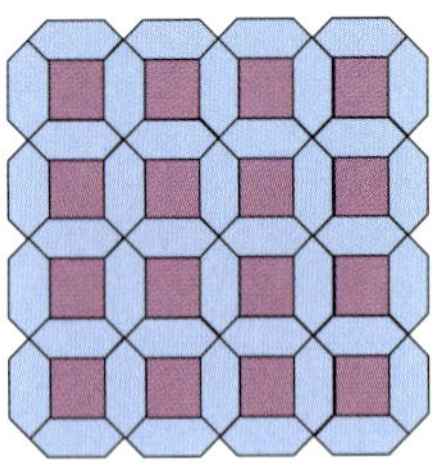

B

C

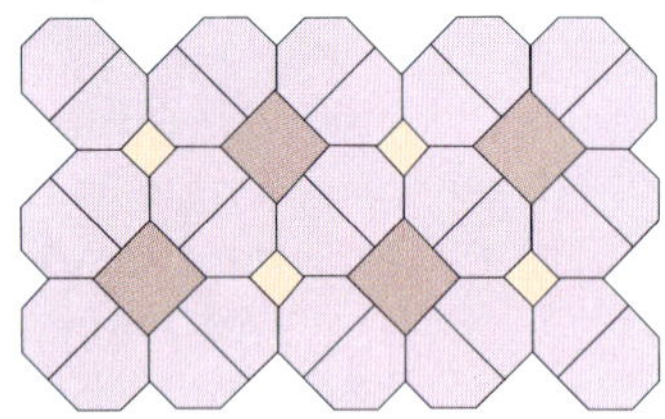

(a) Find the size of all the angles of the hexagon in each design.

(b) Find the sum of the interior angles of each hexagon.

(c) Check that your answers to part (b) agree with your answer to Question 2.

7 Here is another way of finding the size of an interior angle in a regular pentagon. Imagine a very large regular pentagon and walking round it.

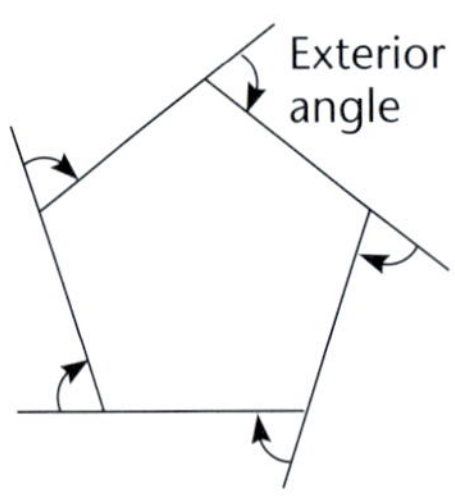

At every vertex, you turn through the *same* amount, the *exterior* angle.
By the time you return to your start, you will have turned through 360°.

(a) There are five vertices. Deduce the size of each exterior angle.

(b) Deduce the size of an interior angle of a regular pentagon.

8 Use the method of Question 7 to deduce the size of each exterior and interior angle of

(**a**) a regular hexagon

(**b**) an equilateral triangle

(**c**) a regular octagon

Making and justifying generalisations

9 Use the method of Question 7 to deduce the size of each exterior and interior angle of a regular polygon with n sides.

10 The method of Question 7 can also be used to find the sum of the angles of non-regular polygons.
Use the method to find the sum of the exterior and interior angles of a non-regular pentagon.

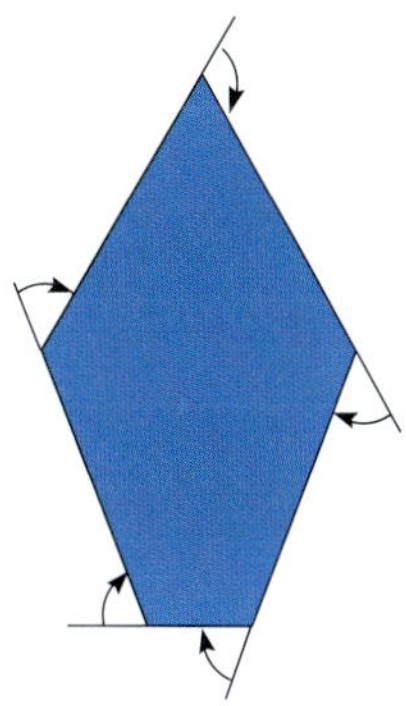

11 Look at this quadrilateral.

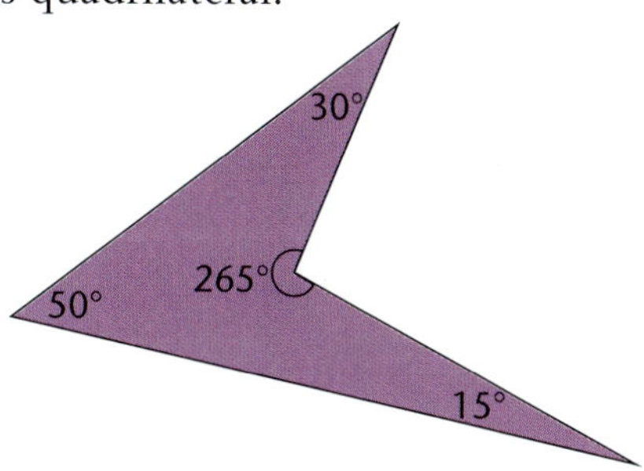

(**a**) What is the sum of the exterior angles of this quadrilateral?
Is there a way of making the sum of the exterior angles 360°?

(**b**) How does this explain why the sum of the interior angles of this quadrilateral is 360°?

Making and justifying generalisations

12 Use the method of Question 7 to find the sum of the exterior and interior angles of any polygon with n sides.

Symmetry

EXERCISE 5

1 Look at these coloured designs.

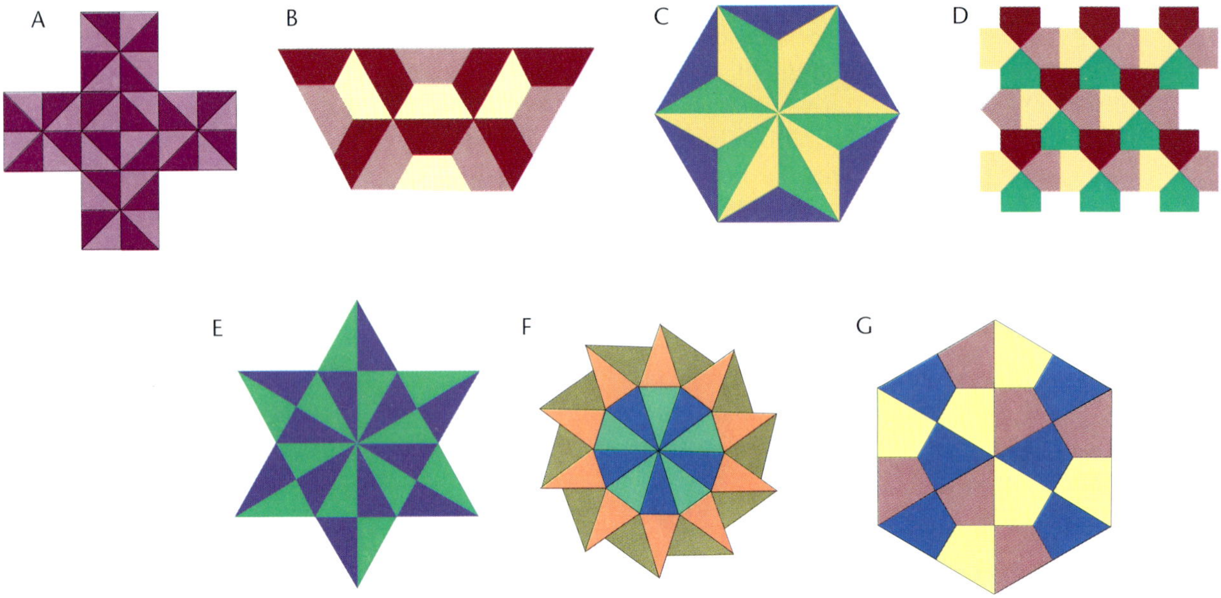

(a) (i) Which of these designs have line symmetry?

(ii) Which of them have line symmetry, if colour is ignored?

(b) (i) Which of these designs have rotational symmetry?
State the order of symmetry.

(ii) Which of them have rotational symmetry if colour is ignored?
State the order of symmetry.

2 Draw a sketch of each of the these triangles (*if* it is possible) marking the lines of symmetry.

A: A triangle with no lines of symmetry

B: A triangle with one line of symmetry

C: A triangle with two lines of symmetry

D: A triangle with three lines of symmetry

E: A triangle with more than three lines of symmetry

3 Draw a sketch of each of these quadrilaterals (*if* it is possible) marking the lines of symmetry.

A: A quadrilateral with no symmetry

B: A quadrilateral with line symmetry but no rotational symmetry

C: A quadrilateral with rotational symmetry of order 2 and line symmetry

D: A quadrilateral with rotational symmetry of order 2 and no line symmetry

E: A quadrilateral with rotational symmetry of order 3

F: A quadrilateral with rotational symmetry of order 4 and line symmetry

G: A quadrilateral with rotational symmetry of order 4 and no line symmetry

4 Sketch, *if* possible, a hexagon with

(**a**) rotational symmetry of order 3 and line symmetry

(**b**) rotational symmetry of order 3 and no line symmetry

(**c**) no rotational symmetry and three lines of symmetry

5 Sketch, *if* possible, an octagon with

(**a**) rotational symmetry of order 2 and line symmetry

(**b**) rotational symmetry of order 4 and line symmetry

(**c**) rotational symmetry of order 4 and no line symmetry

(**d**) no rotational symmetry and four lines of symmetry

6 (**a**) Can a polygon have rotational symmetry of order 4 and just two lines of symmetry?

(**b**) Can a polygon have more than one line of symmetry and no rotational symmetry?

COURSEWORK OPPORTUNITY

Symmetry of polygons

Explore the symmetry properties of polygon with different numbers of sides.

- What is the symmetry of a regular polygon with n sides?
- Is it possible to find a hexagon with two lines of symmetry?
  What other numbers of lines of symmetry can a hexagon have?
  What about rotational symmetry, with or without line symmetry?
- What symmetries are possible for different octagons?
  Pentagons? Polygons with n sides?

You can present your results systematically. Justify some of your results.

▶ Resource Sheet E: *Symmetries of tessellations*

DISCUSSION POINT

Imagine this honeycomb pattern extending forever.

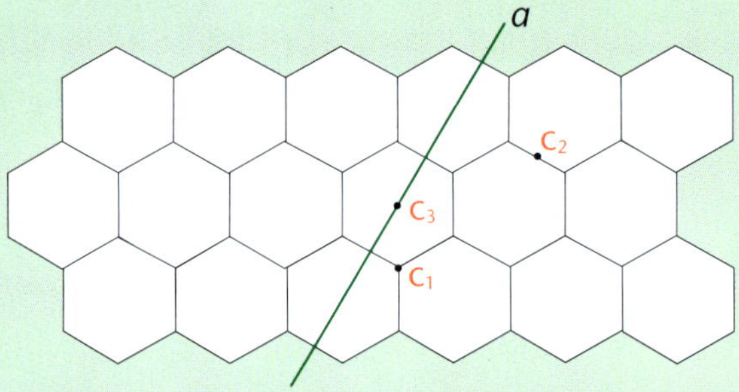

Line *a* is a line of symmetry for the *whole* pattern.

The point C_1 is a centre of symmetry for the *whole* pattern, of order 3, because the pattern lies exactly on top of itself three times during a full turn.

- C_2 is a centre of symmetry. Of what order?
- C_3 is a centre of symmetry. Of what order?
- How many *lines* of symmetry for the whole pattern pass through C_1?
  What are the angles between the lines of symmetry through C_1?
- Answer the same questions for C_2 and C_3.

▶ Resource Sheet E: *Symmetries of tessellations*

EXERCISE 6

1 Look at this pattern. Imagine it extending forever.

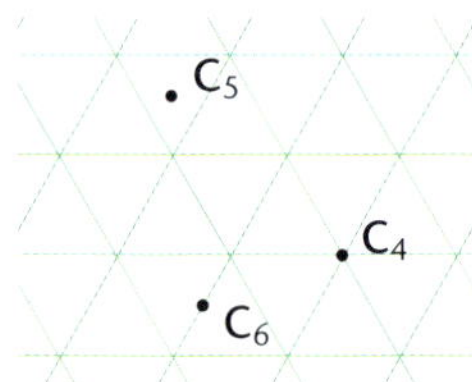

(**a**) How many lines of symmetry go through C_4?
What are the angles between them?
What is the order of rotational symmetry about C_4?
What relationship is there between order and angle?

(**b**) Answer part (a) for C_5 and C_6.

(**c**) Where do all the centres of order 3 lie?

2 Look at this pattern. Imagine it extending forever.

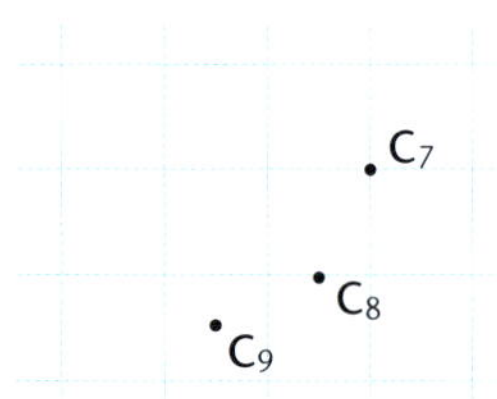

(**a**) How many lines of symmetry go through C_7?
What are the angles between them and what is the order of rotational symmetry about C_7?
What relationship is there between order and angle?

(**b**) Answer part (a) for C_8 and C_9.

(**c**) On this pattern, where do all the centres of order 2 lie?

3 Look at this tessellation.
Imagine it extending forever.

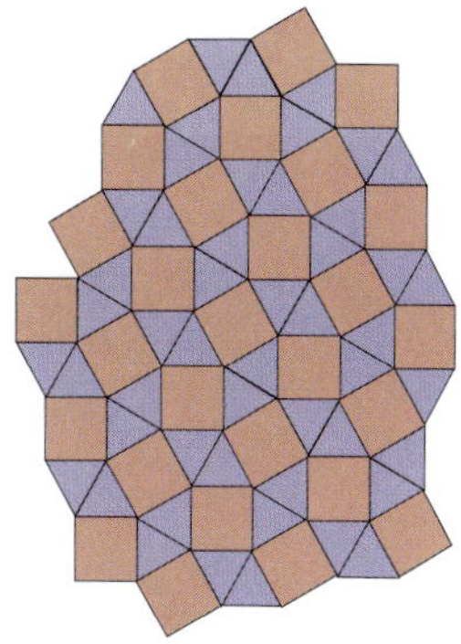

(**a**) On a copy of Resource Sheet E: *Symmetries of tessellations*, draw in two lines of symmetry for this tessellation that are at 90° to each other. Mark the point where they cross as X.

(**b**) Find out whether X is a centre of rotational symmetry.

4 This solid cube is being put into a close-fitting cubical box with face A on top.

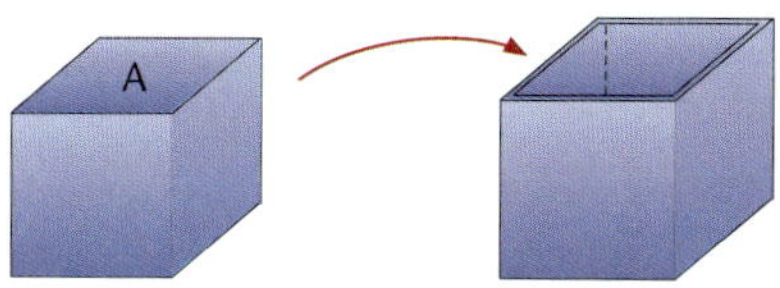

(**a**) Why are there four ways in which this can be done?

(**b**) In how many different ways could the cube be put in, altogether, if face A could go anywhere?

5 If you start with a cube and saw off each corner forming identical equilateral faces, you make a new solid.

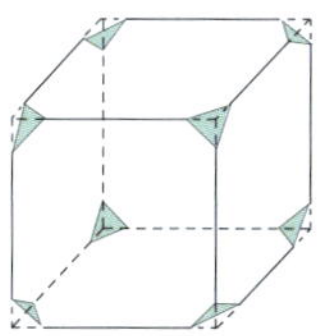

(**a**) Why does it have the same symmetry as the cube?

(**b**) How do you make the cuts so that

(**i**) the other faces are regular octagons?

(**ii**) the other faces are squares?

(**iii**) all the faces of the solid are equilateral triangles?

(**c**) Sketch the shape formed by making the cuts in part (b)(iii).
What is the shape called?

Translations, reflections, rotations and enlargements

DISCUSSION POINT

The red triangle is transformed to the blue triangle by a **translation** of $\begin{pmatrix}3\\-4\end{pmatrix}$. $\begin{pmatrix}3\\-4\end{pmatrix}$ is called the **vector** of the translation.

- What translation is needed to transform the red triangle to the yellow triangle?
- What translation is needed to transform the yellow triangle to the blue triangle?

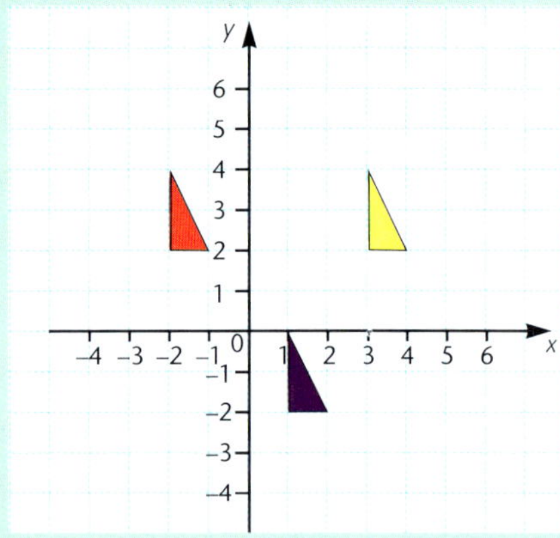

- If triangle ABC is transformed by a **reflection** in the line $x = 1$, where is the image?
- If triangle ABC is transformed by a **rotation** 90° anticlockwise about (1, 1), where is the image?
- What if the **centre of rotation** is the origin?

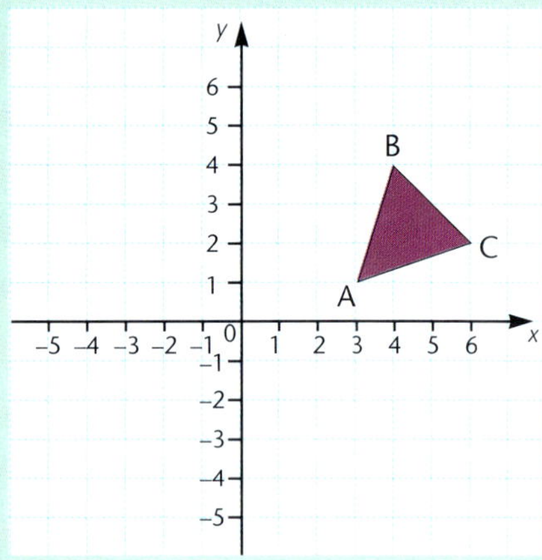

- What transformation is needed to transform the red quadrilateral to the blue quadrilateral?
- What transformation is needed to transform the blue quadrilateral to the yellow quadrilateral?

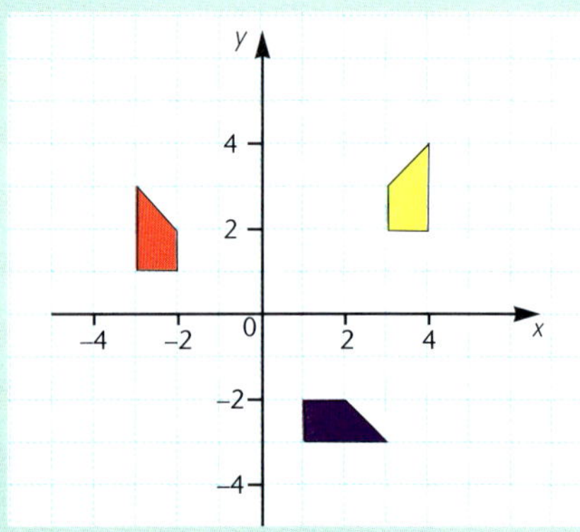

> Resource Sheet A: *Isometric dot*
> Tracing paper

EXERCISE 7

1 In this diagram, the blue parallelogram is surrounded by eight parallelograms which are congruent to it.

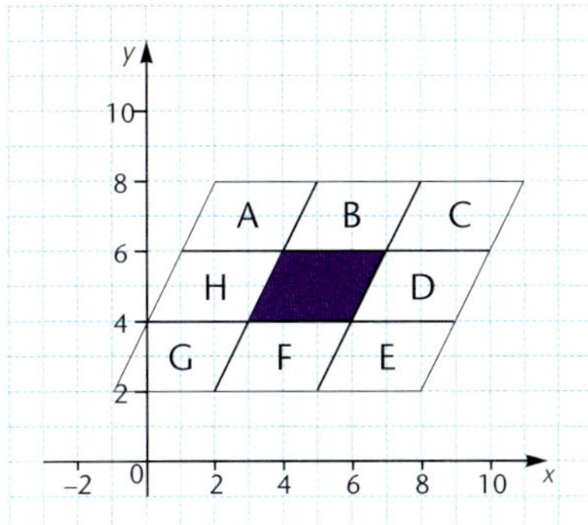

Give the vectors of the eight translations, each of which transforms the blue parallelogram into one of the others.

2 The blue triangle can be translated in many different ways to another triangle on the grid.

What translation is needed if the resulting triangle forms

(**a**) a square with the red triangle?

(**b**) a parallelogram with the red triangle?

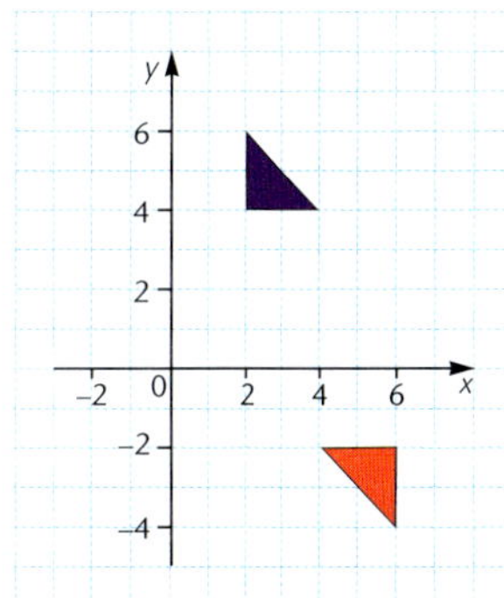

3 The translation $\begin{pmatrix}-3\\2\end{pmatrix}$ transforms Shape A to Shape B. What translation transforms Shape B to Shape A?

4 (**a**) Copy these axes and quadrilateral A on to squared paper.

(**b**) Reflect A in the *x*-axis. Label the image B.

(**c**) Reflect A in the *y*-axis. Label the image C.

(**d**) Reflect A in the line $y = x$. Label the image D.

(**e**) Reflect A in the line $y = -x$. Label the image E.

(**f**) Reflect A in the line $x = 3$. Label the image F.

(**g**) Reflect A in the line $y = -1$. Label the image G.

(**h**) What translation transforms F to C?

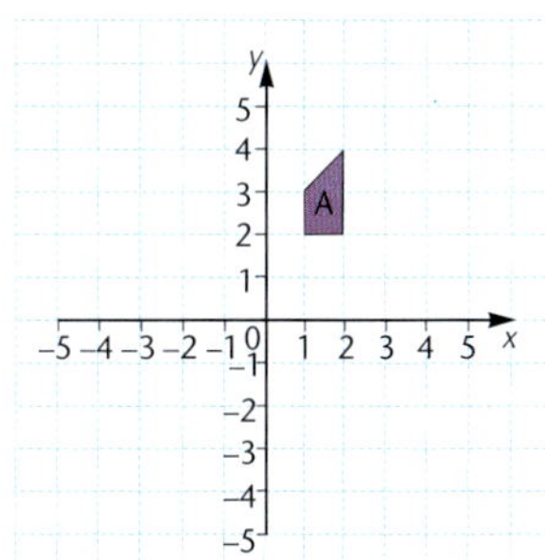

5 (a) Copy these axes and the triangle labelled P on to squared paper.

(b) (i) What sort of triangle is triangle P?
Is triangle P symmetrical?
If so, describe its symmetry.

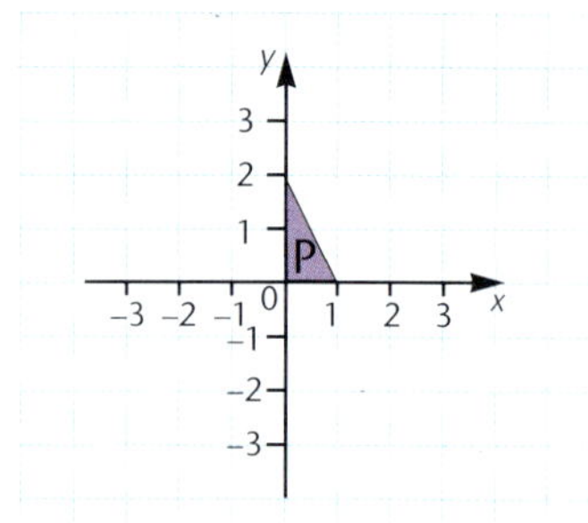

(ii) Reflect triangle P in the x-axis.
Label the image Q.

(c) (i) What shape is produced by triangles P and Q together?
Is this shape symmetrical?
If so, describe its symmetry.

(ii) Reflect triangle Q in the y-axis. Label the image R.

(d) (i) What shape is produced by triangles P, Q and R together?
Is this shape symmetrical? If so, describe its symmetry.

(ii) Reflect triangle R in the x-axis. Label the image S.

(e) What shape is produced by triangles P, Q, R and S together?
Is this shape symmetrical? If so, describe its symmetry.

6 (a) Copy lines p and q and triangle J on to isometric paper.

(b) (i) What kind of triangle is triangle J?
Is triangle J symmetrical?
If so, describe its symmetry.

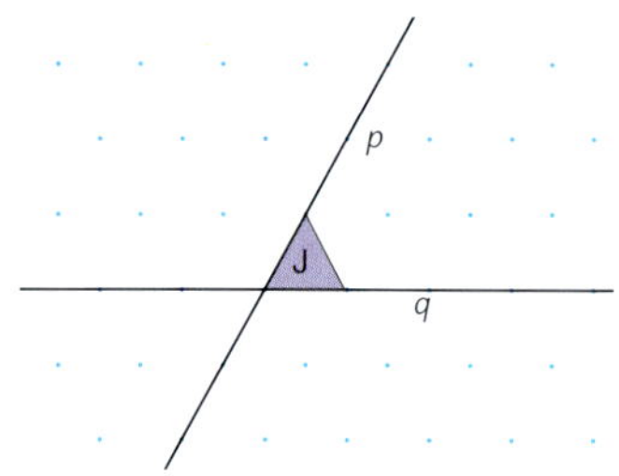

(ii) Reflect triangle J in line p.
Label the image K.

(c) (i) What shape is produced by triangles J and K together?
Is this shape symmetrical? If so, describe its symmetry.

(ii) Reflect triangle K in line q. Label the image L.

(d) (i) Is the shape made from triangles J, K and L symmetrical?
If so, describe its symmetry.

(ii) Reflect triangle L in line p. Label the image M.

(e) (i) Is the shape made from triangles J, K , L and M symmetrical?
If so, describe its symmetry.

(ii) Reflect triangle M in line q. Label the image N.

(f) (i) Is the shape made from triangles J, K, L, M and N symmetrical?
If so, describe its symmetry.

(ii) Reflect triangle N in line p. Label the image O.

(g) Is the shape made from triangles J, K, L, M, N and O symmetrical?
If so, describe its symmetry.

7 In each of these diagrams, the shape Q is the image obtained from shape P by rotation. Copy each diagram, mark the centre of rotation and state the angle of rotation.

A

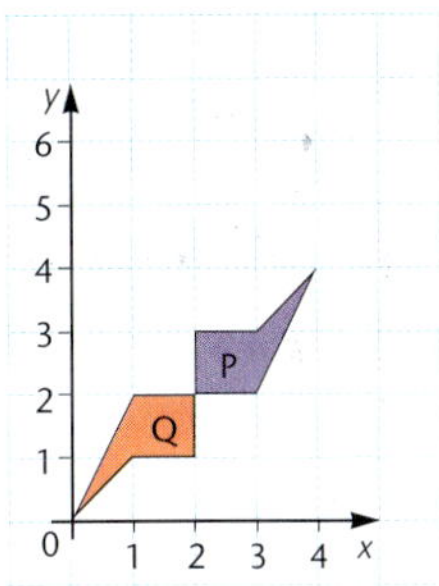

B

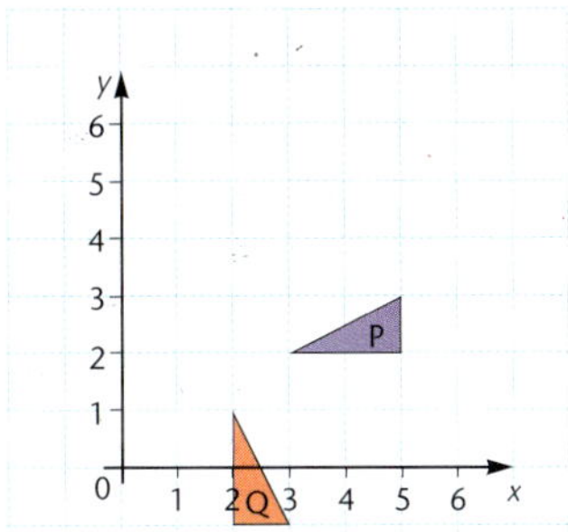

C

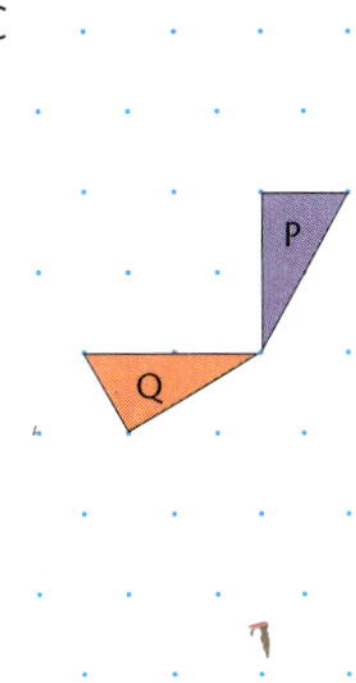

D

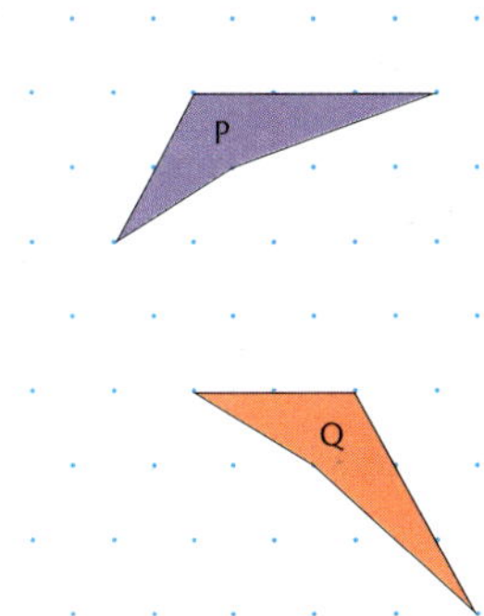

8 On graph paper, using axes with x from –7 to 7 and y from –5 to 5, draw the triangle ABC, where A is (3, 1), B is (4, 4) and C is (6, 2).

(**a**) Reflect triangle ABC in the mirror line $x = y$, labelling the image A′B′C′.

(**b**) Rotate ABC through 180° about the origin, labelling the image A*B*C*.

9 Use the same triangle ABC as in Question 8.

(**a**) Reflect ABC in $y = 2$, labelling the image A′B′C′.

(**b**) Rotate ABC 90° clockwise about (2, 1), labelling the image A*B*C*.

10 Use the same triangle ABC as in Question 8.

(**a**) Reflect ABC in the x-axis, labelling the image A′B′C′

(**b**) Reflect the first image A′B′C′ in the y-axis, labelling this A″B″C″.

(**c**) What *single* transformation maps ABC directly on to A″B″C″?

11 (**a**) Copy this diagram.

Reflect shape S in line m to get S′ and then reflect S′ in line n to get S″.

(**b**) What *single* transformation maps S on to S″ directly?

(**c**) How is the transformation found in part (b) connected to the angle between the two mirror lines?

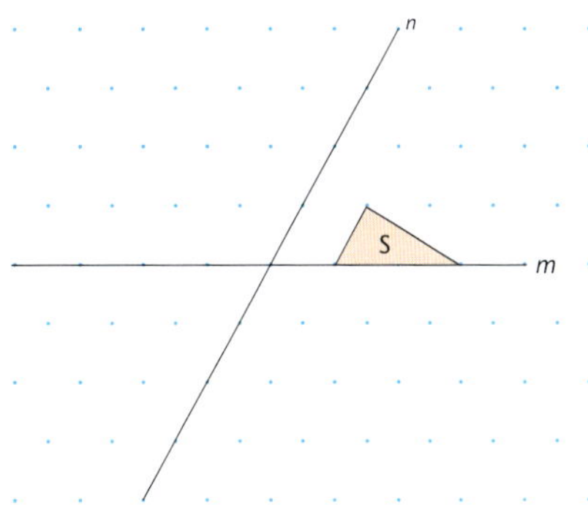

Making and justifying generalisations

12 (a) Reflect the points A (5, –1), B (8, –1), C (8, 5) and D (5, 2) in $y = x$ to produce the points A′, B′, C′ and D′. Write down the coordinates of A′, B′, C′ and D′.

(b) (i) Use your answers to part (a) to predict the image of (p, q) after reflection in $y = x$.

(ii) Justify your predicted result.

(c) Now reflect A′, B′, C′ and D′ in the x-axis to get A″, B″, C″ and D″. Write down the coordinates of A″, B″, C″ and D″.

(d) What single transformation maps ABCD on to A″B″C″D″?

(e) (i) Use your answers to part (c) to predict the image of (p, q) after this single transformation.

(ii) Justify your predicted result.

Enlargement

Enlargement requires a centre of enlargement and a scale factor.
In both of these diagrams, the red shape is the image of the blue shape.

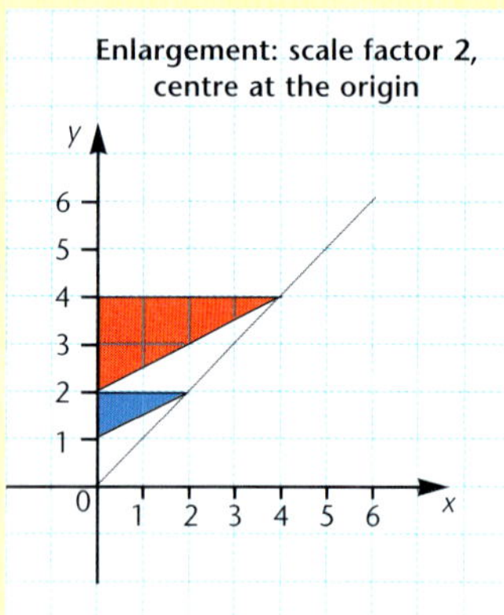

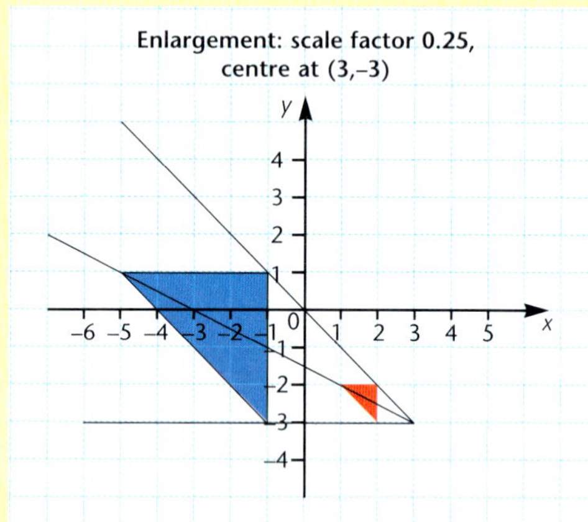

DISCUSSION POINT

In each of these pictures, the red shape is the image of the blue shape after enlargement.

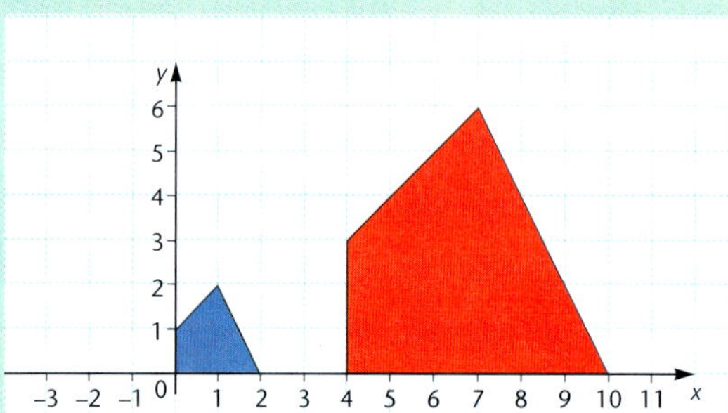

Where is the centre of enlargement and what is the scale factor?

▶ Resource Sheet A: *Isometric dot*

EXERCISE 8

1 The red shape is the image of the blue shape, after enlargement.

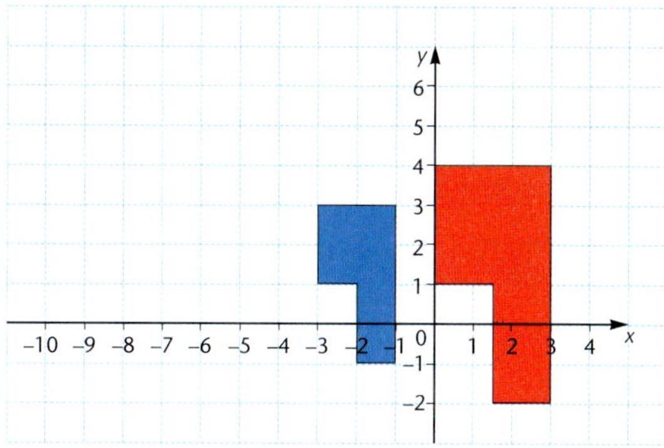

Where is the centre of enlargement and what is the scale factor?

2 (**a**) Copy these axes and the quadrilateral labelled A on to squared paper.

(**b**) Enlarge A with scale factor 2 and with the origin as centre.
Label the image B.

(**c**) Enlarge A with scale factor 3 and with the point (2, 3) as centre.
Label the image C.

(**d**) Enlarge A with scale factor 0.5 and with the point (3, 0) as centre.
Label the image D.

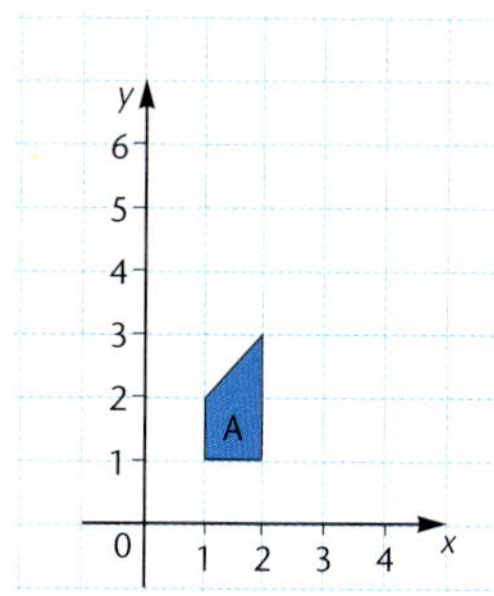

3 (**a**) Copy the shape labelled W and points A, B and C on to isometric paper.

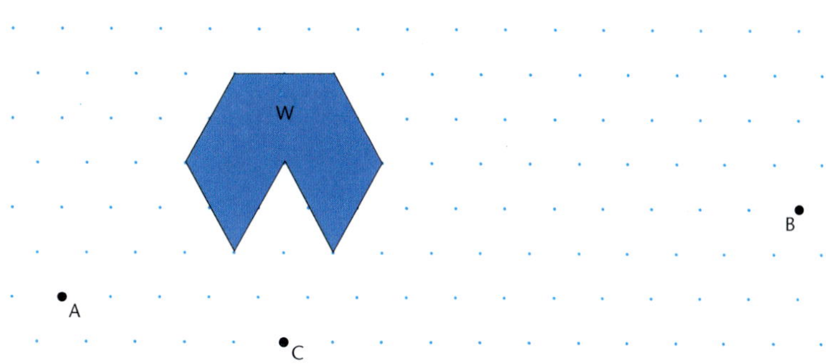

(**b**) Enlarge W with scale factor 2 about point A. Label the image X.

(**c**) Enlarge X with scale factor 1.5 about point B. Label the image Y.

(**d**) Enlarge Y with scale factor $\frac{2}{3}$ about point C. Label the image Z.

(**e**) Why are X and Z the same size?

4 In each of these diagrams, the shape Q is the image of shape P after an enlargement. Copy each diagram, mark the centre of enlargement and state the scale factor.

A

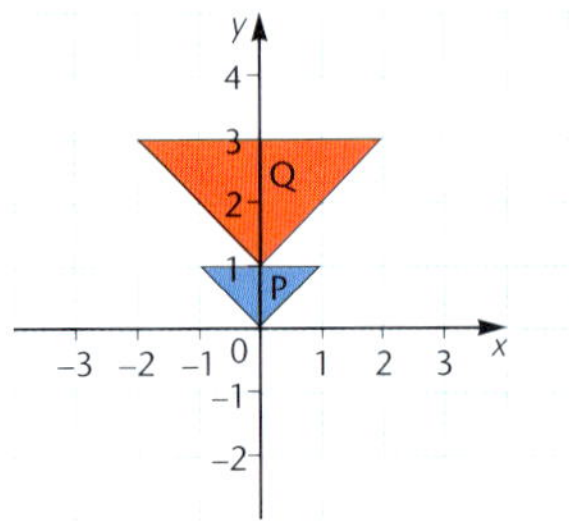

B

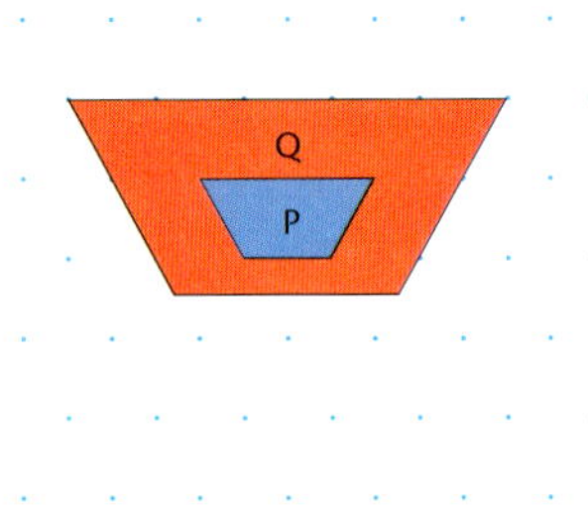

C

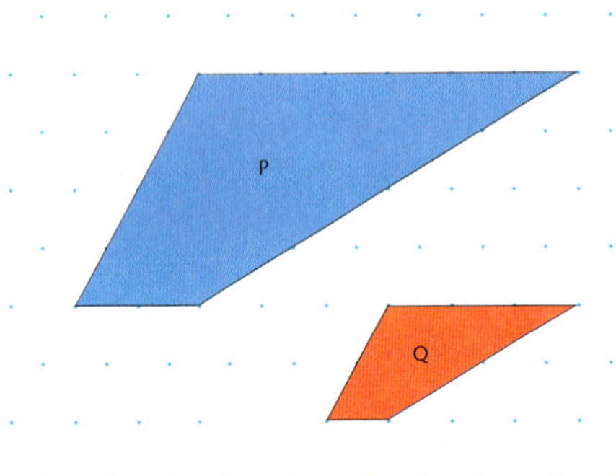

D

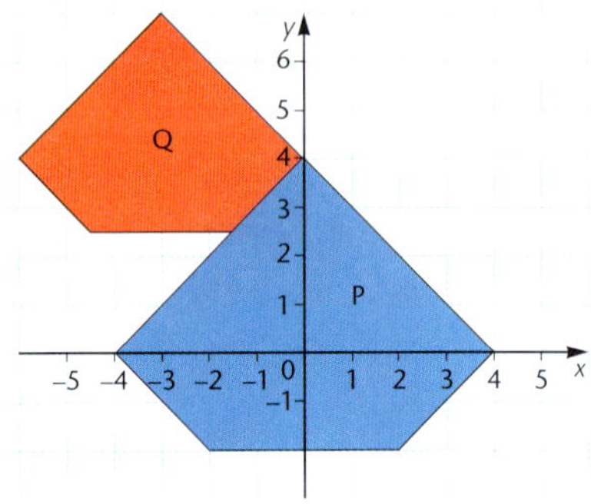

Resource Sheet A: *Isometric dot*

EXERCISE 9

1 Copy this design on to squared paper.

(a) The red triangle can be transformed into the blue triangle by a reflection.
Draw the line of reflection and label it *a*.

(b) The red triangle can be transformed into the yellow triangle by a rotation.
Mark the centre of rotation and label it B.
What is the angle of rotation?

(c) The green square can be transformed into the whole square by an enlargement.
Mark the centre of enlargement and label it C.
What is the scale factor?

2 Copy this design on to isometric paper.

(**a**) The red trapezium can be transformed into the blue trapezium by a reflection.
Draw the line of reflection and label it *a*.

(**b**) The red trapezium can be transformed into the yellow trapezium by a rotation.
Mark the centre of rotation and label it B.
What is the angle of rotation?

(**c**) The whole trapezium can be transformed into the green trapezium by an enlargement.
Mark the centre of enlargement and label it C.
What is the scale factor?

(**d**) The black trapezium can be transformed into the whole trapezium by an enlargement.
Mark the centre of enlargement and label it D.
What is the scale factor?

3 Copy this design on to isometric paper.

(**a**) The red triangle can be transformed into the blue triangle by a reflection.
Draw the line of reflection and label it *a*.

(**b**) The red triangle can be transformed into the yellow triangle by a rotation.
Mark the centre of rotation and label it B.
What is the angle of rotation?

(**c**) The red triangle can be transformed into the black triangle by a rotation.
Mark the centre of rotation and label it C.
What is the angle of rotation?

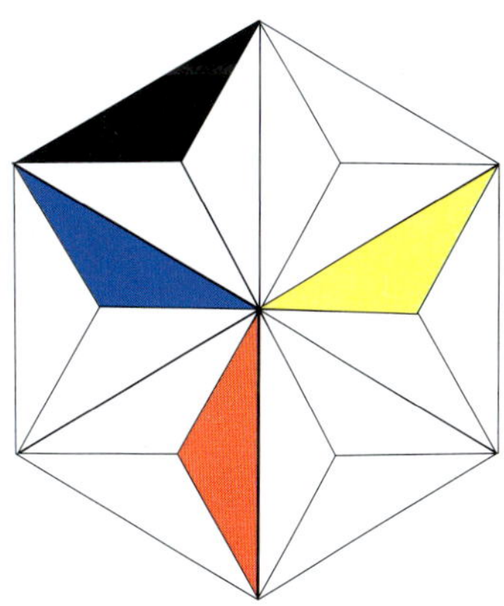

4 Look at this diagram.

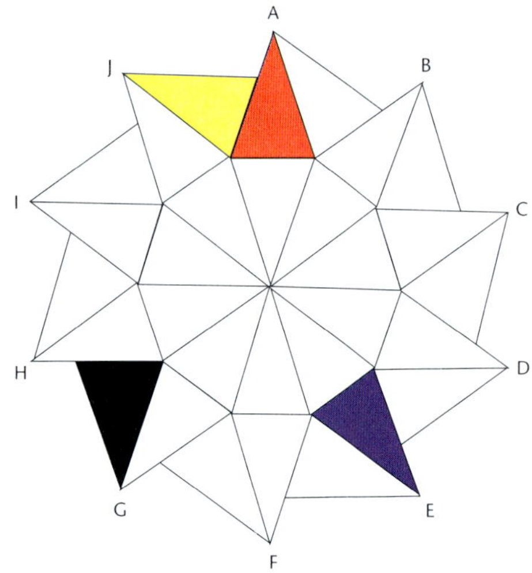

(**a**) The red triangle can be transformed into the blue triangle by a reflection. Where is the line of reflection?

(**b**) The red triangle can also be transformed into the blue triangle by a rotation. Where is the centre of rotation? What is the angle of rotation?

(**c**) The red triangle can be transformed into the yellow triangle by a rotation. Where is the centre of rotation? What is the angle of rotation?

(**d**) The red triangle can be transformed into the black triangle by a rotation. Describe the position of the centre of rotation. What is the angle of rotation?

5 Look at these quadrilaterals.

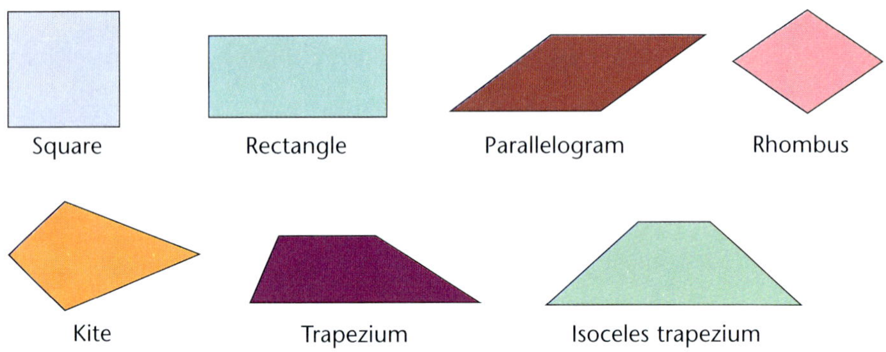

(**a**) Which quadrilaterals can be divided into two pieces in such a way that one piece can be obtained from the other piece by reflection? What does this tell you about the side lengths and angles of this quadrilateral? What does it tell you about its diagonals?

(**b**) Which quadrilaterals can be divided into two pieces in such a way that one piece can be obtained from the other piece by a rotation? What does this tell you about the sides, angles and diagonals of the quadrilateral?

CHAPTER SUMMARY

Quadrilaterals

Shape		Diagonals: same length	cross at right angles	cross at mid-points	bisect angles of quad
Square: Regular quadrilateral; all angles right-angles and all sides equal		YES	YES	YES	YES
Rectangle: All angles right-angles		YES	NO	YES	NO
Rhombus: All sides equal		NO	YES	YES	YES
Parallelogram: Opposite sides parallel		NO	NO	YES	NO
Kite: Two pairs of adjacent sides equal		NO	YES	ONE	ONE PAIR
Trapezium: One pair of opposite sides parallel	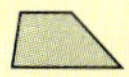	NO	NO	NO	NO
Isosceles trapezium: Trapezium with non-parallel sides equal	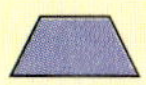	YES	NO	NO	NO

A **regular polygon** has all its sides equal *and* all its angles equal.

Polygons

Each **exterior angle** of a *regular* polygon with n sides is $\frac{360}{n}^{\circ}$

Each **interior angle** of a *regular* polygon with n sides is $(180 - \frac{360}{n})^{\circ}$.

The **angle sum** of *any* **polygon** with n sides is $(180n - 360)°$, proved by splitting the shape into $n - 2$ triangles.

There are only three **regular tessellations**: of equilateral triangles, squares and hexagons. The interior angle of each of these shapes divides exactly into 360°.

Transforming shapes means changing them in some way.

Transformations

A **translation** needs a **vector**. A **reflection** needs a **mirror line**.

A **rotation** needs a **centre of rotation** and an **angle of rotation** and a direction (clockwise or anticlockwise).

An **enlargement** needs a **centre of enlargement** and a **scale factor**.

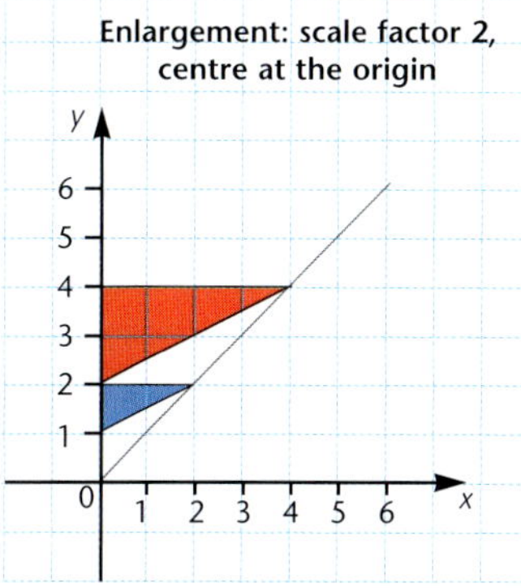

Enlargement: scale factor 2, centre at the origin

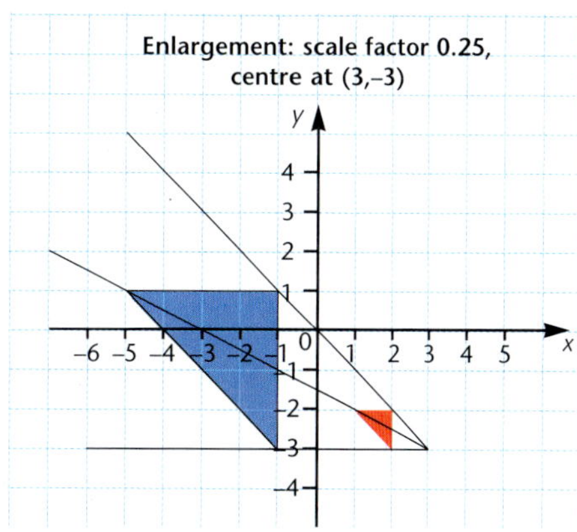

Enlargement: scale factor 0.25, centre at (3,–3)

CHAPTER 3

Algebraic Manipulation

This chapter is about:

- developing mental strategies for long multiplication
- developing skills with manipulating algebra, especially multiplying out brackets and factorising
- developing skills with applying algebra to contexts where it is useful
- justifying and proving generalisations.

Working with brackets

DISCUSSION POINT

Make sure you know how to write expressions like these, *without* brackets. The first has been done for you.

$5(x - 3) - 3(x - 2) = 5x - 15 - 3x + 6$
$= 2x - 9$

$7(x - 2) + 2(x - 3)$ $\quad$ $2(2x + 1) - (x + 2)$
$5x(x - 3) - 3(5 - x)$ $\quad$ $2xy(x - y) - xy(2x - 3y)$

Exercise 1

1 Multiply out the brackets and simplify each of these expressions.

(a) $3(x - 2)$ $\quad$ (b) $-4(y + 3)$

2 Multiply out the brackets and simplify each of these expressions.

(a) $4(x + 5) + 3(2x + 4)$ $\quad$ (b) $2(3z + 4) - 3(z + 2)$
(c) $4(2a - 5) - 3(3a - 6)$ $\quad$ (d) $3(4n - 3) - 2(6n - 5)$
(e) $4 - (x - 3)$

3 Multiply out the brackets and simplify each of these expressions.

(a) $7(x - 2y + 3z) + 4(2x + y - 4z)$ $\quad$ (b) $3(2a - 8b + 4c) - 4(a - 6b + 3c)$
(c) $3(x + 4y) - 4(y - 4x) + 5(6x - 7y)$

4 Multiply out the brackets and simplify each of these expressions.

(a) $x(3x + 7) + 4(x + 3)$
(b) $3x(x - 5) - 2x(x + 4)$
(c) $5y(y + 7) - 7(y - 5)$
(d) $3a(3a - 2b) + 2b(3a + 4b)$
(e) $4p(p - 3q) - 3q(p - 5q)$

5 Multiply out the brackets and simplify each of these expressions.

(a) $x(3x + y - 5) - 6(-2x + 5y + 4)$
(b) $a(b - c) + b(c - a) + c(a - b)$
(c) $pq(p - q) + 2qr(q - r) - 3rp(r - p)$
(d) $x^2(x + y) - x(x^2 - y^2)$
(e) $a^2(a + b - c) + 2b^2(b + c - a) + 3c^2(c + a - b)$

DISCUSSION POINT

In Exercise 1, you multiplied out brackets.
Factorising is the *reverse* of this process.

Make sure you know how to factorise expressions like these. One of them has been done for you.

$4x - 4y$
$3a + 6b$
$4a^2 + 10a = 2a(2a + 5)$
$9x^2y + 12xy^2$

EXERCISE 2

1 Factorise each of these expressions.

(a) $3a + 3b$
(b) $8p - 8q$
(c) $2a + 4$
(d) $3x - 6y$
(e) $y^2 + 4y$
(f) $3z^2 - z$

2 Factorise each of these expressions.

(a) $8a^2 + 4a$
(b) $6x^2 - 12x$
(c) $9b^2 + 15b$
(d) $20a - 30a^2$

3 Factorise each of these expressions.

(a) $pqr - pqs$
(b) $x^2y + xy^2$
(c) $\pi r^2 + 2\pi r$
(d) $3a^3 + 4a^2b$
(e) $9x^2y - 15y^3$
(f) $\pi r + 2r$

4 Factorise each of these expressions.

(a) $a^3b^2c + b^3c^2a - c^3a^2b$
(b) $14x^2y^2 - 49xy^3$
(c) $12a^3b^2c + 16a^4b^2 - 28a^2b^2c^2$
(d) $32x^3 + 64x^2y - 80xy^2$

Multiplying out brackets

DISCUSSION POINT

One way of multiplying 2-digit numbers together is like this.

	20	6
30	600	180
4	80	24

$$26 \times 34 = (20 + 6) \times (30 + 4)$$
$$= 600 + 180 + 80 + 24$$
$$= 884$$

Try this method on other numbers.

A similar method can be used to multiply out brackets with algebra.

For example, this is how $(x + 3)(x + 5)$ can be multiplied out.

	x	3
x	x^2	$3x$
5	$5x$	15

$$(x + 3)(x + 5) = x^2 + 3x + 5x + 15$$
$$= x^2 + 8x + 15$$

Multiply out these brackets.

$(3m - 4n)(m + 5n)$

$(x + 5)^2 = (x + 5)(x + 5)$

To multiply out some brackets, you need more boxes.

For example, to multiply out $(2a - b)(a + b + 1)$, this diagram can be used.

	a	b	1
$2a$	$2a^2$	$2ab$	$2a$
$-b$	$-ab$	$-b^2$	$-b$

In this exercise, use whatever non-calculator method you like.

EXERCISE 3

1 Calculate each of these.

(a) 32×13 (b) 24×43 (c) 57×71 (d) 97×25 (e) 101×68

2 Calculate each of these.

(a) 32^2 (b) 45^2 (c) 87×78 (d) 232×12 (e) 457×68

EXERCISE 4

1 Multiply out the brackets and simplify these expressions.

(a) $(m + 1)(m + 2)$ (b) $(x + 3)(x + 5)$ (c) $(p + 2)(p - 1)$
(d) $(r - 3)(r - 5)$ (e) $(s - 5)(s + 3)$ (f) $(y + 7)(y + 6)$
(g) $(y + 7)(y - 6)$ (h) $(3a + 2)(a + 3)$ (i) $(2n - 3)(3n - 5)$
(j) $(3b - 5)(5b + 3)$ (k) $(x - 4)(x + 4)$ (l) $(3p + 5)(3p - 5)$
(m) $(x + 4)^2$ (n) $(n - 3)^2$ (o) $(3y + 1)^2$
(p) $(2a - 7)^2$

2 Multiply out the brackets and simplify these expressions.

(a) $(x + y)(x + 2y)$ (b) $(x + 3y)(x - 2y)$ (c) $(a - 4b)(a - 5b)$
(d) $(m + 3n)^2$ (e) $(p - 5q)^2$ (f) $(2y + 3z)(3y + 4z)$
(g) $(3p - q)(2p + 3q)$ (h) $(a - 3b)(a + 3b)$ (i) $(2p - 5q)(2p + 5q)$
(j) $(7x + 3y)(7x - 3y)$ (k) $(4m - 3n)(2m - 5n)$ (l) $(x + y)(x + y + 1)$

3 Multiply out the brackets and simplify these expressions.

(a) $(3p - 2q - 2)(2p + 3q)$ (b) $(2a + 3b)(3a + 5b) + (2a - 3b)(3a - 5b)$
(c) $3(2r + 3s)(4r + 3s)$ (d) $(3q + 4r)(2q - 5r) - (3q - 4r)(2q + 5r)$
(e) $a(a + 2b)(a - 3b)$ (f) $(p + q + r)(p - 2q - 3r)$

Using algebra to solve problems

Resource Sheet C: *Hundred square*

EXERCISE 5

1 Look through this 2-by-2 window on to the grid containing the numbers 1 to 100.

The numbers in opposite corners of the window can be multiplied.
$46 \times 57 = 2622$ $47 \times 56 = 2632$
The difference between these two products is 10.

1	2	3	4	5	6	7	8	9	10
11	12	13	14	15	16	17	18	19	20
21	22	23	24	25	26	27	28	29	30
31	32	33	34	35	36	37	38	39	40
41	42	43	44	45	46	47	48	49	50
51	52	53	54	55	56	57	58	59	60
61	62	63	64	65	66	67	68	69	70
71	72	73	74	75	76	77	78	79	80
81	82	83	84	85	86	87	88	89	90
91	92	93	94	95	96	97	98	99	100

(a) The window can be moved to a different position on the grid, e.g. to 62, 63, 72, 73. Multiply the numbers in opposite corners.
What is the difference between the products this time?

62	63
72	73

(b) Move the window to three other positions on the grid. Multiply the numbers in opposite corners.
What is the difference between the products in each case?

Making and justifying a generalisation

(c) Make a hypothesis concerning the difference between the products.

2 Algebra can be used to prove the hypothesis in Question 1 part (c).

(**a**) Here is the window again. The smallest number in the window has been labelled n.

n	

Copy this window and put the numbers in the empty boxes (written in terms of n).

Making and justifying a generalisation

(**b**) Multiply the numbers in opposite corners in this window. Write down the difference between the products and simplify the expression. Prove your hypothesis in Question 1 part (c).

3 Look through this 3-by-2 window on to the same grid.

73	74	75
83	84	85

(**a**) Multiply the numbers in opposite corners. What is the difference between the products this time?

(**b**) Move the window to three other positions on the grid. Multiply numbers in opposite corners. Find the difference between the products.

Making and justifying a generalisation

(**c**) Make a hypothesis concerning the difference between the products in a 3-by-2 window.

Prove your hypothesis by completing this window and working as in Question 2.

n		

Making and justifying a generalisation

4 Answer Question 3 for a 5-by-3 window.

5 Find the *sum* of the numbers in a 2-by-2 window if the smallest number in the window is 32.

32	

6 n is the smallest number in a 2-by-2 window.

n	

Find the sum of the four numbers in the window in terms of n.

7 n is the smallest number in a 4-by-3 window. Find the sum of the numbers in this window in terms of n.

n			

8 n is the smallest number in each of these windows. Copy each window, mark the position of n and write expressions for the numbers in the other squares. Find the sum of the numbers in each window in terms of n.

A
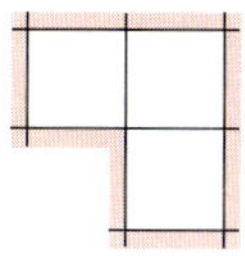

B
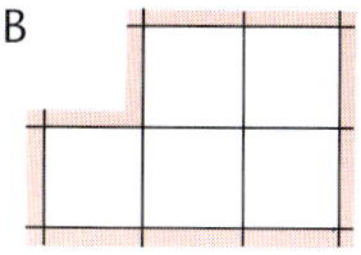

C
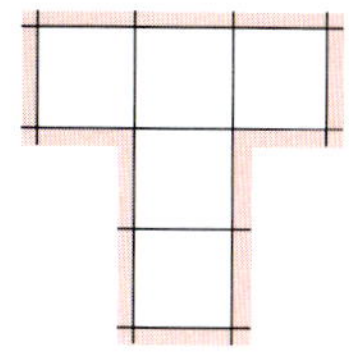

9 Find, *if possible*, a suitable window for each of these formulae.
n is the smallest number in the window.
The formula gives the sum of the numbers in the window.

(a) $3n + 21$ **(b)** $4n + 31$ **(c)** $5n + 41$ **(d)** $5n + 51$

(e) $5n + 61$ **(f)** $5n + 71$ **(g)** $5n + 81$

COURSEWORK OPPORTUNITY

Resource Sheet A: *Isometric dot*

Isometric areas

This coursework opportunity is about shapes drawn on isometric dot paper.

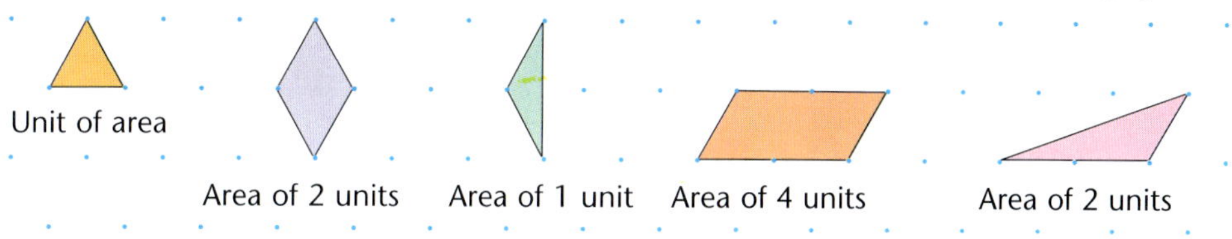

An untilted equilateral triangle

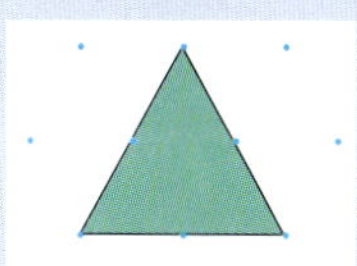

- Find out all you can about the areas of *untilted* equilateral triangles drawn on isometric dot paper.
- Find out all you can about the areas of equiangular hexagons whose side lengths follow the pattern *m, n, m, n, m, n*.
- Find a formula for the area of a hexagon with this side pattern.
- Can you prove your formula?

This is a 1, 2, 1, 2, 1, 2 hexagon. Its area is 13 units.

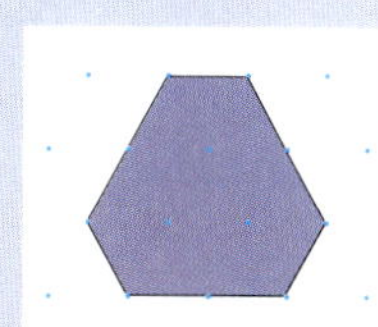

Here are some more ideas.

- Find a formula for the area of *tilted* equilateral triangles. Prove your formula.
- Find and prove a formula for the area of equiangular hexagons with side lengths *m, n, p, m, n, p*.
- Investigate tilted equiangular hexagons.
- Investigate other shapes drawn on isometric dot paper.

1, 2, 3, 1, 2, 3 hexagon

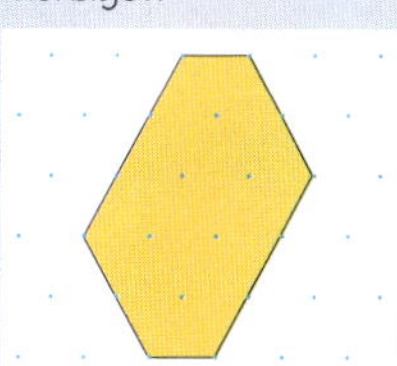

Tilted triangle $\binom{2}{1}$ has area of 7 units.

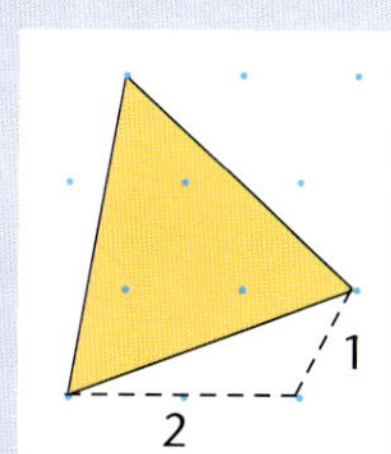

Manipulating formulae and factorising

DISCUSSION POINT

Look through this 3-by-2 window on to a tables square.

1	2	3	4	5	6	7	8	9	10
2	4	6	8	10	12	14	16	18	20
3	6	9	12	15	18	21	24	27	30
4	8	12	16	20	24	28	32	36	40
5	10	15	20	25	30	35	40	45	50
6	12	18	24	30	36	42	48	54	60
7	14	21	28	35	42	49	56	63	70
8	16	24	32	40	48	56	64	72	80
9	18	27	36	45	54	63	72	81	90
10	20	30	40	50	60	70	80	90	100

This diagram shows what numbers are multiplied to obtain the numbers in the window.

5×3	6×3	7×3
5×4	6×4	7×4

Now imagine a 3-by-2 window in any position.

mn	$(m+1)n$	
		$(m+2)(n+1)$

Find expressions for the other numbers in the window.
Multiply out the brackets.

Resource Sheet U: *Tables square*

EXERCISE 6

1 Look through this window on to the tables square.

28	35
32	40

The numbers in opposite corners of the window can be added.
$28 + 40 = 68$
$32 + 35 = 67$
The difference between the sums is 1.

(**a**) Move the window to other positions on the grid.
Add pairs of numbers in opposite corners.
What do you notice?

Making and justifying a generalisation

(**b**) Your observation in part (a) can be proved using algebra.
Copy this window and fill the empty squares with expressions for the missing numbers.
Add pairs of numbers in opposite corners.
Find the difference between the sums and hence prove your observation in part (a).

mn	

Making and justifying a generalisation

2 What happens if you add the pairs of numbers in opposite corners using a 4-by-3 window?
Prove your statement using algebra.

mn			

Making and justifying a generalisation

3 What happens if you add the pairs of numbers in opposite corners of a p-by-q window?
Prove your statement using algebra.

In Question 4, you will need to put the expressions back into brackets.

4 mn is the number in the top left-hand corner of a p-by-q window on a tables square.
Find p and q if the number in the bottom right-hand corner is

(**a**) $mn + m + n + 1$ (**b**) $mn + 2m + 3n + 6$ (**c**) $mn + 5m + 3n + 15$

5 mn is the number in *one* of the corners of a p-by-q window on a tables square.
Find p and q if the number in one of the other corners is

(**a**) $mn - m + n - 1$ (**b**) $mn - 4m + 3n - 12$ (**c**) $mn - 6m - 2n + 12$

6 m^2 is the number in *one* of the corners of a p-by-q window on a tables square.
Find out as much as you can about p and q, if the number in one of the *other* corners is

(**a**) $m^2 + 5m + 4$ (**b**) $m^2 - 5m + 6$ (**c**) $m^2 - 4m$

DISCUSSION POINT

In Exercises 1 and 2, you multiplied out brackets and then **factorised** expressions.

Questions 4, 5 and 6 in Exercise 6 provide more examples of factorising.

Make sure you understand how to do factorisations like these.

$2ab - 3bc + 4ad - 6cd = (2a - 3c)(b + 2d)$ $\qquad a^2 + 4a + 3 = (a + 3)(a + 1)$

$p^2 + 6p + 9 = (p + 3)(p + 3) = (p + 3)^2$ $\qquad n^2 - 5n + 6 = (n - 5)(n - 1)$

$2x^2 + 5x + 2 = (2x + 1)(x + 2)$ $\qquad x^2 - x - 6 = (x - 3)(x + 2)$

EXERCISE 7

1 Factorise each of these expressions.

(a) $xy + x + y + 1$ (b) $pq + q - p - 1$ (c) $ab + 5a + 4b + 20$

(d) $3pq - 9p - 5q + 15$ (e) $ac + bd + ad + bc$ (f) $wy - xz - wz + xy$

(g) $pr - 3qr + 2ps - 6qs$ (h) $8ac - 15bd + 10ad - 12bc$

2 Factorise each of these expressions.

(a) $x^2 + 5x + 4$ (b) $x^2 + 7x + 6$ (c) $x^2 + 5x + 6$

(d) $a^2 + 6a + 8$ (e) $a^2 + 9a + 8$ (f) $x^2 - 5x + 4$

(g) $x^2 - 7x + 6$ (h) $x^2 - 5x + 6$ (i) $a^2 + 8ab + 15b^2$

(j) $a^2 + 2ab + b^2$ (k) $a^2 - 2ab + b^2$ (l) $m^2 - 7mn + 10n^2$

3 Factorise each of these expressions.

(a) $3x^2 + 4x + 1$ (b) $2a^2 + 3a + 1$ (c) $2b^2 + 5b + 2$

(d) $3c^2 + 10c + 3$ (e) $2a^2 - 3a + 1$ (f) $2b^2 - 5b + 2$

(g) $3c^2 - 10c + 3$ (h) $4x^2 + 5xy + y^2$ (i) $2x^2 + 5xy + 2y^2$

(j) $2a^2 + 7ab + 3b^2$ (k) $2a^2 + 5ab + 3b^2$ (l) $4m^2 + 12mn + 9n^2$

4 Factorise each of these expressions.

(a) $y^2 - 3y - 4$ (b) $z^2 - z - 2$ (c) $a^2 - 7a - 8$

(d) $a^2 + 2a - 8$ (e) $x^2 + 5x - 6$ (f) $x^2 + x - 6$

(g) $a^2 - 3ab - 10b^2$ (h) $a^2 + 9ab - 10b^2$

5 Factorise each of these expressions.

(a) $2x^2 + 3x - 2$ (b) $3x^2 + x - 2$ (c) $6x^2 + 11x - 10$

(d) $4x^2 - 4xy - 3y^2$ (e) $4x^2 - 12x + 9$ (f) $16y^2 - 40y + 25$

(g) $4a^2 + 9ab - 9b^2$ (h) $3x^2 - 8xy - 3y^2$

$(a + b)(a - b) = a^2 + ab - ab + b^2 = a^2 - b^2$

So

$(a + b)(a - b) = a^2 - b^2$

This is known as the **difference of two squares**.

You might be asked to factorise a difference of two squares:

$x^2 - y^2 = (x + y)(x - y)$

Exercise 8

1 Rewrite each of these without brackets.

(a) $(p + q)(p - q)$ **(b)** $(x + 4)(x - 4)$ **(c)** $(2m + 5)(2m - 5)$

(d) $(p + 4q)(p - 4q)$ **(e)** $(2a - 3b)(2a + 3b)$ **(f)** $3(x - 5y)(x + 5y)$

(g) $c(c - 4)(c + 4)$ **(h)** $2n(3m + 5n)(3m - 5n)$

2 Factorise each of these.

(a) $m^2 - n^2$ **(b)** $z^2 - 9$ **(c)** $9y^2 - 4$ **(d)** $n^2 - 4m^2$

(e) $p^2 - 25$ **(f)** $s^2 - 36t^2$ **(g)** $4a^2 - 25b^2$ **(h)** $81m^2 - 49n^2$

Sometimes you can take out a common factor before you factorise an expression into two brackets.

$8a^2 - 18b^2 = 2(4a^2 - 9b^2)$

$= 2(2a - 3b)(2a - 3b)$

It is easier to factorise this expression if you take out the common factor first.

$21x^2 - 35x + 14 = 7(3x^2 - 5x + 2)$

$= 7(3x - 2)(x - 1)$

Exercise 9

1 Factorise each of these expressions.

(a) $2x^2 - 8$ **(b)** $45a^2 - 20$ **(c)** $50x^2 - 98$

(d) $12x^2 - 27y^2$ **(e)** $7a^2 - 63b^2$ **(f)** $4x^3 - 25xy^2$

(g) $12a^4 -75a^2b^2$ **(h)** $18abc^3 - 32a^3bc$

2 Factorise each of these expressions.

(a) $7a^2 + 35a + 28$ **(b)** $10x^2 - 25x + 10$ **(c)** $3m^2 - 3mn - 60n^2$

(d) $22x^2 + 33xy - 22y^2$ **(e)** $a^2b + 6abc + 5bc^2$ **(f)** $m^3 - m^2 - 6m$

(g) $6x^3 - 14x^2y + 4xy^2$ **(h)** $5a^4 + 20a^3b + 20a^2b^2$

Exercise 10

1 Factorise each of these expressions.

(a) $x^2 - 9$ (b) $x^2 - 9x$ (c) $x^2 - 9x + 8$

(d) $x^2 - 9x - 10$ (e) $x^2 - 9x + 14$ (f) $x^2 - 9x + 20$

(g) $x^2 - 9x - 22$ (h) $x^2 - 9x - 90$

2 Factorise each of these expressions.

(a) $2a^3 - 8ab^2$ (b) $2a^3 - 8a^2b$ (c) $2a^3 - 8a^2b + 8ab^2$

(d) $2a^3 - 8a^2b + 6ab^2$ (e) $2a^3 - 8a^2b - 10ab^2$ (f) $2a^3 - 8a^2b + 6c^3$

Mental strategies for long multiplication

One strategy for mental arithmetic is doubling.

$$6 \times 8 = 48$$
$$6 \times 16 = 96$$
$$12 \times 16 = 192$$

In this exercise, do these multiplications mentally in whatever way you want. You might find doubling useful.

Exercise 11

1 Calculate these.

(a) 3×14 (b) 9×16 (c) 6×18 (d) 7×32

2 Calculate these.

(a) 18^2 (b) 8×28 (c) 16×28 (d) 7×36

(e) 24^2 (f) 28^2

Sometimes you can use a 'near miss' strategy for doing mental arithmetic.

$$38 \times 99 = 38 \times 100 - 38$$
$$= 3800 - 38$$
$$= 3762$$

Difference of two squares can also be used as a 'near–miss' strategy.
For example, what is 39^2?

$$39^2 - 1 = (39 + 1)(39 - 1)$$
$$= 40 \times 38$$
$$= 1520$$

So, $39^2 = 1520 + 1$
$= 1521$

Here is another example.

$$53 \times 47 = (50 + 3)(50 - 3)$$
$$= 50^2 - 3^2$$
$$= 2491$$

Exercise 12

In Question 1, you might find 'near-miss' strategies useful.

1 Calculate these, mentally, in whatever way you want.

(a) 101×99 (b) 21^2 (c) 37^2 (d) 19×21

(e) 28^2 (f) 999×1001 (g) 99^2 (h) 42×38

(i) 53×47 (j) 49×76

2 Use difference of two squares to help you to write these as the product of prime factors.

(a) 899 (b) 1591 (c) 2451 (d) 4819

Sometimes the 'multiplying out brackets' strategy can be used for multiplication.

To find the square of a number ending in 5, this method can be used.

$$35^2 - 5^2 = (35 + 5)(35 - 5) = 40 \times 30 = 1200$$

So, $35^2 = 1200 + 5^2 = 1225$

To find the product of numbers, this method might be useful, especially with smallish unit digits.

$32 \times 33 = (30 + 2)(30 + 3) = 900 + 150 + 6 = 1056$

Exercise 13

1 Calculate these squares, mentally, in whatever way you want.

(a) 15^2 (b) 25^2 (c) 45^2 (d) 65^2

(e) 195^2 (f) 3.5^2 (g) 7.5^2 (h) 10.5^2

2 Do these multiplications, mentally, in whatever way you want.

(a) 13×12 (b) 21×24 (c) 32^2 (d) 41^2

(e) 42×43 (f) 103×104 (g) 202×201 (h) 3.1×3.3

Exercise 14

In this exercise, a variety of methods can be used.

1 Do these multiplications, in whatever way you want.

(a) 7×14 (b) 3×29 (c) 41×43 (d) 27×33

(e) 48×52 (f) 64×56 (g) 17×13 (h) 59×27

2 Calculate these squares mentally.

(a) 21^2 (b) 31^2 (c) 41^2 (d) 39^2 (e) 55^2

(f) 85^2 (g) 18^2 (h) 36^2 (i) 302^2 (j) 98^2

To solve the first, you could let x be 500 and express 493 and 497 in terms of x.

DISCUSSION POINT

Here are some tricky number problems to round off the chapter.

- Express the number $493 \times 497 - 12$ as the product of prime factors.
- Express the number $909 \times 893 - 80$ as the product of prime factors.

CHAPTER SUMMARY

Multiplying out brackets

To multiply out two brackets, multiply *all* the terms in the first bracket by *all* the terms in the second.

	x	3
x	x^2	$3x$
5	$5x$	15

$$(x + 3)(x + 5) = x^2 + 3x + 5x + 15$$
$$= x^2 + 8x + 15$$

$$(3m - 4n)(m + 5n) = 3m^2 - 4mn + 15mn - 20n^2$$
$$= 3m^2 + 11mn - 20n^2$$

$$(x + 5)^2 = (x + 5)(x + 5)$$
$$= x^2 + 10x + 25$$

	a	b	1
$2a$	$2a^2$	$2ab$	$2a$
$-b$	$-ab$	$-b^2$	$-b$

$$(2a - b)(a + b + 1) = 2a^2 - ab - b^2 + 2a - b$$

Factorising quadratic expressions

Factorising a quadratic expression means rewriting it as the product of two brackets.

$a^2 + 4a + 3 = (a + 3)(a + 1)$

$x^2 - x - 6 = (x - 3)(x + 2)$

$n^2 - 5n + 6 = (n - 2)(n - 3)$

$2x^2 + 5x + 2 = (2x + 1)(x + 2)$

$2ab - 3bc + 4ad - 6cd = (2a - 3c)(b + 2d)$

A particularly important type of factorisation is known as the **difference of two squares**.

$x^2 - 16 = (x + 4)(x - 4)$

$12x^2 - 27y^2 = 3(4x^2 - 9y^2) = 3(2x + 3y)(2x - 3y)$

CHAPTER 4

WORKING WITH DATA

This chapter is about:

- different types of data
- the collection and organisation of data
- representing data by means of frequency polygons and histograms with unequal intervals
- finding the mean of grouped frequency distributions
- cumulative frequency diagrams: median and interquartile range
- calculating standard deviation
- hypothesis testing
- drawing conclusions based on graphs and statistics
- comparing two distributions
- evaluating results critically.

Using statistics

Information is all around us: on television, in papers, in books, in software on computers.

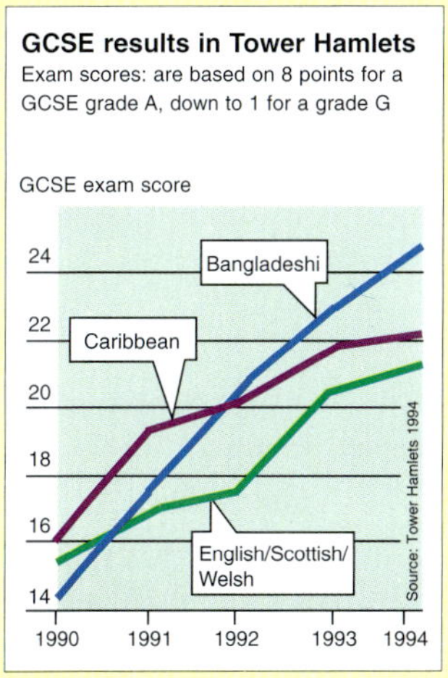

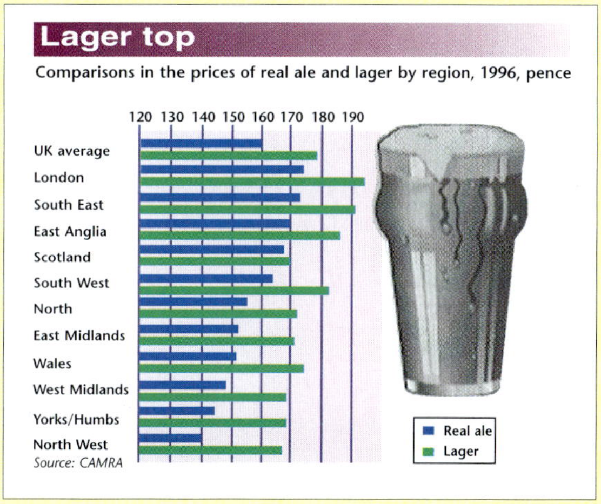

Frankly, everyone gave a damn

Dan Glaister on the biggest movie earners of all time

Go home, ET. Stay in the water, Jaws. The most successful movie of all time is Gone With The Wind. As the latest Hollywood blockbuster, the aliens-are-coming caper Independence Day, breaks records with box-office takings of almost £129 million in two weeks, a survey in New York magazine shows that, at today's prices and with today's potential audience, Gone With The Wind would have taken £1,669 million.

Second place in the re-adjusted rankings is The Sound Of Music, with £629 million, and third the 1956 biblical epic The Ten Commandments, taking £559 million.

The highest placed film of the modern era is Star Wars, made in 1977, which comes in fourth and recent blockbusters such as Jurassic Park and Forrest Gump just make the top 20.

Blockbuster movies

Twenty top earning films	First run in £m	Adjusted figures for '96 in £m
1 **Gone with the wind** (1939)	43.3	1,669
2 **The Sound of Music** (1965)	106	629
3 **The Ten Commandments** (1956)	47.3	559
4 **Star Wars** (1977)	215	511
5 **Ben Hur** (1959)	50.6	492
6 **Jaws** (1975)	173	466
7 **ET** (1982)	266	456
8 **Snow White** (1937)	11.3	434
9 **The Exorcist** (1973)	110	363
10 **Around The World In Eighty Days** (1956)	30.6	361
11 **Doctor Zhivago** (1965)	60	356
12 **The Sting** (1973)	104	325
13 **Raiders Of The Lost Ark** (1981)	161	295
14 **The Empire Strikes Back** (1980)	148	284
15 **Mary Poppins** (1964)	43.3	284
16 **Return Of The Jedi** (1983)	176	278
17 **Cleopatra** (1963)	36	263
18 **Jurassic Park** (1993)	238	260
19 **Forrest Gump** (1994)	220	235
20 **Ghostbusters** (1984)	159	234

With average cinema ticket 19 times the 1939 price, and the available US audience having doubled, most top film lists feature the last three decades. But by adjusting for population growth and inflation these figures show that the guru of the blockbuster is not Steven Spelberg or George Lucas, but David O Selznick, producer of Gone With The Wind. The list includes several other surprises: the 1956 film Around The World in 80 Days is at number 10, with takings of £361 million at today's prices, while The Exorcist, the most controversial film on the list, at number nine with takings of £363 million, is sure to turn heads.

Julie Andrews manages two entries in the top 20, with The Sound Of Music in second place and Mary Poppins at number 15, with takings of £284 million.

Spielberg has four films in the top 20, with total takings of £1,477 million. All of the Star Wars trilogy, made by Spielberg's sometime colleague George Lucas, are in the top 20, with combined takings of £1,073 million.

Outside the top 20, the quality of the films becomes decidely variable. Beverley Hills Cop is at number 21, Grease at number 22, and Animal House at number 24, one place above Home Alone.

The average ticket price in 1939, the year of Gone With The Wind's release, was 15 pence. By the time The Sound Of Music was released in 1965 it had risen to 67 pence and 12 years later, it had more than doubled to £1.48.

Source: New York magazine

Information can be about any topic and be presented in any number of ways: as tables, graphs or charts.

We use statistics to try to make sense of the information that is presented to us.

There are four basic stages to any statistical investigation:

- Deciding on the question to ask or the **hypothesis** to test
- **Collecting** the data
- **Analysing** the data
- **Interpreting** the results

DISCUSSION POINT

Discuss what this diagram means.

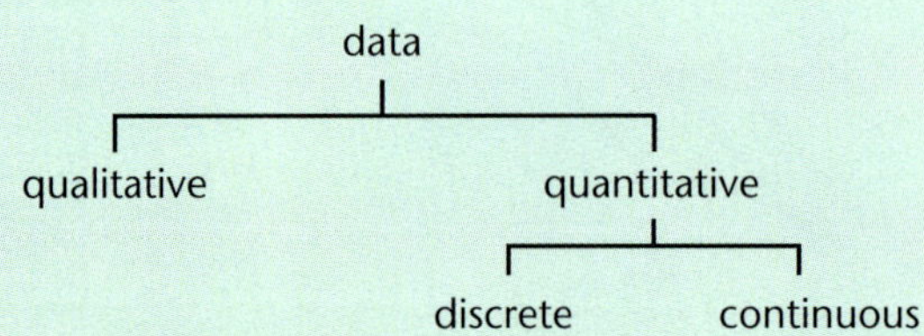

Think of some examples of the different types of data.

▷ Resource Sheet F: *Mental arithmetic speed test*
▷ Resource Sheet G: *Mental arithmetic speed test – answers*

Exercise 1

1 Look at the reports shown on pages 51 and 52 of three different statistical investigations.

(a) For each investigation, state the question you think the researcher was trying to find the answer to.

(b) How do you think the data might have been collected?

(c) What type of data has been collected in each case?

2 Look at the report on page 51 about the prices of real ale and lager.

(a) Which areas charge more than the national average for both lager and real ale?

(b) How much more expensive is real ale in East Anglia than in the North West?

(c) In which area is the biggest difference between the prices of real ale and lager?

3 Write a brief report, suitable for a newspaper, to accompany the graphs about GCSE results in Tower Hamlets (on page 51).

In Question 4, you are going to test your numeracy skills, and then compare your accuracy and speed with the accuracy and speed of other students in your class. You may find it easier to work with a partner who can time you.

4 (a) Do the mental arithmetic speed test, *without* using a calculator, and make a note of the time that you take, to the nearest second.

(b) When you have finished the test, immediately write down the time taken, mark your answers and write down your score. (Give one mark for each correct answer.)

(c) Collect results from other people in your class for both the time taken and the test score.

(d) What type of data are the test scores?

(e) What type of data are the test times?

Keep your data safe as you will need it to answer questions in later exercises.

5 (a) Organise the test scores you have collected in a table like this.

Score (s secs)	Frequency
$0 \le s < 10$	
$10 \le s < 20$	
$20 \le s < 30$	
$30 \le s < 40$	
$40 \le s < 50$	

(b) Draw a bar chart to represent this information.

(c) Add a frequency polygon to your bar chart.

A **frequency polygon** is obtained by joining up the midpoints of the tops of the bars.

6 (**a**) Organise the times taken for your class to do the test into a frequency table. Choose your own **class intervals**.

(**b**) Draw a bar chart to represent this information.

(**c**) Add a frequency polygon to your bar chart.

7 Comment on the similarities and differences between the shapes of your two frequency polygons.
What can you deduce from the shapes of the polygons?

8 Repeat the numeracy skills investigation with another class.
Draw frequency polygons for their results and compare them with those obtained for your class.

Histograms with unequal class intervals

DISCUSSION POINT

A survey measures the height of 100 male students.

Height (x)cm	Frequency (f)
$155 \le x < 165$	10
$165 \le x < 170$	18
$170 \le x < 174$	20
$174 \le x < 177$	12
$177 \le x < 185$	12
$185 \le x < 199$	28

This bar chart is intended to represent the data.

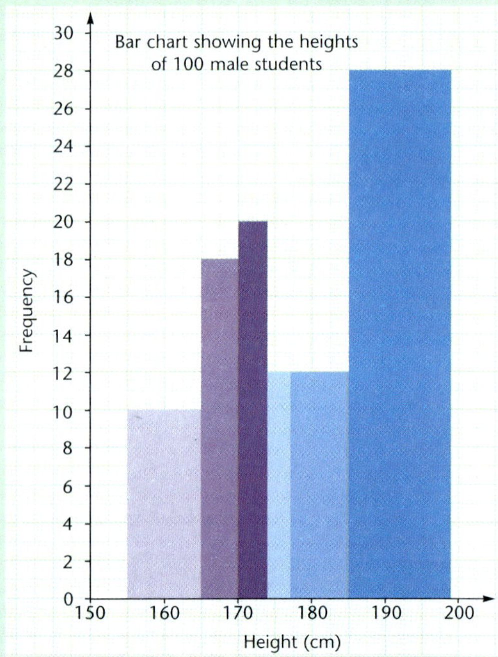

Why might the chart be misleading?

To give a clear representation of data which is organised into *unequal* class intervals, it is necessary to use **frequency density** and to draw a **histogram**. This means that the *areas* of the bars represent the frequencies. This table shows how to calculate frequency density.

Height (x cm)	Frequency (f)	Class width (w)	Frequency density ($f \div w$)
$155 \le x < 165$	10	10	1
$165 \le x < 170$	18	5	3.6
$170 \le x < 174$	20	4	5
$174 \le x < 177$	12	3	4
$177 \le x < 185$	12	8	1.5
$185 \le x < 199$	28	14	2

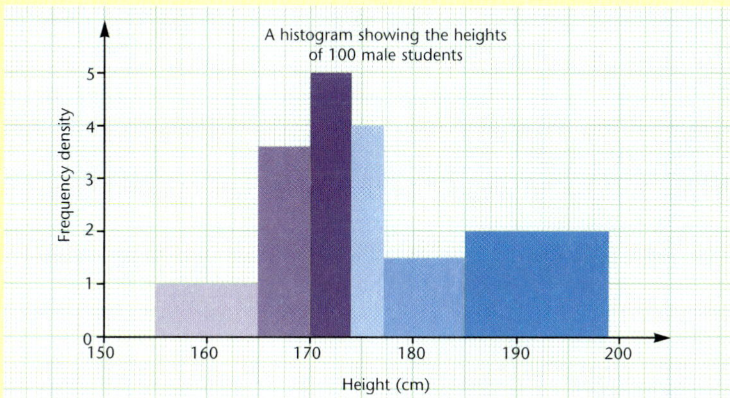

Note that the modal group is the group with the tallest bar, i.e. the highest frequency density, and this is not *necessarily* the group with the highest frequency.

Exercise 2

For Question 1, you need the mental arithmetic speed test scores from Question 4 in Exercise 1.

1 (a) Organise the test scores for your class into these class intervals.

(b) Work out the frequency densities.

(c) Draw a histogram to represent the results.

(d) Compare this histogram with the bar chart you drew for Question 5 in Exercise 1. Which diagram is more helpful?

Score (s secs)	Frequency
$0 \le s < 10$	
$10 \le s < 20$	
$20 \le s < 25$	
$25 \le s < 30$	
$30 \le s < 35$	
$35 \le s < 40$	
$40 \le s < 50$	

2 Draw a histogram to represent this distribution and state the modal class.

Time (secs)	$0 \le t < 6$	$6 \le t < 15$	$15 \le t < 20$	$20 \le t < 30$
Frequency	24	27	24	15

3 Draw a histogram to represent this distribution and state the modal class.

Length (cm)	$20 \le d < 24$	$24 \le d < 30$	$30 \le d < 40$	$40 \le d < 60$
Frequency	16	21	14	29

4 Draw a histogram to represent this data.

Class interval	$0 < x \le 100$	$100 < x \le 300$	$300 < x \le 500$	$500 < x \le 750$	$750 < x \le 1000$
Frequency	2	12	11	14	5

5 The average attendance figures for football league clubs are summarised in this table.

Attendance (n)	Number of clubs
$0 \le n < 2500$	2
$2500 \le n < 4000$	15
$4000 \le n < 6000$	12
$6000 \le n < 10\,000$	15
$10\,000 \le n < 15\,000$	11
$15\,000 \le n < 20\,000$	24
$20\,000 \le n < 30\,000$	10
$30\,000 \le n < 50\,000$	7

Draw a histogram to represent this data.

6 Write out the frequency table which produces this histogram.

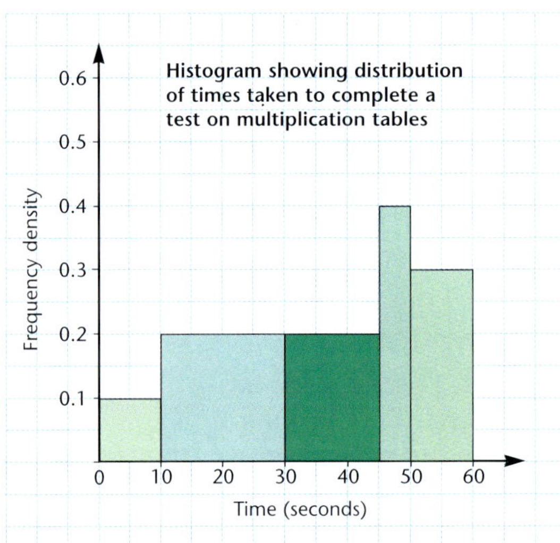

Analysing small sets of data

If there is not too much data, the **median** and **interquartile range** can be found by ordering the data and counting.

Example

Here are the marks obtained by 17 A-level students in a test marked out of 70.

14, 12, 22, 34, 23, 33, 61, 49, 27, 31, 54, 43, 19, 27, 24, 33, 62

List the marks in order of size:

12, 14, 19, 22, 23, 24, 27, 27, 31, 33, 33, 34, 43, 49, 54, 61, 62

lower quartile (between 22 and 23) median (31) upper quartile (between 43 and 49)

The **median** is the middle value: 31 marks.

The **lower quartile** is the median of the data which is below the median. In this case, it lies midway between the values 22 and 23 marks, so a value of 22.5 marks is used.

The **upper quartile** lies midway between the values 43 and 49 marks, i.e. at 46 marks.

The **interquartile range** is the difference between the upper and lower quartiles.

In this example, the interquartile range is
46 marks – 22.5 marks = 23.5 marks

DISCUSSION POINT

- Find the mean and mode for the A-level test marks given above.
  Discuss which might be the most appropriate measure of 'average' mark: mean, median or mode.
- Find the range of the marks.
  What do the range and interquartile range tell you about the marks?
  What are the advantages and disadvantages of using range rather than interquartile range?

EXERCISE 3

1 Look at these five sets of data.

A

The shoe size of students in a class

4	5	5	2	4	4	4	6
4	3	5	5	6	5	6	4
5	6	5	3	5	5	4	4
3	5	6	4	6	5		

B

Students' homework marks

6	8	5	6	4	6	0	7
8	6	6	6	7	0	0	4
5	7	7	5	6	6	6	6
6	10	5	7	7	5	0	

C

The scores of a cricketer during a season's matches

69	6	27	37	5	132	14	51	173	4
14	4	27	0	9	28	25	57	9	8
25	21	38	25	82	60	7	6	16	23

D

Scores obtained when a single die is rolled

4	1	2	5	5	4	3	5	6	6	1	3	5	2
1	4	3	5	1	6	1	4	4	2	5	1	3	6
6	2	6	3	3	2	2	6	3	1	2	4		

E

Minutes spent watching television during one Sunday by a group of students

180	30	0	0	30	180	180	240	300	240
90	0	240	450	30	60	210	30	240	240
270	180	240	0	30	240	240	60	30	390

For each set of data

(a) find the mean, median and mode

(b) state which you consider to be the most appropriate measure of average and give reasons for your answer

(c) find the range and interquartile range

Which do you think is the more appropriate measure of spread?

Why?

2 This line chart shows the number of shots taken by golfers at one particular hole during a competition.

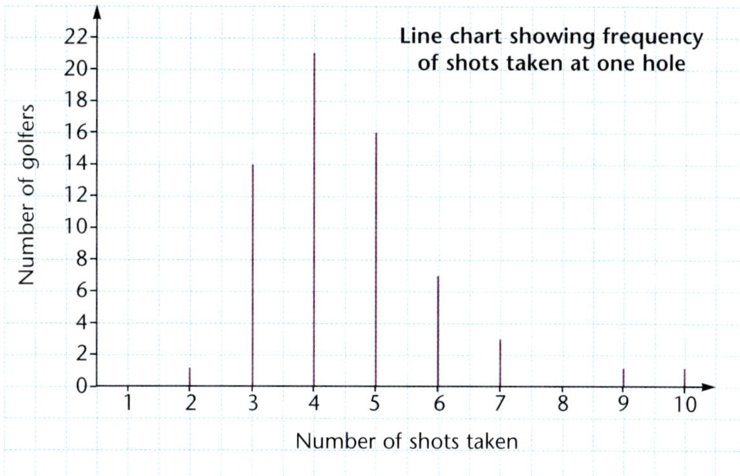

(**a**) Is the line chart an appropriate way of presenting this data?
Give a reason for your answer.

(**b**) Find the mean, mode and median number of golf shots taken.
Which answer best describes the average number of shots taken?

3 This data shows the number of new cars sold during a one-year period by a sample of sales people.

33	15	6	37	46	25	28	24	52	18	26	22
19	54	20	26	31	64	31	18	27	14	32	40
43	27	29	35	30	22	12	34	26	29	47	17

Find the median and interquartile range for the number of cars sold.

Standard deviation

DISCUSSION POINT

A boy scored percentages of 63, 64, 63, 38, 64, 44, 81, 60, 44, 61 for his ten GCSE mock exams.

A girl scored percentages of 68, 48, 47, 48, 68, 49, 68, 48, 90, 48 in the same exams.

Who did better?

Who was more consistent?

To measure consistency you need to know how spread out data is.

The marks of the boy and girl (on page 59) have the same range and the same interquartile range. So neither of these statistics can be used to distinguish between them in terms of consistency.

Yet you might still feel that one is more consistent than the other.

A different way of measuring spread is to use the amount by which *each* of the data items differs from the mean. In this way you take account of *all* the data items.

The **standard deviation** is such a measure of spread.

For standard deviation you work out how far each item of data is from the mean. You then average these 'distances from the mean' by squaring each of them, taking the average of the squares and then taking the square root.

Here is how you can calculate the standard deviation of the boy's marks.

Exam mark (%)	Mean score	Difference from mean	$(\text{Difference})^2$
63	58.2	4.8	23.04
64	58.2	5.8	33.64
63	58.2	4.8	23.04
38	58.2	–20.2	408.04
64	58.2	5.8	33.64
44	58.2	–14.2	201.64
81	58.2	22.8	519.84
60	58.2	1.8	3.24
44	58.2	–14.2	201.64
61	58.2	2.8	7.84
		Total	1455.6

Standard deviation is $\sqrt{\frac{1455.6}{10}} = 12.1$ marks

Exercise 4

1 (a) Calculate the standard deviation of the girl's 10 GCSE mock exam marks given in the discussion point above.

(b) If standard deviation is used as a measure of consistency, which student was more consistent in the mock exams?

2 (**a**) Find the mean and standard deviation for each of these sets of figures.

A

13	18	16
15	11	14
18	16	12

B

150	160	140	140	50
50	190	80	70	120

C

75	80	70
70	80	75
75	75	80

(**b**) Why can you not use standard deviation on its own to say which of these sets of data is more 'spread out'?

3 This table shows the distribution of goals scored by a hockey team in the first eight matches of the season.

Goals scored	0	1	2	3	4	5	6
Number of matches	1	3	1	0	1	0	2

Calculate the mean and standard deviation of the goals scored.

4 (**a**) Find the mean and standard deviation for this set of numbers.

12 17 14 14 16 15 13 13

(**b**) Write down the mean and standard deviation, if

(**i**) you add 10 to each of the numbers in part (a).

(**ii**) you subtract 10 from each of the numbers in part (a).

(**iii**) you add 250 to each of the numbers in part (a).

(**iv**) you double all of the numbers in part (a).

(**v**) you multiply all of the numbers in part (a) by 100.

(**vi**) you divide all of the numbers in part (a) by 4.

5 (**a**) Work out the mean and standard deviation for the number of letters in the words used in this sentence.

(**b**) Now work the same thing out for this sentence.

(**c**) In which of the two sentences is the word length more variable?

6 Six data items have a range of 10.

(a) Find, by experiment, how to choose them so that they have the greatest possible standard deviation.

(b) Find how to choose them so that they have the smallest possible standard deviation.

DISCUSSION POINT

How do the statistics functions on your calculator allow you to calculate the mean and standard deviation?

EXERCISE 5

1 Check your answers to Exercise 4 using the statistics functions on your calculator.

2 Look at the table on page 61 about the twenty top blockbuster movies. Calculate the mean and standard deviation for each set of figures. How do you account for the differences in your results?

COURSEWORK OPPORTUNITY

▶ Resource Sheet H: *Y10 data*

Using statistics to compare two sets of data

Choose a number of male students and a number of female students from the database, or alternatively collect your own data.

- Are males taller than females?
- Are males' or females' heights more variable?
- Who takes the bigger shoe size?

You can make up other questions like these.

Use diagrams to illustrate your findings, as well as calculating measures of average and measures of spread.

Using cumulative frequency diagrams

When there is a lot of data, it is very time-consuming to write out all the data in order of size. Instead, to find the median and inter-quartile range, you can estimate these from a **cumulative frequency diagram**.

The exam results of 200 students are summarised in this table.

Mark (%)	Frequency	Mark less than ...	Cumulative frequency
0–9	1	10	1
10–19	1	20	2
20–29	9	30	11
30–39	23	40	34
40–49	65	50	99
50–59	62	60	161
60–69	26	70	187
70–79	8	80	195
80–89	5	90	200
90+	0	100	200

This diagram is called a **cumulative frequency polygon**, because straight lines have been used to join the points.

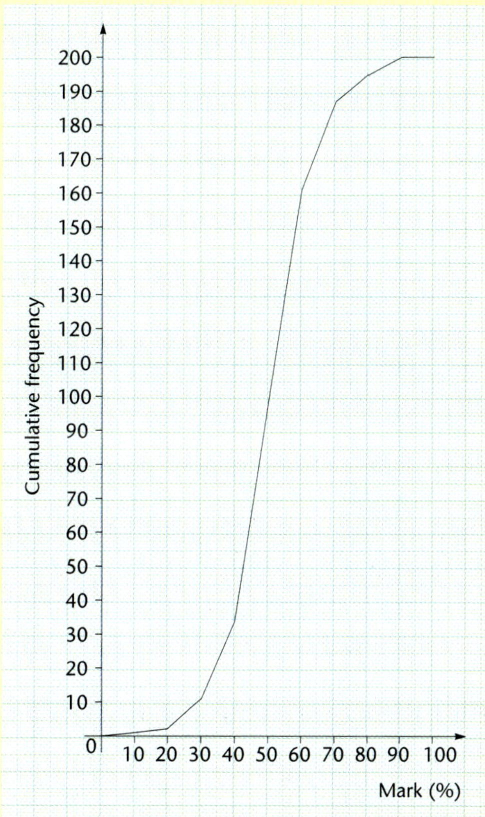

Points can also be joined by a smooth curve to produce a **cumulative frequency curve**.

DISCUSSION POINT

- In the exam results example, why do we plot the points (10, 1), (20, 2), (30, 11), etc.?
- Use the diagram to estimate the median and interquartile range.
- 45% is needed to achieve a grade C.
  Estimate how many students did *not* achieve a grade C.
- 85% is needed to achieve a grade A*.
  Estimate how many students achieved a grade A*.

EXERCISE 6

1 This table contains information about the ages of a sample of people who hold driving licences.

Age (years)	Frequency	Age less than…	Cumulative frequency
17–20	28	21	28
21–25	44	26	72
26–30	57		
31–35	63		
36–40	84		
41–45	87		
46–50	70		
51–55	72		
56–60	65		
61–70	66		
71–80	41		

(**a**) Copy and complete the table.

(**b**) Draw a cumulative frequency diagram for this distribution of drivers' ages.

(**c**) An insurance company offers a discount for drivers between the ages of 23 and 65 inclusive.
Use your graph to estimate the percentage of all drivers eligible for this discount.

For Question 2, you need the data on test scores collected in Question 4 of Exercise 1.

2 (**a**) Draw up a cumulative frequency table for the distribution of test scores.

(**b**) Draw a cumulative frequency diagram and use it to estimate the median and interquartile range for the test scores.

(**c**) What percentage of students achieved a score greater than 35?

(**d**) The top 15% of the students are to be awarded a certificate of merit.
What is the minimum mark you would need, to achieve a certificate of merit?

For Question 3, you need the data on test times collected in Question 4 of Exercise 1.

3 (**a**) Draw a cumulative frequency diagram for the test times.

(**b**) Use your graph to estimate the median and interquartile range for the test times.

(**c**) What percentage of students took longer than 40 seconds?

4 This table shows the weekly wages of staff in a large hotel.

Wage (£w)	Frequency
$0 \le w < 50$	18
$50 \le w < 100$	22
$100 \le w < 150$	28
$150 \le w < 200$	6
$200 \le w < 300$	2
$300 \le w < 500$	1

(**a**) Estimate the median and the interquartile range.

(**b**) Estimate the percentage of the staff who earn more than £180.

Fantasy football is a competition run in some daily newspapers, where you buy and sell players for the prices advertised in the paper.

5 This list shows the values of goalkeepers in a fantasy football competition played in 1997.

GOALKEEPERS

Seaman	ARS	£5m	Beeney	LEE	£1m
Manninger	ARS	£300000	Keller	LEI	£2m
Bosnich	AST	£3m	Poole	LEI	£500000
M Oakes	AST	£500000	James	LIV	£5m
Watson	BAR	£2m	J Nielson	LIV	£500000
Lars Leese	BAR	£500000	Schmeichel	MAN	£6m
Flowers	BLA	£4m	Van Der Gouw	MAN	£1m
Filan	BAR	£500000	Given	NEW	£2m
Branagan	BOL	£2m	Hislop	NEW	£2m
G Ward	BOL	£500000	Pressman	SHE	£3m
Ed De Goey	CHE	£3m	M Clarke	SHE	£500000
Kharine	CHE	£1m	Taylor	SOU	£3m
Ogrizovic	COV	£2m	Paul Jones	SOU	£500000
Hedman	COV	£500000	Beasant	SOU	£500000
Miller	CRY	£2m	I Walker	TOT	£3m
Nash	CRY	£500000	Baardsen	TOT	£500000
Poom	DER	£3m	Miklosko	WES	£2m
Hoult	DER	£1m	Forrest	WES	£500000
Southall	EVE	£2m	Sealey	WES	£500000
Gerrard	EVE	£500000	Sullivan	WIM	£3m
Martyn	LEE	£4m	Heald	WIM	£500000

(**a**) Organise the values of the players into a frequency table with suitable class intervals.

(**b**) Draw up a cumulative frequency table and cumulative frequency diagram.

(**c**) Use your graph to estimate the median and interquartile range.

(**d**) How much does a goalkeeper need to be worth to be in the top 15%?

6 This list shows the values of strikers in the same fantasy football competition.

STRIKERS

Anelka	ARS	£3.5m	Dublin	COV	£2m	Sherringham	MAN	£3.5m
Boamorte	ARS	£2m	Whelan	COV	£2.5	Cole	MAN	£3.5m
Bergkamp	ARS	£5m	Shipperley	CRY	£2.5	Solskjaer	MAN	£6m
I Wright	ARS	£5m	Dyer	CRY	£2m	Shearer	NEW	£12m
Collymore	AST	£5m	Ndah	CRY	£2m	Asprilla	NEW	£5m
Joachim	AST	£3.5m	Freedman	CRY	£2m	Ferdinand	NEW	£6m
Yorke	AST	£5m	Sturridge	DER	£3m	Tomasson	NEW	£3m
Milosevic	AST	£2m	Willems	DER	£2m	Donaldson	SHE	£2m
John Hendrie	BAR	£2m	Wanchope	DER	£2m	Booth	SHE	£3m
Marcelle	BAR	£2m	A Ward	DER	£2m	Hirst	SHE	£2m
Wilkinson	BAR	£2m	Stuart	EVE	£2.5m	Humphreys	SHE	£1.5m
Hristov	BAR	£3m	Branch	EVE	£2m	Ostenstadt	SOU	£2m
Dahlin	BLA	£3m	Ferguson	EVE	£3m	Evans	SOU	£2m
Fenton	BLA	£2m	Barmby	EVE	£2.5m	Oakley	SOU	£2m
Sutton	BLA	£4m	Hasselbaink	LEE	£2m	Kevin Davies	SOU	£2m
Gallacher	BLA	£4m	I Rush	LEE	£1.5m	McVeigh	TOT	£2m
McGinlay	BOL	£3.5m	Lilley	LEE	£2m	Armstrong	TOT	£3m
Blake	BOL	£3.5m	Wallace	LEE	£2m	Allen	TOT	£2m
Scott Taylor	BOL	£2m	Claridge	LEI	£3m	Ginola	TOT	£2m
Paatelainen	BOL	£2m	Marshall	LEI	£2m	Iversen	TOT	£3m
Gunnlaugsson	BOL	£2.5m	Heskey	LEI	£3m	Kitson	WHU	£3m
Vialli	CHE	£2m	Robins	LEI	£1.5m	Dowie	WHU	£2m
Tore Andre Flo	CHE	£3m	Kennedy	LIV	£2m	Hartson	WHU	£3.5m
Mk Hughes	CHE	£3m	Fowler	LIV	£8m	Omoyinmi	WHU	£1m
Zola	CHE	£6m	Berger	LIV	£3m	Holdsworth	WIM	£3m
Lightbourne	COV	£1m	M Owen	LIV	£3m	Ekoku	WIM	£3m
Huckerby	COV	£3m	Erik Nevland	MAN	£2m	Gayle	WIM	3.5m
						Euell	WIM	£2m

(**a**) Organise the values of the players into a frequency table with suitable class intervals.

(**b**) Draw up a cumulative frequency table and cumulative frequency diagram.

(**c**) Use your graph to estimate the median and interquartile range.

(**d**) What percentage of players are worth more than £3.5 million?

7 Use your answers to Questions 5 and 6 to compare the values of goalkeepers and strikers in this fantasy football competition.

Estimating the mean of a grouped frequency distribution

DISCUSSION POINT

How can you estimate the mean from a frequency table like this?

Cost of item (£c)	Frequency (f)
$0 \le c < 1$	3
$1 \le c < 2$	12
$2 \le c < 3$	8
$3 \le c < 5$	7

EXERCISE 7

1 The heights of a group of beech trees and a group of oak trees, correct to the nearest metre, are given in these tables.
Estimate the mean height for each type of tree.

Beech trees height (m)	Frequency
3	0
4	2
5	8
6	5
7	35
8	0
9	0

Oak trees height (m)	Frequency
3	0
4	0
5	0
6	0
7	12
8	17
9	1

2 Estimate the mean wage for the staff at a hotel whose earnings are shown in this table.

Wage (£w)	Frequency
$0 \leq w < 50$	18
$50 \leq w < 100$	22
$100 \leq w < 150$	28
$150 \leq w < 200$	6
$200 \leq w < 300$	2
$300 \leq w < 500$	1

3 Estimate the mean exam score from this table.

Mark (%)	Frequency
0–9	1
10–19	1
20–29	9
30–39	23
40–49	65
50–59	62
60–69	26
70–79	8
80–89	5
90+	0

For Question 4, you need the table of test scores from Question 5 of Exercise 1.

4 **(a)** Estimate the mean test score from your frequency table.

(b) By working out the exact value of the mean, comment on the accuracy of your estimate.

For Question 5, you need the table of test times from Question 6 of Exercise 1.

5 (**a**) Estimate the mean test time from your frequency table.

(**b**) By working out the exact value of the mean, comment on the accuracy of your estimate.

6 This histogram displays data about the running time of a sample of films.

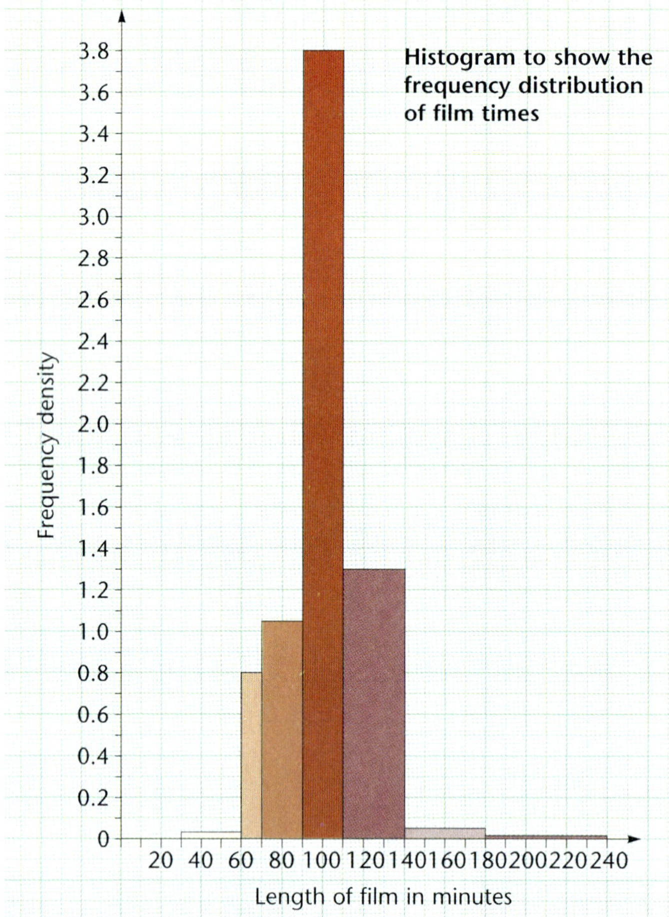

(**a**) Using the histogram, copy and complete this table.

Running time (L mins)	Frequency
$30 \le L < 60$	1
$60 \le L < 70$	
$70 \le L < 90$	
$90 \le L < 110$	
$110 \le L < 140$	
$140 \le L < 180$	5
$180 \le L < 240$	1

(**b**) From your table, estimate the mean running time.

7 (a) Write out the frequency table for this histogram.

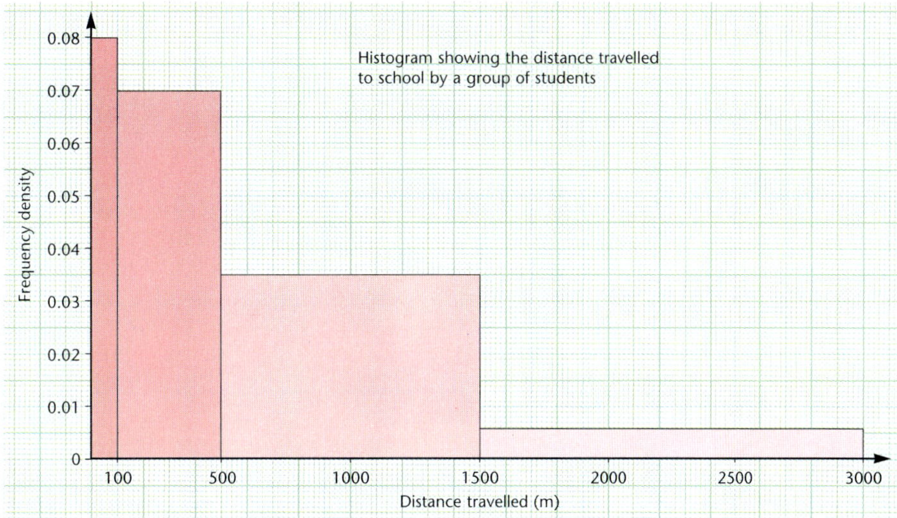

(b) From your table, estimate the mean distance travelled.

8 The manager of a busy supermarket recorded the amount of money spent by each customer during one day.

Amount spent	Number of customers
£0–£4.99	34
£5–£9.99	118
£10–£19.99	203
£20–£29.99	116
£30–£49.99	73
£50–£74.99	50
£75–£99.99	32
£100–£149.99	19
£150–£199.99	4

(a) Draw a histogram to represent this distribution.
Remember the class intervals are not all equal.

(b) Estimate the mean amount of money spent by each customer.

(c) Estimate the median amount of money spent by each customer.

(d) Compare your answers for the mean and median.
Account for any differences.
Which of the two gives the best estimate for the average amount of money spent by each customer?

(e) Estimate the interquartile range.

9 Boxes of drawing pins are advertised as having average contents of 100 pins. In a quality control exercise, 150 boxes are examined and the number of pins more or less than 100 are recorded. These are the results.

0	1	12	−6	−14	0	15	−9	17	0	10	2	−1	0
6	7	9	−8	−14	0	0	−1	−1	4	2	2	−45	13
13	−2	12	−5	1	−7	2	0	−9	15	−8	11	0	−4
−7	−2	0	3	−13	−8	12	−13	1	0	0	−3	−4	5
16	−14	−10	0	1	0	3	−6	−11	−3	8	−12	−5	15
−22	−10	1	−10	6	−7	−10	11	−12	8	6	4	20	8
3	12	9	15	−7	11	0	11	19	0	0	1	−4	1
4	−12	0	−1	10	−4	3	3	−8	12	−12	13	−14	−5
−2	−5	0	−4	−6	−6	16	−18	3	2	1	−5	0	−5
−10	−11	9	0	6	−2	2	0	1	−7	8	−11	6	−2

(**a**) What do the negative numbers signify?

(**b**) Draw a suitable frequency diagram to represent this data.

(**c**) Use a suitable method to estimate the mean number of drawing pins in a box.

(**d**) One of the boxes was recorded as having 45 pins less than the average. This was thought to be a counting error, and so this particular result was discarded. Will ignoring this result make any significant difference to the mean?

10 A number of batteries of two different types were tested to see how long they lasted with continuous use.
This table provides a summary of the results:

Battery life (h hours)	Frequency	
	Type A	Type B
$0 \le h < 1$	7	2
$1 \le h < 1.5$	15	8
$1.5 \le h < 2$	26	38
$2 \le h < 2.5$	31	47
$2.5 \le h < 3$	22	12
$3 \le h < 4$	8	3
$4 \le h < 5$	7	0

(**a**) Draw a cumulative frequency diagram for each type of battery using the same set of axes. Use your graphs to estimate the median and interquartile range for each type.

(**b**) Comment on the differences between Type A and Type B batteries which you can see from your diagram.

(**c**) Estimate the mean for each type of battery. Comment on any differences between your estimates for the means or medians.

CHAPTER SUMMARY

A **statistical investigation** has four stages: questioning; collection; analysis; and interpretation.
A **hypothesis** is an idea that underlies the questions asked in a statistical investigation

Different types of data

Qualitative: e.g. hair colour
Discrete (counting): e.g. number of children in a family
Continuous (measuring): e.g. height in centimetres

Representing data

A **frequency polygon** can be obtained by joining the mid-points of tops of bars on a histogram.

Histogram for unequal class intervals

Frequency density is used instead of frequency.
The *area* of each bar represents the frequency.

Time taken to complete test (t secs)	Frequency (x)	Class width (w)	Frequency density ($f \div w$)
$0 \leq t < 10$	1	10	0.1
$10 \leq t < 30$	4	20	0.2
$30 \leq t < 45$	3	15	0.2
$45 \leq t < 50$	2	5	0.4
$50 \leq t < 60$	3	10	0.3

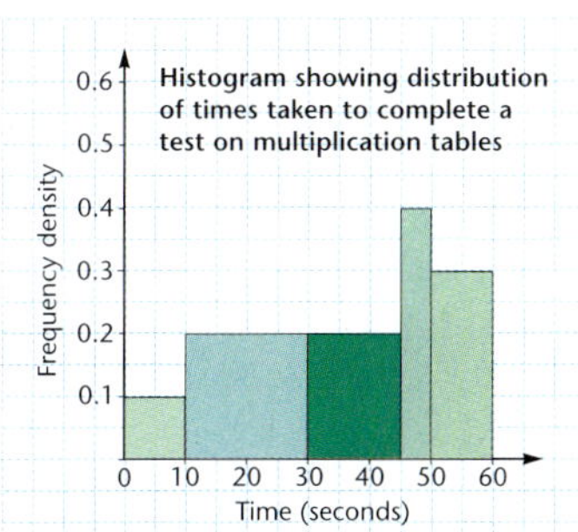

The **modal group** is 45–50 marks, because it has the tallest bar. It is *not* 10–30 marks (which has the highest frequency in the table).

Medians and quartiles

- List all the items in order of size.
- The item in the middle of the list is the **median**. If there are two 'middle' items, the median is half way between them.
- The median of the data below the median (so that one quarter of the items are below it) is the **lower quartile**.
- The median of the data above the median (so that one quarter of the items are above it) is the **upper quartile**.

Measuring the spread of data

Range is the difference between the largest and smallest items of data.
Interquartile range is the difference between the upper and lower quartiles.
Standard deviation:
For small sets of data use this method.

- Find the mean.
- Find the difference between each item of data and the mean.
- Square these differences.
- Add up all these squared differences.
- Divide by the number of items of data.
- Square root the answer.

For larger sets of data, use the statistical functions on your calculator.

Cumulative frequency diagrams

% Mark	Frequency	Mark less than...	Cumulative frequency
0–9	1	10	1
10–19	1	20	2
20–29	9	30	11
30–39	23	40	34
40–49	65	50	99
50–59	62	60	161
60–69	26	70	187
70–79	8	80	195
80–89	5	90	200
90+	0	100	200

The cumulative frequency diagram for this data is shown on page 73.
Note that each cumulative frequency figure is plotted against the *upper* end of each class interval.

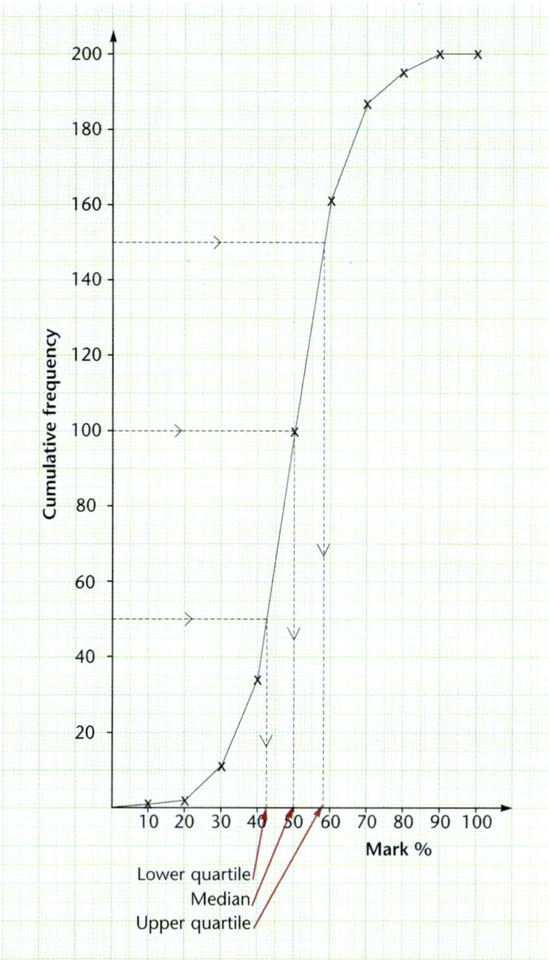

Estimating means from a grouped frequency distribution

Every item in each class interval is assumed to take the middle value of the interval.

Example

Find the mean homework mark for this class of 30 students.

Homework mark	Frequency (x)	Mid-value (x)	$f \times x$
1–5	0	3	0
6–10	3	8	24
11–15	20	13	260
16–20	7	18	126
Total	30		410

Estimated mean = 410 marks ÷ 30

= 13.7 marks

CHAPTER 5

PYTHAGORAS' THEOREM AND SIMILAR SHAPES

This chapter is about:

- understanding and using Pythagoras' theorem
- applying the skills of multiplying out brackets and factorising
- similar shapes and their areas
- using surds.

Proving Pythagoras' theorem

▶ Resource Sheet B: *Square dot*

EXERCISE 1

1 Here is a square drawn on centimetre-squared dot paper. What is the area of this square?

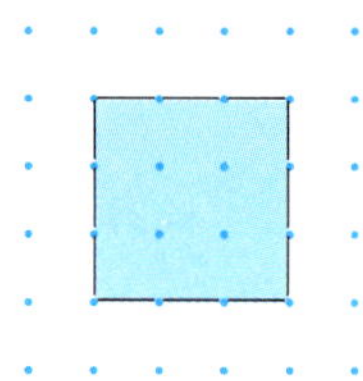

2 Here is another square. Find the area of this square.

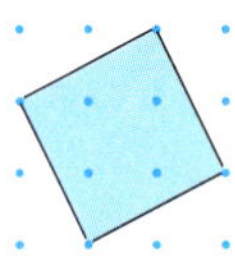

Making a generalisation

3 Draw some more squares with their vertices at dots. Find their areas. Is it possible to draw a square with an area of 10 cm^2? 12 cm^2? Which areas less than 20 cm^2 are possible?

4 One way of telling someone else which tilted square you have drawn is to use vectors.

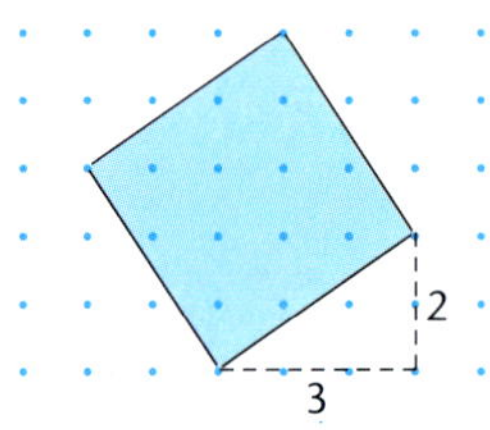

This could be called a $\begin{pmatrix}3\\2\end{pmatrix}$ square.

Can you tell what the area of any tilted square is from its vector? If not, try drawing some more squares.

Justifying a generalisation

DISCUSSION POINT

Use these diagrams to prove the general result you obtained in Question 4 about the area of any $\binom{m}{n}$ square.

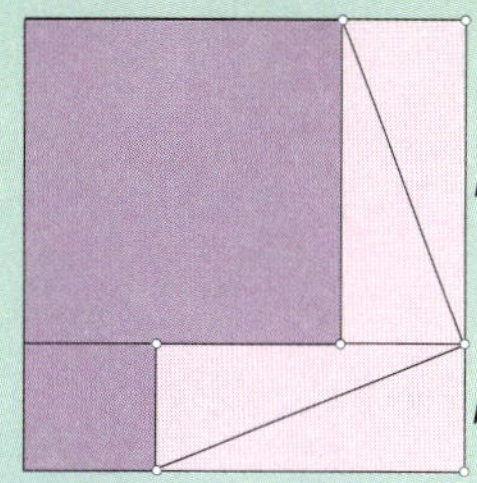

The result you have just proved in the discussion point can be thought of as follows.

When you draw squares on the sides of a right-angled triangle, the area of the square on the longest side (the hypotenuse) is equal to the sum of the areas of the squares on the other two sides.

This is called **Pythagoras' theorem.**

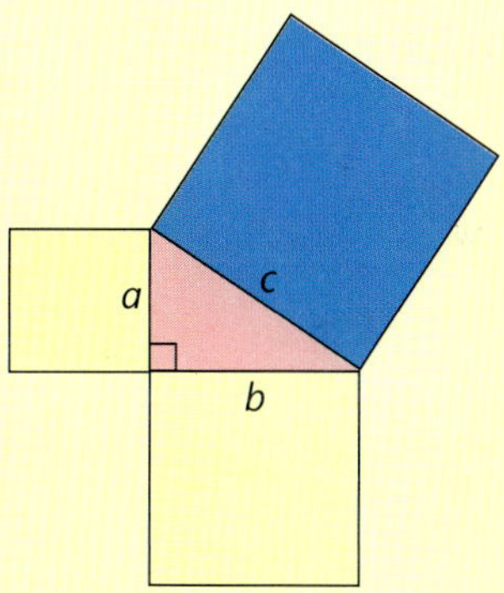

Squares do not have to be drawn on square dot paper for Pythagoras' theorem to be true.
All that is needed is a right-angled triangle.

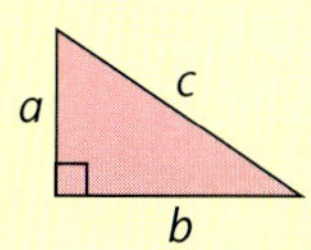

$$a^2 + b^2 = c^2$$

Applying Pythagoras' theorem

This is a right-angled triangle.
The lengths of two of its sides are known.

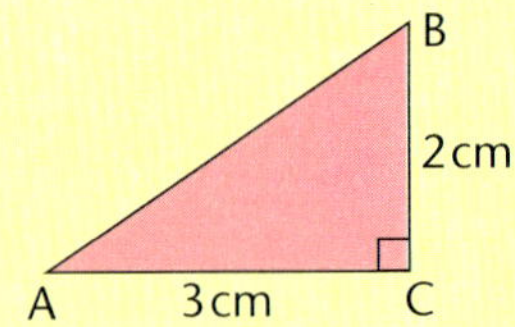

This diagram shows how you can find the length of the third side.

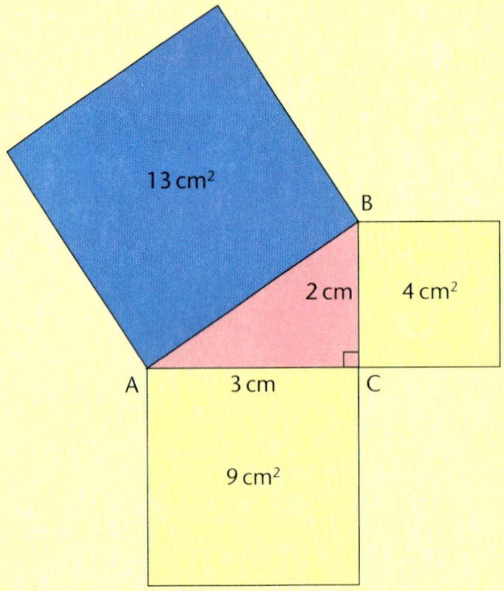

The length of AB is $\sqrt{13}$cm = 3.62cm.

The third side of the triangle can be found *without* drawing the squares, like this.

Length of AB is $\sqrt{2^2 + 3^2}$cm = $\sqrt{13}$cm = 3.61cm

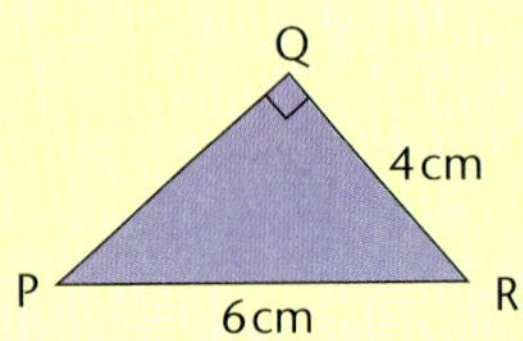

Length of PQ is
$\sqrt{6^2 - 4^2}$cm = $\sqrt{20}$cm = 4.47cm

The questions in this exercise apply Pythagoras' theorem in various contexts.
Give all your answers to a sensible degree of accuracy.

EXERCISE 2

1 When a ladder is propped against the wall of a house, the bottom of the ladder is 2.8m from the wall and the top of the ladder reaches 4.8m up the wall.

How long is the ladder?

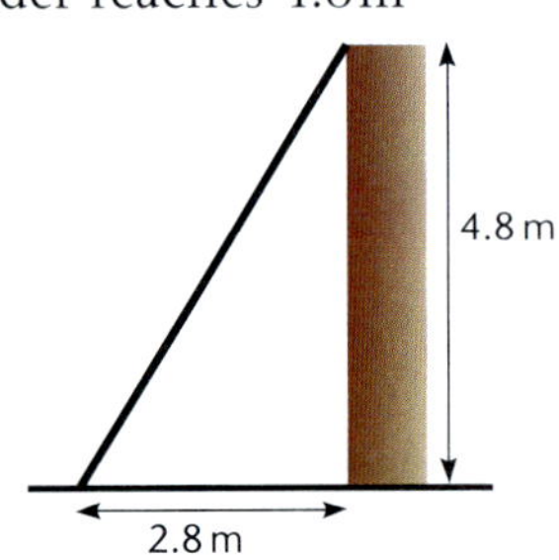

2 A shelf is 25 cm wide. A support for the shelf is fixed to the wall 15 cm below the shelf and to the shelf 7 cm from its outer edge.

Find the length of the bracket.

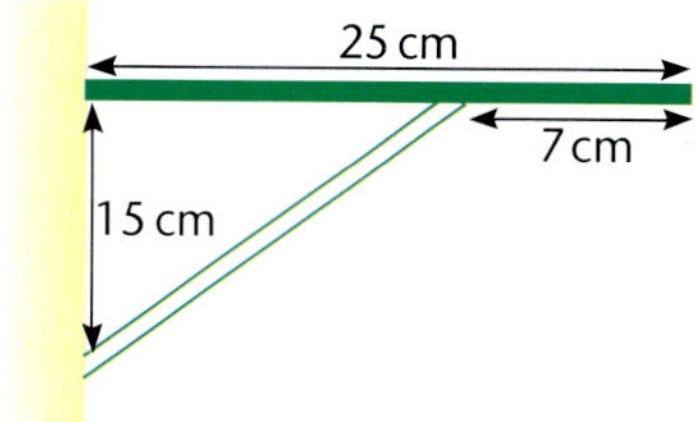

3 The shape of a set square is always a right-angled triangle.

(**a**) The shortest side of a set square is 7.6 cm and the longest side is 15.2 cm. Find the length of the other side.

(**b**) The longest side of a set square is 13.8 cm and the other two sides are equal in length. Find the perimeter of the set square.

4 (**a**) Map A shows part of a field with two straight footpaths across it. Find the length of each footpath.

Map A

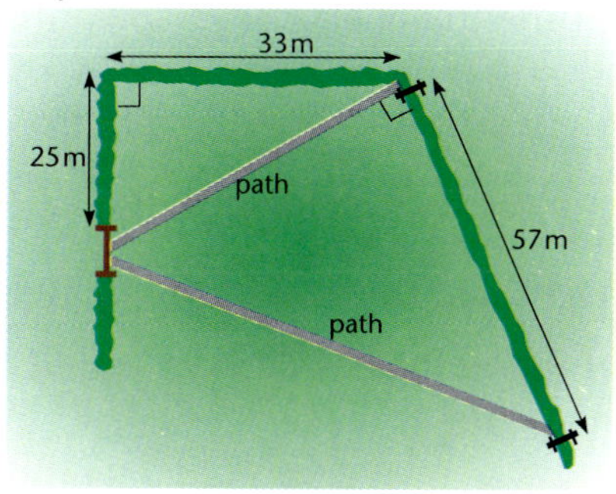

Plan B

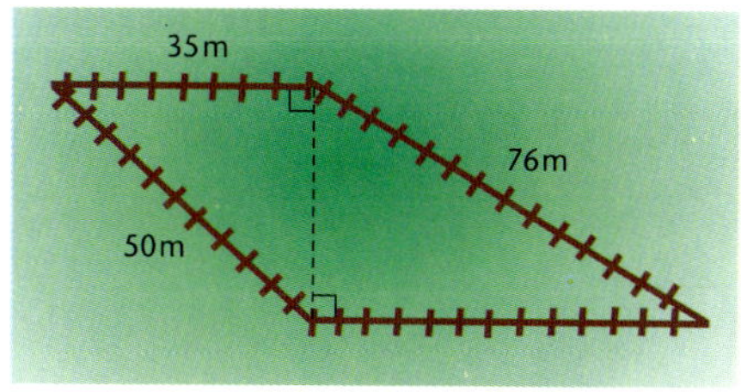

(**b**) Plan B shows part of a field to be fenced off for conservation purposes. Find the length of fence needed.

EXERCISE 3

The questions in this exercise apply Pythagoras' theorem to mathematical shapes.
Give all your answers to a suitable degree of accuracy.

1 What is the length of the diagonal of a rectangle which is 9 cm by 4 cm?

2 For each of these diagrams, find the lengths of the sides marked y.

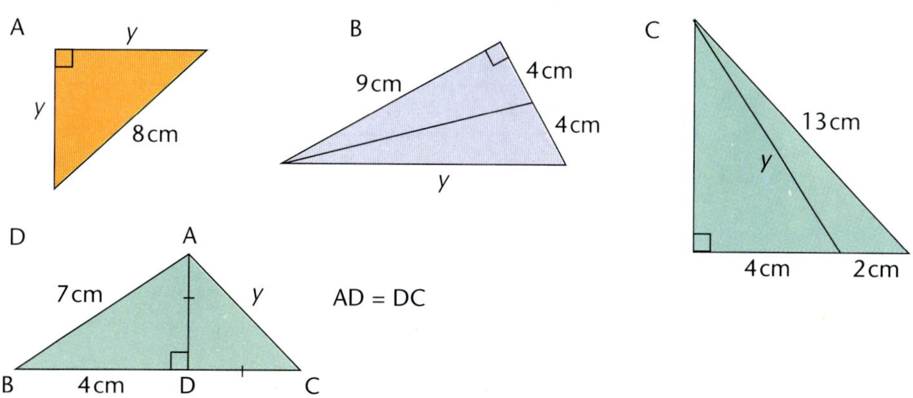

AD = DC

3 The diagonals of a square are 15 cm long. Find the perimeter of the square.

4 Find the length of the side marked x in this diagram.

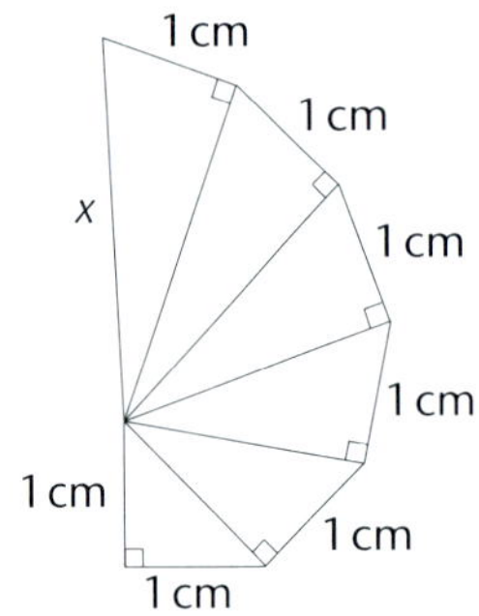

5 The lengths of the sides of an isosceles triangle are 6 cm, 6 cm and 5 cm. Calculate the area of the triangle.

An isosceles triangle

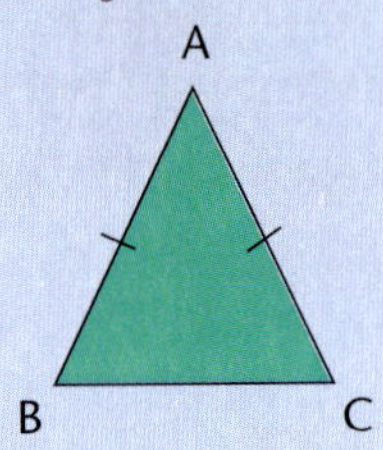

6 In each of these statements, ABC is a different isosceles triangle with AB = AC.

A: AB = 6.5 cm and BC = 4.2 cm.
Calculate the height and the area of the triangle.

B: The perimeter of the triangle is 20.2 cm and BC is 6.3 cm.
Calculate the area of the triangle.

C: The area of the triangle is 1 cm^2 and BC is 1 cm.
Calculate the perimeter.

7 The diagonals of a rhombus are of length 10.2 cm and 7.8 cm. Find

(**a**) the area of the rhombus

(**b**) the perimeter of the rhombus

8 The diagonals of a kite are of length 9.2 cm and 8.4 cm.
Two of the sides of the kite are of length 5.3 cm.
Find *both* possible values for the lengths of the other two sides of the kite.

Exercise 4

This exercise is about using Pythagoras' theorem to estimate the value of square roots. Your estimates will be better if you use a scale larger than 1 cm representing 1 unit.

1 Draw this right-angled triangle accurately.

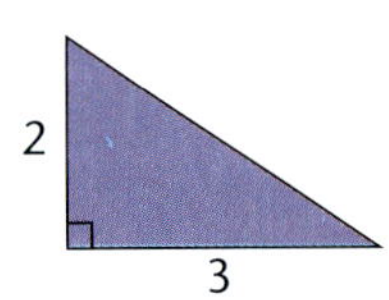

Use your drawing to estimate the value of $\sqrt{13}$.

2 Draw right-angled triangles accurately to estimate these values.

(a) $\sqrt{17}$ (b) $\sqrt{29}$ (c) $\sqrt{41}$

3 (a) Draw an equilateral triangle accurately with sides of length 2.
Use your drawing to estimate $\sqrt{3}$.

(b) Building on part (a), draw a triangle accurately to estimate the value of $\sqrt{7}$.

DISCUSSION POINT

Find the lengths of a_2, a_3, a_4 ... in this diagram

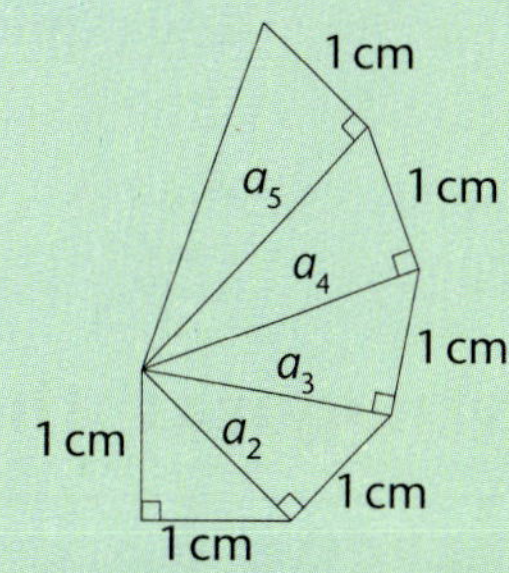

Theoretically, this method can be used to construct a line whose length is the square root of *any* positive whole integer.

- What practical problems would arise if you tried to use this method to construct the square roots of moderately large numbers such as $\sqrt{31}$?
- What short cuts might you take to construct $\sqrt{31}$?

Manipulating square roots

DISCUSSION POINT

It is useful to be able to simplify expressions which contain square roots.
Make sure you understand how these simplifications have been made.

$\sqrt{8} = 2\sqrt{2}$ $(\sqrt{5})^3 = 5\sqrt{5}$ $\sqrt{3}(\sqrt{3} + 1) = 3 + \sqrt{3}$

$\dfrac{\sqrt{8} + \sqrt{32}}{\sqrt{2}} = 6$ $\dfrac{6}{\sqrt{3}} = 2\sqrt{3}$

EXERCISE 5

1 Write each of these as a multiple of $\sqrt{2}$ (e.g. $\sqrt{8} = 2\sqrt{2}$).

(a) $\sqrt{32}$ (b) $\sqrt{50}$ (c) $\sqrt{18} + \sqrt{98}$

2 Which of these numbers are equal?

$\sqrt{12}$ $3\sqrt{2}$ $2\sqrt{3}$ $\sqrt{8}$ $\sqrt{18}$ $\sqrt{81}$ $\sqrt{200} - \sqrt{128}$ $\dfrac{\sqrt{45} + \sqrt{180}}{\sqrt{5}}$ $\sqrt{48} - \sqrt{12}$ $\sqrt{48}$

3 Multiply out the brackets and simplify these expressions.

(a) $(\sqrt{2} + 2)(\sqrt{2} + 3)$ (b) $(\sqrt{3} - 1)^2$

4 Write these expressions with the square root on the top.

(a) $\dfrac{1}{\sqrt{2}}$ (b) $\dfrac{7}{\sqrt{7}}$ (c) $\dfrac{10}{\sqrt{5}}$ (d) $\dfrac{15}{2\sqrt{3}}$

(e) $\dfrac{3 + 2\sqrt{3}}{\sqrt{3}}$ (f) $\dfrac{4 - \sqrt{8}}{\sqrt{2}}$

In Question 5, each answer is a whole number.

5 Simplify these expressions.

(a) $\sqrt{5}(\sqrt{5} + 1) + \sqrt{5}(\sqrt{5} - 1)$ (b) $\sqrt{3}(4 + \sqrt{27}) + \sqrt{12}(\sqrt{75} - 2)$

(c) $(\sqrt{5} + 2)^2 + (\sqrt{5} - 2)^2$ (d) $\dfrac{\sqrt{63} + \sqrt{175}}{\sqrt{28}}$

Pythagoras' theorem without a calculator

Exercise 6

1 In the diagram, D is the midpoint of BC.

Prove that $x^2 + 3y^2 = z^2$.

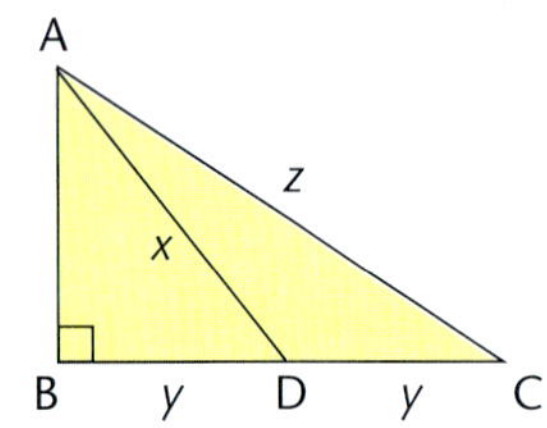

2 ABCD and PQRS are squares.

Prove that $z^2 = 2x^2 + 2y^2$.

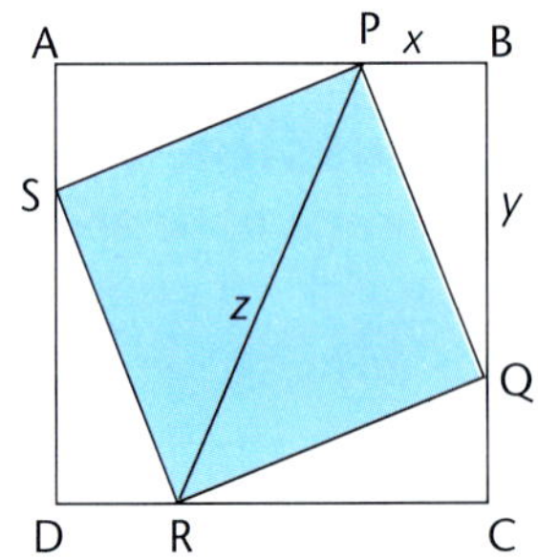

Square roots are sometimes called **surds**. Giving an answer **in surd form** means you do not evaluate the square root.

3 If triangle ABC is equilateral with sides of length 1cm, find the *exact* area of the triangle in surd form.

4 In this diagram, triangle ABC has a right angle at B and BD is perpendicular to AC.

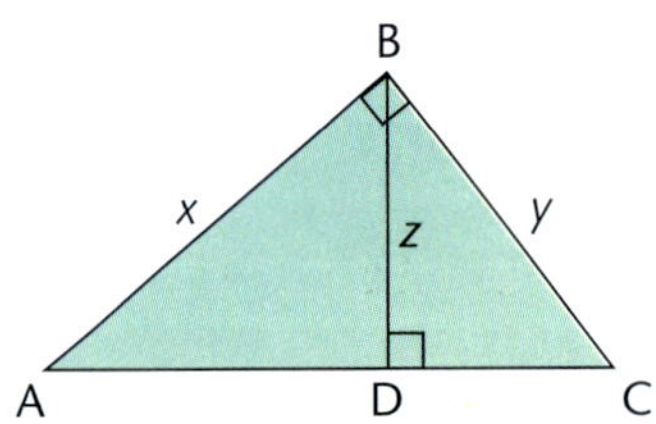

Prove that $z = \dfrac{xy}{\sqrt{x^2 + y^2}}$

5 This picture shows a square inside another square.

The vertices of the inner square are the mid-points of the sides of the outer square. The lengths of the sides of the outer square are 8 units.

(**a**) Find the areas of the two squares. What is the ratio of their areas?

(**b**) Find the perimeters of the two squares. What is the ratio of their perimeters?

6 A square is drawn inside another square so that the vertices of the inner square divide the sides of the outer square in the ratio 1:2.

(**a**) What is the ratio of the areas of these two squares?

(**b**) What is the ratio of the perimeters of these two squares?

7 A square is drawn inside another square so that the vertices of the inner square divide the sides of the outer square in the ratio 3:4.

(**a**) What is the ratio of the area of the two squares?

(**b**) What is the ratio of the perimeters of the two squares?

8 A rectangle (which is not a square) is drawn inside a square so that its vertices divide the sides of the square in the ratio 3:4.

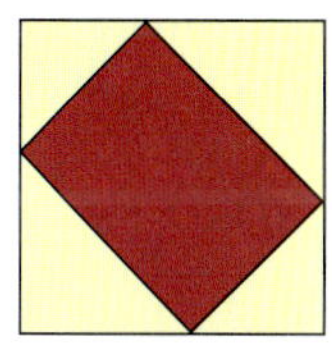

(**a**) What is the ratio of the areas of the square and the rectangle?

(**b**) What is the ratio of the perimeters of the square and the rectangle?

9 An isosceles trapezium (which is neither a square nor a rectangle) is drawn inside a square so that its vertices divide the sides of the square in the ratio 3:4.

(**a**) What is the ratio of the areas of the square and the trapezium?

(**b**) What is the ratio of the perimeters of the square and the trapezium?

10 A quadrilateral (which is neither a square, a rectangle nor an isosceles trapezium) is drawn inside a square so that its vertices divide the sides of the square in the ratio 3:4.

(**a**) What is the ratio of the areas of the square and the quadrilateral?

(**b**) What is the ratio of the perimeters of the square and the quadrilateral?

DISCUSSION POINT

A **Pythagorean triangle** is a right-angled triangle with whole number lengths for its sides.

- Use Pythagoras' theorem to check that each of the triangles shown is right-angled.

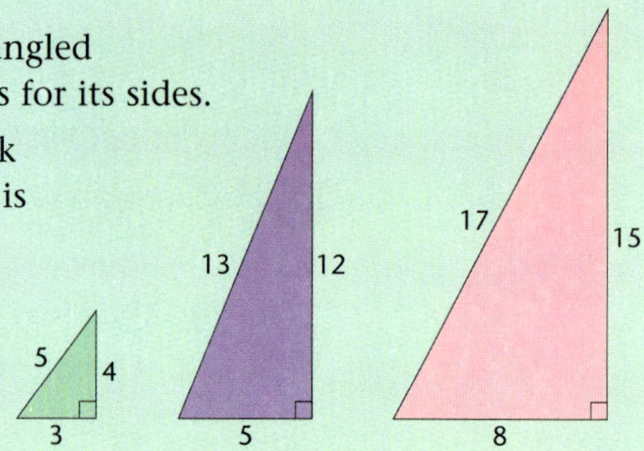

Three whole numbers which are the side lengths of a Pythagorean triangle are called a **Pythagorean triad**.

If you know a Pythagorean triad, such as (3, 4, 5), you can obtain another Pythagorean triad simply by making the triangle bigger. For example, (6, 8, 10), (9, 12, 15) (12, 16, 20), ... are all Pythagorean triads.

There are various methods of finding other Pythagorean triads. One is to use a formula.

$(m^2 - n^2, 2mn, m^2 + n^2)$ is a Pythagorean triad, if m and n are integers.

- Substitute some values for m and n and write down some Pythagorean triads.
- Explain why m must be bigger than n.
- Use algebra to prove that $(m^2 - n^2, 2mn, m^2 + n^2)$ is a Pythagorean triad.

EXERCISE 7

For Question 1, you can use the Pythagorean triads given above.

1 Find the value of x for each of these right-angled triangles.

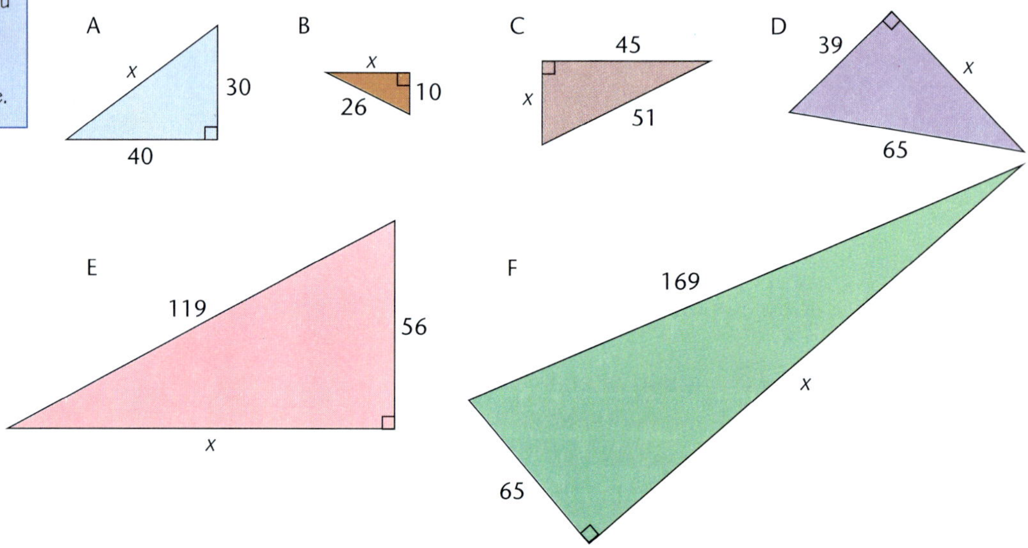

2 Find integer values for a and c in each of these triangles.
There is sometimes more than one answer.

A
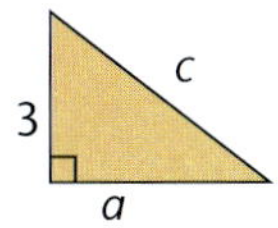

B
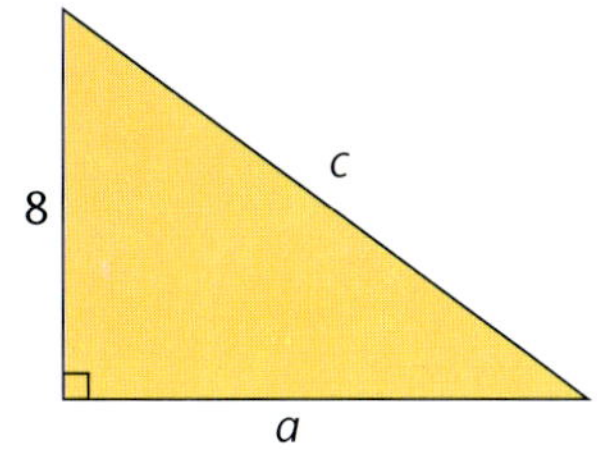

C
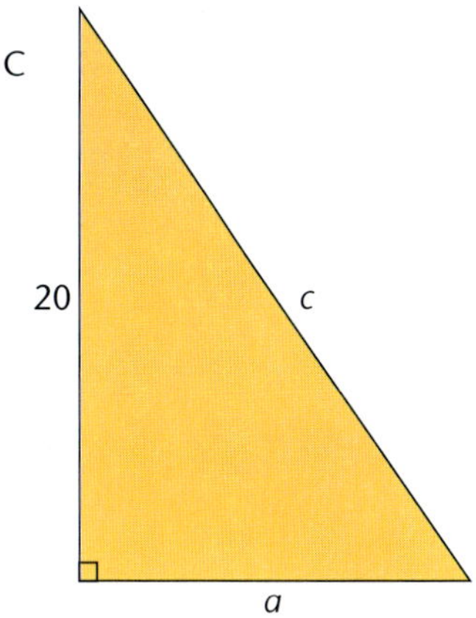

3 This table lists some Pythagorean triads.

a	b	c	$c^2 - b^2$	$c + b$
3	4	5		
5	12	?		
7	?	?		
9	40	?		
11	?	?		
13	?	?		

(**a**) Copy and complete the table.

(**b**) Make a note of any patterns you observe in your table.

For Question 4, use the formulae for a Pythagorean triad: ($m^2 - n^2$, $2mn$, $m^2 + n^2$).

4 By choosing suitable pairs of values for m and n, find several Pythagorean triads in which one of the numbers in the triad is 40.

5 People who write text books often use Pythagorean triads to make up questions about geometrical shapes in such a way that the answers are whole numbers.

For example, since (8, 15, 17) is a Pythagorean triad, the area of this isosceles triangle is a whole number.

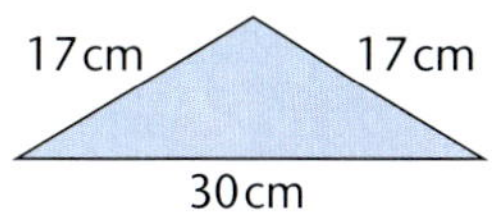

(**a**) Find the area of the triangle.

(**b**) Choose a different Pythagorean triad.
Make up a similar question about an isosceles triangle which has a whole number for its area.

(**c**) Suppose you use the Pythagorean triad (a, b, c) to make up a question about an isosceles triangle.
What is the area of the triangle?

6 (**a**) The diagonals of a rhombus are of length 8cm and 15cm.

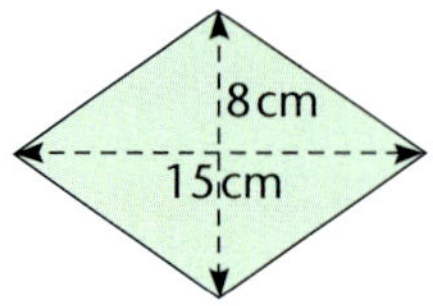

Since (8, 15, 17) is a Pythagorean triad, the area and the perimeter of this rhombus are both whole numbers.

Find the area and perimeter of the rhombus.

(**b**) Choose a different Pythagorean triad.
Make up a similar question about a rhombus which has a whole number for its area and perimeter.

(**c**) Suppose you use the Pythagorean triad (a, b, c) to make up a question about the area and perimeter of a rhombus.
What are the area and perimeter of the rhombus?

7 (**a**) The diagonals of a kite are of length 16 cm and 21 cm, and one of its sides is of length 17 cm.

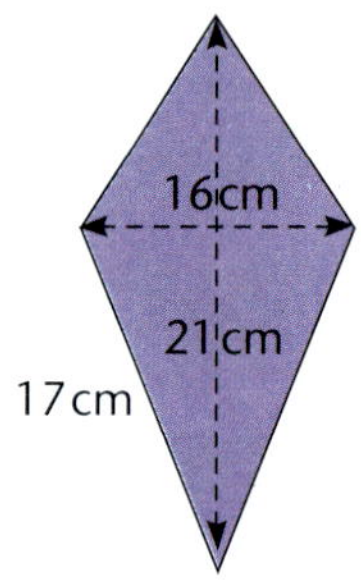

Since (8, 15, 17) and (6, 8 10) are Pythagorean triads, the other side lengths of this kite are whole numbers.

Find the other side lengths of the kite, and the area of the kite.

(**b**) Choose a different pair of suitable Pythagorean triads.
Make up a similar question about a kite which has whole numbers for its side lengths.

(**c**) Suppose you use the Pythagorean triads (a, b, c) and (d, a, e) to make up a question about a kite.
What are the side lengths of the kite?
What is the area of the kite?

Similarity

In Mathematics, two shapes are **similar** if they are the same shape. They can be a different size.

All squares are similar.

Two different rectangles might or might not be similar.

Two similar rectangles

Two rectangles which are not similar

If two shapes are similar, then the angles in one shape are equal to the corresponding angles in the other shape.

For example, these two triangles are similar.
Both have angles of 50°, 60° and 70°.

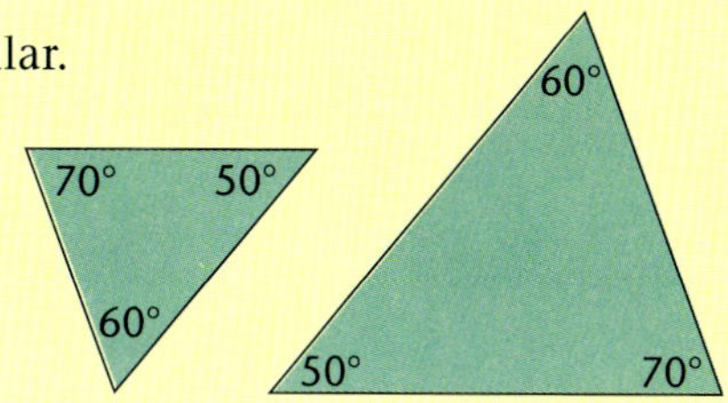

EXERCISE 8

1 Each of these statements is *true* or *false*. If the statement is *false*, give three examples of the shape: two which are similar and one which is not.

A: All equilateral triangles are similar.

B: All rhombuses are similar.

C: All circles are similar.

D: All right-angled triangles are similar.

E: All trapeziums are similar.

F: All isosceles trapeziums are similar.

G: All isosceles triangles are similar.

H: All kites are similar.

I: All regular hexagons are similar.

J: All right-angled, isosceles triangles are similar.

2 Each of these statements is *true* or *false*. If the statement is *false*, give three examples of the shape: two which are similar and one which is not.

A: All cubes are similar.

B: All cuboids are similar.

C: All cylinders are similar.

D: All spheres are similar.

E: All tetrahedra are similar

F: All regular tetrahedra are similar.

G: All triangular prisms are similar.

H: All equilateral triangular prisms are similar.

I: All square-based pyramids are similar.

J: All cones are similar.

The pictures in Questions 3 to 5 are drawn accurately. You can measure them if you need to.

3 Which of these shapes are similar?

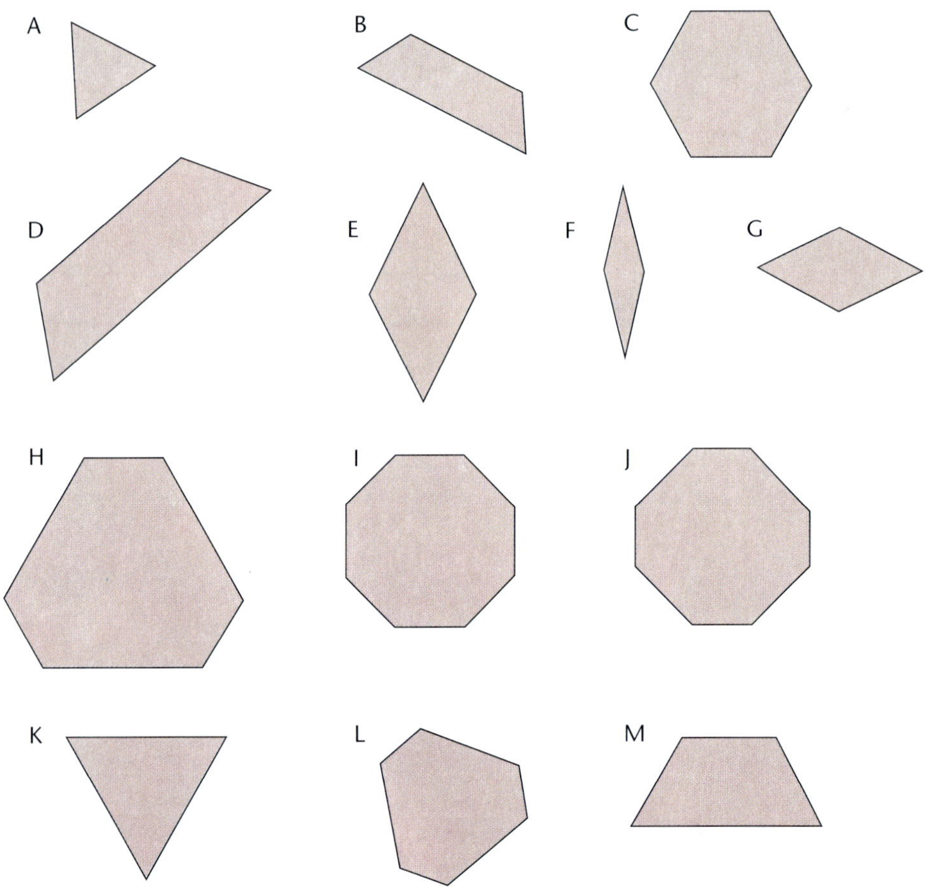

4 Which of these triangles are similar?

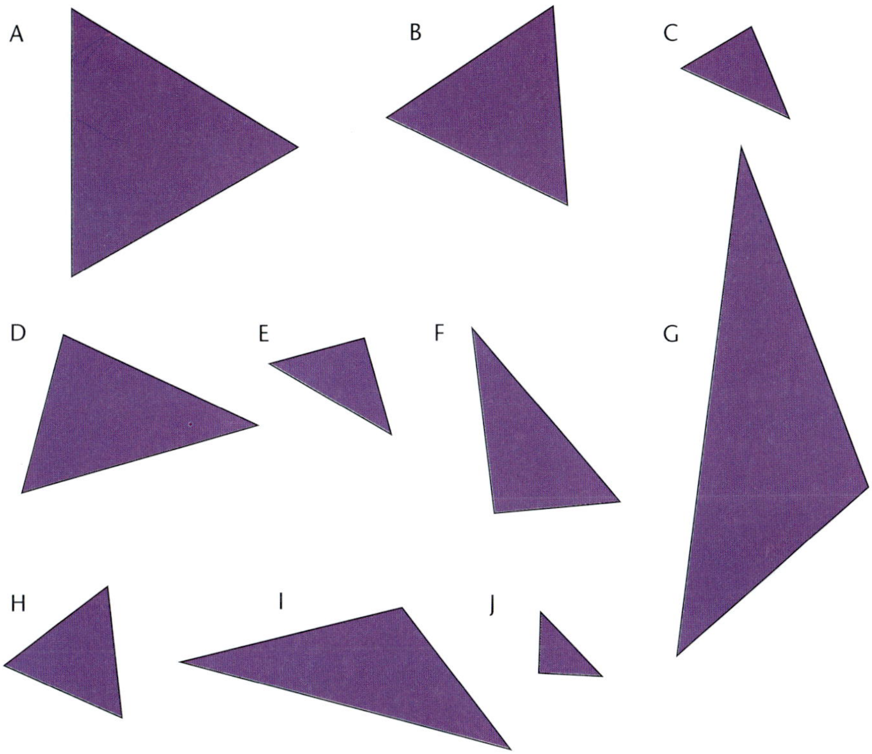

5 In which of these diagrams is the inside triangle similar to the outside triangle?

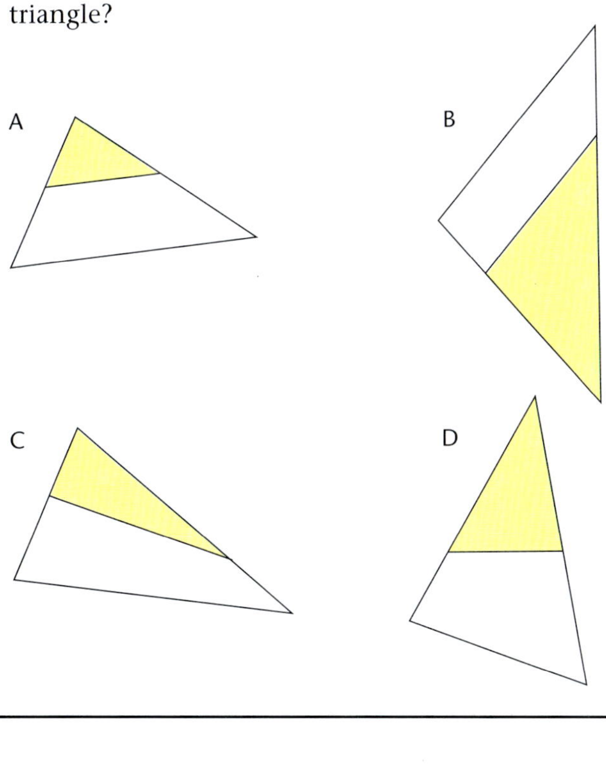

6 (**a**) Explain why these two rectangles are similar.

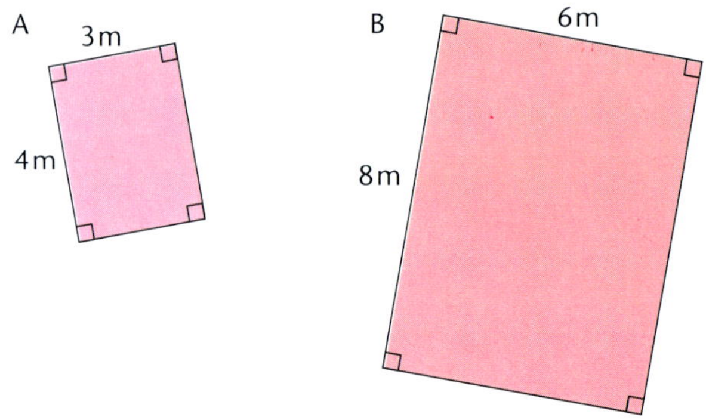

(**b**) Use Pythagoras' theorem to find the length of the diagonal of rectangle A.

(**c**) Use the fact that the rectangles are similar to find the length of the diagonal of rectangle B without using Pythagoras' theorem.

(**d**) Check your answer to part (c) by using Pythagoras' theorem in rectangle B.

> If the sides of one rectangle are twice the length of the sides of the others, then, the diagonal is also twice the length.

7 (**a**) Explain why these two rectangles are similar.

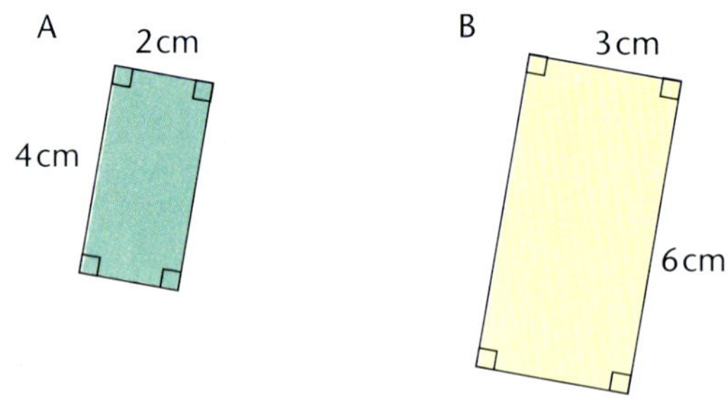

(**b**) Use Pythagoras' theorem to find the length of the diagonal of rectangle A. (Leave your answer in surd form.)

(**c**) Use the fact that the rectangles are similar to find the length of the diagonal of rectangle B without using Pythagoras' theorem.

(**d**) Check your answer to part (c) by using Pythagoras' theorem.

8 This right-angled triangle can be dissected into two right-angled triangles.

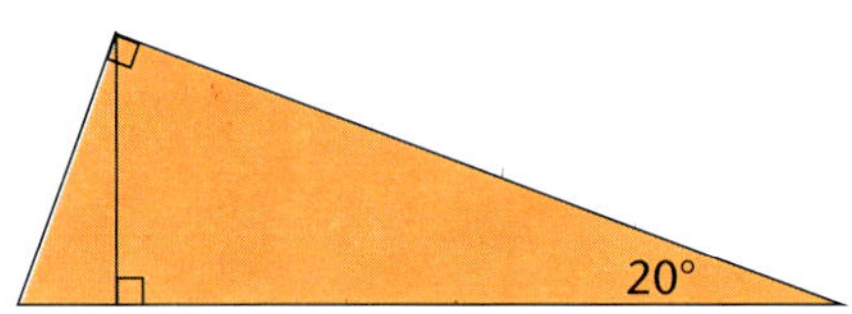

(**a**) Prove that the two new right-angled triangles are similar to each other and to the original triangle.

(**b**) Is the same true for *any* right-angled triangle?

Areas of similar shapes

DISCUSSION POINT

If the sides of one rectangle are 3 times the corresponding sides of the other, prove that the area of one is 9 times the area of the other.

If the sides of one rectangle are k times the corresponding sides of the other, prove that the area of one is k^2 times the area of the other.

Discuss why the same also applies to parallelograms and to triangles.

Given any two shapes which are similar, if the lengths in one shape are k times the corresponding lengths in the other shape, the area of one shape is k^2 times the area of the other shape. k does not have to be a whole number.

EXERCISE 9

1 These two triangles are similar.

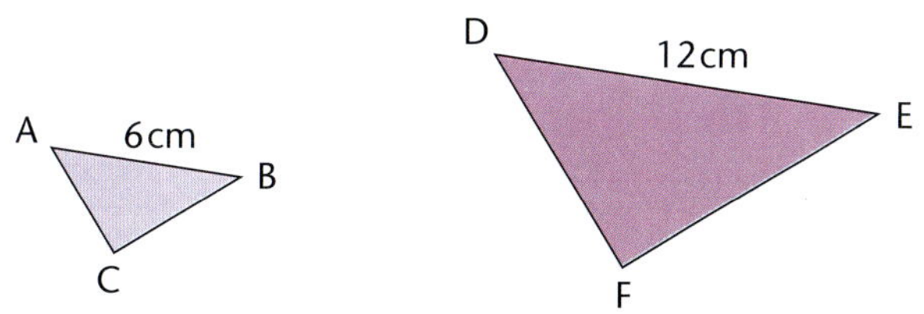

AB is the longest side of triangle ABC, and DE is the longest side of triangle DEF. The area of triangle ABC is 8 cm².
What is the area of triangle DEF?

2 These two parallelograms are similar.

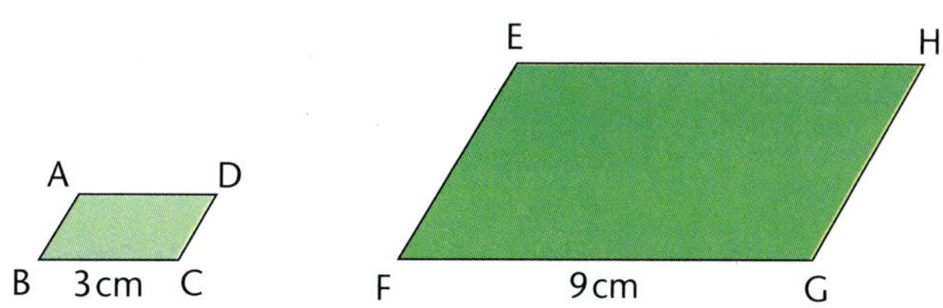

The area of parallelogram EFGH is 27 cm².
What is the area of parallelogram ABCD?

3 These two hexagons are similar. The length of AB is 5 cm and the length of GH is 15 cm

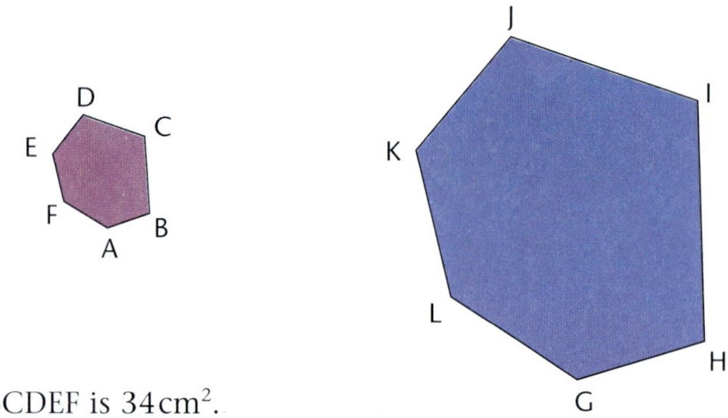

The area of hexagon ABCDEF is $34\,\text{cm}^2$.
What is the area of hexagon GHIJKL?

4 Rectangles A and B are similar.
The perimeter of rectangle A is 30 cm and of rectangle B is 40 cm.
The area of rectangle B is $80\,\text{cm}^2$.
What is the area of rectangle A?

5 D and E are the midpoints of the sides BC and CA of triangle ABC.
The area of triangle ABC is $56\,\text{cm}^2$.
What is the area of triangle EDC?

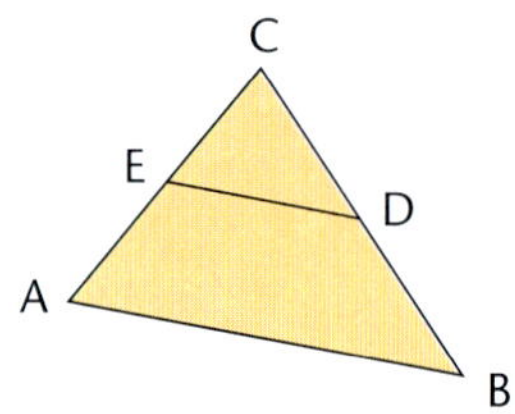

6 Two isosceles triangles are similar. Their areas are $16\,\text{cm}^2$ and $100\,\text{cm}^2$.
The perimeter of the smaller triangle is 24 cm.
What is the perimeter of the larger triangle?

7 In this diagram, ST is parallel to PQ. $\angle SRT = 70°$. $\angle RQP = 50°$.

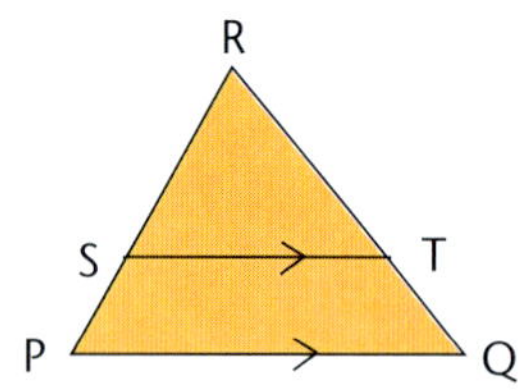

(**a**) Find all the angles of triangle STR and triangle PQR.

(**b**) Explain why triangle STR is similar to triangle PQR.

(**c**) The area of triangle STR is $40\,\text{cm}^2$ and the area of triangle PQR is $90\,\text{cm}^2$. What is the ratio of the length of ST to the length of PQ?

(**d**) Find the ratio in which the point S divides PR and the ratio in which the point T divides QR.

8 This equilateral triangle has sides of length 2 units and is dissected into two 'set-square' triangles.

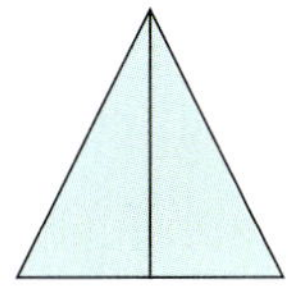

Four of these triangles are used to make this pattern.

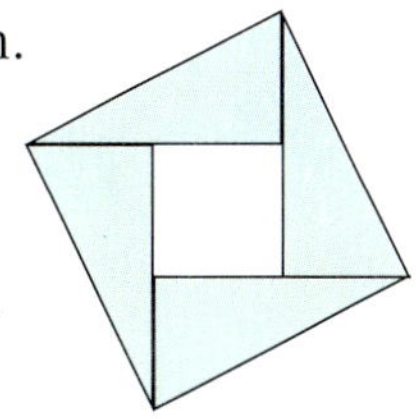

(**a**) Find the area of the large square.

(**b**) Find the area of one of the 'set square' triangles.

(**c**) Find the area of the small unshaded square.

COURSEWORK OPPORTUNITY

Set-square triangles

Four identical set-square triangles (with angles of 30°, 60° and 90°) are used to make each of the following three patterns. The size of the four triangles in each pattern are the same.

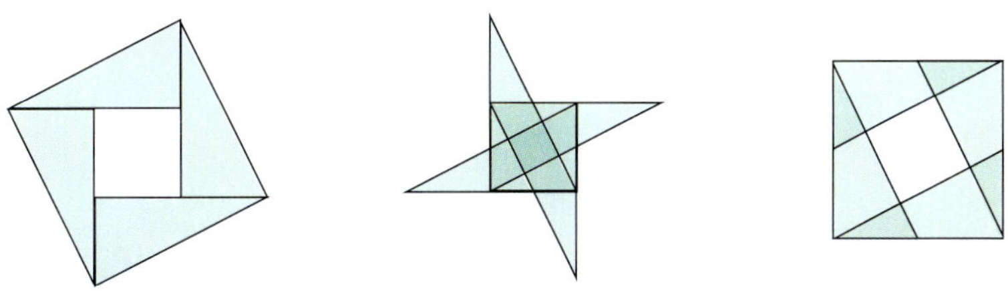

Describe and investigate these three patterns and the connections between them.

It is suggested that you do *not* use a calculator: if you find lengths or areas in terms of square roots then try to work with the square roots themselves.

You might want to consider these questions.

- What similar triangles can be seen in these three patterns?
  What other similar shapes can be seen?
- What are the relationships between the areas of the squares in these three patterns?
  What about the areas of other shapes?
- Explain some of the relationships between lengths and areas.

Create designs of your own, involving similar shapes and explore the relationships between them.

CHAPTER SUMMARY

Pythagoras' theorem

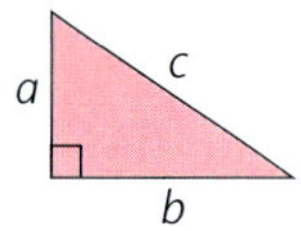

$a^2 + b^2 = c^2$

Examples of the use of Pythagoras theorem

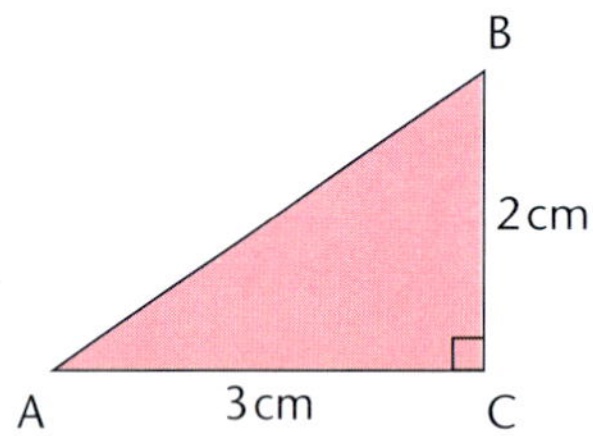

Length of AB is $\sqrt{2^2 + 3^2}$ cm
$= \sqrt{13}$ cm
$= 3.61$ cm

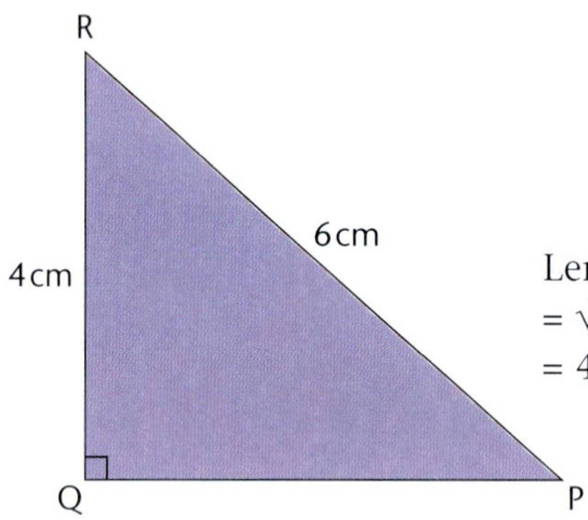

Length of PQ is $\sqrt{6^2 - 4^2}$ cm
$= \sqrt{20}$ cm
$= 4.47$ cm

It is useful to remember these **Pythagorean triads**.

3, 4, 5   5, 12, 13   8, 15, 17

Manipulation of square roots (or surds)

Here are some examples.

$\sqrt{12} = \sqrt{4} \times \sqrt{3} = 2\sqrt{3}$

$(\sqrt{7})^3 = 7\sqrt{7}$

$\sqrt{2}(\sqrt{2} + 3) = 2 + 3\sqrt{2}$

$(2 - \sqrt{3})^2 = 4 - 4\sqrt{3} + 3 = 7 - 4\sqrt{3}$

$\frac{\sqrt{12} + \sqrt{27}}{\sqrt{3}} = \frac{\sqrt{12}}{\sqrt{3}} + \frac{\sqrt{27}}{\sqrt{3}} = \sqrt{4} + \sqrt{9} = 5$

$\frac{8}{\sqrt{2}} = 4\sqrt{2}$

Similar shapes

In Mathematics, two shapes are **similar** if they are the same shape; they can be a different size.

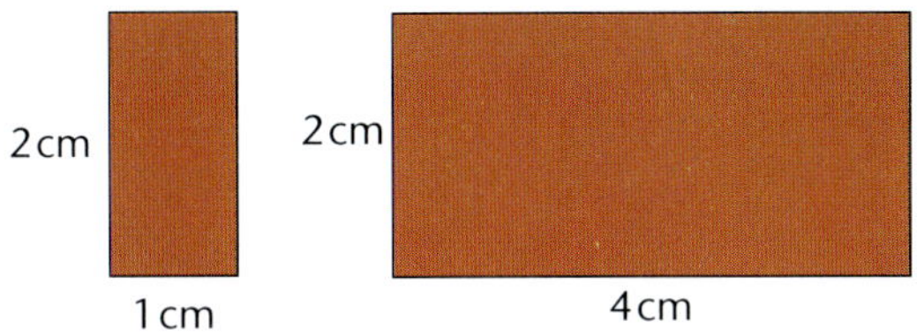

Two similar rectangles

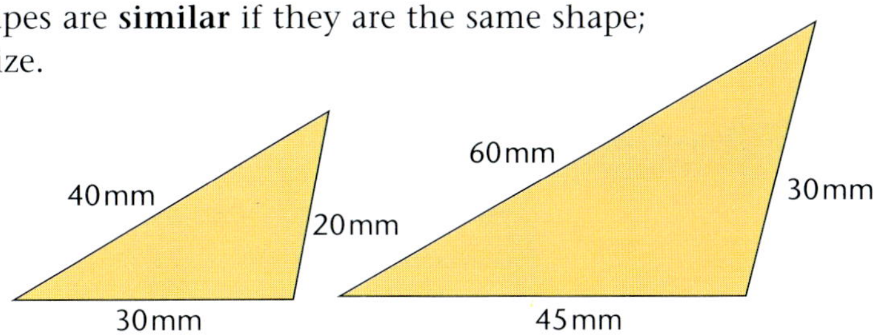

Two similar triangles

If two shapes are similar, their angles are equal and their sides are in the same ratio.

Areas of similar shapes

If two shapes are similar and if the lengths in one shape are 2 times the corresponding lengths in the other shape, the area of one shape is 4 times the area of the other shape.

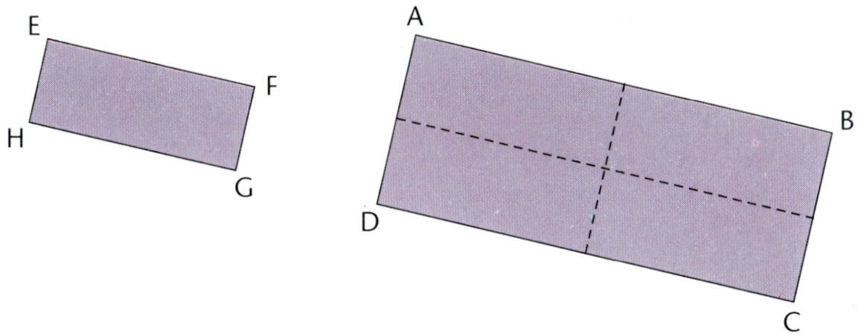

Rectangle ABCD is 4 times the area of rectangle EFGH.

If the lengths in one shape are 3 times the corresponding lengths in the other, the area is 9 times the area of the other.

Triangle ABC is 9 times the area of triangle DEF.

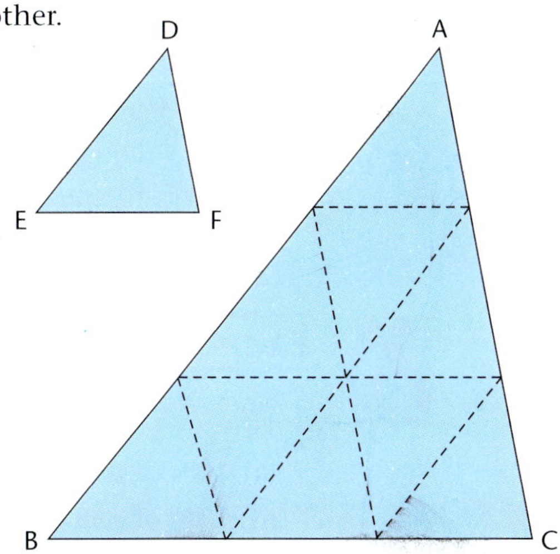

If the lengths in one shape are k times the corresponding lengths in the other the area is k^2 times the area of the other.

CHAPTER 6

PERCENTAGES

This chapter is about:

- using percentages
- scale factors for percentage change
- reverse percentages
- repeated percentage change.

Using percentages

DISCUSSION POINT

- Check that you know how to work out easy percentages, *without* your calculator.

  What is 50%, 25%, ... of £270?

  What is 10%, 20%, 5%, ... of £38.60?

  What is the VAT (at 17.5%) on £36?

- Check that you know how to work out percentages using a calculator.

  What is 37% of £530?

- Check that you know how to find one quantity as a percentage of another.

  What percentage of £5 is £1.30?

- Check that you know how to work out percentage changes.

  What is £80 increased by 15%?

  What is the percentage change when £65 is decreased to £61?

EXERCISE 1

1 Find

(a) 10% of £560 (b) 5% of £70 (c) 50% of £17

(d) 75% of £38 (e) 20% of £27 (f) 90% of £280

2 Find

(a) 3% of £20 (b) 7% of £12 (c) 20% of an hour

(d) $33\frac{1}{3}$% of £75 (e) $17\frac{1}{2}$% of £320 (f) 150% of 28

3 Increase each of these amounts by the percentage given.

(a) £2 by 6% (b) £20 by 10% (c) £50 by 8%

4 Decrease each of these amounts by the percentage given.

(a) £5 by 5% (b) £30 by 8% (c) £22 by 9%

EXERCISE 2

1 VAT (value added tax) has to be added on to all these invoices before they are paid. Use this year's rate to work out the final total for each invoice.

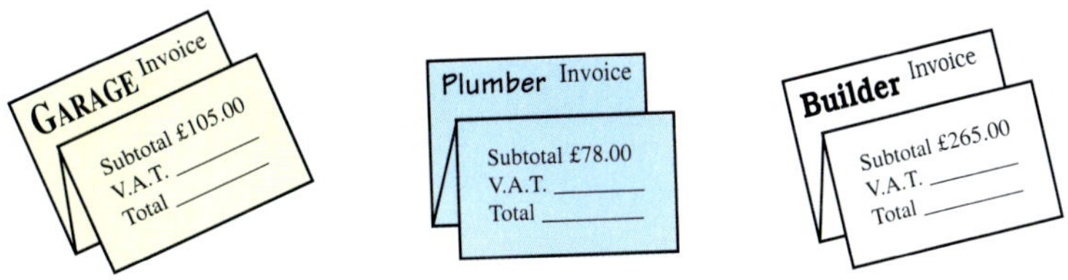

2 Find the percentage that

(a) 50p is of £8 (b) £3 is of £12

(c) 24 minutes is of an hour (d) 8 minutes is of 2 hours

(e) 3 minutes is of $\frac{3}{4}$ hour (f) 70 minutes is of 1 hour

3 These are the January and April phone bills for three households.

Household	January	April
A	£48	£58
B	£72	£82
C	£35	£28

Find the change for each household and what percentage it is of the January bill.

4 These are the prices of goods before and during a sale

Goods	Before sale	In the sale
TV	£168	£130
Freezer	£360	£275
Cooker	£620	£470

What was the percentage reduction in each case?

5 An old bike was bought for £50 and another £80 was spent on the parts and labour to get it working.
It was then sold for £165.
What was the percentage profit on the total outlay?

6 In a village, 60% of the men are married to 40% of the women.
What percentage of the adult population is married?

Percentage scale factors

DISCUSSION POINT

These problems can be solved using the scale factors shown in the flow charts.

Increase £70 by 4%.

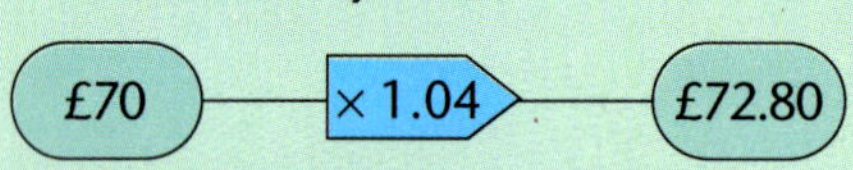

Decrease £250 by 5%

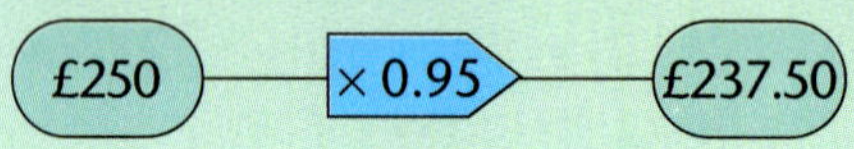

What scale factors would you use to solve these problems?
Increase by 7%.
Decrease by 15%.

EXERCISE 3

1 Copy and complete this table of percentage changes and their equivalent scale factors.

Percentage change	Scale factor
increase by 5%	× 1.05
	× 0.92
decrease by 25%	
	× 1.2
	× 1.5
decrease by 50%	
	× 2

2 Increase each of these amounts by the percentage given.

(a) £75 by 25% (b) £200 by $17\frac{1}{2}$% (c) £50 by 120%

3 Decrease each of these amounts by the percentage given.

(a) £93.75 by 20% (b) £235 by 14.9% (c) £40 by 90%

4 A settee is priced at £570. During a year, its price increases by 5%, decreases by 20% and then increases by 10%.

(a) What is the final price?

(b) What is the overall percentage change?

5 Prices in a stationery store are decreased by 8%, then increased by 5% and finally increased by 10%.
What is the overall percentage change?

6 Prices in a DIY store are increased by 8%, then decreased by 10% and finally decreased by 5%.
What is the overall percentage change?

7 The sides of a rectangle measure 4 cm and 3 cm.
Both lengths are increased by 10%.

(a) Find the new area.

(b) What is the percentage increase in the area?

8 The sides of a rectangle measure a cm and b cm.
Both lengths are increased by 10%.

(a) Find the new area.

(b) What is the percentage increase in the area?

9 The lengths of the sides of a rectangle are a and b.

(a) Both lengths are increased by 5%.
What is the percentage increase in the area?

(b) What happens if both lengths are increased by 20% instead?

(c) What percentage should both lengths be increased by to produce an 80% increase in the area?

10 The lengths of the sides of a rectangle are a and b.

(a) Both lengths are decreased by 5%.
What is the percentage decrease in the area?

(b) What happens if both lengths are decreased by 7% instead?

(c) What percentage should both lengths be decreased by to produce a 60% decrease in the area?

11 One side of a rectangle is increased by 10% and the other side is decreased by 10%.
What is the percentage change in its area?

Reversing a percentage change

After a number is increased by 10%, the answer is 26.4. What was the number?

Increasing by 10% is equivalent to multiplying by a scale factor of 1.1.

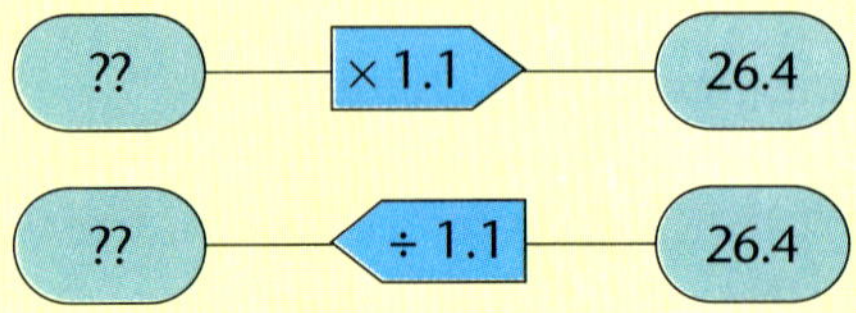

Working backwards on the flowchart, the number was 26.4 ÷ 1.1 = 24.

EXERCISE 4

1 After the annual stock check, all the prices were increased by 8%.

If these are the new prices, what were the old prices?

(a) £27 (b) £81 (c) £40.50

(d) £93.96 (e) £285 (f) 10p

2 In a sale, all the goods were reduced by 30%.

If these are the new prices, what were they before the sale?

(a) £35 (b) £56 (c) £147

(d) £6.30 (e) £3.50 (f) 14p

3 The special offer shampoo container said '25% extra'.

It had 600ml of shampoo in it.

How much shampoo was in the original bottle?

4 A drink can offers '13% EXTRA FREE'.

The volume of drink in the can is 500ml.

What was the volume of drink in the can before this free offer?

5 The label on a jar of barbecue sauce says '50% FREE – 284ml for the price of 184ml'.

How accurate is the percentage given on the label?

Do you think the label is misleading?

6 The nutrition information on a packet of breakfast cereal shows the quantity of each vitamin in either 100 g or in a 37.5 g helping, and what proportion it is of the recommended daily allowance, the RDA.

	per 100 g	per 37.5g serving
energy	1439kJ	540kJ
	339kcal	127kcal
protein	11.5g	4.3g
carbohydrate	67.3g	25.2g
(of which sugars)	(4.7g)	(1.8g)
fat	2.7g	1.0g
(of which saturates)	(0.7g)	(0.3g)
fibre	10.9g	4.1g
soluble	3.2g	1.2g
insoluble	7.7g	2.9g
sodium	0.3g	0.1g
vitamins		
thiamin B1	1.2mg / 85%RDA	0.4mg / 32%RDA
riboflavin B2	1.4mg / 85%RDA	0.5mg / 33%RDA
niacin	15.3mg / 85%RDA	5.7mg / 32%RDA
folacin (folic acid)	170.0µg / 85%RDA	63.8µg / 32%RDA
iron	11.9mg / 85%RDA	4.5mg / 32%RDA

(**a**) Estimate the RDA of thiamin, riboflavin, niacin and folacin from both the 100 g data and the 37.5 g data.

(**b**) Comment on your results.

Repeated percentage change

Exercise 5

1 A television is priced at £270. In January, its price is increased by 10%. In April, it is increased by 10% again. What percentage reduction must be made in June for its price to return to the original £270?

2 A population of bugs increases by 18% a year. If the population is 2000 now, how many years will it take to double in size?

3 £1000 is deposited in a new savings account which adds 4.2% interest each year. The money is left in the account.
How much will be in the account after

(**a**) 5 years? (**b**) 10 years?

4 After an audit, office equipment and furniture is valued at £25000. It is estimated that it loses 10% of its value every year through depreciation. What will be its value after five years?

5 The contents of a house are valued at £20000 for insurance purposes.
It is expected that the value will depreciate at 6% a year.
How much will the contents be worth after three years?

6 A lottery winner puts half a million pounds in a savings account earning 7% interest a year. If it is left there until it is worth a million pounds, how long does that take?

7 A bank charges interest at the rate of 1.4% a month for a loan of £3000.

(**a**) If nothing is paid, how much is owed after 12 months?

(**b**) What is the APR equivalent to a rate of 1.4% a month?

The APR (annual percentage rate) is the percentage of a loan charged as interest after one year.

DISCUSSION POINT

Paying back a loan

£2000 is borrowed and has to be repaid over two years at the rate of £99.85 a month.

The interest rate is 1.5% per month.

This table shows the results of the calculations for each month.

Month	Amount	With interest	Less payment
1	2000.00	2030.00	1930.15
2	1930.15	1959.10	1859.25
3	1859.25	1887.14	1787.29
4	1787.29	1814.10	1714.25
5	1714.25	1739.96	1640.11
6	1640.11	1664.72	1564.87
7	1564.87	1588.34	1488.49
8	1488.49	1510.82	1410.97
9	1410.97	1432.13	1332.28
10	1332.28	1352.26	1252.41
11	1252.41	1271.20	1171.35
12	1171.35	1188.92	1089.07
13	1089.07	1105.41	1005.56
14	1005.56	1020.64	920.79
15	920.79	934.60	834.75
16	834.75	847.27	747.42
17	747.42	758.64	658.79
18	658.79	668.67	568.82
19	568.82	577.35	477.50
20	477.50	484.66	384.81
21	384.81	390.58	290.73
22	290.73	295.10	195.25
23	195.25	198.17	98.32
24	98.32	99.80	–0.05

Check that you understand how the table was worked out.

APR (annual percentage rate) is the rate of interest that would have been due if no repayments were made until the end of the year.
On this loan, since $1.015^{12} = 119.56$, the APR is 19.56%.

How much more than the £2000 you borrowed, do you pay back?

However else they advertise their services, money lenders are obliged by law to quote the APR they are charging so that borrowers can make comparisons more easily.
Look in newspapers and collect leaflets from banks and building societies to find up-to-date information on loans and APRs.

CHAPTER SUMMARY

Finding a percentage of a number

15% of £320 = 15 ÷ 100 × £320 = £48

Finding one number as a percentage of another

What percentage is 3 of 12?
3 ÷ 12 × 100% = 25%

Percentage change

£15 decreased by 10% is £13.50 (because 10% of £15 is £1.50 and £15 – £13.50 = £1.50).

Using scale factors to work out percentage changes

What is £60 increased by 7%?
£60 × 1.07 = £64.20
What is £15 reduced by 10%?
£15 × 0.90 = £13.50

Finding overall percentage change without knowing (or using) the quantity

A price is increased by 10%. It is then decreased by 8%. What is the overall percentage change?
1.10 × 0.92 = 1.012
So, the overall change is an increase by 1.2%.

Reversing a percentage change

If, after a 10% reduction, the new price is £13.50, what was the original price?
A 10% reduction is found by multiplying by 0.90.
So divide by 0.90 to find the original price.
£13.50 ÷ 0.9 = £15

Repeated percentage change

If £15 is increased by 12% a year for five years, what is the new amount?
£15 × 1.12^5 = £26.44
A bank charges 1.3% interest per month. What is the APR (annual percentage rate)?
1.013^{12} = 1.168 (to 3 d.p.)
The APR is 16.8%.

CHAPTER 7

CUBES AND SEQUENCES

This chapter is about:

- exploring properties of volumes and surface area of cube models
- making difference tables for sequences
- finding the rule for the *n*th term of linear, quadratic and other sequences
- volumes and surface areas of similar solids
- Pythagoras' theorem in 3D shapes
- justifying generalisations.

Linear sequences

DISCUSSION POINT

Look at this sequence of cube models.

- Write down the number of cubes in each model. Continue the sequence.
- Explain how you know how to continue the sequence.
- How many cubes are needed to make the *n*th model?

This table may help you.

Model no.	Number of cubes
1	1
2	$1 + 4$
3	$1 + 4 + 4 = 1 + 2 \times 4$
4	$1 + 4 + 4 + 4 = 1 + 3 \times 4$
n	? ...

Check that your formula is correct by substituting a value for *n* and then comparing your answer with the appropriate model.

A **linear sequence** is one which goes up (or down) in equal steps.

EXERCISE 1

1 Find and check a formula for the *n*th term of each of these linear sequences.

(a) 5, 8, 11, 14, 17, ...
(b) 4, 9, 14, 19, 24, ...
(c) 13, 9, 5, 1, –3, ...`
(d) 0, 2.5, 5, 7.5, 10, ...
(e) 50, 41, 32, 23, 14, 5, ...
(f) –10, –6, –2, 2, ...
(g) 12, 13.8, 15.6, 17.4, 19.2, ...

2 Find and check a formula for each of these sequences.

(a) $\frac{1}{3}, \frac{2}{5}, \frac{3}{7}, \frac{4}{9}, \frac{5}{11}, \ldots$
(b) $\frac{3}{10}, \frac{5}{13}, \frac{7}{16}, \frac{9}{19}, \frac{11}{22}, \ldots$
(c) $\frac{7}{15}, \frac{7}{21}, \frac{7}{27}, \frac{7}{33}, \frac{7}{39}, \ldots$
(d) $\frac{3}{8}, \frac{2}{11}, \frac{1}{14}, 0, -\frac{1}{20}, \ldots$
(e) $\frac{1}{9}, \frac{1}{3}, \frac{5}{9}, \frac{7}{9}, 1, \ldots$
(f) $\frac{1}{5}, \frac{1}{3}, \frac{3}{7}, \frac{1}{2}, \frac{5}{9}, \ldots$

3 (a) Is 100 a member of the linear sequence 9, 12, 15, 18, 21, ... ?
Give a reason for your answer.

(b) Is 10 000 a member of the linear sequence 1, 10, 19, 28, 37, ... ?
Give a reason for your answer.

(c) Is 5432 a member of the linear sequence 8, 14, 20, 26, 32, ... ?
Give a reason for your answer.

(d) What is the first member of the linear sequence 32, 49, 66, 83, 100, ... which is bigger than a million?

(e) What is the first member of the linear sequence 2843, 2820, 2797, 2774, 2751, ... which is less than zero?

4 The linear sequence 7, 15, 23, 31, 39, ... ends with 1943.
How many terms are there in the sequence?

5 (a) 50 is one term in the linear sequence 6, 10, 14, ...
Which term is it?

(b) What other linear sequences of *whole* numbers which start with the number 6 have 50 in them?
Which term is 50 in each of these sequences?

DISCUSSION POINT
Why do you think that sequences which go up (or down) in equal steps are called linear sequences?

Difference patterns

In linear sequences, the step from one term to the next is always the same. This is shown by the difference pattern.

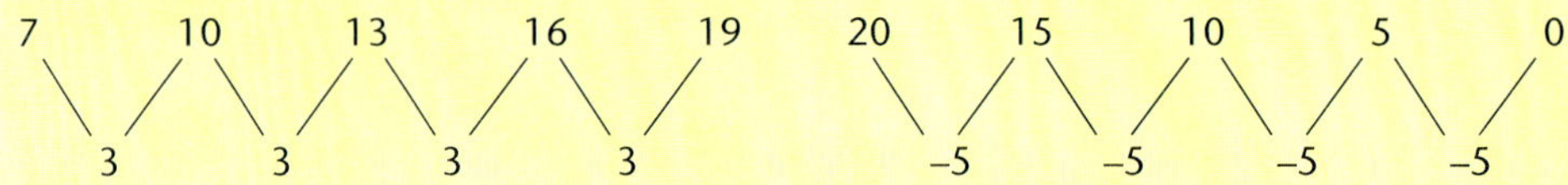

Difference patterns can sometimes be helpful with more complicated sequences.

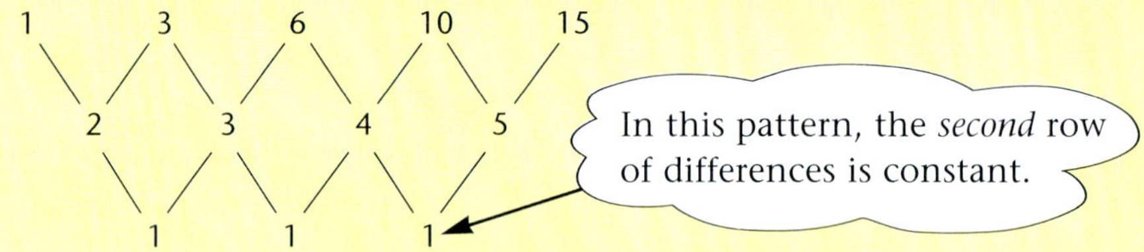

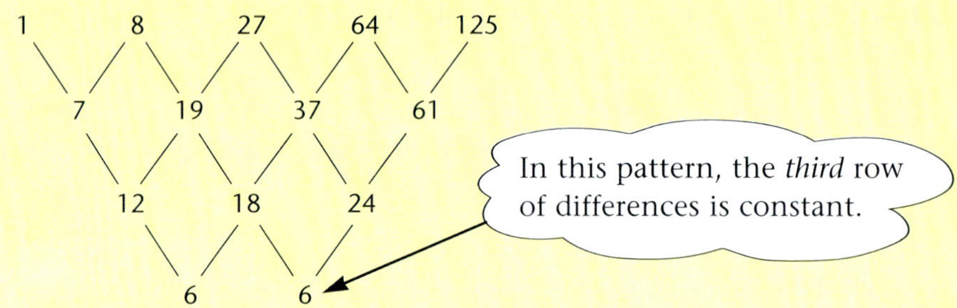

Exercise 2

1 Write out the difference pattern for the first ten triangular numbers 1, 3, 6, 10, 15....

2 Write out the difference pattern for the first ten cube numbers 1, 8, 27, ...

3 Write out the difference pattern for each of these sequences, and find the next two terms of each sequence.

(**a**) 3, 6, 11, 18, 27, ...

(**b**) 3, 12, 27, 48, 75, ...

(**c**) 4, 10, 18, 28, 40, ...

(**d**) 1, 2, 8, 22, 47, ...

(**e**) 1, 5, 6, 4, –1, ...

(**f**) 1, 5, 11, 22, 42, 76, 130, ...

4 Use difference patterns to help you make up some sequences of your own. Ask someone else to continue your sequences.

5 Find the next three terms for each of these sequences.
Do difference patterns help?

(a) 1, 2, 4, 8, 16, ...
(b) 4, 12, 36, 108, 324, ...
(c) 1, 1, 2, 3, 5, ...
(d) 3, –6, 12, –24, 48, ...
(e) 80, 40, 20, 10, 5, ...
(f) 512, 128, 32, 8, 2, ...
(g) 2, 5, 7, 12, 19, ...
(h) 10, 26, 18, 22, 20, ...

6 Write out the difference pattern for the sequence whose nth term is

(a) $n^2 - 2n + 1$
(b) $n(n + 1)(n - 1)$
(c) $n^3 + n^2 + n + 1$
(d) $\frac{1}{2}n(n + 1)$
(e) $\frac{1}{2}n^2(n - 1)$
(f) $\frac{1}{6}n(n + 1)(2n + 1)$

Using difference patterns to find the *n*th term of a quadratic sequence

Exercise 3

1 Write out the difference pattern for the sequence whose nth term is

(a) n^2
(b) $n^2 + 3n$
(c) $5n^2 - 2n + 7$
(d) $\frac{1}{2}n^2$
(e) $-2n^2$
(f) $8 - 3n^2$

Making and testing a generalisation

2 For each sequence in Question 1, look at your second row of differences.
What connection is there between these and the formula for the nth term?

3 Test the prediction you made in Question 2 on some sequences of your own.

Sequences containing an n^2 term but no higher power of n are called **quadratic** sequences.
The number in front of n^2 or n is called the **coefficient**.

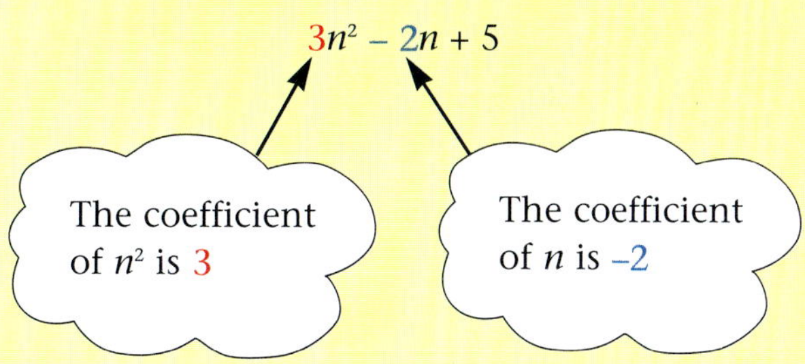

In Exercise 3, you might have discovered that, in a *quadratic* sequence, the second row of differences is constant. *Halving* this constant gives the coefficient of n^2 in the formula.

This rule can be used to find the nth term of a seauence.

Example

Find the nth term of the sequence 4, 13, 26, 43, 64, … .

First, write out the difference pattern.

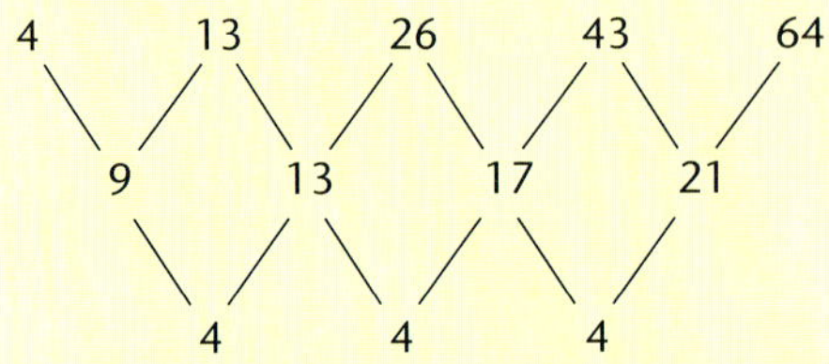

This second row of constant differences of 4 means that the formula is quadratic and contains a $2n^2$ term.

Now subtract this $2n^2$ from the given sequence and see what is left.

Sequence:	4	13	26	43	64
$2n^2$:	2	8	18	32	50
	2	5	8	11	14

Now find the rule for what is left. This is $3n - 1$.

So, the complete formula for the original sequence is $2n^2 + 3n - 1$.

It is always worth checking your answer.

For example, substituting $n = 3$ gives $18 + 9 - 1 = 26$, which is correct.

EXERCISE 4

1 Find the formula for the nth term of each of these sequences.

(a) 3, 12, 27, 48, 75, 108, …

(b) 4, 16, 36, 64, 100, 144, …

(c) $\frac{1}{2}$, 2, $4\frac{1}{2}$, 8, $12\frac{1}{2}$, 18, …

(d) 3, 6, 11, 18, 27, 38, …

(e) 11, 14, 19, 26, 35, 46, …

(f) –2, 1, 6, 13, 22, 33, …

2 Find the formula for the nth term of each of these sequences.

(a) 2, 6, 12, 20, 30, 42, …

(b) 4, 10, 18, 28, 40, 54, …

(c) 3, 10, 21, 36, 55, 78, …

(d) 6, 13, 24, 39, 58, 81, …

(e) 6, 12, 20, 30, 42, 56, …

(f) 2, 9, 18, 29, 42, 57, …

(g) –1, 0, 3, 8, 15, 24, …

(h) 2, 2, 0, –4, –10, –18, …

(i) $1\frac{1}{2}$, 4, $7\frac{1}{2}$, 12, $17\frac{1}{2}$, 24, …

(j) 2, 3, 3, 2, 0, –3, …

3 Find the formula for the nth term of each of these sequences.

(a) $\frac{1}{4}, \frac{4}{9}, \frac{9}{16}, \frac{16}{25}, \frac{25}{36}, \ldots$

(b) $\frac{2}{5}, \frac{6}{11}, \frac{12}{21}, \frac{20}{35}, \frac{30}{53}, \ldots$

(c) $\frac{1}{1}, \frac{1}{3}, \frac{1}{6}, \frac{1}{10}, \frac{1}{15}, \ldots$

(d) $\frac{1}{9}, \frac{3}{16}, \frac{6}{25}, \frac{5}{18}, \frac{15}{49}, \ldots$

Justifying a generalisation

4 This formula can be used to represent the nth term of *any* quadratic sequence: $an^2 + bn + c$.

(a) Write down the first six terms of the sequence whose nth term is given by this formula.
(Each of your terms will be an expression involving a, b and c.)

(b) Complete a difference pattern for this sequence.

(c) What does your difference pattern prove about the second row of differences of *any* quadratic sequence?

Finding the *n*th term of cubic and other sequences

Exercise 5

1 Write out the difference pattern for the sequence whose nth term is

(a) n^3 (b) $n^3 - n$ (c) $2n^3 + n$ (d) $3n^2 - n^3$ (e) $\frac{3}{2}n^3$ (f) $\frac{1}{6}n^3$

2 For each sequence in Question 1, look at your *third* row of differences. What connection is there between these and the formula for the nth term?

3 Test the prediction you made in Question 2 on some sequences of your own.

Making and testing a generalisation

Sequences like those in Exercise 5 are called **cubic** sequences. They all contain an n^3 term.

You might have discovered that, for a *cubic sequence,* the *third* row of differences is constant. *Dividing* this constant by 6 gives the coefficient of n^3 in the formula.

Exercise 6

1 Find the formula for the nth term of each of these cubic sequences.

(a) 0, 7, 26, 63, 124, ...

(b) 3, 12, 33, 72, 135, ...

(c) 0, 4, 18, 48, 100, ...

2 Find the formula for the nth term of each of these cubic sequences.

(a) 4, 21, 64, 145, 276, ...

(b) 0, –6, –24, –60, –120, ...

(c) 1, 6, 19, 44, 85, ...

For help with part 3(a), look at Question 4 in Exercise 4.

Making and justifying generalisations

3 (a) What formula can be used to represent the nth term of *any* cubic sequence?

(b) Write down the first six terms of the sequence with this formula for its nth term.

(c) Complete a difference pattern for this sequence.

(d) What does your difference pattern prove about the third row of differences of *any* cubic sequence?

Making and justifying generalisations

4 (a) Investigate the difference patterns for the sequence whose nth term is

(i) $\frac{1}{2}n(n + 1)$ (ii) $\frac{1}{6}n(n + 1)(n + 2)$

(iii) $\frac{1}{24}n(n + 1)(n + 2)(n + 3)$

(b) How does the sequence of sequences in part (a) continue?
How does the sequence of difference patterns continue?

Making and justifying generalisations

5 Investigate the difference patterns for quartic sequences (containing an n^4 term).

Making and justifying generalisations

6 Investigate the difference patterns for quintic sequences (containing an n^5 term).

Making and justifying generalisations

7 Generalise the results of Questions 3, 5 and 6.

DISCUSSION POINT

These sequences are called **geometric sequences.**

1, 2, 4, 8, ... 2, 6, 18, 54, ...

1, $\frac{1}{5}$, $\frac{1}{25}$, $\frac{1}{125}$, ... 144, 72, 36, 18, ...

- What is the common property shared by all these sequences?
- Find a formula for the nth term of each sequence.
  Difference patterns will not help!

Sometimes it is useful to find the sum of the first n terms of a geometric sequence.

Look at this pattern.

- What fraction of the square is coloured orange?
- The drawing contains triangles of eight different sizes.
  Suppose nested squares were added so that triangles of n different sizes were coloured orange.
  What fraction of the area of the square would be orange then?
- Suppose the nested squares were continued forever ...

EXERCISE 7

1 Look at these six geometric sequences.

A: 1, 4, 16, 64, ... B: 1, 10, 100, 1000, ... C: 3, 6, 12, 24, ...

D: 10, 30, 90, 270, ... E: 1, $\frac{1}{4}$, $\frac{1}{16}$, $\frac{1}{64}$, ... F: 1000, 250, 62.5, ...

For each sequence

(**a**) find the next three terms

(**b**) find a formula for the *n*th term

2 Repeat Question 1 for these sequences.

A: 1, $\frac{1}{3}$, $\frac{1}{9}$, $\frac{1}{27}$, ... B: 8, 4, 2, 1, ... C: 100, 20, 4, ...

3 For each of the sequences in Question 2, find

(**a**) the *sum* of an infinite number of terms

(**b**) a formula for the *sum* of the first *n* terms

4 Look at this pattern of isoceles triangles. It is composed of triangles obtained by repeatedly halving one of the central triangles.

(**a**) What is the total area of the shaded triangles (if the area of the square is one unit)?

(**b**) Suppose the pattern is continued so that there are shaded triangles of *n* different sizes.
What is the total area now?

(**c**) Suppose the pattern is continued *forever*.
What is the total area now?

5 Look at these sequences.

A: –2, 4, –8, 16, ... B: 1, –3, 9, –27, ... C: –6, 12, –24, 48, ...

D: 1, $-\frac{1}{3}$, $\frac{1}{9}$, $-\frac{1}{27}$, ... E: 100, –50, 25, –12.5, ...

For each sequence

(**a**) explain why the sequence is a geometric sequence

(**b**) find the next three terms

(**c**) find a formula for the *n*th term

Sequences of cube models

Exercise 8 shows how formulae for sequences can be used to explain some properties of cube models.

Making and justifying generalisations

EXERCISE 8

1 Look at this sequence of cube models.

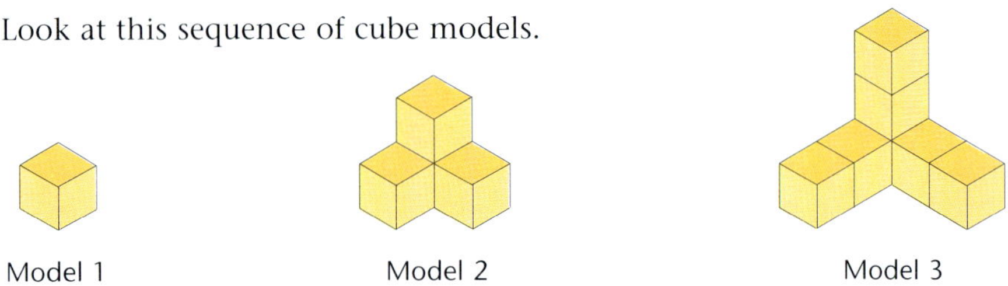

(a) Write down the numbers of cubes in the first six models.

(b) Find the nth term of the sequence of numbers of cubes.

(c) By considering the nth model, explain how you know that your formula is correct.

2 (a) Find the surface areas of the first six models in Question 1.

(b) Find the nth term of the sequence of surface areas.

(c) By considering the nth model, explain how you know that your formula for surface areas is correct.

3 Look at this sequence of cube models.

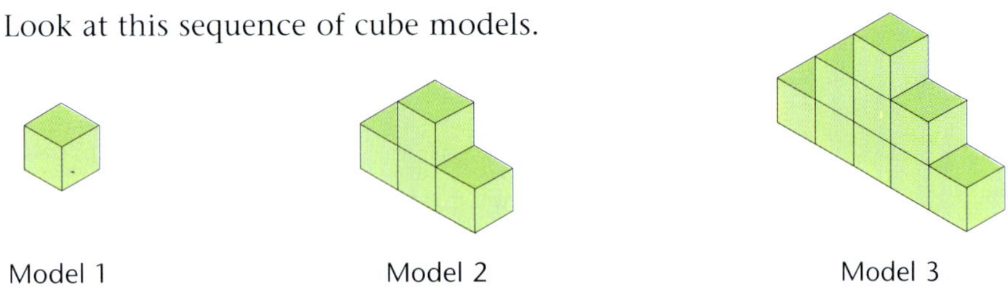

(a) Write down the numbers of cubes in the first six models of the sequence.

(b) Find the nth term of the sequence of numbers of cubes.

(c) Use this picture to help you to explain why your formula for part (b) is correct.

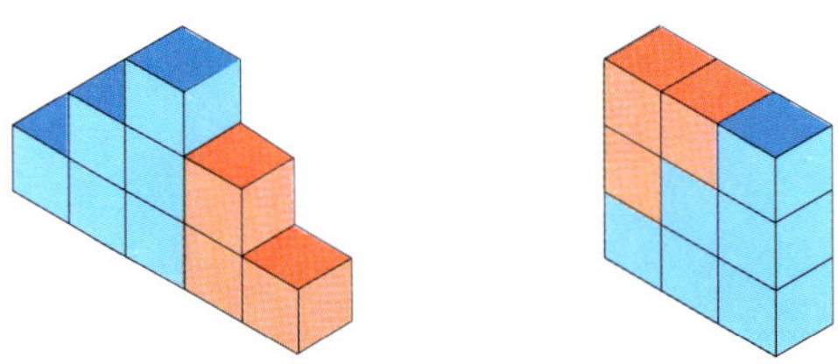

4 (a) Find the surface areas of the first six models in Question 3.

(b) Find the nth term of the sequence of surface areas.

(c) Explain how you know that your formula for surface areas is correct.

5 Look at this sequence of cube models.

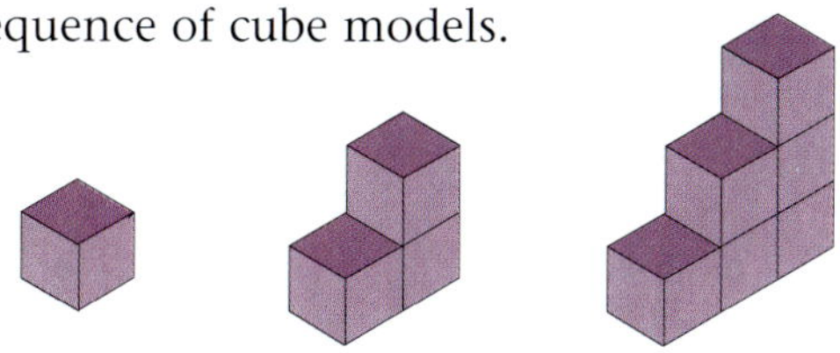

(**a**) Write down the numbers of cubes in the first six models of the sequence.

(**b**) Find the nth term of the sequence of numbers of cubes.

(**c**) This diagram shows how two copies of Model 3 can be fitted together to make a cuboid.

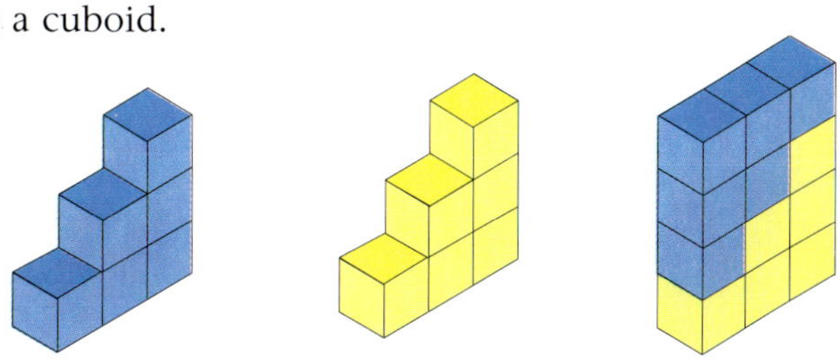

Use this to help you to explain why your formula for part (b) is correct.

6 (**a**) Find the nth term of the sequence of surface areas of the models in Question 5.

(**b**) Explain how you know that your formula for surface areas is correct.

COURSEWORK OPPORTUNITY

Sequences of cube models

Investigate your own sequence of cube models. You could consider

- the number of cubes used to make the models
- the surface areas of the models
- the total edge lengths of your models
- the number of edges in your models (you will need to define what you mean by an edge)
- the number of vertices in your models (you will need to define what you mean by a vertex).

For each property you investigate

- find a formula for model number n
- explain how you know your formula is correct by considering the geometry of the model.

Sequences of similar cube models

Resource Sheet A: *Isometric dot*

In Exercise 9, Questions 1 to 6 are about the same sequence of cubes.

Exercise 9

1 Find a formula for the number of cubes (volume) for Model n in this sequence of cubes.

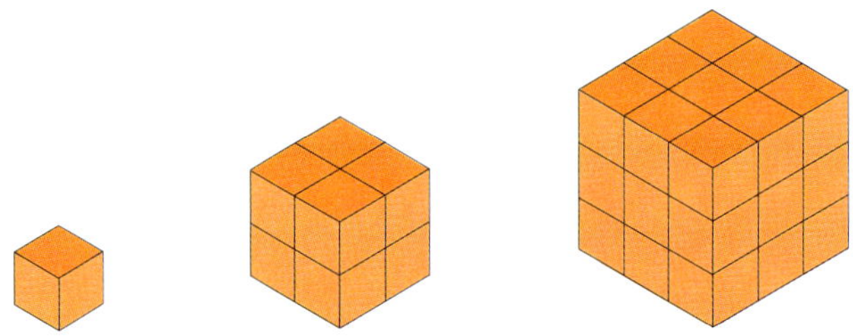

Model 1 Model 2 Model 3

All these models are the same shape. They differ only in size. They are **similar solids.**

2 Find a formula for the surface area of Model n, in the sequence of cubes in Question 1.

3 Model 2 has an edge length which is twice that of Model 1.
What is the relationship between

(**a**) their volumes? (**b**) their surface areas?

4 Compare the edge lengths, volumes and surface areas of Model 3 and Model 1.

5 A large cube has an edge length which is four times bigger than the edge length of a smaller cube.
How much bigger is its volume? What about its surface area?

6 A large cube has an edge length which is k times bigger than the edge length of a smaller cube.

(**a**) How much bigger is its volume and its surface area?

(**b**) Use your formulae for Model n, obtained in Questions 1 and 2, to show that your answers to part (a) are correct.

7 This is the first model in a sequence of similar models.

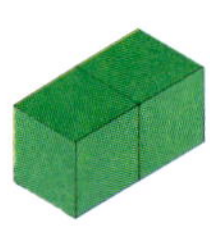

Model 2 is made by doubling all the edge lengths of the first model.
Model 3 is made by multiplying all edge lengths of the first model by 3, and so on.

(**a**) Draw a sketch of Model 2.

(**b**) Work out the volume and surface area of Model 1 and Model 2.

(**c**) Predict, and check, the volume and surface area of Model 3.

8 This is the first model in another sequence of similar models.

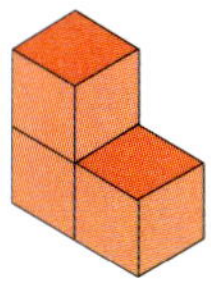

Model 2 and Model 3 are made by multiplying the edge lengths of the first model by 2 and by 3 (as in Question 7), and so on.

(**a**) Draw a sketch of Model 2.

(**b**) Work out the volume and surface area of the first three models in the sequence.

(**c**) Find formulae for the volume and for the surface area of Model *n*.

Making generalisations

9 (**a**) Explore how the volume and surface area change when the edge lengths of any model are doubled, trebled, ...

(**b**) Consider a model which has edge lengths *k* times those of a similar model.
What is the ratio of their volumes?
What is the ratio of their surface areas?

Proving theorems about the surface areas of cube models

Interlocking cubes
Resource Sheet A: *Isometric dot*

Unit cubes have edge lengths of 1 unit, a volume of 1 cubic unit and a surface area of 6 square units.

EXERCISE 10

This exercise is about models that can be made from unit cubes. The models are made by joining cubes by complete faces. You might need to make models with interlocking cubes to help you answer the questions.

1 (**a**) Consider models made from four unit cubes.
What different surface areas are possible?

(**b**) Repeat for five, six, seven and eight cubes.

2 Prove that the surface area of any cube model is an even number of square units.

Making and justifying generalisations

3 What is the maximum surface area for a model made of *n* cubes?
Prove your result.

4 Look again at the results you obtained for Question 1.
Decide whether this statement is true.

For a given number of cubes, for any even number between the minimum surface area and the maximum surface area, it is possible to find a cube model with this surface area.

5 **(a)** 343 cubes are used to make one large cube.
What is its surface area?

(b) The surface area of a large cube made from unit cubes is 1014 square units.
How many unit cubes does it contain?

6 The surface area (in square units) and volume (in cubic units) of a cuboid are both 288.
None of its faces are squares.
Find the lengths of the edges of the cuboid.

7 What is the minimum surface area for cube models made from these numbers of cubes?

(a) 27 **(b)** 26 **(c)** 30

8 Find *cuboid* models which have these surface areas.

(a) 22 square units **(b)** 32 square units **(c)** 52 square units

9 **(a)** Find out whether this statement is true.

There are no *cuboid* models with a surface area of 20 square units.

(b) Find which numbers, less than 20, *cannot* be the surface area for a cuboid model.

10 Find three cuboid models, each of which has a surface area of 128 square units.

11 **(a)** Is it possible to make a large cube from unit cubes so that its surface area is numerically equal to its volume?

(b) Find n such that a 4-by-5-by-n cuboid has surface area numerically equal to its volume.

(c) One of the edges of a cuboid is 4 units long.
Two of the faces of the cuboid are squares.
Its volume is numerically equal to its surface area.
Find its volume.

12 Two of the faces of a cuboid are squares.
Its surface area (in square units) and its volume (in cubic units) are both 250.
Find the lengths of the edges of the cuboid.

COURSEWORK OPPORTUNITY

Surface areas of cube models

Several of the ideas suggested in Exercise 9 could be explored further.

- What are the minimum surface areas of models made from different numbers of unit cubes?
- Which even numbers cannot be the surface area of a cuboid made from unit cubes?
- It is not possible to make a model with eight cubes which has a surface area of 26 square units (even though surface areas of 24 and 28 square units are possible). Find other impossibilities like this.

Exploring volumes, surface areas and lengths in cuboids

In this exercise, the cuboids are not necessarily made of unit cubes. The side lengths might not be whole numbers.

EXERCISE 11

1 Find the surface area of a cube with volume

(a) 10 cubic units (b) 100 cubic units (c) 1000 cubic units

2 Find the volume of a cube with surface area

(a) 30 square units (b) 60 square units (c) 100 square units

3 (a) Find a cuboid with a volume which is an even number of cubic units and a surface area which is an even number of square units.

(b) Describe a method for finding many different cuboids with this property. Prove that your method always works.

4 (a) Find a cuboid with a volume which is an odd number of cubic units and a surface area which is an even number of square units.

(b) Describe a method for finding many different cuboids with this property. Prove that your method always works.

5 (a) Find a cuboid with a volume which is an odd number of cubic units and a surface area which is an odd number of square units.

(b) Describe a method for finding many different cuboids with this property. Prove that your method always works.

6 (a) Find a cuboid with a volume which is an even number of cubic units and a surface area which is an odd number of square units.

(b) Describe a method for finding many different cuboids with this property. Prove that your method always works.

EXERCISE 12

A **face diagonal** of a cuboid is a diagonal drawn on one face of a cuboid.

A **space diagonal** of a cuboid is a diagonal joining opposite vertices of the cuboid.

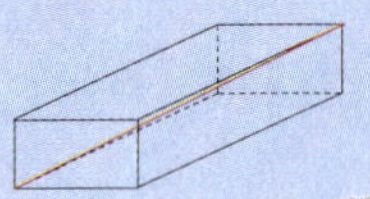

1 A cuboid has edges of lengths 3 cm, 4 cm and 5 cm.

(**a**) Find the surface area of the cuboid.

(**b**) Find the length of the longest face diagonal.

(**c**) Find the length of the shortest face diagonal.

(**d**) Find the length of a space diagonal.

2 A cuboid has edges of length 6 cm, 8 cm and 15 cm. Find the total length of all its diagonals (face diagonals and space diagonals).

3 This cube has edges of length 2 cm. M is the mid-point of BF and N is the mid-point of DH.

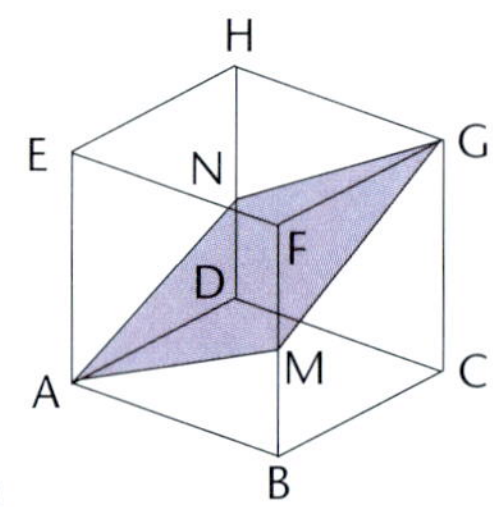

(**a**) What is the distance between A and G?

(**b**) What type of quadrilateral is AMGN?

(**c**) What is the perimeter of AMGN?

(**d**) What is the area of AMGN?

4 A cuboid has faces with areas 32 cm^2, 36 cm^2 and 72 cm^2. Find the volume of the cuboid.

5 A cuboid has volume 2156 cm^3. Two of its faces are squares. The total length of its edges is 156 cm. Find its surface area.

6 A cuboid has volume 6400 cm^3 and surface area 2080 cm^2. Two of its faces are squares. Find the distance between opposite vertices of the cube.

CHAPTER SUMMARY

Linear sequences

In linear sequences, the step from one term to the next is always the same. To find the formula for the nth term of the sequence 1, 5, 9, 13, ...

1st term = 1

2nd term = 1 + 4

3rd term = 1 + 4 + 4

nth term = $1 + (n - 1) \times 4 = 1 + 4n - 4 = 4n - 3$

Difference patterns

These diagrams help you to see how sequences change.

```
1       8       27       64       125
   7       19       37       61
      12       18       24
          6        6
```

Quadratic sequences

The formula for the nth term of a quadratic sequence is of the form $an^2 + bn + c$.
The second row of differences is constant and equal to $2a$.
Halving this constant gives the **coefficient** of n^2 in the formula.

Example

Find the nth term of the sequence 2, 13, 30, 53, 82, ...
First, write out the difference pattern.

2		13		30		53		82
	11		17		23		29	
		6		6		6		

This second row of constant differences of 6 means that the formula is quadratic and contains a $3n^2$ term.

Now subtract this $3n^2$ from the given sequence and see what is left.

Sequence:	2	13	30	53	82
$3n^2$:	3	12	27	48	75
	–1	1	3	5	7

Now find the rule for what is left. This is $2n - 3$.
So, the complete formula for the original sequence is $3n^2 + 2n - 3$.

Cubic sequences

The formula for the nth term of a cubic sequence is of the form $an^3 + bn^2 + cn + d$.
The third row of differences is constant and equal to $6a$.
Dividing this constant by 6 gives the coefficient of n^3 in the formula.

Geometric sequences

In a geometric sequence, each term is obtained by multiplying the previous term by a constant.
Difference patterns do *not* help with finding the next terms of the sequence.

Example

Find the nth term of this sequence: 2, 6, 18, 54, ... The sequence can be written as 2, 2×3, 2×3^2, 2×3^3, ... So, the nth term is $2 \times 3^{n-1}$.

Similar solids

If the edge lengths of two similar solids are in the ratio k:1, then the surface areas are in the ratio k^2:1. The volumes are in the ratio k^3:1.

Pythagoras' theorem in three dimensions

The space diagonal of a cuboid can be found by using Pythagoras' theorem twice.
Space diagonal = $\sqrt{a^2 + b^2 + c^2}$

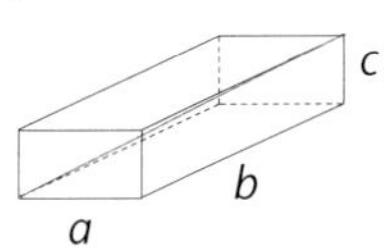

CHAPTER

8 Ratio, Rate and Proportion

This chapter is about:

- ratios
- rates including speed and density
- direct and inverse proportion.

Using ratios

DISCUSSION POINT

- In this family, the toddler weighs 15kg and her mother weighs 60kg.

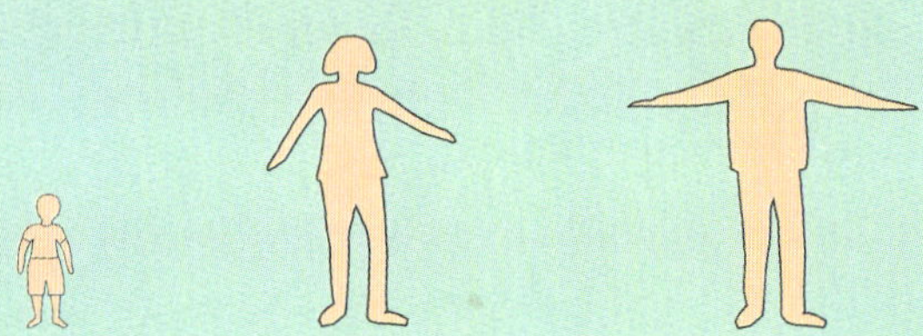

Their weights are in the ratio 1:4.

Another way to describe this is to say the toddler's weight is $\frac{1}{4}$ of her mother's.

The ratio of father's weight to mother's weight is 3:2.

What does the father weigh?

What is the ratio of the father's weight to the toddler's weight?

There are no units in a ratio, just numbers.

The quantities being compared must be in the *same* units.

- The ratio of 1 hour to 10 minutes is *not* 1:10.
  What is the correct ratio?
- Check that you know how to divide £60 in the ratio 3:2.
- Two points A and B lie 6cm apart on an infinite line and P is also a point on the line.

  The ratio AP:PB is 3:1.

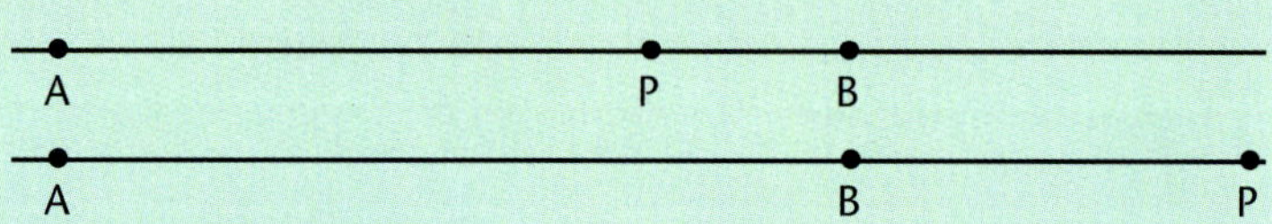

Check that you know how to find the two possible positions for P.

EXERCISE 1

1 Write these ratios in their simplest form.

(a) 10:6 (b) 64 cm:96 cm (c) 1 week:1 day

(d) 3 hours:40 mins (e) 75p:£2 (f) $1\,m^2:1000\,cm^2$

2 Divide £96 in the ratio

(a) 3:1 (b) 5:11 (c) 7:5 (d) 4:3:1 (e) 1:2:3 (f) 4:7

3 The scale on a map is 1:50 000.
The route from home to school measures 12.5 cm on the map.
How long is the journey to school, in kilometres?

4 The scale on a map is 1:25 000.

(a) How many centimetres on the map represent 1 km?

(b) The map is a rectangle 40 cm by 80 cm.
What is the area of the land represented by it?

5 A street map of London has a scale of 6 inches to 1 mile.

There are 1760 yards in a mile.

(a) What is the scale of this map in the form 1:*n*?

(b) The walking distance from Marble Arch to the Science Museum across Hyde Park measures about 25 cm on the map.
How long is the journey in kilometres?

6 Three points, A, B and Q, lie on a line. A and B are 6 cm apart.
AQ:QB is 1:3.
Find the two possible lengths of AQ.

7 Three points, C, D and R, lie on a line. C and D are 12 cm apart.
CR:RD is 5:3.
Find the two possible lengths of CR.

The line drawn in Question 8 is the **locus** of all points P such that LP:PM is 1:1.

8 L and M are two points, 9 cm apart. P is another point.

Draw a diagram with L and M on it.

Mark some possible positions for P so that LP:PM is 1:1.

Draw a line to show *all* the points which are the same distance from L as from M.

9 L and M are points 9 cm apart.
Find some positions for P so that LP:PM is 2:1.
What do you think the locus of P is?

10 A brother and sister invest their money in a business together.
The brother invests £25 000 and the sister invests £30 000.
They agree to share the profit in the same ratio as their investments.
The profit at the end of the first year is £10 923.

(**a**) How much do they each receive?

(**b**) What is the percentage profit on their investments?

11 Scientists wish to estimate the number of seals in the North Sea.
One year, in May, they capture 200, tag them and release them back into the sea. In August, they capture another 200 and find the ratio of tagged to untagged seals is 7:193. They assume the ratio of tagged:untagged in the whole population of seals is the same.
What do you think is their estimate of the number of *untagged* seals?

12 An environmentalist wants to estimate the number of fish in a lake.
She nets 150, tags them and puts them back. Two days later, she nets 80 and finds there are 11 tagged and 69 untagged in the sample.
Estimate the number of fish in the lake.

Rates: speed and density

Speed $= \dfrac{\textbf{distance}}{\textbf{time}}$

Units for speed include ms^{-1} (metres per second), m.p.h. (miles per hour) and k.p.h. (kilometres per hour).
The formula for speed gives the average speed.
Usually, speeds vary throughout a journey.

Density $= \dfrac{\textbf{mass}}{\textbf{volume}}$

Units for density include gcm^{-3} (grams per cubic centimetre) and kgm^{-3} (kilograms per cubic metre).

Exercise 2

1 A girl delivers papers for 45 minutes every morning, Monday to Saturday and earns a weekly rate of £8.10.

(**a**) What is her hourly rate of pay?

(**b**) One week she works for only four mornings. How much will she earn?

2 Some factory staff are paid 'piecework' rates.
The payment for a machinist is £1 for sewing hems on 20 skirts.

(**a**) How much is she paid for sewing 480 hems, one morning?

(**b**) She earned £40 altogether that day. How many more hems did she sew?

3 Brisk walking uses up about 20kJ of food energy per minute.
A cereal breakfast provides 540kJ in one portion.
For how long will this meal keep you walking?

4 Grass seed is to be scattered at the rate of 50g per square metre.
How big a lawn can be covered with a 2-kg bag of seed?

5 The exchange rate for American dollars is \$1.61 per £1 (or you could use today's rate).

(**a**) How many dollars will you get in exchange for £150?

(**b**) How many pounds would you get in exchange for \$1?

(**c**) The exchange rate goes up; in other words, you get more dollars to the pound.
Who will be better off for the change: an American student about to come to the UK, or a UK student about to go to America?

6 A4 paper is described as 80gsm which means it weighs 80 grams per square metre.

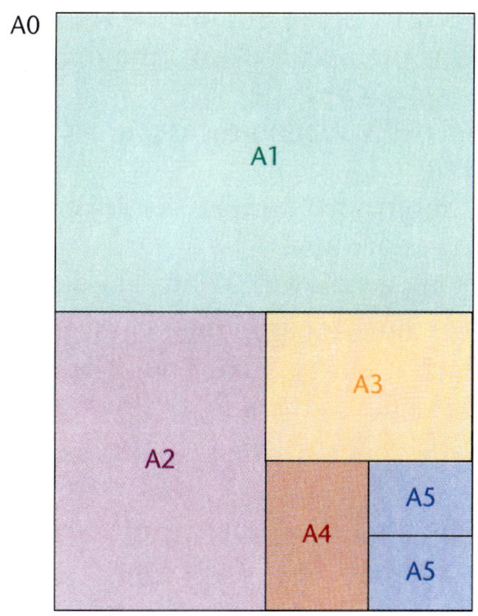

A0 paper has an area of $1\,\text{m}^2$.

(**a**) How much does one sheet of A4 paper weigh?

(**b**) How much does a ream (516 sheets) of A4 paper weigh?

7 A train leaves a station at 3.15 p.m. and arrives at a station 75 miles away at 4.30 p.m.
What is the average speed of the train?

8 A train leaves a station at 2.05 p.m. and arrives at 2.55 p.m. having travelled at an average speed of 90 m.p.h.
How far away is the station?

9 Most people can walk comfortably at a speed of $2\,\text{m}\,\text{s}^{-1}$, and swim at a speed of $1\,\text{m}\,\text{s}^{-1}$.

(a) How long would it take to cover 1 km walking, and 1 km swimming?

(b) How far would I travel if I kept walking for 30 minutes?
How far would I swim if I kept swimming for 30 minutes?

10 The density of fresh water is 1 gram per cubic centimetre (or $1\,\text{g}\,\text{cm}^{-3}$).
What is the mass of a litre of water?

11 The density of pure gold is $19\,\text{g}\,\text{cm}^{-3}$.
What is the volume of gold which weighs 50 g?

12 A cuboid of iron has a volume of $25\,\text{cm}^3$. It weighs 195 g.
What is the density of iron?

13 The density of aluminium is $11\,\text{g}\,\text{cm}^{-3}$.
What is the weight of an aluminium rod with a volume of $50\,\text{cm}^3$?

14 A car covers a round-town journey using petrol at the rate of 6.5 miles per litre.
On a motorway journey, the driver gets a better consumption rate of 8.5 miles per litre.
The tank is full with 35 litres of petrol.

(a) Use the data to estimate how far the car can travel before the fuel tank is empty. Give a range of answers to reflect the fact that you do not know what kind of driving will be done.

(b) How much petrol is needed for a motorway journey of 800 miles?

15 A route-finding computer program suggests this route for the journey from Leicester to Manchester.

Clock	Milometer	Road
0:00	0	From Leicester take M1
1:02	72	Take A road over Pennines
1:40	99	Join M67
1:45	104	Take A road into city
1:59	108	Arrive in Manchester centre

(a) What is the average speed for each stage of the journey?

(b) What is the average speed for the whole journey?

A distance of 5 miles is equivalent to 8 kilometres.

16 (a) How many kilometres are equivalent to 1 mile?

(b) How many miles are equivalent to 1km?

(c) Some UK speed limits are 30 m.p.h., 50 m.p.h. and 70 m.p.h. What are these limits, in k.p.h.?

(d) European cars warn the driver when the car is exceeding the speed limit of 120 k.p.h. How fast is this, in m.p.h.?

(e) How many $m s^{-1}$ are equivalent to the speed of 30 m.p.h.?

(f) World class runners finish the 100m race in under 10 seconds. What is their speed in m.p.h.?

17 The distance from the Earth to the Sun is approximately 150 million kilometres.
The speed of light is $300000 km s^{-1}$.
How long does it take for light to travel from the Sun to the Earth?

18 (a) Find the volumes of the Earth and the Moon.

(b) Find the ratio of the volume of the Moon to that of the Earth, in the form 1:*n*.

	Density	Mass
Earth	$5517 kg m^{-3}$	5.972×10^{24} kg
Moon	$3330 kg m^{-3}$	7.33×10^{22} kg

COURSEWORK OPPORTUNITY

Scout's pace

To cover a long distance on foot and still arrive in a state to talk, some people use 'scout's pace'. It involves alternately running and walking to cover the distance.
In one version of scout's pace, the person runs 100m, then walks 100m, runs 100m, walks 100m, and so on.

- Collect some data about running and walking speeds.
- How long would it take to cover 5km using scout's pace?
- How will the time taken vary with the distance?

In a different version of scout's pace, a person runs for 100 strides, walks for 100 steps, runs for 100 strides and so on.

- Collect some data about stride and step lengths.
- How long would it take to cover 5km using this version of scout's pace?
- How will the time taken vary with the distance?

A different version of scout's pace involves running for a minute, then walking for a minute, then running for a minute, and so on.
Investigate this version.

Direct proportion

DISCUSSION POINT

When quantities increase in the same ratio, they are in **direct proportion**.
Suppose 15 packets of crisps cost £3.45.
Copy and complete this table.

N (number of packets)	5	10	15	20	30	60	120
C (cost in £)	1.15		3.45		6.90		

We say the cost is directly proportional to the number of packets.
This is written as $C \propto N$.
The ratio $\frac{C}{N}$ is constant, so $C = kN$ where $k = 0.23$.

What does 0.23 represent?
k is called the **constant of proportionality**.

If values of *C* were plotted against values of *N*, what shape graph would you expect? Why?

EXERCISE 3

1 A car is being driven at a constant speed of 70 m.p.h.
The distance travelled in miles, *d*, is proportional to the time in minutes, *t*.

(**a**) Write down an equation connecting *d* and *t*.

(**b**) What is the value of the constant of proportionality?
What does this represent?

(**c**) Copy and complete this table

t (minutes)		1	3	6	12	30	48	60
d (miles)	1							70

2 The perimeter of this shape, *P*, is proportional to the length of an edge, *L*.

(**a**) Write down an equation connecting *P* and *L*.

(**b**) What is the value of the constant of proportionality?
What does this represent?

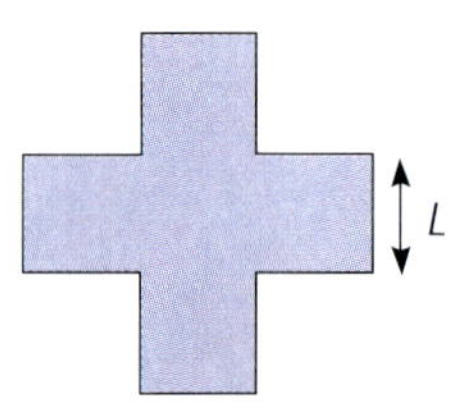

(**c**) Copy and complete this table.

L	1	2	3	10	20	37		
P							500	750

For Question 3, leave your answers in surd form.

3 The perimeter, P, of a square is proportional to the length, D, of its diagonal.

(**a**) Show that when $D = 5$cm, $P = 10\sqrt{2}$cm.

(**b**) Calculate the value of the constant of proportionality.

(**c**) Copy and complete this table.

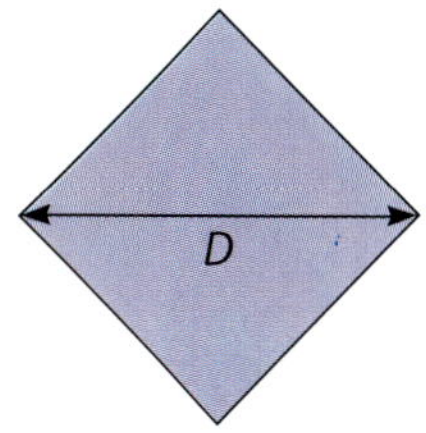

D	1	2	4	5	20	50	$\sqrt{2}$
P				$10\sqrt{2}$			

(**d**) What is D, when $P = 30$cm?

4 The perimeter of this semi-circular shape, P, is proportional to the length of the base B.

(**a**) Show that when $B = 10$cm, $P = 25.708$ (to 3 decimal places).

(**b**) Calculate the value of the constant of proportionality.

(**c**) Copy and complete this table.
Round your answers to 2 decimal places.

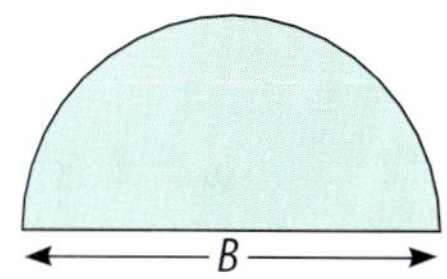

B	1	2	4	5	10	15	30
P					25.71		

(**d**) What is B when $P = 360$?

5 These tables all show sets of numbers which are in direct proportion.

A	3	4	5	6	20
B				7.8	

C	0.2	0.3	0.5	0.9	1
D		5.1			

E	3		10	25	
F		14	35		140

G			6		
H	1.9	3.8	5.7	9.5	11.4

For each table, write an equation using k, the constant of proportionality, and then find the value of k.
Copy and complete the tables.

6 These tables show sets of numbers which may be in direct proportion.

J	3	4	5	6
L	7	$9\frac{1}{3}$	$11\frac{2}{3}$	14

M	7	8	9	10
N	13	15	17	19

P	4	6	8	10
Q	27	29	31	33

R	8	11	14	17
S	88	121	154	187

For those which are, write an equation using *k*, the constant of proportionality, and then find the value of *k*.

7 $Y \propto X$.

(**a**) What happens to the *Y* value if the *X* value is multiplied by *n*?

(**b**) What happens to the *Y* value if the X value is increased by 10%?

8 In which of these situations are the sets of numbers in direct proportion?

A: The perimeter of a rectangle *and* the length of its longest side

B: The number of dollars *and* the number of pounds exchanged for them

C: The distance a car travels *and* the number of revolutions of a wheel

D: The cost of a telephone bill *and* the number of units used

E: The area of a circle *and* its diameter

DISCUSSION POINT

Suppose the area of a circle, *A* (in cm²), is compared with its radius, *R* (in cm).

R (cm)	1	2	3	4	5	6	7	8	9	10
A (cm²)	3.14	12.57	28.27	50.27	78.54	113.10	153.94	201.06	254.97	314.16

Notice that $\frac{A}{R}$ is not a constant and so *A* is not directly proportional to *R*. When *R* goes from 5 to 10, *A* goes from 78.54 to 314.16.

- So when the value of *R* is multiplied by 2 what happens to the value of *A*? Is this always true?
- What happens when the value of *R* is multiplied by 3 or by some other number?

DISCUSSION POINT

This table compares R^2 with A.

R^2	1	4	9	16	25	36	49	64	81	100
A	3.14	12.57	28.27	50.27	78.54	113.10	153.94	201.06	254.97	314.16

- If R^2 is multiplied by 4 what happens to A?
- What happens if R^2 is multiplied by some other number?

Compare the graph of A against R with the graph of A against R^2.

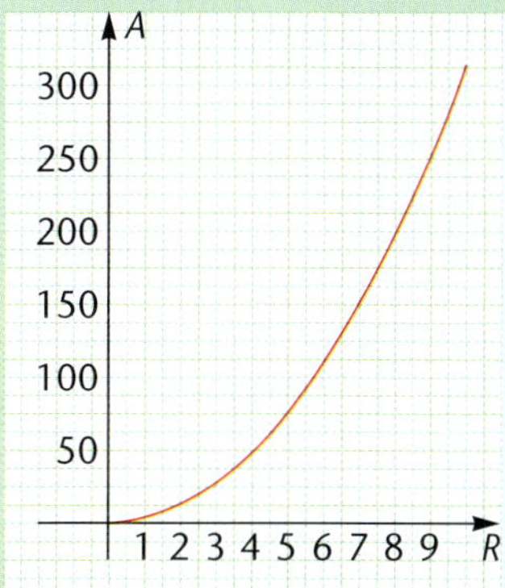

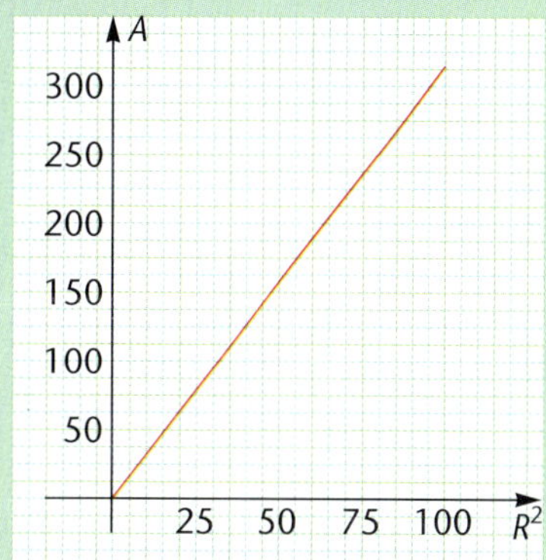

Compare these sets C and D.

D	2	3	4	5	6	10
C	5.6	18.9	44.8	87.5	151.2	700

- When D increases by a factor of 2 what happens to C?
- What about when D increases by a factor of 3?
- Instead of comparing C with D, what would you compare C with, to get direct proportion?

As you have seen in the discussion point above, sometimes there is a relationship between numbers other than direct proportion.

Here are three examples.

A is proportional to the square of B	$A \propto B^2$	$A = kB^2$
C is proportional to the cube of D	$C \propto D^3$	$C = kD^3$
E is proportional to the square root of F	$E \propto \sqrt{F}$	$E = k\sqrt{F}$

EXERCISE 4

1 A student times a ball rolling a distance down an inclined plane. Here are the results.

Distance, *d* (metres)	0.5	0.75	1.00	1.25	1.50
Time, *t* (seconds)	1.32	1.60	1.83	2.05	2.25

The teacher suggested that the connection was $d = kt^2$, where k was a constant.

(a) Calculate t^2 and draw the graph of d against t^2.

(b) What shape is the graph? Find the gradient of the graph.

(c) Find k and write the equation for d in terms of t.

2 In this table, $Z = kW^2$.

W	2	4	6	10	24	
Z	1.6	6.4				360

(a) Find the value of k.

(b) Copy and complete the table.

3 In this table, $Y = kX^3$.

X	2	5	6	10		
Y			32.4		259.2	500

(a) Find the value of k.

(b) Copy and complete the table.

4 This table compares the volume of a sphere, V (in cm^3), with the radius, R (in cm).

R (cm)	2	3	4	5	6	8	10
V (cm^3)	33.51	113.10	268.08	523.60	904.78	2144.66	4188.79

(a) To what power of R is V proportional?

(b) What is the value of the constant of proportionality?

5 In this table, $E \propto \sqrt{F}$ and so $E = k\sqrt{F}$.

F	4	9	16	36	64	100		
E			1.2		2.4		5.1	10

(a) Find the value of k.

(b) Copy and complete the table.

(c) Describe the graph of E against $\sqrt{F}$.

6 You are told that $Y \propto X^3$, and that $Y = 675$ when $X = 15$.

(a) What is Y when $X = 20$?

(b) What is X when $Y = 200$?

(c) What happens to the Y value when the X value is doubled?

(d) What happens to the Y value when the X value is halved?

7 $Y \propto X^2$.

What happens to the Y value if the X value is

(a) multiplied by n?

(b) increased by 10%?

(c) divided by n?

(d) decreased by 10%?

8 A swinging pendulum is timed.

The length L is varied and the time for one swing, T, is recorded.

When $L = 1.21$ m, $T = 2.2$ s, and when $L = 0.64$ m, $T = 1.6$ s.

(a) Suppose you think that $T \propto \sqrt{L}$.
Do these results fit?

(b) How long would you make the pendulum for a swing of 1 second?

Inverse proportion

DISCUSSION POINT

M	1	2	3	4	5	6	7	8	9	10
N	24	12	8	6	4.8	4	3.4286	3	2.6667	2.4

- What happens to N when M is multiplied by 2?
- What is the relationship between M and N?

N is **inversely proportional** to M, i.e. N is proportional to $\frac{1}{M}$.

In symbols, this is written as

$N \propto \frac{1}{M}$ or $N = \frac{k}{M}$

- What is k in this case?
- What shape is the graph of N against M?
- What happens when $M = 0$?

Other cases can be considered. Here are two examples.

D is inversely proportional to A^2 $\quad D \propto \frac{1}{A^2} \quad D = \frac{k}{A^2}$

P is inversely proportional to R^3 $\quad P \propto \frac{1}{R^3} \quad P = \frac{k}{R^3}$

EXERCISE 5

1 These tables all show sets of numbers which are in inverse proportion.

A	3	4	5	6	20
B				3	

C	0.2	0.3	0.5	0.8	1
D		0.2			

E	3		10	25	
F		7.5	3		0.8

G			6		
H	1.5	3.0	5.5	9.6	11

For each, write an equation using a constant *k*, and then find the value of *k*.
Copy and complete each table.

2 Top class runners complete a 100-metre race in about 10 seconds.
Their average speed is about $10\,ms^{-1}$.
This table shows the time, *T*, taken to cover 100m for different average speeds, *S*.

	Stroll	Walk	Jog	Jog-run	Run	Run	Run	Top class	Car in town
S (ms^{-1})	1	2	2.5	4	5	6	8	10	13.3
T (secs)								10	

T is inversely proportional to *S*.

(**a**) Write down an equation connecting *T* and *S*, using a constant *k*.

(**b**) What is the value of *k*?
What does this represent?

(**c**) Copy and complete the table.

(**d**) What happens to the time when the average speed is doubled?

(**e**) An increase in average speed from $4\,ms^{-1}$ to $5\,ms^{-1}$ is an increase in average speed of 25%.
What is the corresponding percentage change in the time?

(**f**) A decrease in average speed from $10\,ms^{-1}$ to $8\,ms^{-1}$ is a decrease in average speed of 20%.
What is the corresponding percentage change in the time?

3 $Y \propto \frac{1}{X}$. What happens to the Y value if the X value is

(**a**) multiplied by n?

(**b**) increased by 10%?

(**c**) decreased by 10%?

4 $Y \propto \frac{1}{X}$.

Use scale factors to find the corresponding percentage changes to complete this table

Change in X	Equivalent scale factor	Scale factor for Y	Change in Y
Increase by 2%			
Increase by 5%			
Increase by 20%			
Increase by 25%	× 1.25	1 ÷ 1.25 = 0.8	Decrease by 20%
Increase by 50%			
Decrease by 7%			
Decrease by 20%			
Decrease by 25%			
Decrease by 50%			

5 In each of these tables, the second variable is in inverse proportion to the square of the first.

So $B \propto \frac{1}{A^2}$, $D \propto \frac{1}{C^2}$, and so on.

A	2	3	4	5	6	12
B	36				4	

C	0.2	0.3	0.5	0.6	0.9	1
D		2				

E	0.2	0.25		2.5		5
F			2.5	1.6	1	

G	5					
H	0.024	0.009375	0.006	0.0026667	0.0015	0.0011342

For each table, write an equation using k, and then find the value of k.
Copy and complete the tables.

6 The volume of this cuboid is W^2L.

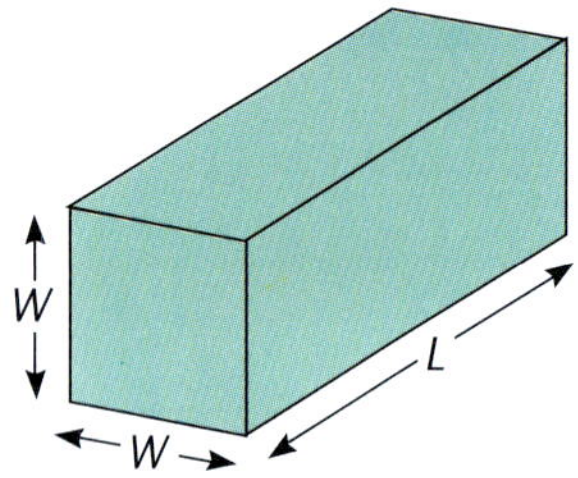

The volume is fixed at 400 cm³.

(**a**) Write an equation for L in terms of W.

(**b**) Copy and complete this table.

***W* (cm)**	5	6	7	8	9	10
***L* (cm)**	16					

(**c**) Write an equation for W in terms of L.

(**d**) What is W proportional to, and what is the value of the constant of proportionality?

7 The volume of a cylindrical can of soup must be 500 cm³.

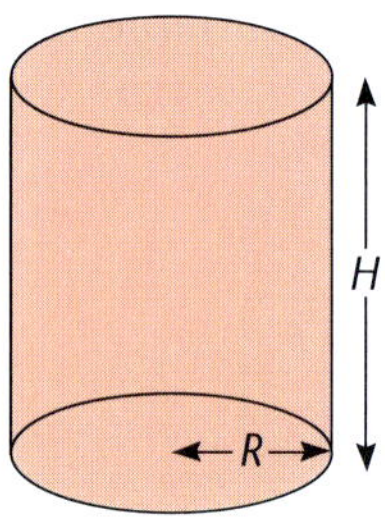

(**a**) Copy and complete this table.

***R* (cm)**	3		4	4.3		5	6
***H* (cm)**	17.7	13			8		

(**b**) If $H = \frac{k}{R^2}$, use the table to find the value of k.

(**c**) Show that $k = \frac{500}{\pi}$, by using the formula for the volume of a cylinder.

(**d**) What is special about the can which has a radius of 4.3 cm?

8 Look at these graphs.

A

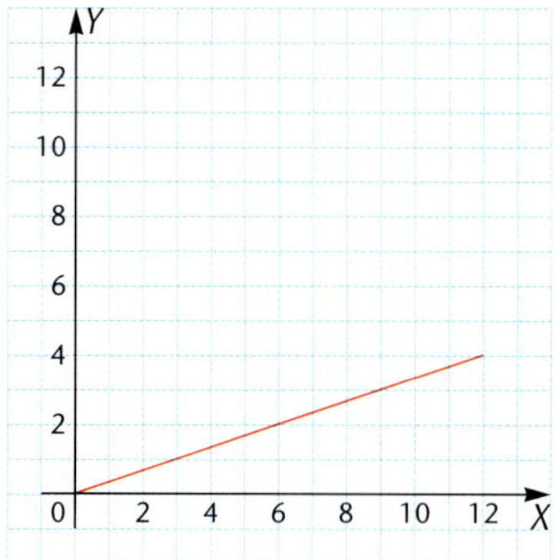

B

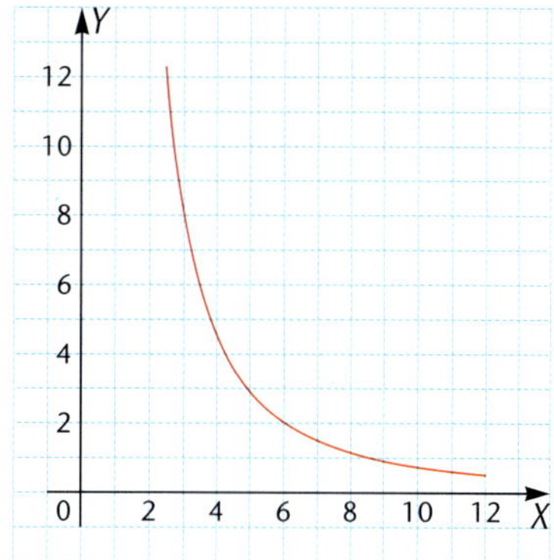

C

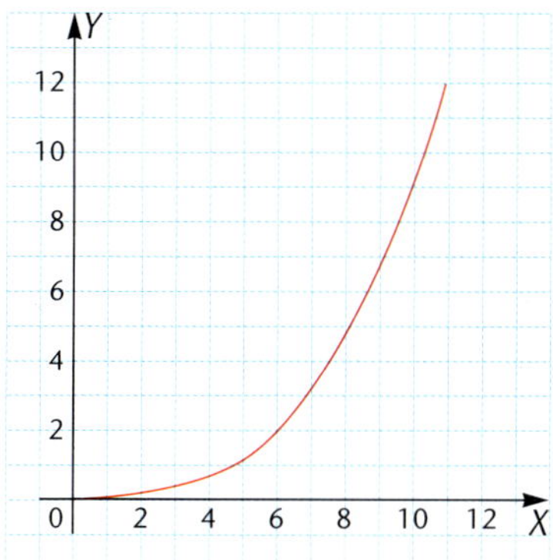

D

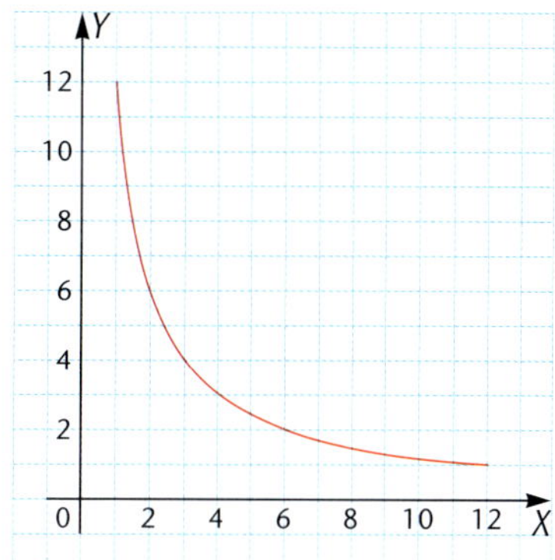

E

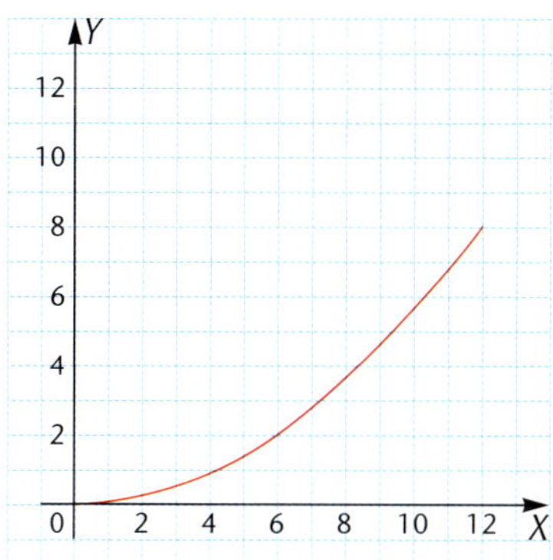

F

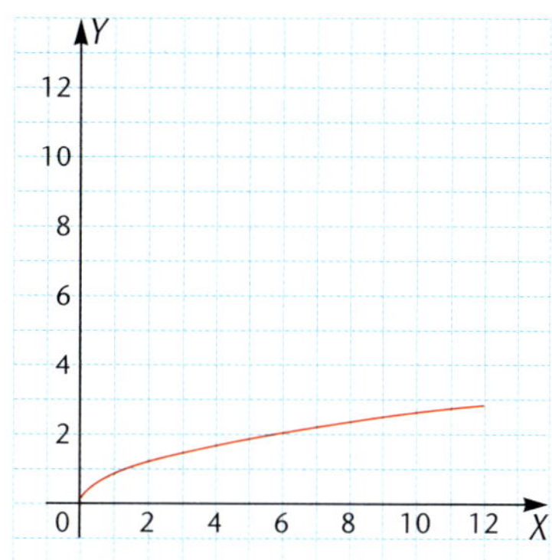

Each graph goes through the point (6, 2).
For each graph, decide which of these equations describes it, and find the value of k.

$Y = \frac{k}{X^2}$ $\quad Y = \frac{k}{X}$ $\quad Y = k\sqrt{X}$ $\quad Y = kX$ $\quad Y = kX^2$ $\quad Y = kX^3$

CHAPTER SUMMARY

Ratios

Comparing quantities
6 minutes: $\frac{1}{2}$ hour = 1:5

Sharing out a total
£56 in the ratio 2:5 = £16:£40

Interpreting map distances
1:50000 means 2cm represents 1km.

Rates

Speed = distance ÷ time

4000 miles in 8 hours = 500 m.p.h.
⇒ In 3 hours, travel 1500 miles
⇒ 900 miles in 1 hour 48 minutes

Density = mass (weight) ÷ volume

The density of pure gold is $19\,\text{g}\,\text{cm}^{-3}$
⇒ Mass of a 4-cm cube of gold is 1.2kg.

Direct proportion

These all mean the same: A is directly proportional to B.

$A \propto B$ $\frac{A}{B}$ is constant A = kB B halved ⇒ A halved

k is called the **constant of proportionality.**

Sometimes one variable is directly proportional to a power of another.

Example
$N \propto M^2$ means the same as $N = kM^2$

If M increased by 10% (× 1.1) then N increased by 21% (× 1.1^2).
$T \propto \sqrt{Q}$ means the same as $T = k\sqrt{Q}$.

Inverse proportion

These mean the same: C is inversely proportional to D.

$C \propto \frac{1}{D}$ $C \times D$ is constant $C = \frac{k}{D}$ D doubled ⇒ C halved

k is called the **constant of proportionality.**

Sometimes one variable is inversely proportional to a power of another.

Example
$H \propto \frac{1}{R^2}$ means the same as $HR^2 = k$

If R is decreased by 10% (× 0.9) then H is increased by 23.5% (÷ 0.9^2)

Graphs

Direct proportion can be represented by a straight-line graph.

Example

If $A \propto B$, plotting A against B will give a straight line.

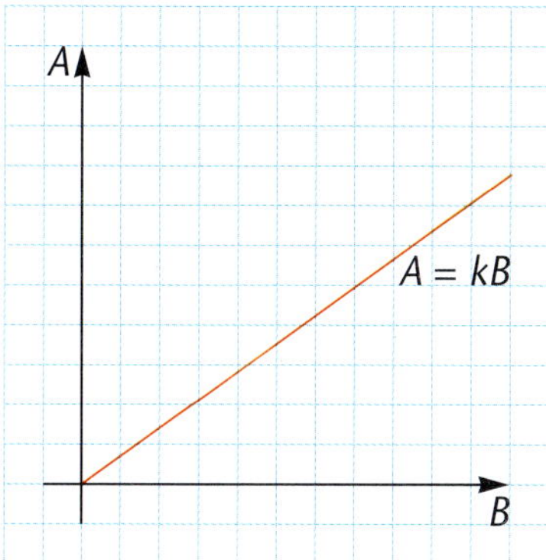

If $N \propto M^2$ plotting N against M^2 will give a straight line.
The gradient of the line is the constant of proportionality.

Inverse proportion can be represented by a **hyperbola** graph.

Example

If $C \propto \frac{1}{D}$, plotting C against D will give a curve (hyperbola), but plotting C against $\frac{1}{D}$ will give a straight line.

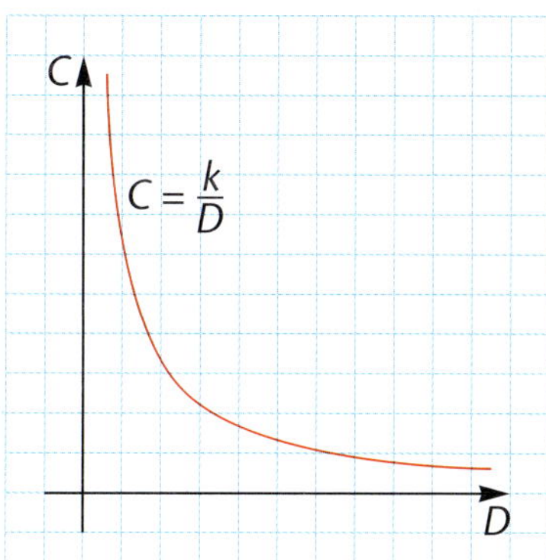

CHAPTER

9 Trigonometry

This chapter is about:

- sine, cosine and tangent in a right-angled triangle
- solving trigonometric problems using an appropriate degree of accuracy
- sine, cosine and tangent of angles of any size, and their graphs.

Sine, cosine and tangent as multipliers

In a right-angled triangle, the longest side of the triangle (which is opposite the right-angle) is called the **hypotenuse** (H).

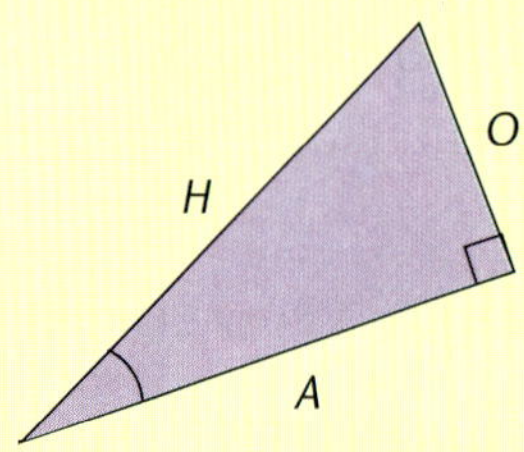

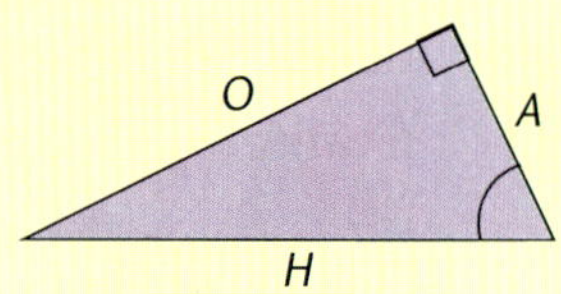

If one of the acute angles is marked, the side (which is not the hypotenuse) next to that angle is called the **adjacent side** (A), and the side opposite the angle is called the **opposite side** (O).

▶ Resource Sheet I: *60° right-angled triangles*
▶ Resource Sheet J: *40° right-angled triangles*

EXERCISE 1

1 In a right-angled triangle, one of the angles is a right angle.
Explain why the other two angles must be acute angles.

2 One of the angles of a right-angled triangle is 20°.

(a) Draw a sketch of the triangle and mark the 20° angle.

(b) Mark the hypotenuse with the letter *H*.
Mark the side opposite the 20° angle with the letter *O*.
Mark the side adjacent to 20° angle with the letter *A*.

(c) Say which side (*H*, *O* or *A*) is the longest side of the triangle and which is the shortest side.

3 Repeat Question 2 with one of the angles of the triangle being

(a) 60° (b) 50° (c) 42°

4 Draw a sketch of a right-angled triangle for which there is not one shortest side. What are the angles of this triangle?

5 (a) Using a copy of Resource Sheet I: *60° right-angled triangles,* label the sides of each triangle *H, O* and *A*.

(b) Measure the sides of each triangle. Copy and complete this table.

Triangle	*H* (cm)	*O* (cm)	*A* (cm)
A	1		
B	2		
C	4		
D	8		
E	3		
F	6		
G	9		

(c) What are the rules connecting the numbers in the three columns?

(d) The patterns you might have found when answering part (c) are probably not exact. Why is this?

Making general statements

6 Repeat Question 5 for the triangles on the Resource Sheet J: *40° right-angled triangles*.

7 Compare your answers to Questions 5 and 6.
What is the same? What is different?

The number you have to multiply the length of the hypotenuse by to get the length of the opposite side is called the **sine** multiplier.

The number you have to multiply the length of the hypotenuse by to get the length of the adjacent side is called the **cosine** multiplier.

The number you have to multiply the length of the adjacent side by to get the length of the opposite side is called the **tangent** multiplier.

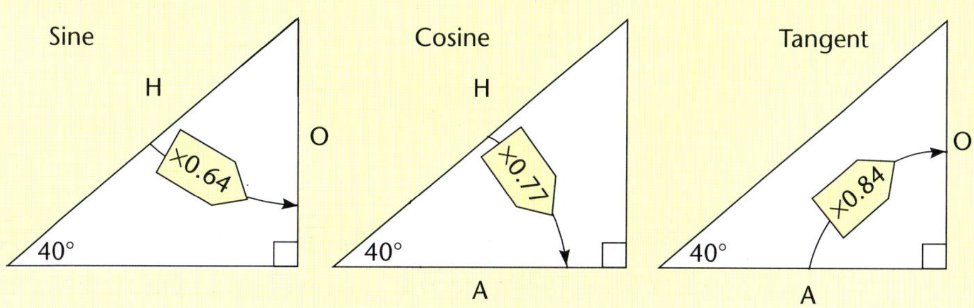

The size of the sine, cosine and tangent multipliers depends on the angle.

DISCUSSION POINT

Imagine two 60° right-angled triangles: one big and one small. Why does the same sine multiplier work for both?

If you know the length of the *hypotenuse* of a right-angled triangle, you can find the length of the *adjacent* side by multiplying by the cosine multiplier. If you know the length of the *adjacent* side, how do you find the length of the *hypotenuse*?

▷ Resource Sheet K: *Right-angled triangles*

The sine multiplier for the angle 40° is called **the sine of 40°** and written as **sin 40°**.

The cosine multiplier for the angle 40° is called **the cosine of 40°** and written as **cos 40°**.

The tangent multiplier for the angle 40° is called **the tangent of 40°** and written as **tan 40°**.

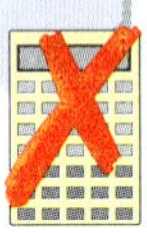

EXERCISE 2

1 (a) On a copy of Resource Sheet K: *Right-angled triangles*, label the sides of each triangle H, O and A.

(b) Measure the sides of the triangles. Copy and complete this table.

Triangle	Marked angle	H (cm)	O (cm)	A (cm)
A	10°		1	
B	20°		2	
C	30°		3	
D	40°			4
E	50°			6
F	60°	6		
G	70°			3
H	80°			2

2 Use your table to find approximate values for the sine, cosine and tangent multipliers for the angles 10°, 20°, ..., 80°.

EXERCISE 3

1 (a) Explain why the sine of any acute angle is *always* less than 1.

(b) What can you say about the cosine of any acute angle? Why?

2 (a) Draw a sketch of an isosceles right-angled triangle. What is the value of tan 45°?

(b) What can you say about the value of the tangent of

(i) an angle *less* than 45°?

(ii) an angle *greater* than 45°?

3 (a) What happens to the sine of an angle as the acute angle gets bigger?

(b) What happens to the cosine of an angle as the acute angle gets bigger?

(c) What happens to the tangent of an angle as the acute angle gets bigger?

For Question 4, you might find it helpful to draw sketches of triangles.

4 For each of these pairs, say which is bigger.

(a) $\sin 20°$, $\cos 20°$ (b) $\sin 40°$, $\cos 40°$ (c) $\sin 60°$, $\cos 60°$

(d) $\sin 30°$, $\tan 30°$ (e) $\sin 50°$, $\tan 50°$ (f) $\sin 30°$, 1

(g) $\sin 70°$, 1 (h) $\tan 30°$, 1 (i) $\tan 70°$, 1

(j) $\cos 70°$, 1 (k) $\sin 40°$, $\cos 50°$

$8\sin 40°$ means $8 \times \sin 40°$
$7\cos 70°$ means $7 \times \cos 70°$
and so on.

5 For each of these, arrange the numbers in order of size, starting with the smallest.

(a) $\frac{8}{\cos 70°}$, $8\cos 70°$, 8 (b) 5, $5\tan 60°$, $\frac{5}{\tan 60°}$

(c) $13\sin 20°$, $\frac{13}{\sin 20°}$, 13 (d) 6.3, $\frac{6.3}{\cos 30°}$, $6.3\cos 30°$

(e) $9.4\tan 40°$, $\frac{9.4}{\tan 40°}$, 9.4

6 What happens to the size of a number when it is

(a) multiplied by the sine of any angle?

(b) multiplied by the cosine of any angle?

(c) divided by the sine of any angle?

(d) divided by the cosine of any angle?

7 This triangle has one very small acute angle and one very large acute angle.

By thinking about this triangle, write down the value of each of these.

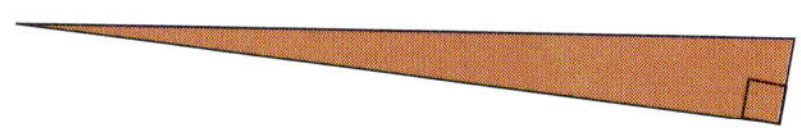

(a) $\sin 0°$ (b) $\cos 0°$ (c) $\tan 0°$

(d) $\sin 90°$ (e) $\cos 90°$ (f) $\tan 90°$

8 Explain why the tangent of any acute angle is always bigger than the sine of that angle.

DISCUSSION POINT

You can use your calculator to find the sine, the cosine or the tangent of an angle. Exactly how you do this, varies from calculator to calculator.

Find out how it works on your calculator.

Use your calculator to find each of these, correct to 3 significant figures.

$\cos 65°$ $\tan 85°$ $\sin 53°$
$\cos 37°$ $\tan 28°$ $\sin 88°$

Solving right-angled triangles

To find the length of c in this triangle, first label each side O, A and H (either on paper or in your mind).

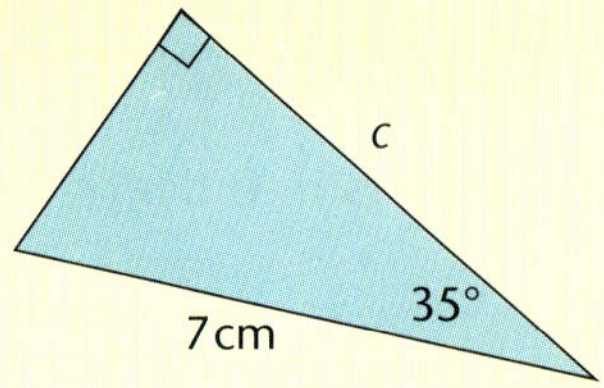

The side length you know is H, and the side length you want to know is A.

A and H are involved and so you use the cosine multiplier to find A.

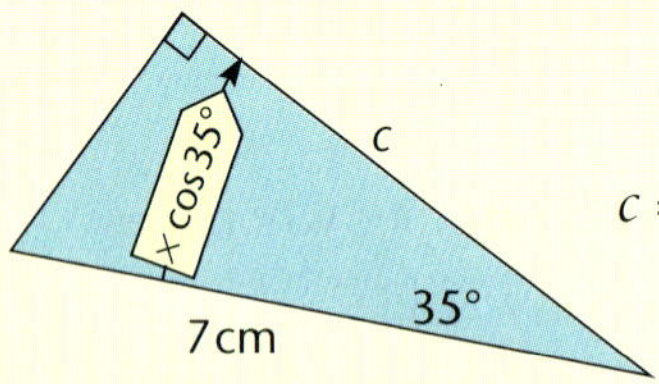

$c = 7\,\text{cm} \times \cos 35° = 5.73\,\text{cm}$ (3 s.f.)

Here is another example.

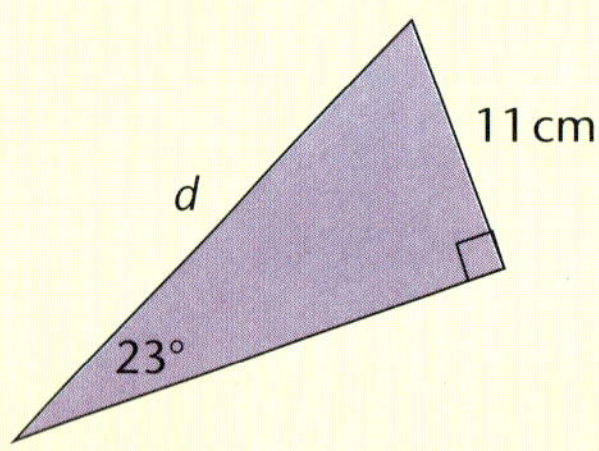

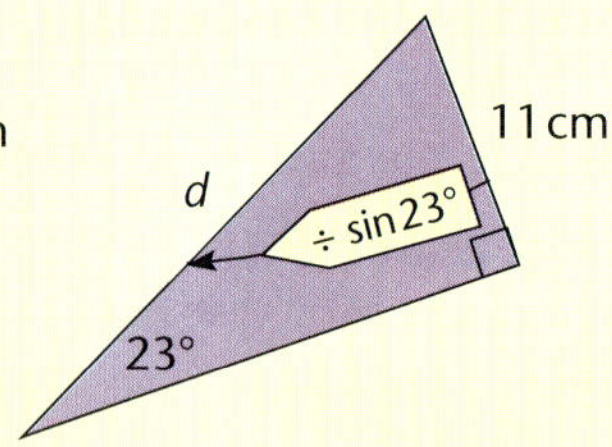

The side length you know is O, and the side length you want to know is H.

The sine *multiplier* converts H to O. You want to convert O to H and so you *divide*.

$d = 11\,\text{cm} \div \sin 23° = 28.2\,\text{cm}$ (3 s.f.)

One way of checking whether you need to multiply or divide is to think whether you want a side length longer or shorter than the side length you start with.

These diagrams may help you to decide when to multiply and when to divide.

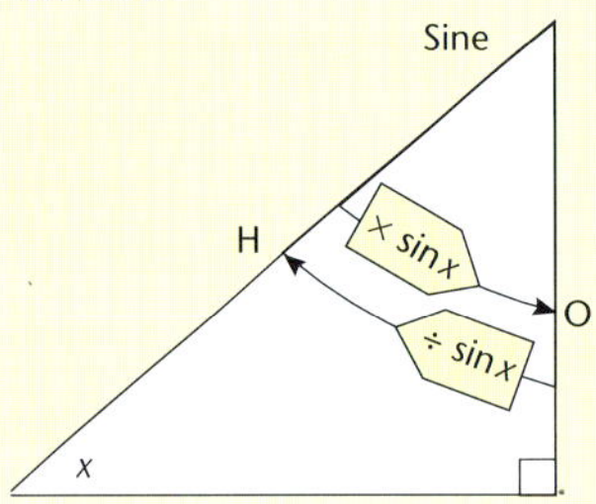

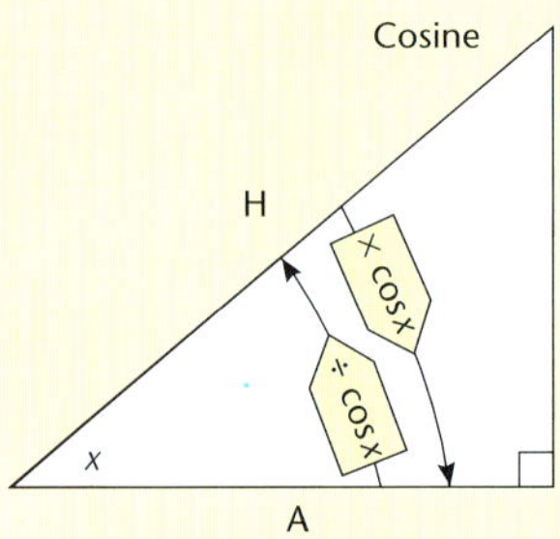

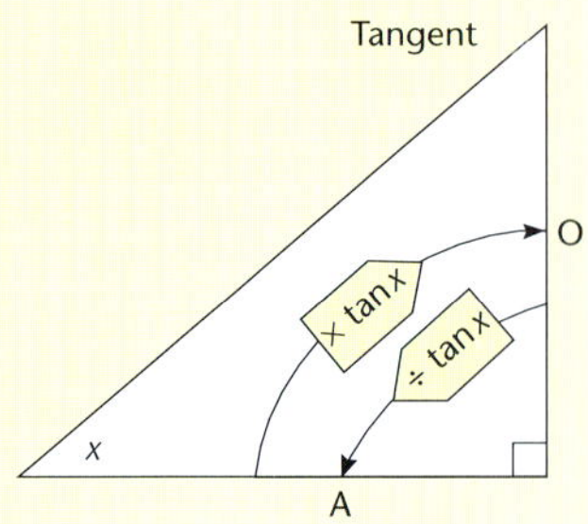

Exercise 4

1 For each of these triangles, find the length of the side marked *a*, correct to 3 significant figures.

A

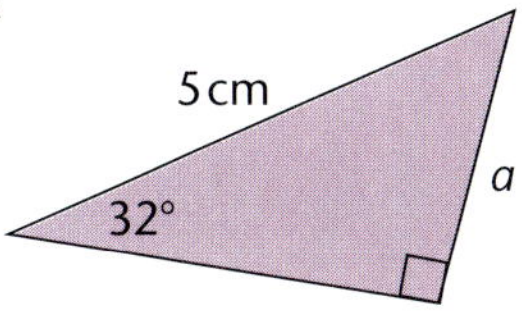

B

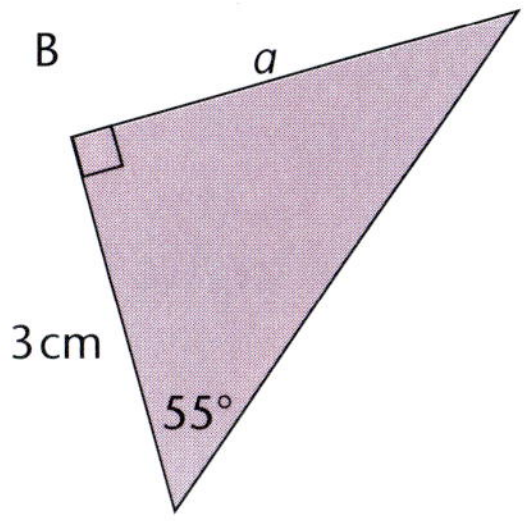

C

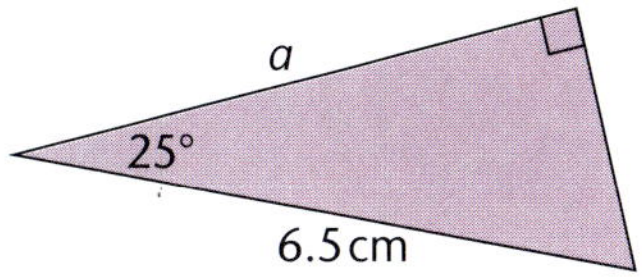

D

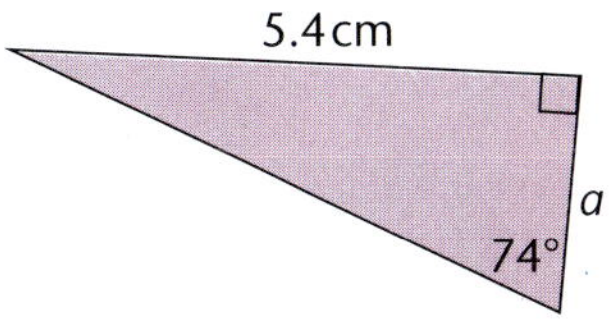

E

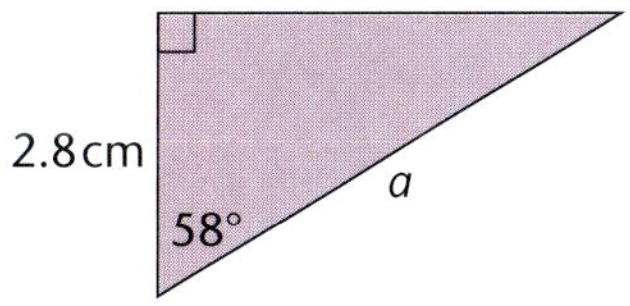

F

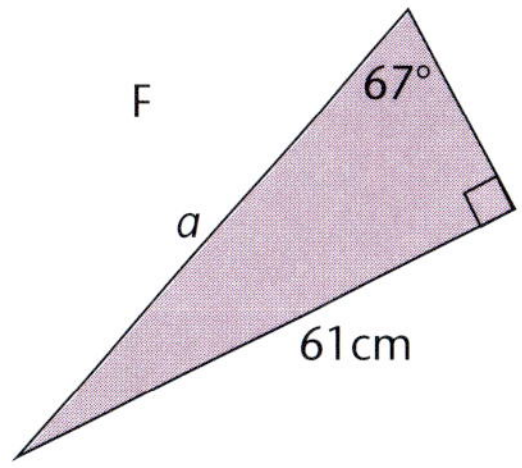

G

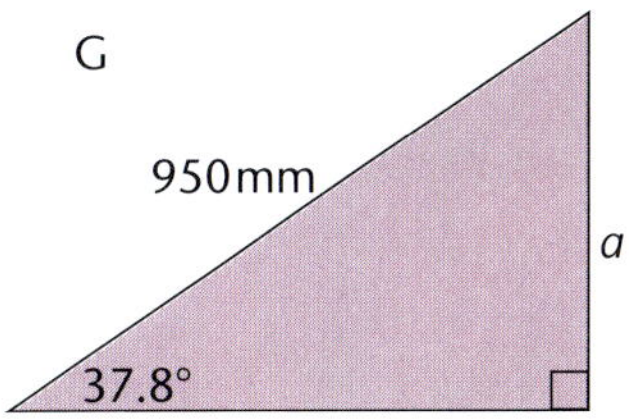

H

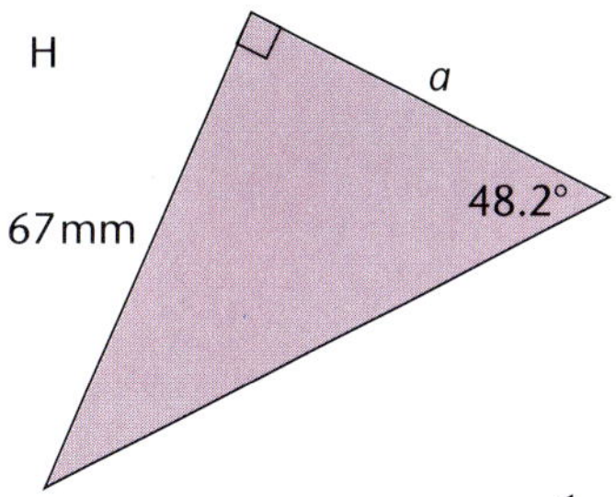

I

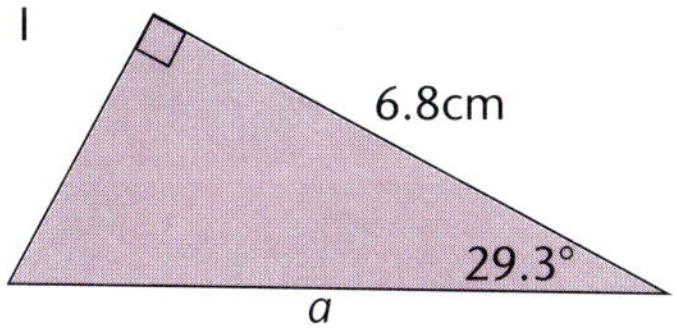

J

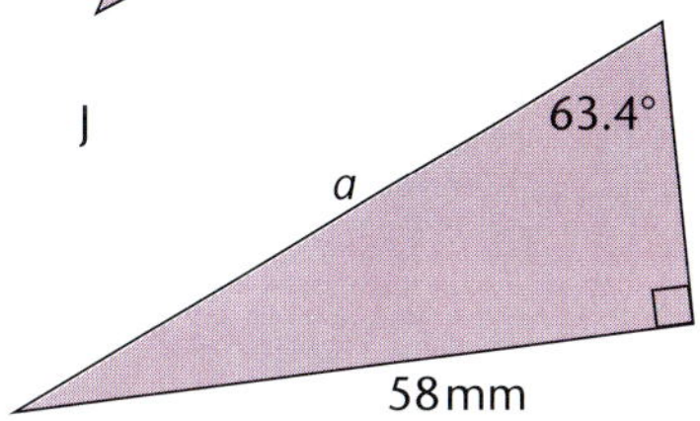

2 Find the perimeter of each of these isosceles triangles, correct to 3 significant figures.

A

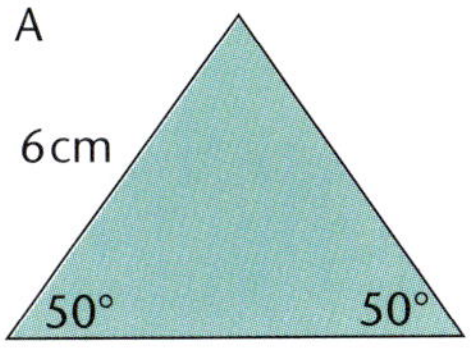

B

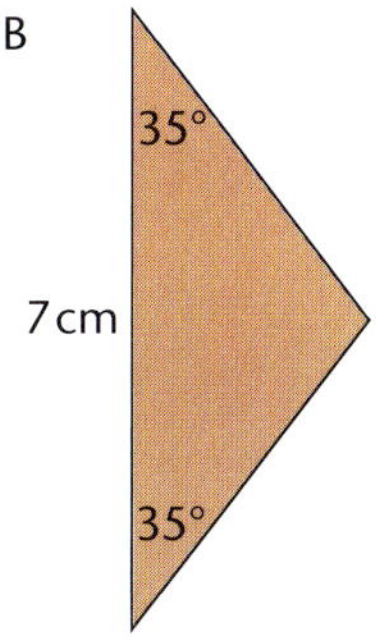

C

D

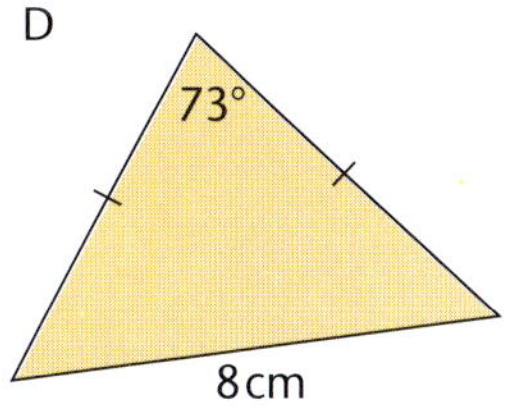

3 Find the perimeter of each of these quadrilaterals, correct to 3 significant figures.

(**a**) A rhombus with an angle of 58° and a diagonal of length 11cm (two possible answers)

(**b**) A kite with two sides of length 12cm, and angles of 90°, 50°, 90° and 130° (two possible answers)

DISCUSSION POINT

The multiplier for going from hypotenuse (H) to adjacent side (A) is cosine.

So $H \times \cos x = A$.

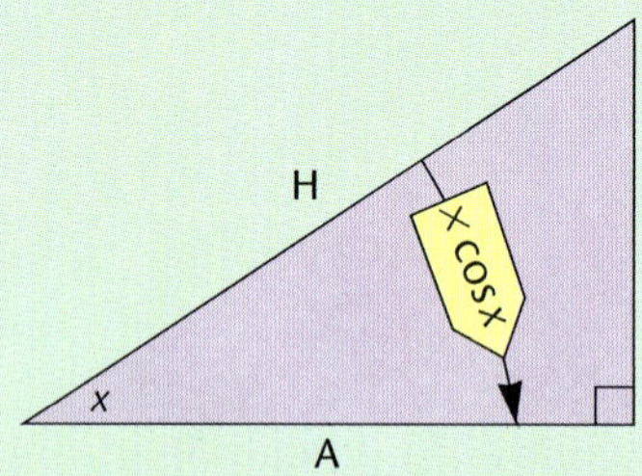

Explain why this means that

$\cos x = \dfrac{A}{H}$

In the same way, find formulae for $\sin x$ and $\tan x$.

If you know the lengths of two sides of a right-angled triangle, you can use your calculator to find the angles of the triangle.

Example

Suppose you want to find the angle x.

The sides you are told are the adjacent (A) and the hypotenuse (H), and so you need to use cosine.

You know that $\cos x = \frac{5}{7}$.

You need to know how use your calculator to work out cos 'backwards', to find the angle whose cosine is $\frac{5}{7}$.

Find out how to do this on your calculator.

You should then find that $x = 44.4°$.

EXERCISE 5

1 For each of these triangles, find the angle marked x, correct to the nearest degree.

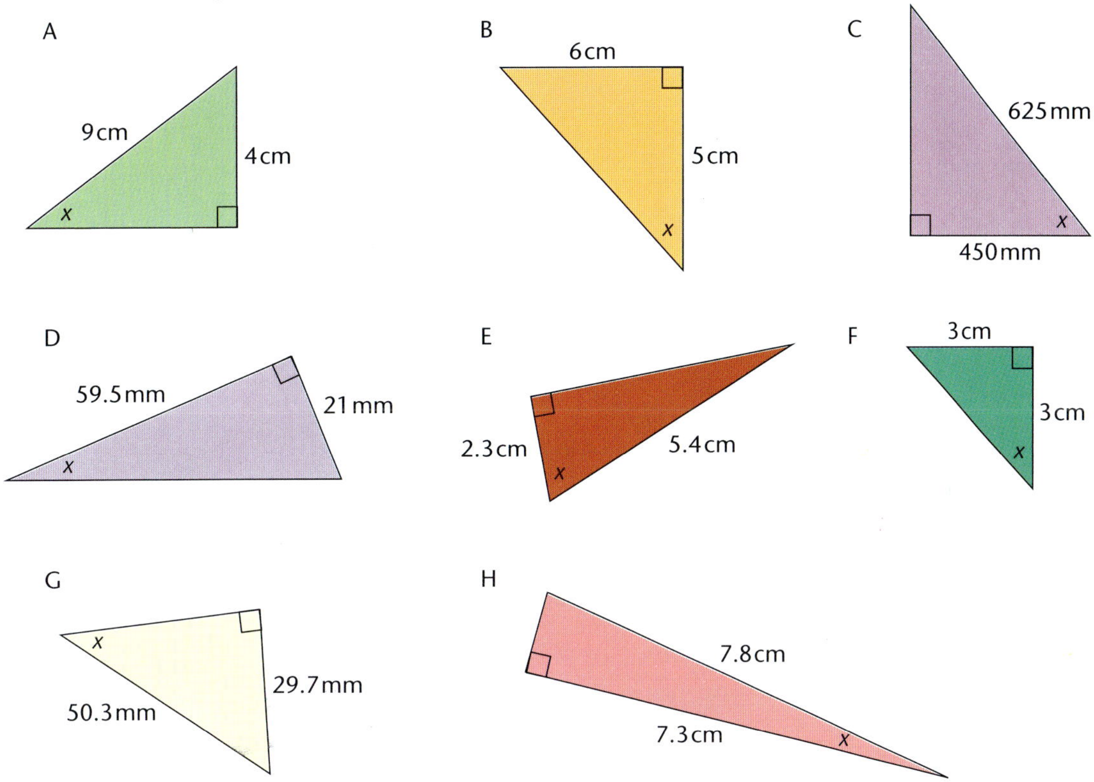

2 Find all three angles of each of these isosceles triangles, correct to the nearest degree.

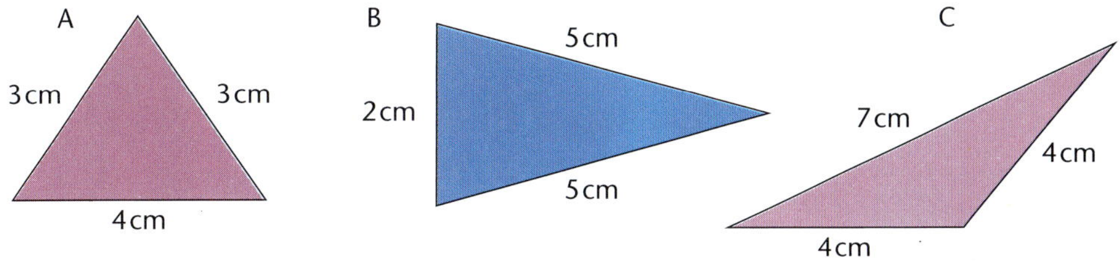

3 Find, correct to the nearest tenth of a degree, the angles of each of these polygons.

(**a**) A rhombus with sides of length 5 cm and a diagonal of length 8 cm

(**b**) An isosceles trapezium with sides of lengths 7 cm, 5 cm, 3 cm and 5 cm

Using trigonometry to solve problems

Angles of elevation and depression are measured from the horizontal.

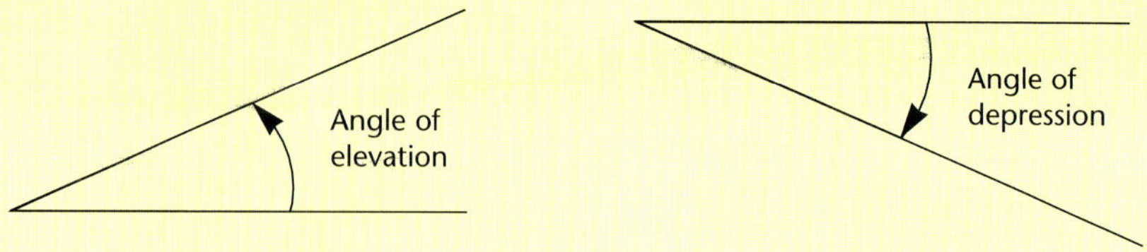

DISCUSSION POINT

What is the bearing of B from A? What is the bearing of A from B?

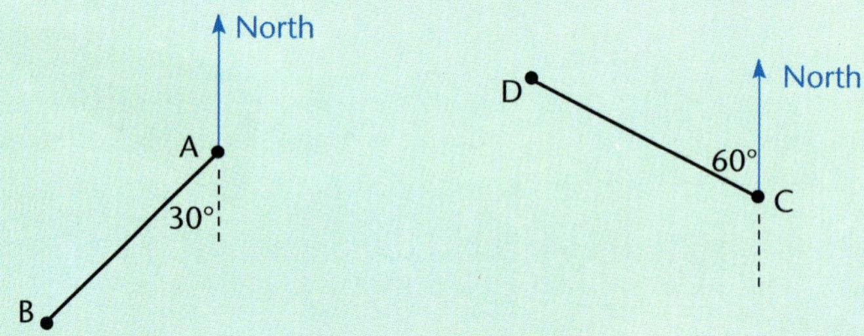

What is the bearing of D from C? What is the bearing of C from D?
What do you notice?

Give your answers to a sensible degree of accuracy.
In some of these questions, you need to make assumptions to get a right-angled triangle to solve.
Say what these assumptions are.

EXERCISE 6

Drawing a sketch may be helpful.

1 A kite is flying on the end of a string 38 m long.
The angle between the string and the horizontal is 38°.
How high is the kite above the ground?

2 From a distance of 125 m from the base of a tower, the angle of elevation of the tower is measured as 16°.
How high is the tower?

3 A ladder of length 4 metres is placed against a wall.
The ladder makes an angle of 70° with the ground.
How far is the foot of the ladder from the base of the wall?

4 A ship travels North for 5.8 miles and then travels West for 4.6 miles.
It then returns straight to its starting point.
What bearing does it follow for the return journey?

5 A ramp is to be provided as an alternative access to a flight of steps. The height of the flight of steps is 1.8 metres. The maximum safe angle for a ramp is judged to be 8°. What is the minimum length of the ramp?

There are 5280 feet in a mile

6 A path up a mountain is $1\frac{1}{2}$ miles long. The path ascends 1750 feet. What is the average angle between the path and the horizontal?

7 This picture shows the side elevation of a house.

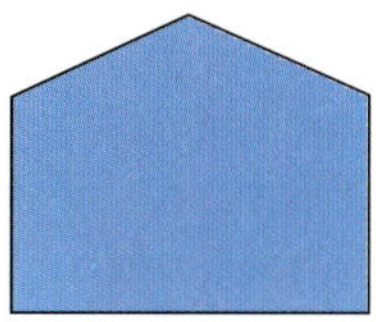

The pitch of the roof (the angle it makes with the horizontal) is 25°.

Find the height of the house.

8 An orienteer walks 700m on a bearing of 128°. She then walks 500m due East.

(**a**) How far is she from her starting point?

(**b**) If she walks straight back to her starting point, what is the *total* length of her walk?

9 A coastline runs due East-West. From the top of a cliff 80 metres high on this coastline, a ship is sighted by a coastguard at an angle of depression of 6°.

(**a**) How far is the ship from the coastguard?

(**b**) The coastguard's sighting of the ship is on a bearing of 335°. How far is the ship from the coastline?

10 The minute hand of a clock is 53cm long and the hour hand is 38cm long. What is the distance between the tips of the hands

(**a**) at six o'clock?

(**b**) at three o'clock?

(**c**) at five o'clock?

(**d**) at half past seven?

11 A ship sails 13.6 miles on a bearing of 187° and then docks. A second ship leaves the same starting point and sails 10.5 miles on a bearing of 136°, and then 12.8 miles on a bearing of 212°.

(**a**) How far is the second ship from its starting point?

(**b**) On what bearing should it sail to dock in the same harbour as the first ship?

(**c**) How far will it need to sail on this bearing?

12 The height of a vertical radio mast is 35 m.

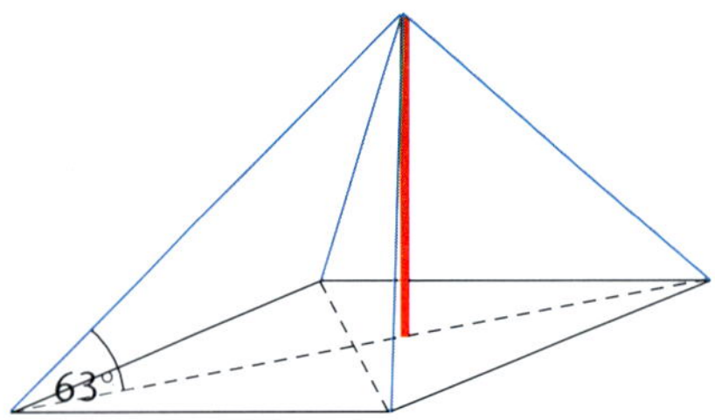

The mast is supported by four wires.

The points where the wires meet the ground are the vertices of a rhombus with diagonals of length 32 m and 19 m.
The angle the longest wire makes with the ground is 63°.
The two shortest wires are of equal length.
Find the angle each wire makes with the mast.

13 A helicopter is flying horizontally.
It is sighted due East of the point A with an angle of elevation of 58°.
A minute later, it is sighted, still due East, at an angle of elevation of 45°.
It is known that the helicopter is travelling at a speed of 150 kilometres per hour.
At what height is the helicopter flying?

14 A vertical mast stands on level ground.
A man measures the angle of elevation of the top of the mast as 40°.
He then walks 50 metres towards the mast and measures the angle of elevation as 60°.
Find the height of the mast.

Trigonometry and polygons

Exercise 7

For Question 1, there are two possible answers.

1 An isosceles triangle has one side of length 8 cm and another side of length 10 cm.
Find the three angles of the triangle.

2 The length of the shorter diagonal of this kite is 8 cm.

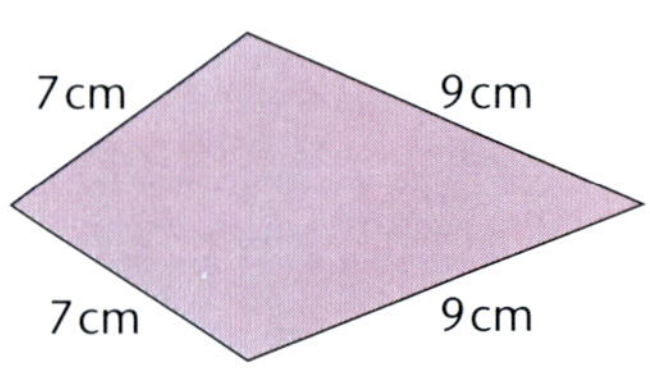

Find the four angles of the kite.

3 This picture shows a regular heptagon with perimeter 28cm.

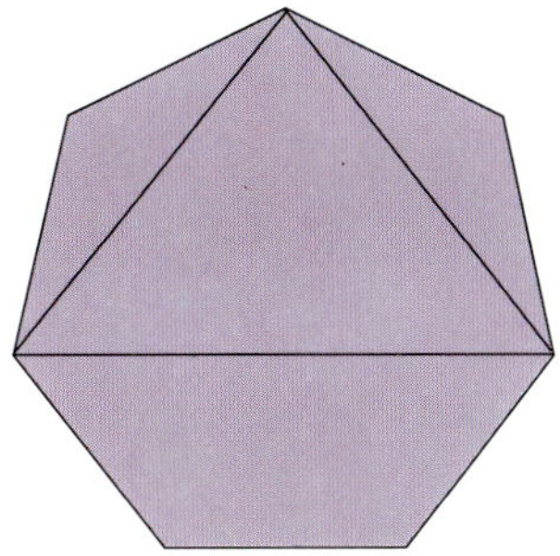

(**a**) What is the size of an interior angle of a regular heptagon?

(**b**) Make a sketch of the heptagon shown above and mark in the sizes of all the angles.

(**c**) Find the length of each of the marked diagonals.

(**d**) Find the area of each of the triangles.

(**e**) Find the area of the trapezium.

(**f**) Find the area of the heptagon.

4 The picture shows a regular nonagon with perimeter 90cm.

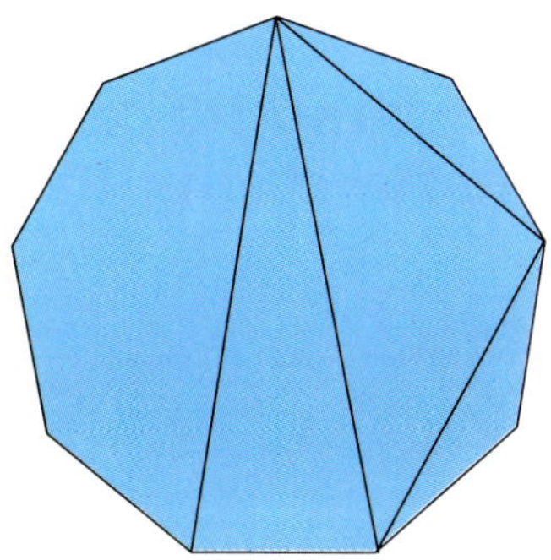

(**a**) What is the size of an interior angle of a regular nonagon?

(**b**) Find the length of each of the marked diagonals.

(**c**) Find the area of each of the triangles.

(**d**) Find the area of the nonagon.

5 (**a**) A regular pentagon has a perimeter of 120cm.
Calculate the length of one of its diagonals, and its area.

(**b**) A regular octagon has the same area as the pentagon.
Calculate its perimeter.

6 One of the angles of a right-angled triangle is 50°.

(**a**) If the length of the hypotenuse is x cm, find expressions for the lengths of the other two sides.

(**b**) The perimeter of the triangle is 20 cm.
Find the lengths of its sides.

(**c**) Find the area of the triangle.

For Question 7, there are two possible answers.

7 One angle of an isosceles triangle is 72°, and its perimeter is 50 cm^2.
Find its area.

8 One of the angles of an isosceles triangle is 104°.
The area of the triangle is 40 cm^2.
Find the lengths of the sides of the triangle.

9 An isosceles trapezium has two sides of length 8 cm, and two angles of 70°.
The area of the trapezium is A cm^2.

(**a**) Find, if possible, its perimeter when

(**i**) $A = 40$

(**ii**) $A = 20$

(**b**) What is the smallest possible value of A, and what does the trapezium look like for this value of A?

Angles greater than 90° and the graphs of trigonometric functions

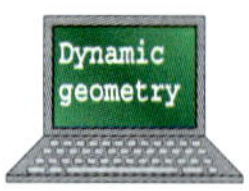

DISCUSSION POINT

The radius of this circle is 1 unit and its centre is at the origin O. The line OP makes an angle t with the x-axis, as shown.

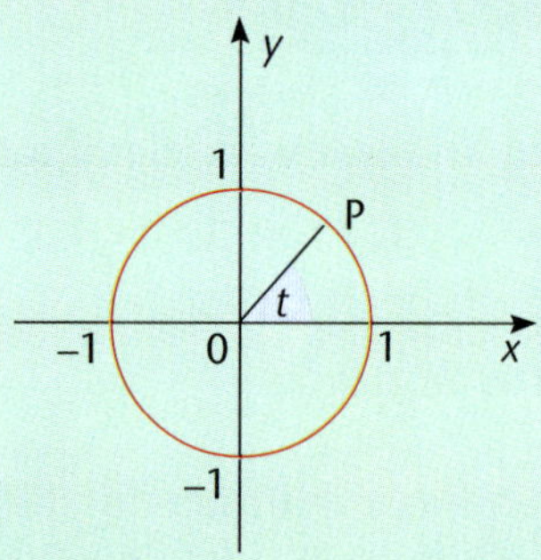

When t is an acute angle, explain why **cos** t is the **x-coordinate** of P and why **sin** t is the **y-coordinate** of P.

If t is *any* angle, **cos** t can be defined to be the **x-coordinate** of P.

If t is *any* angle, **sin** t can be defined to be the **y-coordinate** of P.

sine and **cosine** are sometimes called **circular functions**. These definitions explain why.

sin30° = 0.5
cos30° = 0.866

Exercise 8

1 Look at these diagrams.

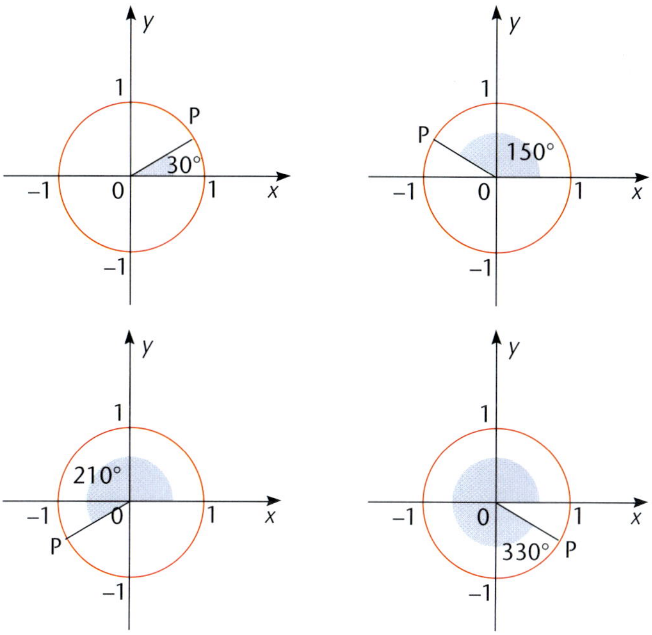

Without using a calculator, copy and complete this table.

t	$\cos t$	$\sin t$
0°		
30°	0.866	0.5
90°		
150°		
180°	–1	0
210°		
270°		
330°		

2 Use a calculator to check your answers to Question 1.

3 By making suitable interpretations of the angle between OP and the x-axis find these, *without* using a calculator.

(**a**) sin 360° (**b**) cos 360° (**c**) cos 390° (**d**) sin 450°
(**e**) sin 510° (**f**) cos 540° (**g**) cos 720° (**h**) cos (–30°)
(**i**) sin (–150°) (**j**) cos (–210°)

DISCUSSION POINT

The radius of this circle is 1 unit and its centre is at the origin O.

The line L is the tangent to the circle at the point where the circle meets the x-axis.

The line OP makes an angle t with the x-axis, as shown. Q is the point where the line L meets the line OP.

Explain why the y-coordinate of Q is $\tan t$.

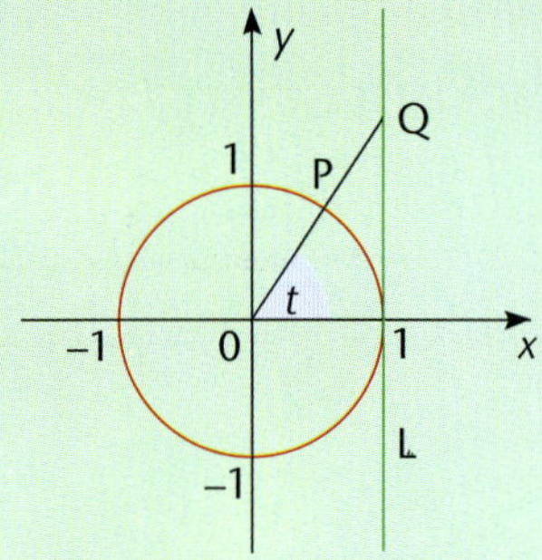

You have just explained that, when t is an acute angle **tan*t*** is the ***y*-coordinate** of Q.

If t is *any* angle **tan*t*** can be defined to be the ***y*-coordinate** of Q. (This explains why the word *tangent* is used in this way.)

EXERCISE 9

1 Look at these diagrams.

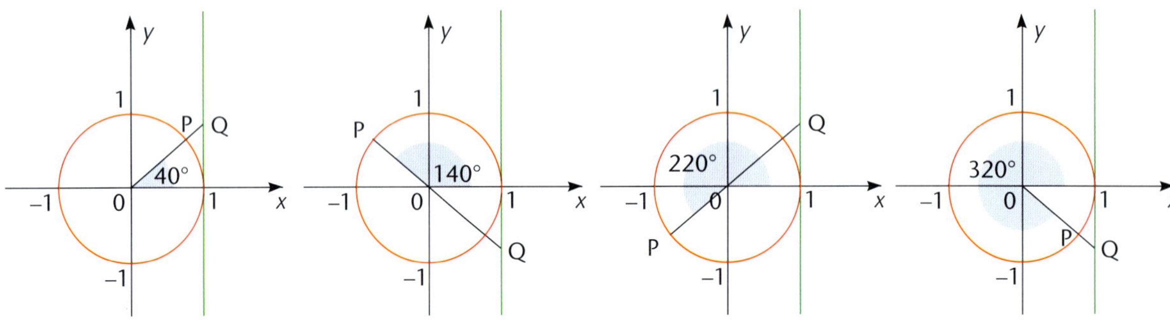

Copy and complete this table, *without* using a calculator.

t	$\tan t$
40°	0.839
140°	
220°	
320°	

2 Look at these diagrams.

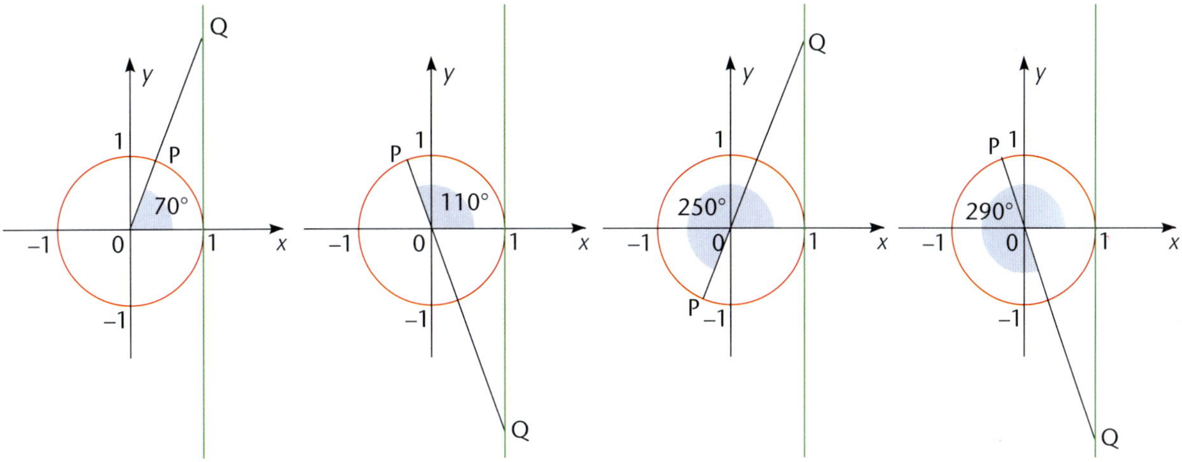

Copy and complete this table, *without* using a calculator.

t	tan t
70°	2.75
110°	
250°	
290°	

3 Copy and complete this table, *without* using a calculator.

t	tan t
0°	
45°	
90°	
135°	
180°	
225°	
270°	
315°	

tan40° = 0.839
tan70° = 2.75

4 Find these, *without* using a calculator.

(**a**) tan 360° (**b**) tan 400° (**c**) tan 450°
(**d**) tan 470° (**e**) tan 540° (**f**) tan 720°
(**g**) tan (–40°) (**h**) tan (–110°) (**i**) tan (–540°)

Resource Sheet L: *Graphs of trigonometric functions*

Exercise 10

1 The Resource Sheet L: *Graphs of trigonometric functions* shows that part of the graph $y = \sin x$ between $x = 0°$ and $x = 90°$.
Complete the graph from $-360°$ to $360°$.

2 The Resource Sheet L: *Graphs of trigonometric functions* shows that part of the graph $y = \cos x$ between $x = 0°$ and $x = 90°$.
Complete the graph from $-360°$ to $360°$.

3 The Resource Sheet L: *Graphs of trigonometric functions* shows that part of the graph $y = \tan x$ between $x = 0°$ and $x = 90°$.
Complete the graph from $-360°$ to $360°$.

4 **(a)** Write down three values of x for which $\sin 39° = \sin x$.

(b) Write down three values of y for which $\cos 63° = \cos y$.

(c) Write down three values of z for which $\tan 38° = \tan z$.

5 **(a)** $\sin 28° = \cos x$, and x is an acute angle. What is x?

(b) $\sin 64° = \cos x$, and x is an acute angle. What is x?

(c) $\sin 45° = \cos x$, and x is an acute angle. What is x?

(d) $\sin y = \cos x$, and x and y are acute angles.
What is the connection between x and y?

6 **(a)** $\tan 36° \times \tan x = 1$, and x is an acute angle. What is x?

(b) $\tan 51° \times \tan x = 1$, and x is an acute angle. What is x?

(c) $\tan 89° \times \tan x = 1$, and x is an acute angle. What is x?

(d) $\tan y \times \tan x = 1$, and x and y are acute angles.
What is the connection between x and y?

7 **(a)** Evaluate each of these.

(i) $(\sin 28° \times \sin 28°) + (\cos 28° \times \cos 28°)$

(ii) $(\sin 57° \times \sin 57°) + (\cos 57° \times \cos 57°)$

(iii) $(\sin 19° \times \sin 19°) + (\cos 19° \times \cos 19°)$

(b)(i) Using your answers to part (a), what general result might you guess for the angles $\sin x$ and $\cos x$?

(ii) Express $\sin x$ and $\cos x$ in terms of a, b and c.

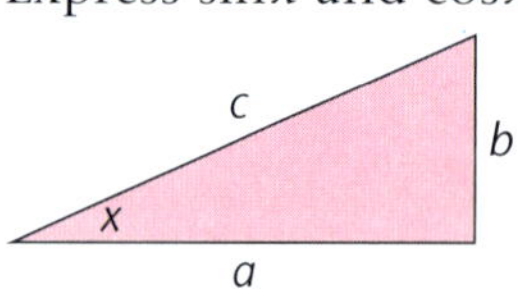

(iii) Hence, by using Pythagoras' theorem, prove the general result you wrote down in part (i).

Making and justifying a generalisation

CHAPTER SUMMARY

The trigonometric formulae

$\sin x = \frac{O}{H}$

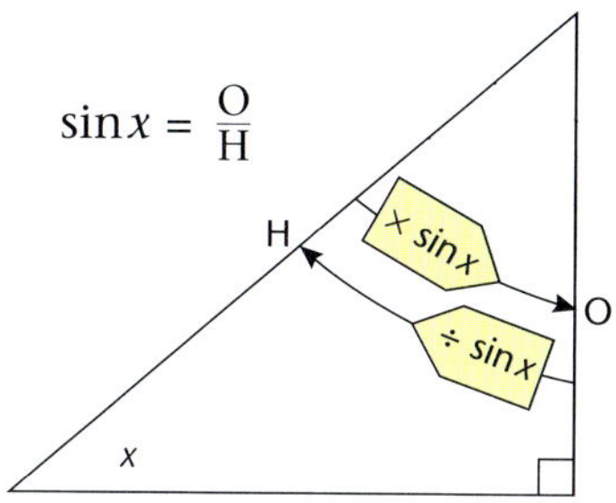

$\cos x = \frac{A}{H}$

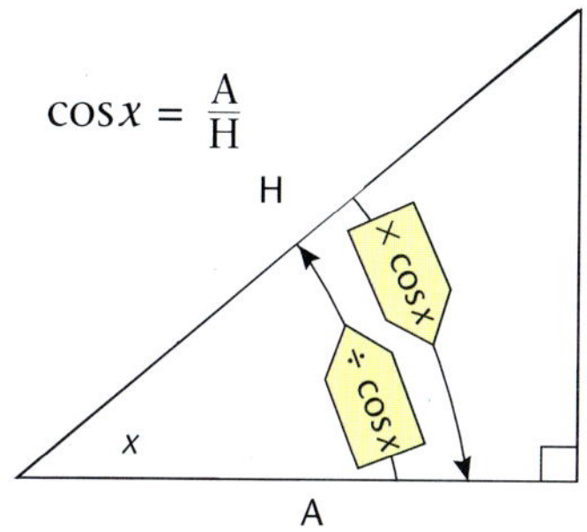

$\tan x = \frac{O}{A}$

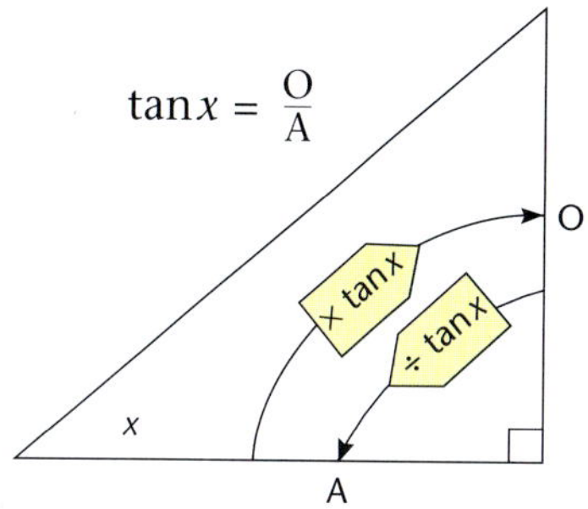

Finding sides of right-angled triangles

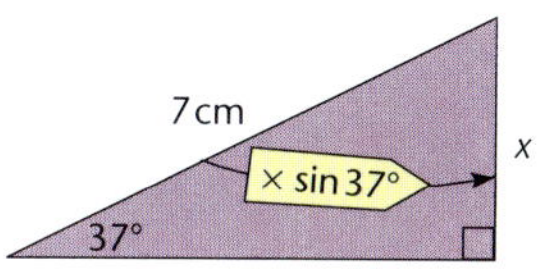

$x = 7\,\text{cm} \times \sin 37° = 4.21\,\text{cm}$

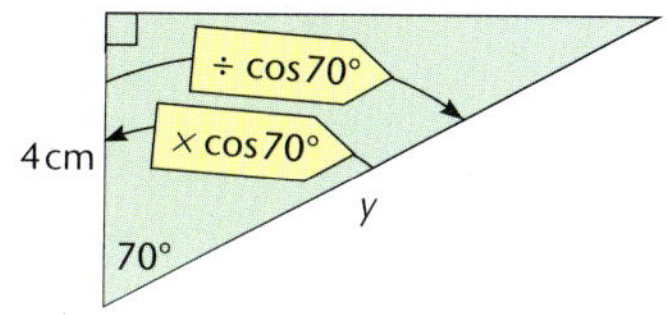

$y = 4\,\text{cm} \div \cos 70° = 11.7\,\text{cm}$

Finding angles in right-angled triangles

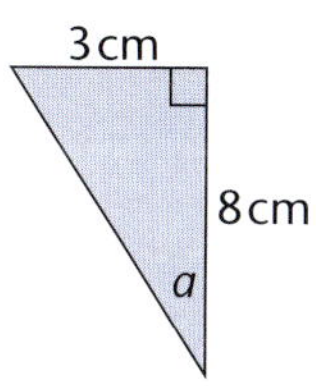

$\tan a = \frac{3}{8}$

$a = 20.6°$

Elevation and depression

Angles of elevation and depression are measured from the horizontal.

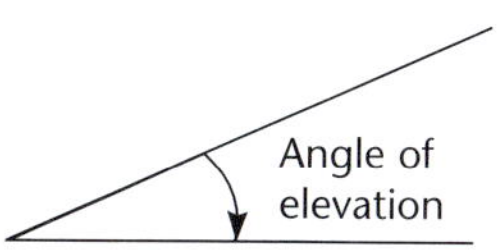

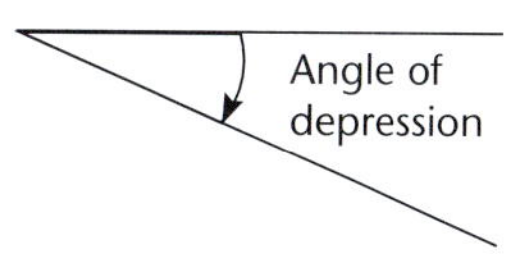

Bearings

A **bearing** is used to define a compass direction. The bearing is the number of degrees turned clockwise from North to the direction.

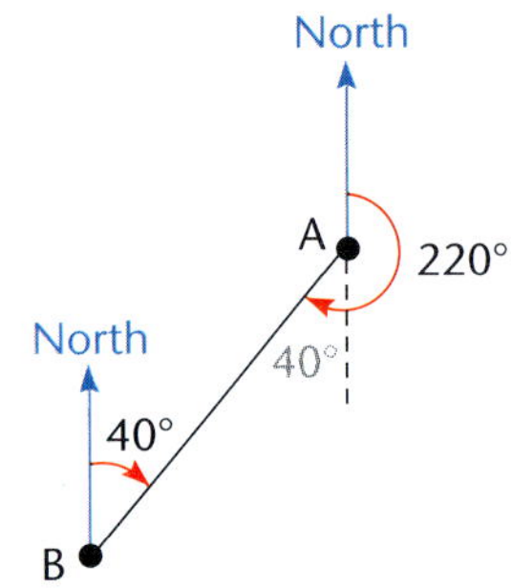

The bearing of A from B is 040°.
The bearing of B from A is 220°.

Sine, cosine and tangent for angles greater than 90°

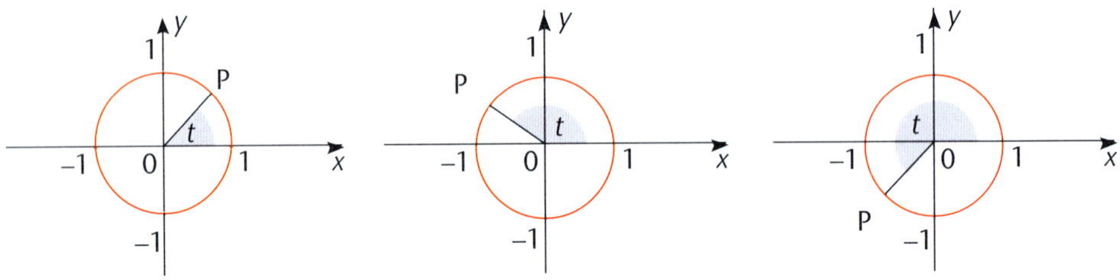

The coordinates of any point P on the circle of radius 1 are ($\cos t$, $\sin t$).

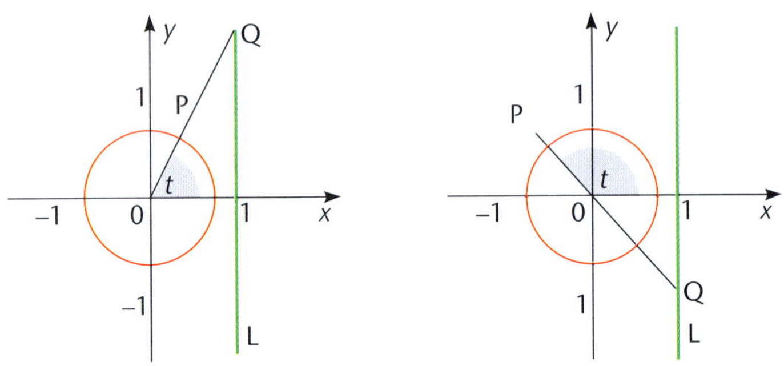

The coordinate of Q is $\tan t$.

Graphs of trigonometric functions

$y = \sin x$

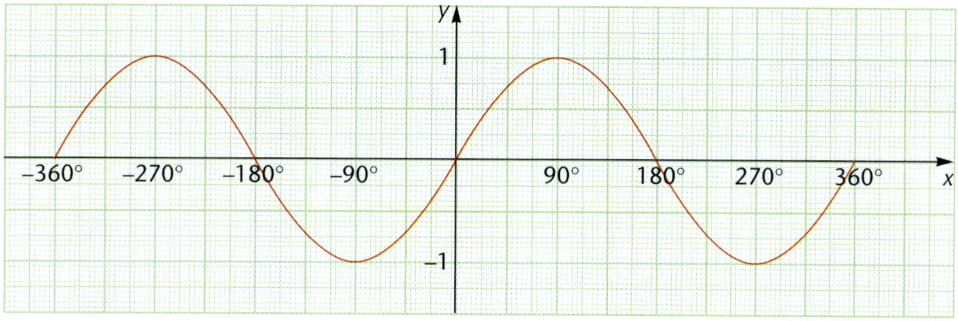

$y = \cos x$

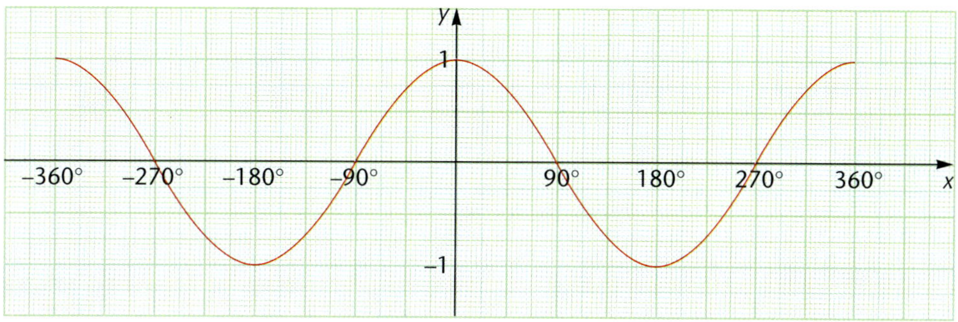

$y = \tan x$

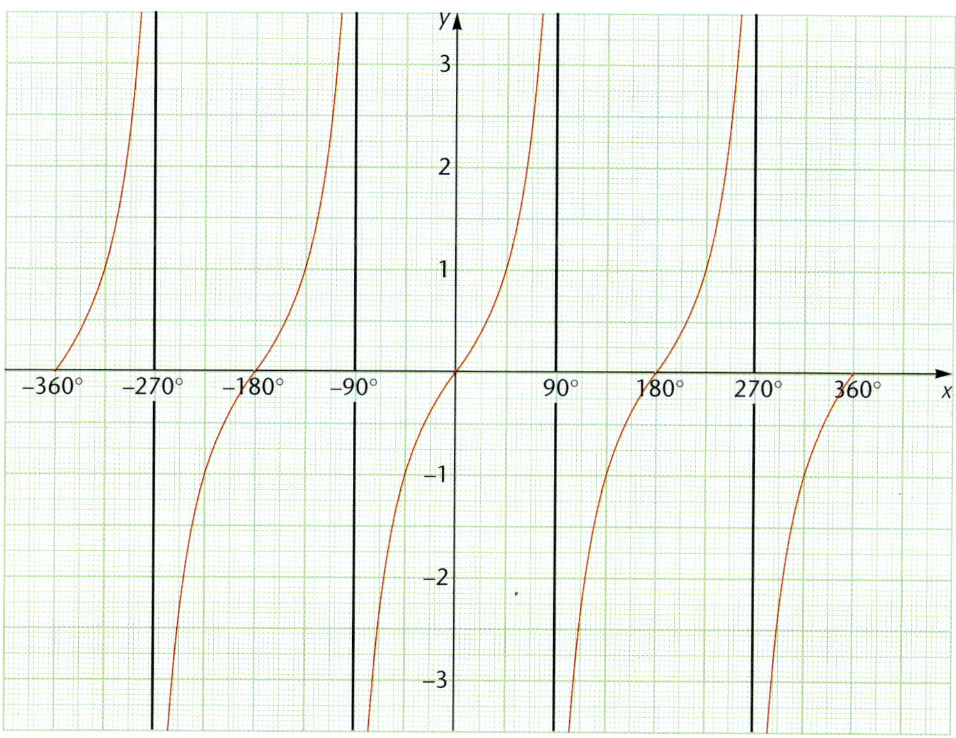

CHAPTER

10 PROBABILITY

This chapter is about:

- relative frequency, including graphical representation
- using equally likely outcomes and experimental evidence
- comparing estimated and theoretical probability
- using two-way tables
- identifying all the outcomes of a combination of two experiments
- using possibility space diagrams
- relative frequency
- using tabulation and tree diagrams
- calculating the probabilities associated with AND and OR
- conditional probability.

Drawing conclusions from experiments

▶ Cubes

DISCUSSION POINT

Ask a partner to put eight cubes in a bag.
They should be cubes of just three colours (say red, blue and yellow) but your partner will not say how many of each. You must not look in the bag.

As an experiment, draw a cube at random from the bag.
Write down its colour. Replace it in the bag.

- Do this experiment four times. From the four colours you have written down, forecast how many of each colour there are in the bag. Still do not look at the cubes in the bag.
- Now do the experiment four more times. You should now have eight colours written down altogether. From these eight colours, forecast again how many of each colour there are in the bag.
  Still do not look at the cubes in the bag.
- Do the experiment eight more times. From the 16 colours you have written down, forecast again how many of each colour there are in the bag.
- Now look at the cubes in the bag.
  Which of your three forecasts was most accurate?

Now repeat the whole experiment, but this time your partner can use a different mix of coloured cubes in the bag.

For the second experiment, your partner might not even tell you how many colours are being used.

EXERCISE 1

1 A bag contains four cubes. Someone draws a cube from the bag and then puts it back. She does this ten times.
These are the colours she pulls from the bag:
RED BLUE RED YELLOW BLUE RED YELLOW RED RED BLUE
For each of these seven statements, write if it is *impossible*, *possible* or *certain*.

A: There are exactly two red cubes in the bag.

B: There are exactly two blue cubes in the bag.

C: There are exactly three red cubes in the bag.

D: There is at least one yellow cube in the bag.

E: There is a green cube in the bag.

F: There are more blue cubes than yellow cubes in the bag.

G: There are more yellow cubes than red cubes in the bag.

2 A bag contains 40 cubes. Someone draws a cube from the bag and then puts it back. He does this ten times.
These are the colours he pulls from the bag:
RED BLUE RED YELLOW BLUE RED YELLOW RED RED BLUE
For each of these six statements, say if it is *impossible*, *possible* or *certain*.

A: There are exactly 20 red cubes in the bag.

B: There are exactly eight blue cubes in the bag.

C: There are more than 20 red cubes in the bag.

D: There is at least one yellow cube in the bag.

E: There is at least one green cube in the bag.

F: There are more green cubes than red cubes in the bag.

3 A bag contains a number of cubes. Someone draws a cube from the bag and puts it back. She does this ten times.
These are the colours she pulls from the bag:
RED BLUE YELLOW BLUE RED BLUE BLUE YELLOW BLUE YELLOW

(**a**) For each of these four statements, say if it is *impossible*, *possible* or *certain*.

A: There are exactly two cubes in the bag.

B: There are exactly ten cubes in the bag.

C: There are more blue cubes than red cubes in the bag.

D: The number of yellow cubes in the bag is a multiple of three.

(**b**) You are now told that there are in fact 36 cubes in the bag.

(**i**) Estimate the number of red cubes, the number of blue cubes and the number of yellow cubes in the bag.

(**ii**) How certain are you about your estimates?

Relative frequency

DISCUSSION POINT

Here are the results of five Y10 students who each threw the same dice six times.

Student A	6	1	3	6	2	4
Student B	5	2	5	5	3	5
Student C	4	1	6	3	2	4
Student D	5	4	3	2	1	6
Student E	3	1	3	6	1	3

Do you think the dice the students are using is fair?
The students then threw the dice 60 times each, and began to accumulate their scores, counting how many sixes they got.

Total number of throws so far	Number of sixes	Total number of sixes so far	Relative frequency (3 s.f.)
60	8	8	$\frac{8}{60} = 0.133$
120	9	17	$\frac{17}{120} = 0.142$
180	12	29	$\frac{29}{180} = 0.161$
240	10	39	$\frac{39}{240} = 0.163$
300	8	47	$\frac{47}{300} = 0.157$

These results can be shown in a graph.

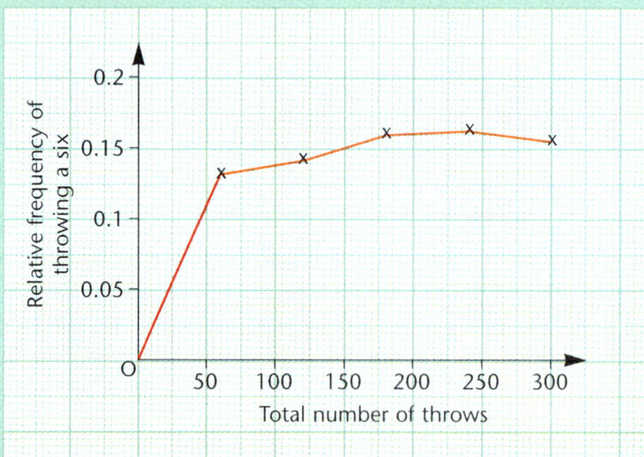

If the dice was fair, how many sixes would you expect them to have thrown?

Do you think the dice was fair?

Dice

EXERCISE 2

1 (a) Throw two ordinary dice 50 times and record the sum of the two scores shown.

(b) Compare your resulting relative frequencies with the theoretical probabilities, assuming that the dice are unbiased.

(c) Combine the class results. How do the class relative frequencies compare with the theoretical probabilities?

2 A drawing pin is dropped ten times and a note is taken of how it lands: point up or point down.

Number of drops	Point up	Point down
10	5	5

The experiment is repeated another ten times. Here are the results.

Number of drops	Point up	Point down
20	12	8

The experiment is repeated many more times. All of the results are shown in this table.

Number of drops	Point up	Point down
10	5	5
20	12	8
30	19	11
40	24	16
50	28	22
60	34	26

(a) Copy and complete this table.

Number of drops	10	20	30	40	50	60
Percentage of times drawing pin lands point up						

(b) Plot these results on a graph.

(c) Estimate the probability of the drawing pin landing point up.

(d) What happens to the points on the graph as the number of drops increases?

3 In a particular town, someone recorded the colour of cars passing him as he stood at the side of the road. Here are the results.

White	43
Black	37
Red	58
Blue	31
Grey	28
Other colours	26

(**a**) Estimate the probability that the next car passing is

(**i**) black

(**ii**) either red or grey

(**iii**) *not* blue

(**b**) The adult population of the town is about 200000.
Given that about 35% of the adults in the town own a car, estimate the number of red cars owned by people in the town.

4 In a local survey of voting intentions, 300 people were questioned. This is how they said they would vote.

Conservative	83
Labour	66
Liberal Democrat	105
Don't know	46

(**a**) Estimate the probability that the next person asked would say they would vote Labour.

(**b**) The electorate of the local constituency is 75418.
Assume that the 'Don't knows' do not vote at all.
Forecast which candidate would win the election and estimate their majority over their nearest competitor to a sensible degree of accuracy.

5 A firm has a fleet of 40 lorries.
Over a period of 30 working weeks, i.e. 150 days, a record was kept of how many lorries needed maintenance each day. Here are the results.

Number of lorries needing maintenance	0	1	2	3	**Total**
Number of days that number occurred	30	60	45	15	150

What is the relative frequency that, on a particular day,

(**a**) two lorries needed maintenance?

(**b**) at least two lorries needed maintenance?

6 Here is an extract from data about deaths in 1992.

Age	0–1	1–5	5–15
Females population (1000s)	339	1345	3104
Number of female deaths	1933	387	413

(**a**) Estimate the relative frequency of a 12-year-old female dying.

(**b**) Estimate the relative frequency of a 4-year-old girl dying.

(**c**) Compare the relative frequency of death for females who were aged 1–5 with those aged 5–15 in 1992.

(**d**) Within the 1–5 age group, 82 of the 387 deaths resulted from violence and 15 from circulation problems. Within the 5–15 age group, 121 of the 413 deaths resulted from violence and 19 from circulation problems. Compare the relative frequencies of these two causes of death for the two different age groups.

Two-way tables

DISCUSSION POINT

A Maths set were asked whether they studied German for GCSE and whether they studied Music for GCSE. Their replies are summarised in this **two-way table.**

	Study German	Don't study German
Study Music	2	5
Don't study Music	16	3

- How many students study German, but not Music?
- How many study *both* subjects?
- If a student were selected randomly, why is the probability that he/she studies Music but not German $\frac{5}{26}$?
- Make up and answer other questions that can be answered from this table.

Sometimes, it can be useful to show row and column totals.

	Study German	Don't study German	Total
Study Music	2	5	7
Don't study Music	16	3	19
Total	18	8	26

- A student is selected at random. It is discovered that this student studies German. What is the probability that this student also studies Music?
- What is the probability that a student selected at random is studying both German and Music?

EXERCISE 3

1 Here is a two-way table about a group of A-level students.

	Study Chemistry	Don't study Chemistry
Study Biology	21	9
Don't study Biology	11	7

What is the probability that a student chosen at random

(**a**) studies both Chemistry and Biology?

(**b**) studies neither Chemistry nor Biology?

(**c**) studies Chemistry?

(**d**) studies Biology but not Chemistry?

(**e**) who studies Chemistry, also studies Biology?

(**f**) studies Chemistry *or* Biology?

In Question 1 (f), 'or' means the student may study one or both subjects.

2 A new ointment for treatment of a skin disease was tested on some patients at a skin clinic while other patients were kept on a previous treatment.
Here are the results.

	Cured within a month	Not cured within a month
New treatment	42	6
Old treatment	118	74

(**a**) What is the probability that a patient, chosen at random, was cured within a month?

(**b**) If a patient who had been given the new treatment was chosen at random, what is the probability that this patient was cured within a month?

(**c**) A patient is chosen at random.
It is then found that this patient was cured within a month.
What is the probability that this patient was on the new treatment?

(**d**) If a patient who had been given the old treatment was chosen at random, what is the probability that this patient was cured within a month?

(**e**) Is there evidence that the new treatment is better than the old? Explain your answer.

For Questions 3 and 4, draw a two-way table to answer the questions.

3 Some former school friends had a reunion to which they brought partners and offspring, if they had any. There were 26 adults and 24 children; there were 20 females of whom 12 were adults.

(**a**) One of the people at the reunion was chosen at random to win a prize. What is the probability that the prize winner was

(**i**) a female child?

(**ii**) a male adult?

(**b**) One of the children at the reunion was chosen at random to win a prize. What is the probability that this prize winner was female?

4 In a child's sorting game, there are 15 red shapes. There are five small red shapes, and two of these have four sides. There are ten red shapes that do not have four sides. One of the shapes is selected at random.

(**a**) What is the probability that the selected shape is

(**i**) a small 4-sided red shape?

(**ii**) a red shape which is either small or *not* 4-sided?

(**b**) It is found that the selected shape is a small red shape. What is the probability that it is 4-sided?

(**c**) It is found that the selected shape is a red 4-sided shape. What is the probability of it being small?

5 In a set of dominoes, each piece has two 'numbers' on it, represented by spots. Each number is between 0 (blank) and 6. All the dominoes in the set are different. Here are four examples.

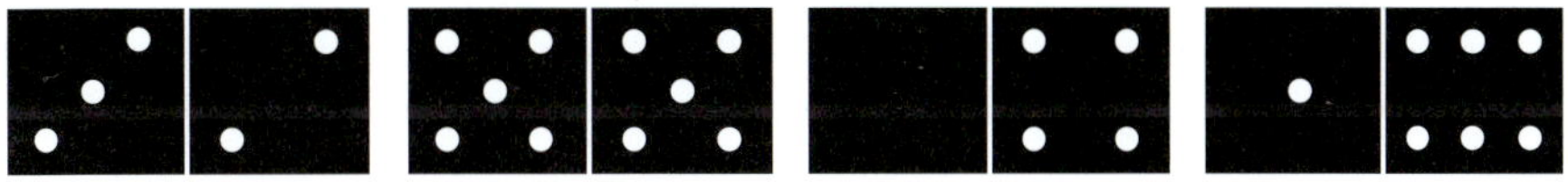

(**a**) How many dominoes are there in a complete set?

(**b**) Compile a two-way table for the categories 'the domino is a double' and 'the domino has a total of 4 or more spots'.

(**c**) What is the probability that a domino chosen at random from a complete set is

(**i**) a double?

(**ii**) a double with four or more spots altogether?

(**iii**) a double when it has a total of four or more spots?

(**iv**) a double or has a total of four or more spots?

Identifying all the possible outcomes

In a bag are three counters, of which two are black and one is red.
One counter is picked out at random.

Two counters are taken out in succession, *the first being replaced before the second is chosen.*
These diagrams show all the equally likely possible outcomes:

A two-way table

		2nd counter		
		Black	Not black (= red)	Totals
1st counter	Black	4	2	6
	Not black (= red)	2	1	3
	Totals	6	3	9

A possibility space diagram

		2nd counter		
		B_1	B_2	R
1st counter	B_1	B_1B_1	B_1B_2	B_1R
	B_2	B_2B_1	B_2B_2	B_2R
	R	RB_1	RB_2	RR

A tree diagram

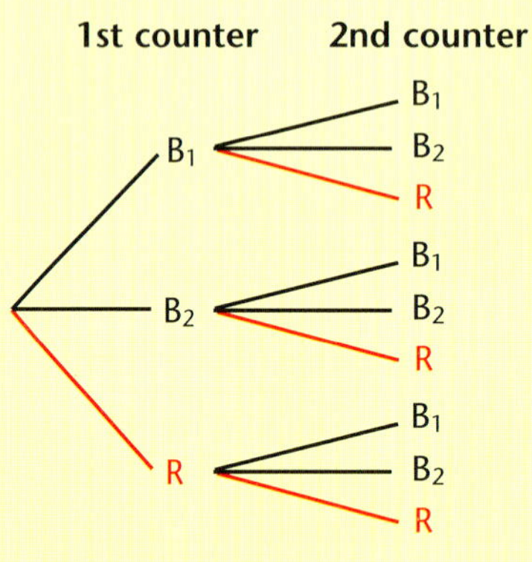

Any of these three diagrams can be used to show that the probability of

- taking out two black counters is $\frac{4}{9}$
- both counters being the same colour is $\frac{5}{9}$
- taking out one counter of each colour is $\frac{4}{9}$

EXERCISE 4

1 In a bag, there are two black counters and two white counters.
Two counters are taken from this bag at random.
The first one is replaced in the bag before the second one is taken.
What is the probability that

(a) the counter is black *both* times?

(b) the *same* colour is drawn both times?

(c) different colours are drawn?

(d) the first counter is white and the second is black?

2 **(a)** Draw a possibility space diagram to show the 36 possible outcomes when two ordinary dice, one red and one blue, are thrown.

(b) Use your diagram to find the probability of

(i) a total of 8 or more when the two scores are added

(ii) a difference of 2 between the two scores

(iii) a total of 8 or more, and a difference of 2

(iv) a total of 8 or more, when the difference is 2

(v) a difference of 2 when the total is 8 or more

(vi) a total of 8 or more, or a difference of 2

(c) Someone throws the two dice and the blue dice rolls under a chair.
The red dice shows a four.
Given this score on the red dice, what is the probability that the sum of the scores on the two dice is 9 or more?

3 In my pocket there are three coins: a 1p, a 2p and a 5p.
My friend also has three coins – a 1p, 2p and a 5p – in her pocket.
We each take one coin at random from our pocket.

(a) Draw either a tree diagram or a possibility space diagram to show all the outcomes.

(b) Use your diagram to find the probability that

(i) the total value of the two coins drawn is 6p or more

(ii) the two coins drawn are the *same*

(iii) the two coins are the same *and* their total value is 6p or more

(iv) the total value of the two coins is 6p or more, or they are the same

(v) the two coins are the same when their sum is 6p or more

(vi) the total value is 6p or more when the two coins are the same

(vii) the total value is 6p or more when my coin is a 2p

(viii) the total value is 6p or more when my friend's coin is a 5p

4 From a sports club committee comprising three women and two men, a chairperson and a vice-chairperson are to be selected at random.
No one, of course, can be both.
Find the probability that

(**a**) two females are chosen

(**b**) one of each sex is chosen

5 A card is drawn from a normal pack of playing cards. It is replaced and a second card drawn.
Find the probability that

(**a**) both cards are hearts

(**b**) both cards are the same suit

(**c**) at least one card is a heart

6 There are two red cubes and two black cubes in a bag.
Two are drawn at random, the first being replaced before the second is selected.
Find the probability that

(**a**) the cube drawn is red *both* times

(**b**) the first cube drawn is red

(**c**) the second cube drawn is red

(**d**) the second cube drawn is red when the first is red

(**e**) the second cube drawn is black when the first is red

(**f**) the second cube drawn is black *and* the first is red

(**g**) the first cube drawn is red *or* the second is black

(**h**) the same colour is drawn each time

7 Answer the same questions as in Question 6 for a bag containing *three* red and two black cubes.

DISCUSSION POINT

Imagine the situation where a bag contains m red cubes and two black cubes.
Find probabilities like those in Questions 6 and 7 above.
Generalise to the situation where there are m red and n black cubes in the bag.

Making and justifying a generalisation

Combining probabilities

Independent events

A bag contains five cubes: three red and two blue. Imagine that someone draws a cube from the bag at random, replaces the cube in the bag and then draws a cube from the bag a second time.

There are 25 possible outcomes, as shown in this table.

Second draw

First draw	R	R	R	B	B
R	RR	RR	RR	RB	RB
R	RR	RR	RR	RB	RB
R	RR	RR	RR	RB	RB
B	BR	BR	BR	BB	BB
B	BR	BR	BR	BB	BB

What is the probability that the first cube drawn is red and the second cube is blue?

This question can be answered by looking at the block of six outcomes (RB). There are 25 outcomes altogether and so the probability required is $\frac{6}{25}$.

Another way of looking at this is to think about the shapes of the blocks. The (RB) block is a 3-by-2 rectangle. The block of all outcomes is a 5-by-5 square. So, the probability of drawing red cube first time and a blue cube second time is $\frac{3 \times 2}{5 \times 5}$

This is the same as

$$\frac{3}{5} \times \frac{2}{5}$$

The probability of the first cube being red is $\frac{3}{5}$.

The probability of the second cube being blue is $\frac{2}{5}$.

So, the probability of both events happening can be worked out by *multiplying* the probabilities that each of them will happen.

This is only possible because the two events are **independent**. In other words, whatever colour is drawn the first time does not change the chance of drawing a particular colour the second time (as long as you shake the bag!). Cubes have no memory.

The rule for probabilities of independent events can be extended to three or more events. You can work out the probability of several events *all* happening by multiplying the probabilities that *each* of them will happen.

You would certainly want to use this rule, rather than drawing up a table, if there were 40 cubes in the bag of several different colours. It is also straightforward to use the rule, but difficult to use a table, if you are combining, not just two events, but three or more.

EXERCISE 5

1 A bag contains five cubes, identical except for colour. Four of the cubes are red and one is blue.
A cube is drawn from the bag at random and replaced.
A second cube is then drawn at random from the bag.
What is the probability that

(**a**) the first cube is red *and* the second cube is blue?

(**b**) both cubes are red?

2 A bag contains eight cubes, identical except for colour. Four of the cubes are blue, three are green and one is yellow.

(**a**) A cube is drawn from the bag at random and replaced.
A second cube is then drawn at random from the bag. What is the probability that the first cube is green *and* the second cube is blue?

(**b**) In another experiment, a cube is drawn at random from the bag and replaced. Next, a second cube is drawn at random and replaced.
Then, a third cube is drawn at random.
What is the probability that the first cube is yellow, the second cube is blue, and the third cube is green?

3 A bag contains 20 cubes, identical except for colour.
Eight of the cubes are red, five are yellow, and seven are blue.

(**a**) A cube is drawn from the bag at random and replaced.
A second cube is then drawn at random from the bag.
What is the probability that

(**i**) the first cube is red *and* the second cube is blue?

(**ii**) one of the cubes drawn is red and the other cube drawn is yellow?

(**b**) A cube is drawn from the bag at random and replaced.
Then a second is drawn and replaced. Then a third is drawn.
What is the probability that

(**i**) the first cube drawn is red, the second is blue and the third is yellow?

(**ii**) one cube of each colour is drawn?

4 A normal pack of playing cards is shuffled. A card is drawn from the pack and replaced. Then a second card is drawn from the pack.
What is the probability that

(**a**) the first card is a red card *and* the second card is a spade?

(**b**) one card is a red card and the other card is a spade?

(**c**) one card is an ace and the other card is a picture card (King, Queen or Jack)?

Mutually exclusive events

A bag contains nine cubes: four red, three blue and two green.
A cube is drawn at random and replaced. Another cube is then drawn at random.

Question: What is the probability that one cube is red and one cube is blue?

Answer: For this question, there is a combination of two events: RB or BR

If the first cube is red and the second cube is blue, the probability is

$\frac{4}{9} \times \frac{3}{9} = \frac{12}{81}$

If the first cube is blue and the second cube is red, the probability is

$\frac{3}{9} \times \frac{4}{9} = \frac{12}{81}$

The probability of the **combination** of these two events is

$\frac{12}{81} + \frac{12}{81} = \frac{24}{81} = \frac{8}{27}$

You can add the probabilities *only* because the events are **mutually exclusive.**

In other words, it is not possible for both events to happen at the same time.

Question: What is the probability that *either* both cubes are red *or* both cubes are green?

Answer: The probability that both cubes are red is

$\frac{4}{9} \times \frac{4}{9} = \frac{16}{81}$

The probability that both cubes are green is

$\frac{2}{9} \times \frac{2}{9} = \frac{4}{81}$

So the probability that either both cubes are red *or* both cubes are green is

$\frac{16}{81} + \frac{4}{81} = \frac{20}{81}$

Question: What is the probability that *both* cubes are the *same* colour?

Answer: This is a combination of *three* events: RR, BB, GG.

If both cubes are red, the probability is

$\frac{16}{81}$

If both cubes are blue, the probability is

$\frac{9}{81}$

If both cubes are green, the probability is

$\frac{4}{81}$

So, the probability that both are the same colour is

$\frac{16}{81} + \frac{9}{81} + \frac{4}{81} = \frac{29}{81}$

EXERCISE 6

1 A bag contains five cubes, identical except for colour. Four of them are blue and one is yellow.
A cube is drawn from the bag at random and replaced.
Then a second cube is drawn. What is the probability that

(**a**) *both* cubes drawn are the *same* colour?

(**b**) the two cubes drawn are *different* colours?

2 A bag contains ten cubes, identical except for colour. Five of them are blue, three are red and two are green.
A cube is drawn from the bag at random and replaced.
Then a second cube is drawn. What is the probability that

(**a**) one cube is red and one cube is green?

(**b**) the cubes are different colours?

(**c**) at least one of the cubes is blue?

3 A normal pack of playing cards is shuffled.
A card is drawn from the pack and replaced. Another card is then drawn from the pack.
What is the probability that

(**a**) both cards are the *same* colour?

(**b**) both cards are the same *suit*?

(**c**) *neither* card is a picture card?

(**d**) at least one card is a diamond?

4 A particular drawing pin has a probability of 0.4 of landing point down when it is thrown and a probability of 0.6 of landing point up.

(**a**) The drawing pin is thrown twice. What is the probability of its landing

(**i**) point up twice?

(**ii**) point up once and point down once?

(**b**) The drawing pin is thrown three times. What is the probability that it lands the same way each of the three times?

5 Two different drawing pins are thrown.
One has a probability of 0.4 of landing point down when it is thrown; the other has a probability of 0.3 of landing point down when it is thrown.
Two players play a game. Player A wins if *both* drawing pins land the same way (both point down or both point up). Player B wins if the drawings pins land in different ways (one point down and the other point up).
What is the probability that

(**a**) player A wins?

(**b**) player B wins?

Who is more likely to win?

DISCUSSION POINT

A bag contains five red cubes and seven blue cubes.
One cube is drawn at random.
It is then replaced in the bag and a second cube is drawn.

A **tree diagram** can be used to describe this situation.

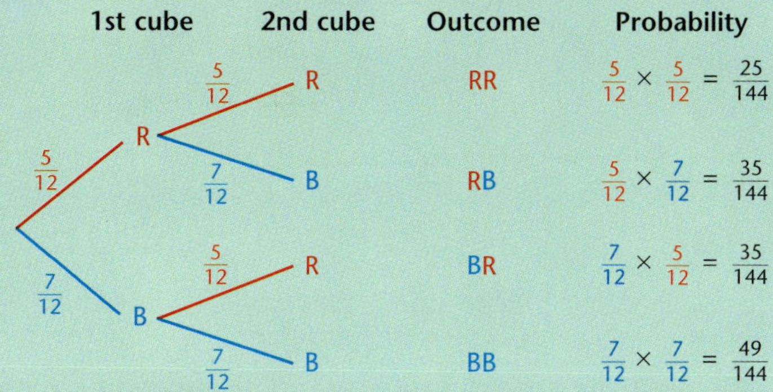

How does the tree diagram help you to find the probability that

- both cubes are red?
- the first cube is red and the second is blue?
- both cubes are blue?
- there is one of each colour?
- there is at least one red?

EXERCISE 7

1 A bag contains five green and two yellow cubes, identical except for colour. Two cubes are drawn in succession, the first being replaced before the second is chosen.

(**a**) Draw a tree diagram to represent this situation, showing all the outcomes.

(**b**) What is the probability that

(**i**) the same colour is drawn each time?

(**ii**) one of each colour is drawn?

2 Draw a tree diagram to show all the possible combinations for three flips of an unbiased coin, and use it to work out the probability that

(**a**) the first two flips are heads and the last is tails

(**b**) there are two heads and one tail in any order

(**c**) there are at least two heads

3 This spinner is spun twice.

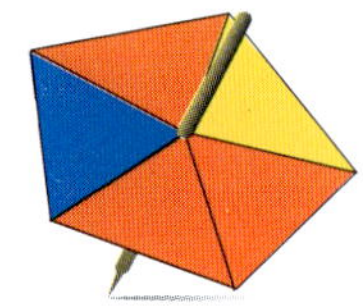

(**a**) Copy and complete this tree diagram.

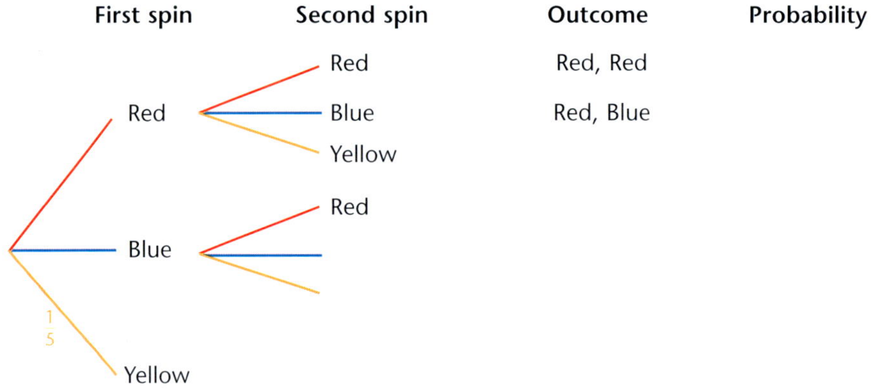

(**b**) What is the probability that the spinner lands on red once and on blue once?

(**c**) What is the probability that it does *not* land on yellow exactly once?

4 A card is drawn at random from a normal pack of playing cards.
This card is replaced and another card is drawn.

(**a**) Draw a tree diagram to find the probability that both cards are picture cards.

(**b**) Use your tree diagram to find the probability that at least one of the cards drawn is a picture card.

5 In a bag, there are four red, three yellow and six blue cubes, identical except for colour.
Two are drawn at random, in succession, with replacement.

(**a**) Draw a tree diagram for this situation, listing all the outcomes.

(**b**) What is the probability that one cube drawn is blue and one is yellow?

(**c**) What is the probability that both cubes drawn are the same colour?

(**d**) A red cube scores 1, a yellow cube scores 2 and a blue cube scores 3.
What is the probability that the sum of the score for the two cubes is 4?

6 In a game with a dice, these are the rules.

You lose if your first throw of the dice does not show a five or a six.

If it shows a six, you throw again and win unless the dice shows one.

If it shows a five, you throw again and win if the dice shows five or six.

Draw a tree diagram to find the probability of winning the game.

7 A bag contains four white and six blue cubes.
Three are drawn at random, in succession, with replacement.

(**a**) Draw a tree diagram for this situation, listing all the outcomes.

(**b**) What is the probability that

(**i**) the cube is blue all three times?

(**ii**) the same colour is drawn each time?

(**iii**) at least one of the cubes drawn is blue?

(**iv**) *exactly* one of the cubes drawn is blue?

8 Someone is interested in the possibility of obtaining sixes when a dice is thrown three times. With or without drawing a suitable tree diagram, find the probability of obtaining

(**a**) three sixes

(**b**) no sixes

(**c**) at least one six

(**d**) exactly one six

9 (**a**) What is the probability of getting *exactly* three sixes when a dice is thrown four times?

(**b**) What is the probability of getting *exactly* four sixes when a dice is thrown five times?

10 A coin is biased so that the probability of it showing a head is $\frac{5}{8}$.
What is the probability that

(**a**) in two flips, it shows heads *both* times?

(**b**) in two flips, it shows one head and one tail?

(**c**) in three flips, it shows *only* tails?

(**d**) in three flips, it shows two heads?

(**e**) in *n* flips, it shows *exactly* one tail?

Conditional probability

DISCUSSION POINT

A bag contains five cubes: three red and two black.
One cube is taken from the bag. It is *not* replaced.
A second cube is taken from the bag.

- What is the probability that *both* cubes taken are red?
- What is the probability that the two cubes taken are *different* colours?

This is an example of **conditional probability**.

The probability of the second cube being a black cube is **conditional** on the colour of the first cube.

EXERCISE 8

1 A bag contains two green and two yellow cubes.
Two are taken out in succession, *without* replacement.

(a) Draw a tree diagram to represent this, showing the probability on each branch and the outcomes.

(b) What is the probability that

(i) the cubes are *both* green?

(ii) the cubes are the *same* colour?

(iii) the first cube is yellow and the second is green?

(iv) one cube of *each* colour is drawn?

2 A bag contains four white and six blue cubes.
Two are taken in succession, *without* replacement.

(a) Draw a tree diagram to represent this.

(b) What is the probability that

(i) they are *both* blue?

(ii) they are the *same* colour?

(iii) there is at least one blue one?

(iv) the first *or* the second is blue?

(v) *neither* is blue?

3 A bag contains five red and three black cubes.
Two are taken in succession, *without* replacement.
Which is larger, the probability that they are both the same colour, or the probability that there is one of each colour?

Making and justifying a generalisation

4 There are m red cubes and n black cubes in a bag, from which two are taken *without* replacement.

(a) What is the probability that they are

(i) both red?

(ii) the same colour?

(iii) different colours?

(b) Is it possible to determine whether the answer to part (a)(ii) is larger than the answer to part (a)(iii)?
Are these two answers ever equal?

A standard set of dominoes has 28 dominoes.

5 Someone picks three dominoes at random from a standard set.

(a) What is the probability that they are all 'doubles'?

(b) What is the probability that each domino has a six on it?

6 A magazine competition consists of choosing four features in order of priority from a given list of seven.
You win if your order is the same as that of the judges.

(**a**) Find the probability of your order being completely correct.

(**b**) If the competition involved choosing *six* features in order of priority from a list of *ten*, what would be the probability of winning?

7 Someone picks two cards at random from a pack of playing cards.
What is the probability that they are

(**a**) both red?

(**b**) both aces?

(**c**) both from the same suit?

8 Someone picks three cards at random from a pack of playing cards.
What is the probability that

(**a**) they are all spades?

(**b**) two of them are spades?

(**c**) no two are from the same suit?

9 Five cubes are taken in succession from a bag containing six red and four black cubes.
What is the probability of taking exactly four cubes of one colour?

10 In the National Lottery, six numbers are drawn, without replacement, from 49. Suppose you have chosen 7, 11, 24, 30, 39 and 42.

(**a**) What is the probability that

(**i**) the first two numbers drawn are 7 and then 11?

(**ii**) the first three numbers drawn are 7, then 11 and then 24?

(**iii**) the first two numbers drawn are your smallest two?

(**iv**) the first three numbers drawn are your smallest three?

(**b**) What is the probability that the six numbers drawn are the same as your six?

DISCUSSION POINT

In a television game show, there are three boxes to choose from.
The show's host knows what is in each box. One box holds the key to a new car, the other two each contain booby prizes: a cold kipper and a balloon.

You are the participant in the game. You first select one of the boxes, which is not yet opened. The host then opens one of the *other* boxes which she knows contains a booby prize, and invites you to think again.

What is the your best course of action – should you stick with your first choice, or should you change your mind? Or does it make no difference?

Further problems

DISCUSSION POINT

The quality control department in a factory collects samples of light bulbs and tests for standard of quality.
In one large sample, 3% of the bulbs were found to be substandard.
What does this tree diagram about a sample of two bulbs assume?

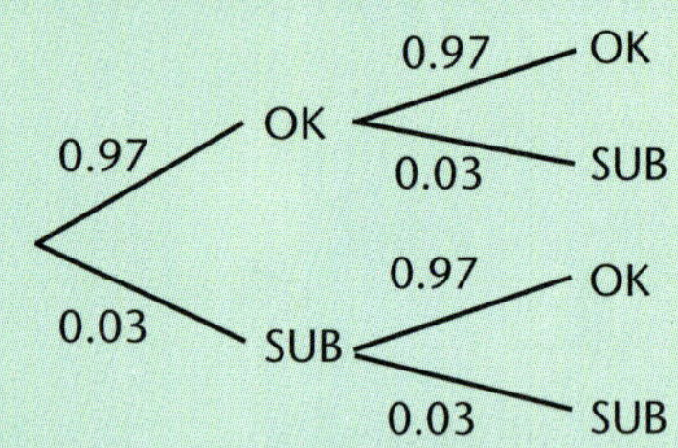

What would be the probability of two substandard bulbs in a pack of three?

Is **independence** a reasonable assumption in these examples – would the probabilities on subsequent branches *really* stay the same?

Many answers to probability problems can only be realistically calculated on the assumption of **independence**, i.e. that the probabilities on subsequent branches do *not* depend on what has preceded them.

EXERCISE 9

1 The probability of a violent death for a female aged between 1 and 5 is approximately 3.1×10^{-6}. A 4-year-old and her 2-year-old sister die as a result of violence. Is the probability of this happening $(3.1 \times 10^{-6})^2$? Explain your answer.

2 A passenger estimated that the probability of an aeroplane having a bomb on it was one in a million.

(**a**) On this basis, what is the probability of an aeroplane having *two* bombs on it?

(**b**) In view of the answer to part (a), the passenger reasoned that the likelihood of the plane being blown up would be greatly reduced if he took a bomb on the aeroplane with him!
Is his reasoning sound?

3 A firm has a fleet of 40 lorries.
Over a period of 30 working weeks, i.e. 150 days, a record was kept of how many lorries needed maintenance each day.
These were the results.

Number of lorries needing maintenance	0	1	2	3	Total
Number of days that number occurred	30	60	45	15	150

Calculate the probability that at least two lorries need maintenance on

(a) two consecutive days

(b) three consecutive days

(c) two days out of three consecutive days

(d) four days out of five consecutive days

4 **(a)** A particular drawing pin has a probability of 0.43 of landing 'point up'. If it is dropped three times, estimate the probability of it landing 'point up'

(i) once

(ii) at least once

(b) Answer parts (a)(i) and (a)(ii) if the drawing pin is dropped 20 times.

5 A wholesaler has received a large consignment of saucepans.
Past experience suggests that the probability of a badly fitting lid on any saucepan is 0.034.

(a) If a sample of five pans were checked, estimate the probability of

(i) five badly fitting lids

(ii) no badly fitting lids

(iii) one badly fitting lid

(b) What would be your advice if five badly fitting lids *were* found?

6 Past experience suggests that, for a particular examination, the probability of passing first time is 68%.
Of those who fail, 35% pass the second time. Of those who fail the second time as well, 18% pass the third time.
There is, of course, no need to re-sit once the examination has been passed.

(a) Show that the probability that the examination is passed in at most two tries is 0.792.

(b) Calculate the probability that the examination is passed

(i) at the third attempt

(ii) not later than the third attempt

7 A particular coin appears to be biased because in 200 flips it landed tails 150 times.

(**a**) Use this information to estimate the probability of getting a head with one flip.

(**b**) Using your answer to part (a) estimate the probability that

(**i**) you have to flip it at least three times to get the first head

(**ii**) at least one head appears in the first three flips

COURSEWORK OPPORTUNITY

String

The matchmaker

In some Russian villages during the 1800s, if a man and a woman wanted to marry, they had to seek the permission of a professional matchmaker.
This person, usually an elderly unmarried woman, would carry out a test to see whether the couple were suited.
In one of these tests, the matchmaker would cut three pieces of string, fold them and then hold them so that just the six loose ends were visible.

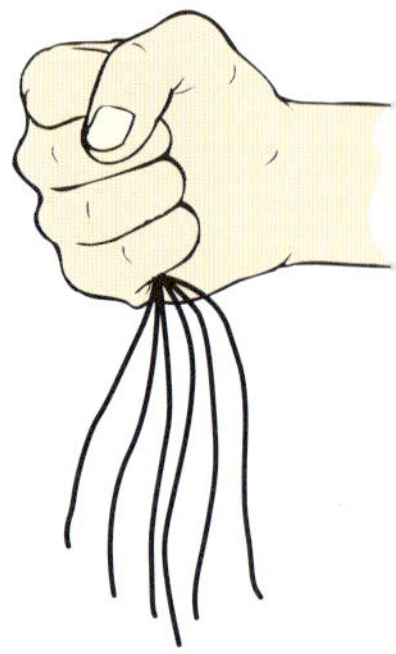

The couple then had to tie pairs of loose ends together.
When they had made their three knots, the matchmaker would open her hand to see what had happened to the pieces of string.
If there was just one large loop, the matchmaker would give them permission to marry; but if the matchmaker found two or three loops, the couple would not be allowed to marry.

- What is the probability that a couple would pass this test?
- What happens for different numbers of pieces of string?
- What are the alternatives to getting one large loop and what is the probability of getting these alternatives?

CHAPTER SUMMARY

Relative frequency

$$\text{Estimated probability} = \frac{\text{number of times the event occurs}}{\text{number of times experiment took place}}$$

Example: If 40 identical drawing pins are dropped on a table and 26 of them land point up, the probability of a drawing pin landing point up is estimated to be $\frac{26}{40}$ or 0.65 or 65%.

Probabilities of more than one event

Example: A bag contains two red cubes, one blue cube and one yellow cube. One cube is drawn and replaced. Then another cube is drawn.

1st draw \ Second draw	R	R	B	Y
R	RR	RR	RB	RY
R	RR	RR	RB	RY
B	BR	BR	BB	BY
Y	YR	YR	YB	YY

The probability of drawing a red followed by a blue is $\frac{2}{16} = \frac{1}{8}$.

The probability of drawing one red and one yellow is $\frac{4}{16} = \frac{1}{4}$.

This problem can also be solved using a **tree diagram**.

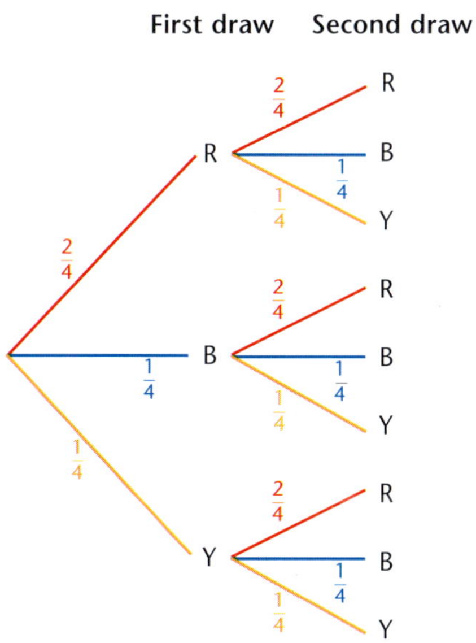

Outcome	Probability
RR	$\frac{2}{4} \times \frac{2}{4} = \frac{4}{16}$
RB	$\frac{2}{4} \times \frac{1}{4} = \frac{2}{16}$
RY	$\frac{2}{4} \times \frac{1}{4} = \frac{2}{16}$
BR	$\frac{1}{4} \times \frac{2}{4} = \frac{2}{16}$
BB	$\frac{1}{4} \times \frac{1}{4} = \frac{1}{16}$
BY	$\frac{1}{4} \times \frac{1}{4} = \frac{1}{16}$
YR	$\frac{1}{4} \times \frac{2}{4} = \frac{2}{16}$
YB	$\frac{1}{4} \times \frac{1}{4} = \frac{1}{16}$
YY	$\frac{1}{4} \times \frac{1}{4} = \frac{1}{16}$

The probability of drawing a red followed by a blue is $\frac{2}{16} = \frac{1}{8}$.

The probability of drawing one red and one yellow is $\frac{2}{16} + \frac{2}{16} = \frac{4}{16} = \frac{1}{4}$.

These probabilities can also be calculated by using the fact that the events are independent (see below).

Independent events

If a red dice and a blue dice are thrown, getting a six on the red dice is **independent** of getting a six on the blue dice.
When events are independent, the probability of *both* of them happening is found by *multiplying* the probabilities.
The probability of a six on both dice is

$\frac{1}{6} \times \frac{1}{6} = \frac{1}{36}$

Mutually exclusive events

If a dice is thrown, getting a six and getting an odd number are **mutually exclusive** events.
When events are mutually exclusive, the probability that either one *or* the other happens is found by *adding* the probabilities.
The probability of a six or an odd number is

$\frac{1}{6} + \frac{1}{2} = \frac{2}{3}$

Conditional probability

Sometimes the outcome of one event affects the outcome of another.
For example, a card is drawn at random from a normal pack, and then a second card is drawn without replacing the first.
The probability that the second card is an ace depends on whether the first card is an ace. This is an example of **conditional probability**.

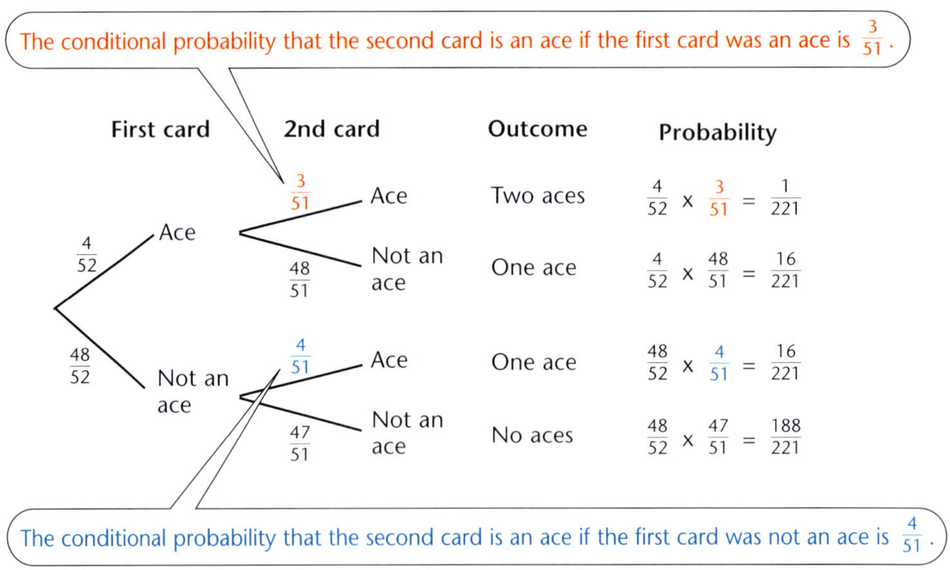

The probability of getting, for example, one ace is

$\frac{16}{221} + \frac{16}{221} = \frac{32}{221}$

CHAPTER 11

GRAPHS

This chapter is about:

- straight line graphs and their equations
- interpreting everyday graphs
- non-linear graphs.

Equations of straight lines

This table and the graph show why the gradient of the straight line through the points (2, 3) and (7, 13) is $10 \div 5 = 2$.

x	2	7
y	3	13

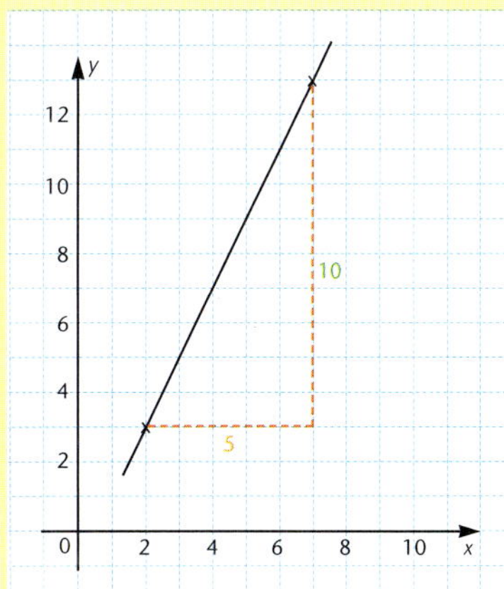

DISCUSSION POINT

Do the three points (2, 3), (5, 9) and (7, 13) lie in a straight line?

How can you use gradient to find out?

Find one more point on the same straight line.

If you choose any pair of points on this line, explain why the gradient between them should be the same.

Find an equation relating x and y for any point (x, y) on the line.

DISCUSSION POINT

Find the gradient of the line joining the points (–2, 14) and (4, 2).

Use gradient to discover whether the points (–2, 14), (1, 8) and (4, 2) lie on a straight line.

Find an equation relating x and y for any point (x, y) on the line.

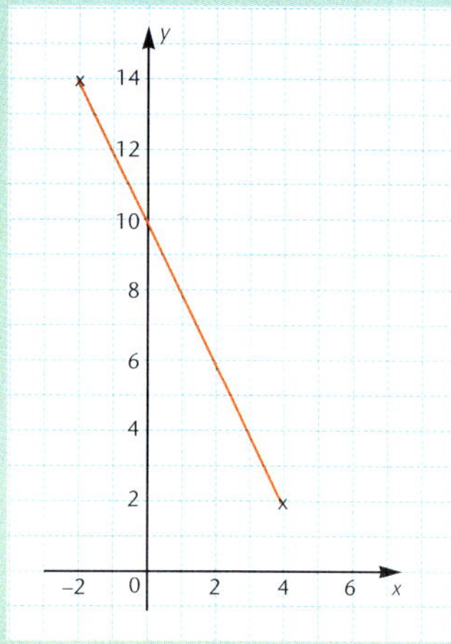

Exercise 1

1 Find the gradient of the straight line between each of these pairs of points.

(**a**) (0, 4) and (2, 10) (**b**) (–3, 2) and (3, 20) (**c**) (2, 2) and (11, 5)

(**d**) (0, 2) and (4, 0) (**e**) (–4, 10) and (1, 0) (**f**) (2, –4) and (4, 4)

(**g**) (3, –1) and (9, 2) (**h**) (2, –1) and (5, –7)

2 For each of these, use gradients to decide whether all three points lie on a straight line.

(**a**) (3, 5), (6, 11), (18, 35) (**b**) (–2, 6), (1, 9), (3, 15)

(**c**) (–5, –2), (5, 2), (12.5, 5)

3 (**a**) Find the gradient of the line

(**i**) joining (–6, –7) to (3, –1) (**ii**) joining (7, 2) to (13, 6)

(**b**) What do you notice about your two answers to part (a)?

(**c**) Why does your answer to part (b) not prove that the points (–6, –7), (3, –1), (7, 2) and (13, 6) all lie on a straight line?
Do these point all lie on a straight line?

4 In each of these, a point and a gradient are given.
Find two more points on the line with this gradient through this point.
Then find an equation for the line.

(**a**) (0, 0); gradient 4 (**b**) (0, 0); gradient –5 (**c**) (0, 3); gradient 2

(**d**) (0, –1); gradient –3 (**e**) (1, 3); gradient 2 (**f**) (2, 5); gradient –4

(**g**) (–2, 5); gradient 2 (**h**) (–1, –2); gradient $\frac{1}{3}$ (**i**) (4, 0); gradient $-\frac{1}{2}$

5 Find an equation for the line through each of these sets of points in the form $y = \ldots$.

A

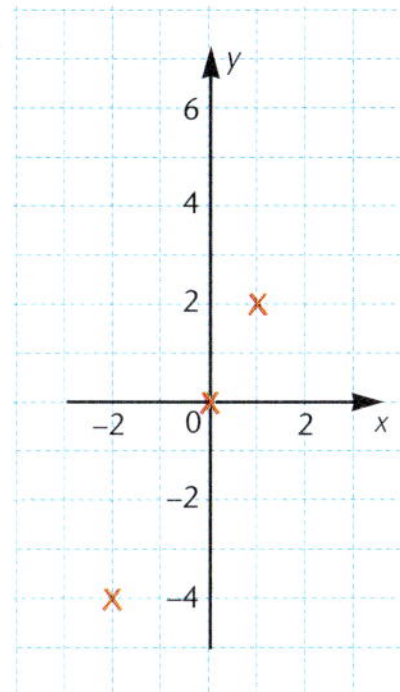

B

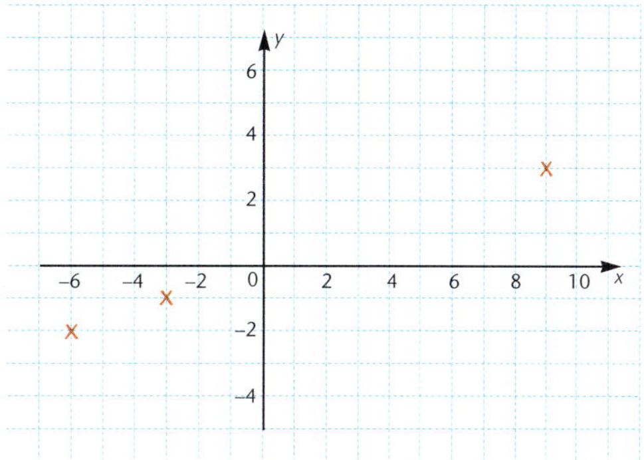

C

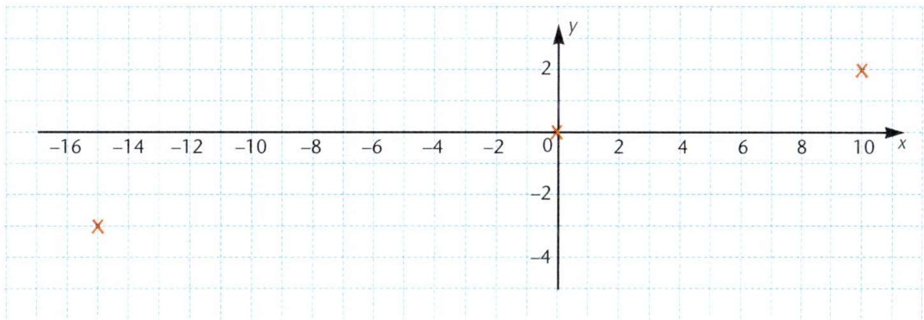

6 Find an equation for the line through each of these sets of points in the form $y = \ldots$.

(a)

x	–5	–1	3
y	2	–2	–6

(b) (–3, –4), (0, –1) and (4, 3)

(c) (–4, 2), (3, –1.5) and (6, –3)

Instead of talking about 'the line with equation $y = 2x - 3$', it is often called 'the line $y = 2x - 3$' for short.

DISCUSSION POINT

Look at your answers to Question 4 in Exercise 1. Where does the gradient feature in the equation?

In $y = 3x + 5$, what is the gradient? What does the '+5' tell you about the line?

Now explore the equation $y = mx + c$ by drawing more lines or using a graphical calculator.

What do m and c tell you about the line?

Resource Sheet P: *Sorting straight lines*

DISCUSSION POINT

Find where each of these lines meets the x-axis and the y-axis.

Then sketch the line.

$2x + y = 4$ $\quad$ $2x - y = 4$ $\quad$ $y - 2x = 6$

$3x + 2y = 12$ $\quad$ $5x - 3y = 15$

Where does the line $2x + 3y = 7$ meet the x-axis and the y-axis?

Find three points with integer coordinates on this line.

Find an equation for this line.

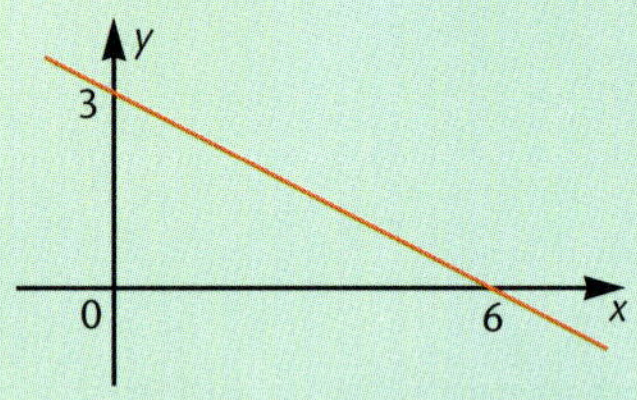

Now play the sorting game: *Sorting straight lines*.

EXERCISE 2

1 Write down the gradient of each of these lines and also the point where the line crosses the y-axis.

(a) $y = 2x + 5$ $\quad$ **(b)** $y = 3x - 6$ $\quad$ **(c)** $y = -x + 7$

(d) $y = -5x - 2$ $\quad$ **(e)** $y = \frac{1}{2}x + 5$ $\quad$ **(f)** $y = \frac{4 - x}{3}$

2 Sketch these lines on the same set of axes.

$x + y = 10$ $\quad$ $x + y = 5$ $\quad$ $x + y = 0$

$x + y = -10$ $\quad$ $x + y = -5$

3 For each of these lines, find an equation of the form $ax + by = c$.

A

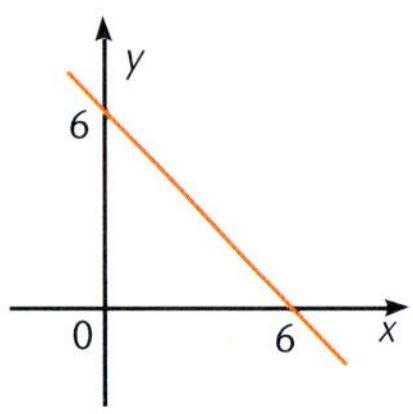

B

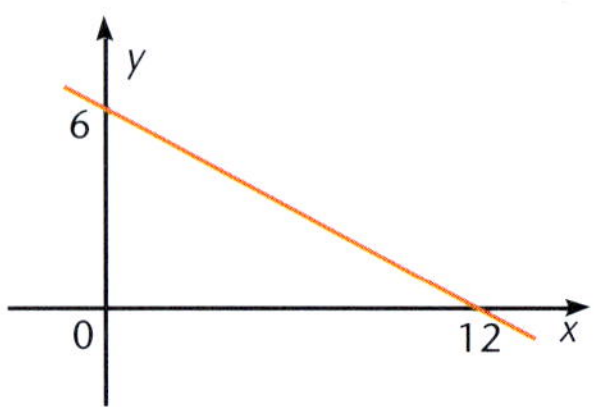

C

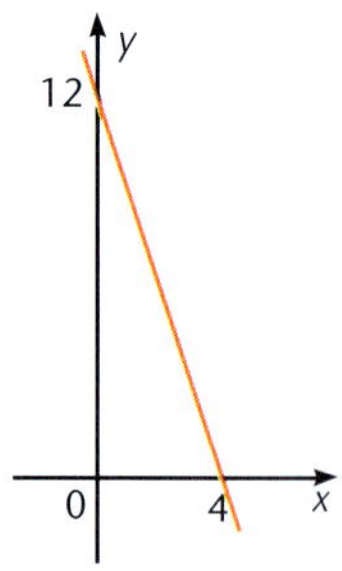

4 For each of these lines, find an equation of the form $ax + by = c$.

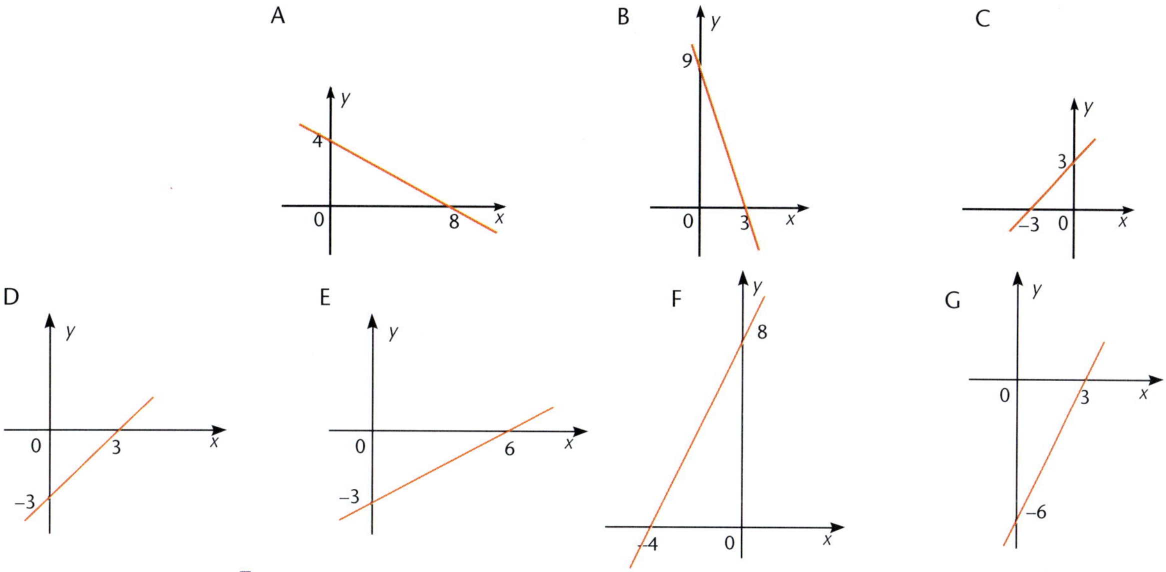

5 Sketch the graph of each of these lines and find its gradient.

(a) $x + y = 6$ **(b)** $2x + y = 6$ **(c)** $3x - 2y = 18$

(d) $4x - 5y = -20$ **(e)** $3x + 2y = 11$ **(f)** $3x - 2y = 11$

6 Find the gradient of each of these lines.

(a) $3x + y = 12$ **(b)** $\frac{1}{2}x + y = 6$ **(c)** $y - 3x = 7$

(d) $5x + 3y = 20$ **(e)** $2x - y = 5$ **(f)** $x - 3y = 6$

7 **(a)** Which pairs of these four lines are parallel?

A: $x - 4y = 8$ B: $x - 4y = 12$

C: $4x + y = 8$ D: $4x + y = 12$

(b) Which pairs are perpendicular?

8 The equations of two of the sides of a parallelogram are $5y + 3x = 13$ and $2y - 7x = 11$. One of the vertices of the parallelogram is at (3, 4). Find the equations of the other two sides of the parallelogram.

9 The equation of one side of a square is $3x + 4y = 12$. One of the vertices of the square is at (6, 11). Find the equations of the other three sides of the square.

DISCUSSION POINT

If you are given the equations of two lines, how can you tell whether the lines are perpendicular?

Practical uses of straight-line graphs

▶ Graph paper

For part (a) of Question 1, make sure you choose a scale for your graph so that you can answer the remainder of the question.

EXERCISE 3

The freezing point of water is 0° on the Celsius scale and 32° on the Fahrenheit scale. Its boiling point is 100°C and 212°F.

1 **(a)** Draw a conversion graph for converting from degrees Celsius to degrees Fahrenheit.

(b) At –40°C, it is very cold. What is this temperature on the Fahrenheit scale?

(c) 35°C is a lot warmer. What is this temperature in degrees Fahrenheit?

(d) Where does your conversion graph cross the Fahrenheit axis? What does this tell you?

(e) Find the gradient of your graph. What does your gradient tell you about a temperature rise of 1°F compared with a temperature rise of 1°C?

(f) What is the formula for your graph?

2 This table shows the length of a spring when different masses were hung from it.

Mass in g	20	40	60	80	100	120
Length in mm	72	89	104	119	136	152

(a) How can you tell, *before* plotting the graph, that this data will be roughly in a straight line when plotted on a graph?

(b) Plot the points on the graph and draw a line of best fit.

(c) What is the length of the spring with *no* mass hung on it?

(d) How much does the length of the spring change per gram?

(e) What is the equation of the line of best fit you have drawn?

3 When a weighing machine was checked for accuracy with some standard masses, these results were obtained.

Standard mass (g)	10	20	30	40	50
Mass shown (g)	8	19.6	31.1	42.6	54.2

(a) Plot this data on a graph with 'standard mass' on the horizontal axis.

(b) Estimate where the machine was inaccurate by less than 0.2g.

(c) What standard mass would be on the machine when it registers 0?

(d) Draw a line of best fit and find an equation for your line.

(e) What does the gradient of the line of best fit tell you about the weighing machine?

4 (a) Draw a graph of distance against time for travelling at a steady speed of 50 m.p.h. for three hours.

(b) Use your graph to find the distance travelled in 1 hour 45 minutes.

(c) Use your graph to find how long it takes to travel 80 miles.

(d) What is the gradient of the graph and what does it represent?

5 An object is thrown up at 50 metres per second.
Its speed then reduces by 10m/s every second because of the pull of gravity.

(a) Draw a graph of speed against time for the first five seconds.

(b) Find a formula for the speed, vm/s, after t seconds.

(c) Interpret the answer for speed when a time of six seconds is substituted into the formula.

6 An object is dropped down a deep well.
Its speed increases by 10m/s every second.

(a) How fast is the object travelling after six seconds?

(b) The distance in metres travelled by the object after t seconds is given by the formula $d = 5t^2$.
Draw a graph of d against t^2 (*not* against t).
What is the shape of this graph?

7 If a vehicle starts from rest with constant acceleration (a metres per second per second), the distance (d metres) it has travelled after time t seconds is given by this formula.

$d = \frac{1}{2}at^2$

This table shows the progress of a vehicle starting from rest.

t (seconds)	0	5	10	15	20	25
d (metres)	0	11	47	108	190	303

(a) Plot these values on a graph of d against t^2.

(b) Draw a line of best fit.

(c) Use your line of best fit to estimate the approximate acceleration of the vehicle during the first 25 seconds.

A **simple pendulum** is a string suspended from a point with a weight fixed to the bottom of the string.
The **period** of a simple pendulum is the time taken for a complete swing, forwards and back.

8 An experiment was carried out to find how the period, T, of a simple pendulum depended on the length, L, of the string.
Here are the results.

Length of string (L metres)	0.2	0.4	0.6	0.8	1.0
Period (T secs)	0.8	1.2	1.5	1.7	1.9

Theory suggests that T is proportional to $\sqrt{L}$.

(a) Plot of a graph of T against $\sqrt{L}$ for the results in the table above.

(b) Draw a line of best fit to go through the origin.
Why should it go through the origin?

(c) Do you think the results support the theory that T is proportional to $\sqrt{L}$?

(d) Use your line of best fit to obtain an approximate formula for T in terms of L.

9 Here are some results concerning the periods, T, of various planets and their mean distances, D, from the Sun.

Planet	Mercury	Venus	Earth	Mars	Jupiter
Period (T days)	87.7	224	365	687	4330
Mean distance (Dkm)	58	108	150	228	780

Theory suggests that T^2 is proportional to D^3.

(a) Plot of a graph of T against $D^{3/2}$ for the results in the table above.
Leave out the data for Jupiter.

(b) Draw a line of best fit.
Should it go through the origin?

(c) Do you think the results support the theory that T^2 is proportional to D^3?

(d) Use your line of best fit to obtain an approximate formula connecting T and D.
Check that the data for Jupiter fits your formula approximately.

Non-linear graphs

DISCUSSION POINT

The black graph is a graph of $y = x^2$.

The translation $\begin{pmatrix} 0 \\ 3 \end{pmatrix}$ maps the black graph on to the blue graph.

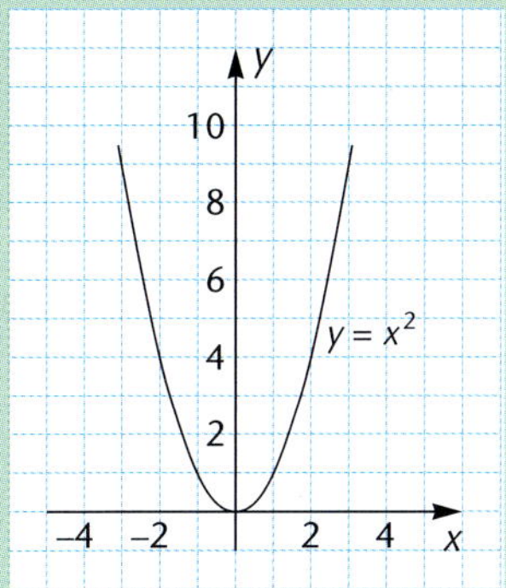

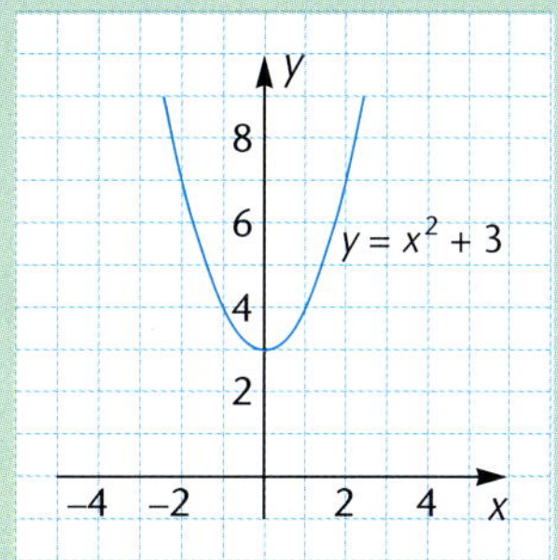

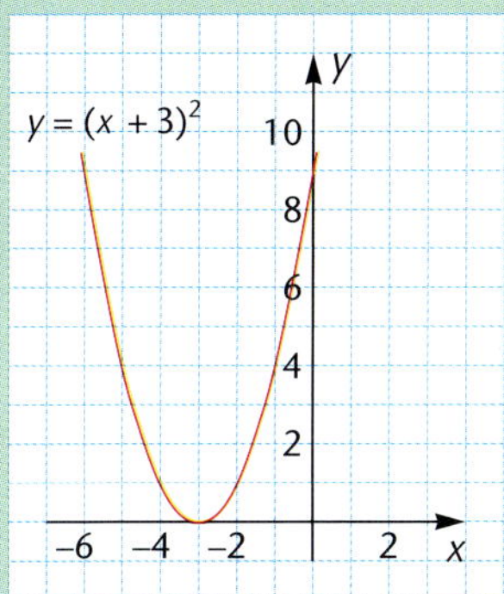

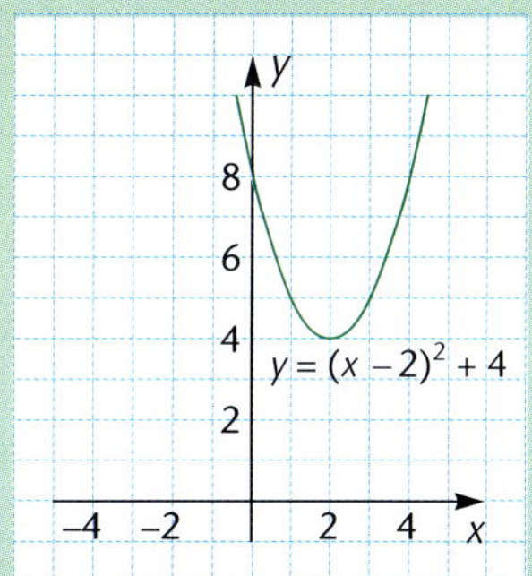

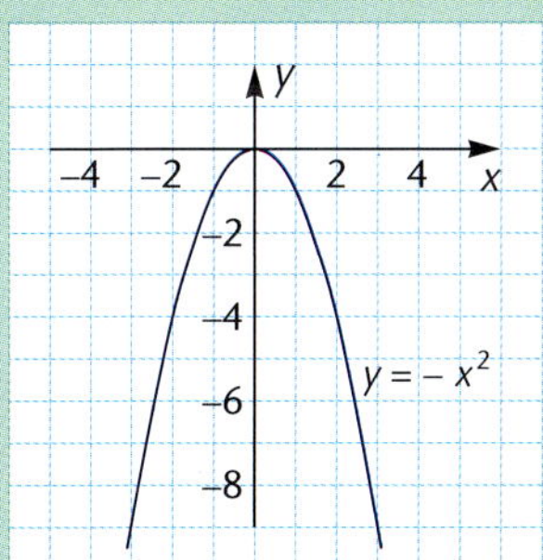

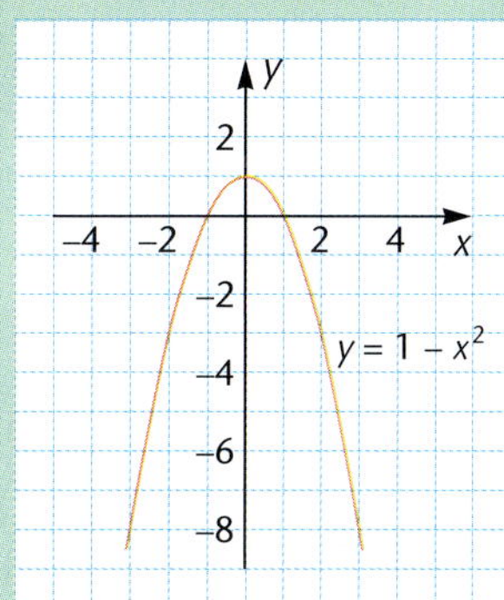

What transformation maps the black graph on to

- the red graph?
- the green graph?
- the purple graph?
- the orange graph?

EXERCISE 4

1 (a) Draw the graphs of $y = 3x^2$ and $y = 3x^2 + 4$ on the same axes, using x values from –3 to 3.

(b) What translation maps the first graph to the second?

(c) On each graph, find the values of x when $y = 15$.

(d) On the $y = 3x^2$ graph, for what values of x is y less than 10?

2 (a) Draw the graphs of $y = x^2$ and $y = 2x^2$ on the same axes, using values of x between –3 and 3.

(b) On the graph $y = 2x^2$, find x when $y = 15$. What is the value of y for these same values of x on the graph $y = x^2$?

(c) For each graph, state the values of x for which y is greater than 8.

3 *Sketch* the graphs $y = 2x^2$ and $y = 2x^2 - 4$ on the same axes.
What transformation maps $y = 2x^2$ on to $y = 2x^2 - 4$?

4 (a) Draw the graphs of $y = x^2$, $y = x^2 + 2$ and $y = (x + 2)^2$ on the *same* axes using x values from –3 to 3.

(b) What transformation maps the graph of $y = x^2$ on to the graph of $y = x^2 + 2$?
What transformation maps $y = x^2$ on to $y = (x + 2)^2$?

5 (a) Using values of x between –3 and 3, draw the graph of $y = 4 - x^2$.

(b) On the graph, find x when $y = -1$.

(c) On the graph, what x values make y positive?

(d) On the graph, what x values make y lie between –2 and 3?

(e) What transformation maps the graph $y = 4 - x^2$ on to the graph of $y = x^2 - 4$?

(f) What transformation maps the graph $y = 4 - x^2$ on to the graph of $y = x^2$?

Making a generalisation

6 (a) How is the graph of $y = x^2 + c$ related to the graph of $y = x^2$?

(b) How is the graph of $y = (x + c)^2$ related to the graph of $y = x^2$?

(c) How is the graph of $y = c - x^2$ related to the graph of $y = x^2 - c$?

(d) How is the graph of $y = c - x^2$ related to the graph of $y = x^2$?

For Question 6, you might want to draw or sketch some graphs, or use a graphical calculator or a graph drawing program.

7 Give a set of possible equations to produce the graphs in each of these sketches.

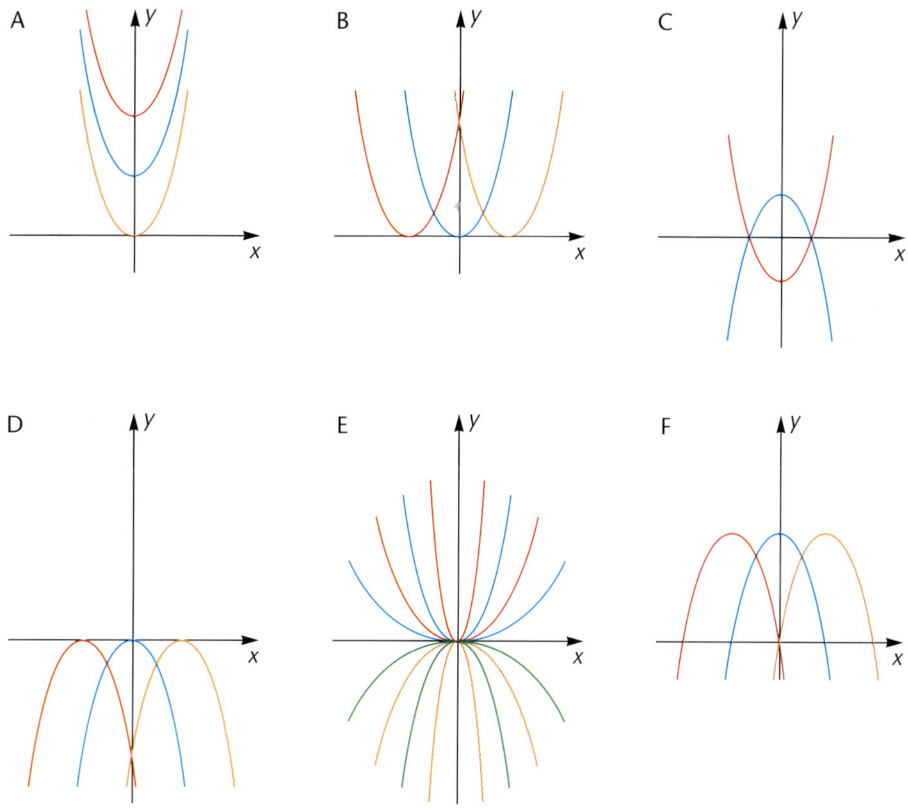

8 Find equations that fit these sketches.

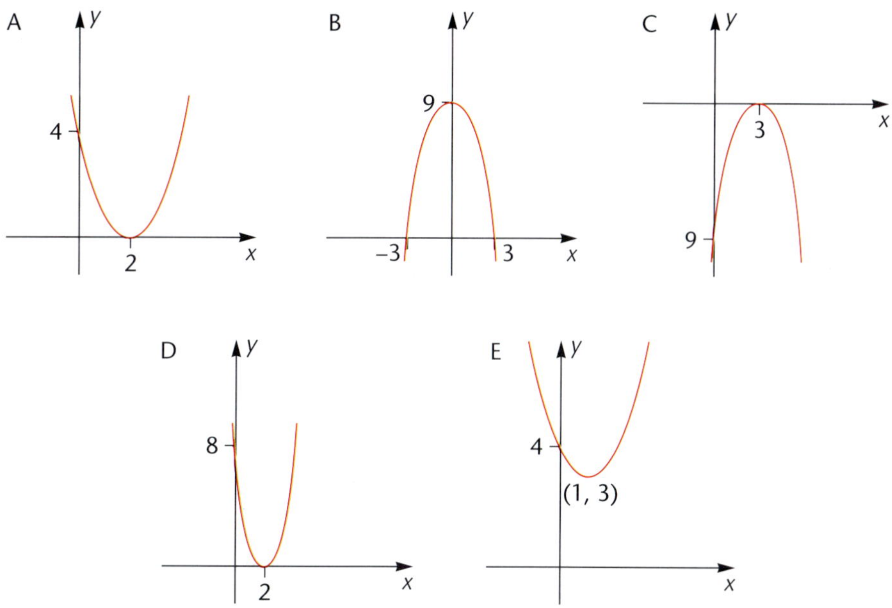

9 (a) Draw the graph of $y = x^2 + 3x$ for $-5 \le x \le 3$.
(b) For what values of x is y greater than 0 on the graph?
(c) For what values of x is y less than 6 on the graph?

10 (a) Draw the graph of $y = x^2 + 2x - 4$ for $-4 \le x \le 3$.
(b) For what values of x is $0 \le y \le 4$?

11 What kind of symmetry do all the graphs in Questions 1 to 10 have?

12 Consider the graphs of $y = x^2$ and $y = 2x^2$.

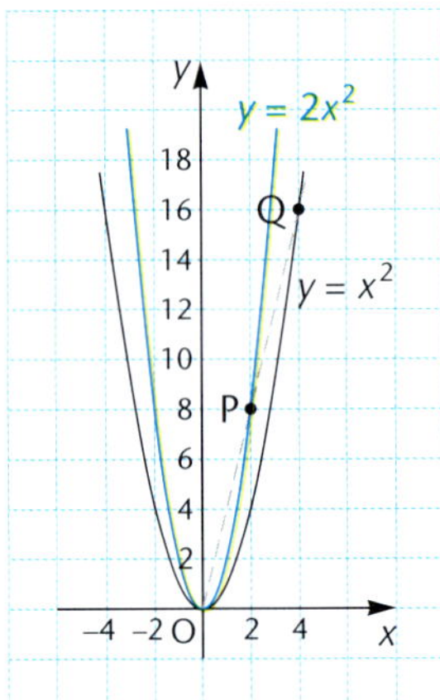

(a) (i) Check that the point P(2, 8) lies on the graph $y = 2x^2$.
(ii) The line through the origin O and P meets the graph of $y = x^2$ again at Q. What are the coordinates of Q?
(iii) What is the ratio of the distances OP and OQ?
(b) (i) Check that the point R(3, 18) lies on the graph $y = 2x^2$.
(ii) The line OR meets the graph of $y = x^2$ again at S. What are the coordinates of S?
(iii) What is the ratio of the distances OR and OS?
(c) (i) The point T has x-coordinate k. T lies on the graph $y = 2x^2$. OT meets the graph $y = x^2$ again at U. What are the coordinates of T and U?
(ii) What is the ratio of the distances OT and OU?
(d) What transformation maps the graph $y = 2x^2$ on to the graph $y = x^2$?

13 What transformation maps the graph $y = ax^2$ on to the graph $y = x^2$?

14 What transformation maps the graph $y = 2x^2$ on to the graph $y = \frac{1}{3}x^2$?

All the curves in Exercise 4 had equations involving x^2.
These 'U shaped' curves are called **parabolas**.
Parabolas occur in a variety of everyday situations.
For example, the path of a stone thrown is a parabola.

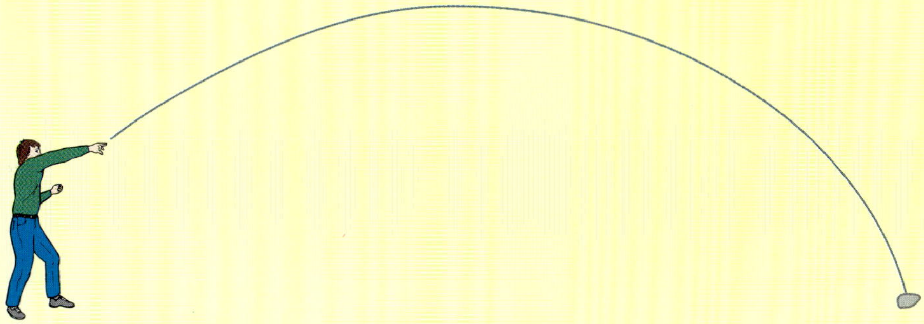

Also, the shape of the reflector in car headlamps is obtained by rotating a parabola about its line of symmetry. The reflector is made in this shape because this shape happens to produce a parallel beam of light.

S is light source

All parabolas are **similar**, as suggested by Question 12 in Exercise 4. Other types of equation produce curves with different shapes as Exercise 5 shows.

DISCUSSION POINT

Consider the formula $y = \frac{4}{x}$.

- What happens if you try to substitute $x = 0$?
- What can you say about the value of y if x is close to 0 and positive?
- What can you say about the value of y if x is close to 0 and negative?
- What can you say about the value of y if x is very large and positive?
- What can you say about the value of y when x is very large and negative (e.g. $x = -100$)?

What does this tell you about the shape of the graph of $y = \frac{4}{x}$?

Describe the symmetry of the graph.

You might find a graphical calculator or graph drawing program useful with some of this exercise. When drawing graphs in this exercise you can plot non-integer values of x as well as integers to obtain a good curve.

For Question 3, use x values from -6 to 6.

Exercise 5

The graph $y = \frac{6}{x}$ is an example of a **rectangular hyperbola**.

1 (a) Draw the graph of $y = \frac{6}{x}$ for $-6 \leq x \leq 6$.

(b) Find x on the graph when

(i) $y = 3.2$ (ii) $y = -2.5$

(c) For what values of x on the graph is

(i) y positive but greater than 2? (ii) y negative but less than -3?

(iii) $-4 \leq y \leq 4$?

2 If a is a number, what happens to the graph $y = \frac{a}{x}$ when a changes? What happens when a is negative?

3 (a) Draw the graphs of $y = \frac{12}{x}$ and $y = \frac{12}{x} + 4$ on the *same* axes.

(b) What transformation maps the first graph on to the second?

(c) What transformation maps the graph $y = \frac{a}{x}$ on to the graph $y = \frac{a}{x} + c$?

4 (a) Draw these three graphs on the same axes using x values between -4 and 4.

$y = \frac{4}{x}$ $y = \frac{4}{x + 2}$ $y = \frac{4}{x - 2}$

(b) How are these graphs related?

(c) Describe the graph $y = \frac{a}{x + b}$. What happens when a and/or b is negative?

5 Suggest equations for these graphs.

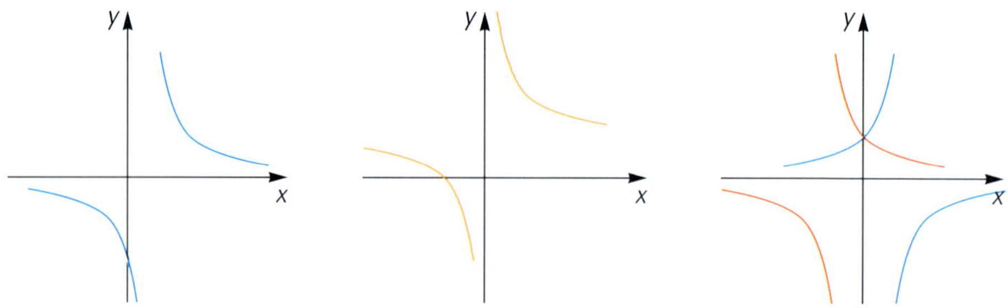

6 What kind of symmetry do all the graphs in Questions 1 to 5 have?

7 (a) Draw accurately a graph of $y = x^3$ for $-2 \leq x \leq 2$.

(b) Where would the graph of $y = x^3 + 2$ be in relation to that of $y = x^3$?

(c) Where would the graph of $y = (x + 3)^3$ be in relation to $y = x^3$?

8 (a) Using x values between -3 and 3, draw the graph of $y = x^3 + x$. Where does this graph cross each axis?

(b) Draw the graph of $y = x^3 - x$. Where does this graph cross each axis?

(c) What are the similarities and differences in the graphs of $y = x^3$, $y = x^3 + x$ and $y = x^3 - x$?

9 (a) Using x values between –4 and 2, draw the graph of $y = x^3 + 3x^2$.

(b) Factorise $x^3 + 3x^2$.

Use this factorisation to explain the shape of the graph.

10 What kind of symmetry do all the graphs in Questions 6 to 9 have?

11 What kinds of equations would produce graphs like these?

A

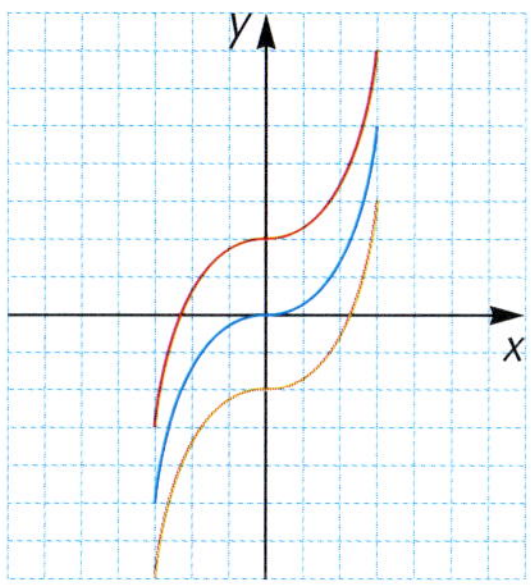

B

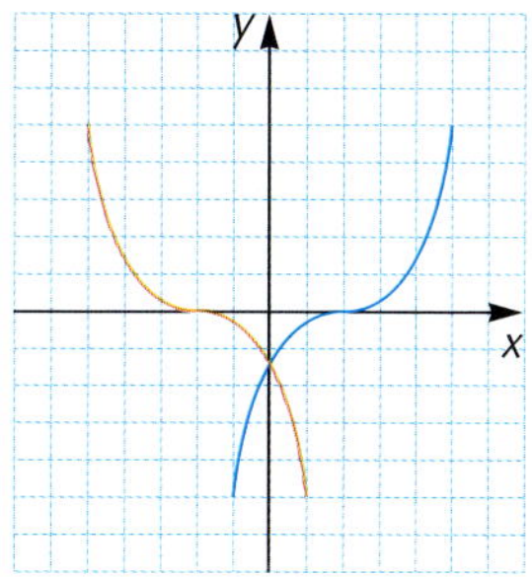

12 Match each equation with the right type of graph.

$y = x^2 - 4$ $\quad$ $y = 2x - 4$ $\quad$ $y = 4 - x$

$y = \frac{4}{x}$ $\quad$ $y = 4 - x^2$ $\quad$ $y = x^3 - 4$

A

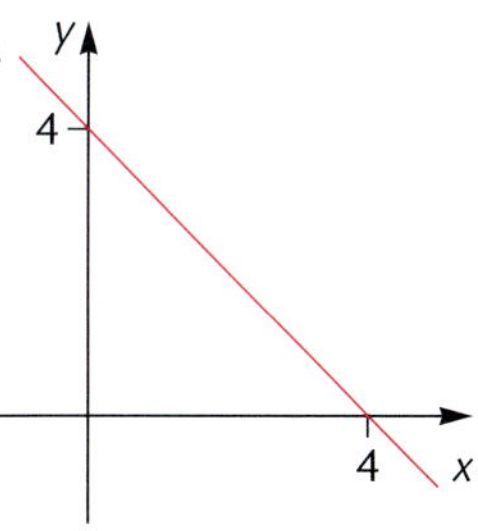

B

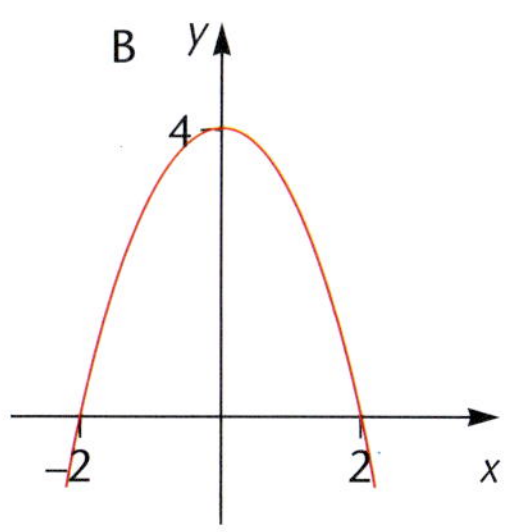

C

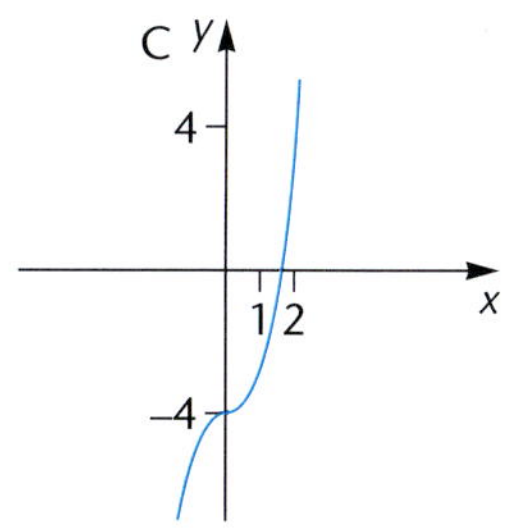

D

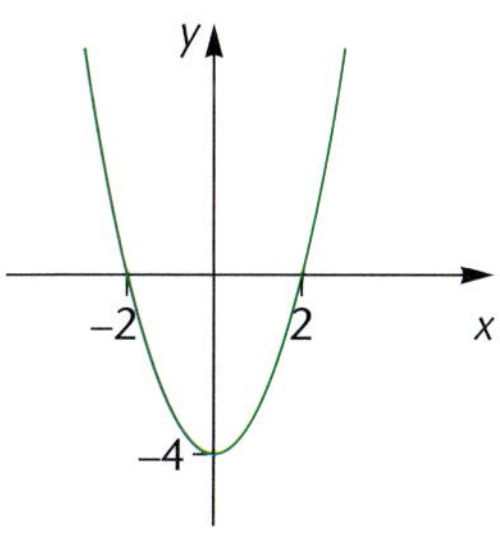

E

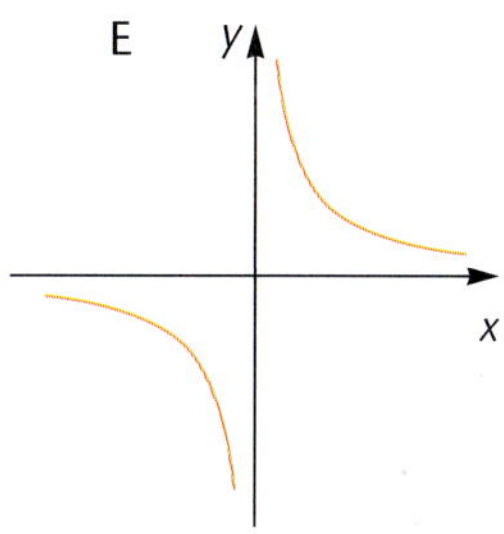

F

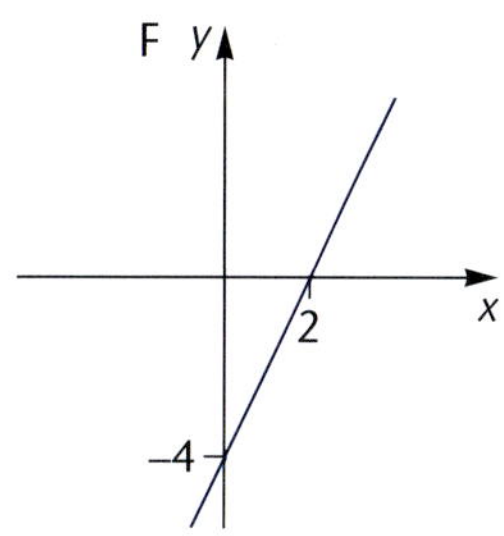

Making a generalisation

13 Sketch graphs of $y = x^n$ for different positive integer values of n.
Describe how the shape of the graph changes as n changes.
Describe the symmetry of the graphs.

▶ Resource Sheet Q: *Sorting non-linear graphs*

DISCUSSION POINT

Play the second sorting game: *Sorting non-linear graphs*.

Interpreting graphs of real-life situations

DISCUSSION POINT

This vase has different girths, or distances around it, at different heights.

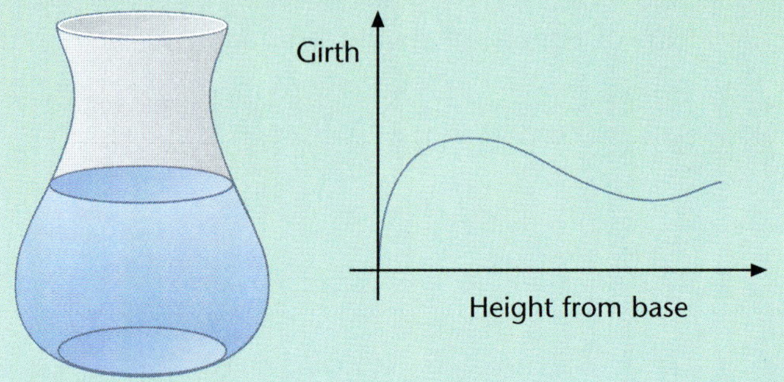

Explain the relationship between the shape of the vase and the shape of the graph.

What would a graph of cross-sectional area plotted against height from base look like?

Suppose you were filling the vase with water flowing at a steady rate of, say, 150ml per sec.
What would the graph of depth of water against time look like?

EXERCISE 6

1 For each of these containers, draw sketch graphs of girth plotted against height from base.

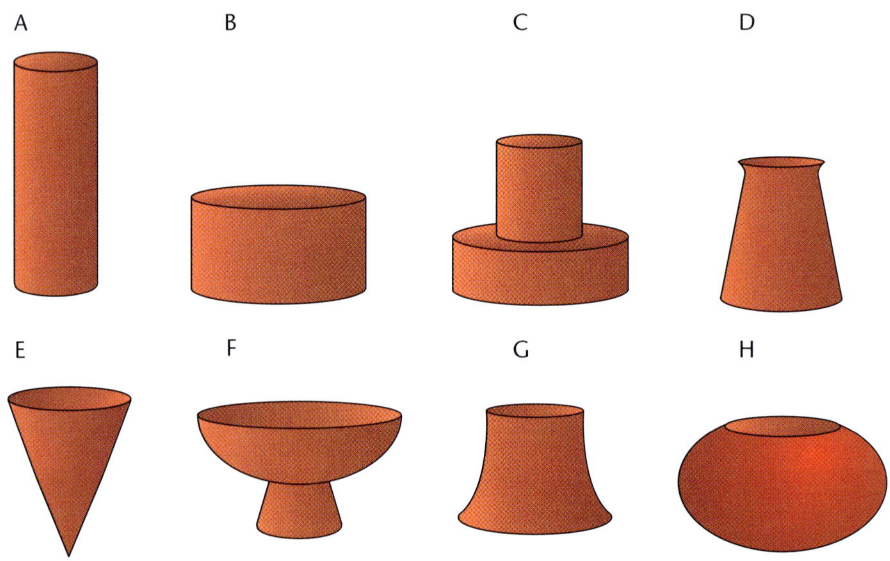

2 These sketch graphs show girth plotted against height from base for different containers. Sketch each container.

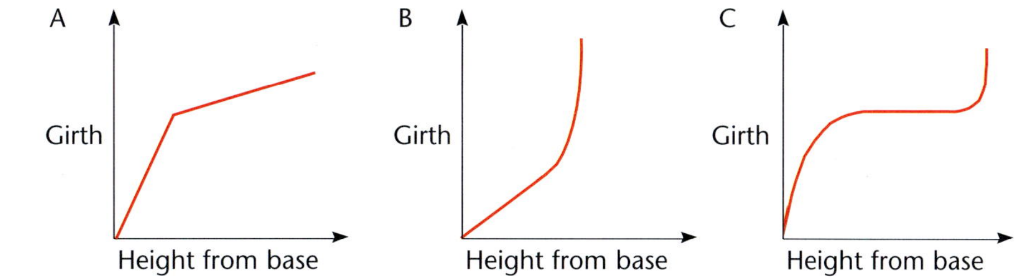

3 Draw a sketch graph to show cross-sectional area plotted against height for each container in Question 1.

4 Each of the containers in Question 1 is filled with water flowing in at a constant rate. For each container, draw a sketch graph of the depth of water against time.

5 These are graphs for containers being filled with water at a steady rate.

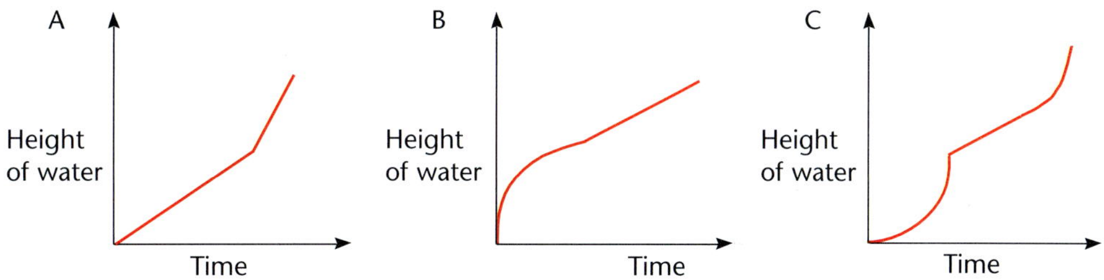

Sketch a possible container for each.

6 These are plans of race tracks.

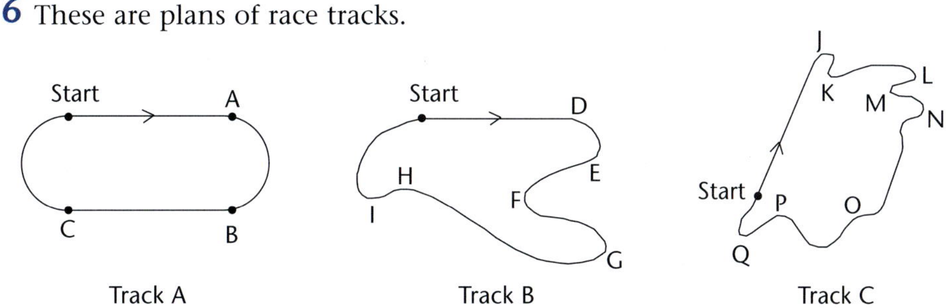

Sketch a graph of speed against time for each track. Indicate on your graph the places related to the points marked.

7 These are sketch graphs of speed against time for two race tracks.

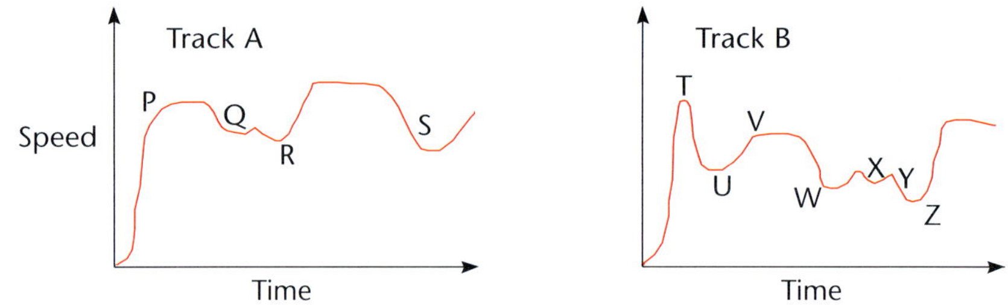

Draw a possible track for each, labelling the points marked.

COURSEWORK OPPORTUNITY

Cubic and quartic graphs

Cubic graphs are graphs of equations of the form $y = ax^3 + bx^2 + cx + d$, where a, b, c and d are numbers. Such equations can sometimes be conveniently written as $y = a(x - e)(x - f)(x - g)$, where e, f and g are numbers.
Quartic graphs are graphs of equations of the form $y = ax^4 + bx^3 + cx^2 + dx + e$.
Investigate the shapes of different cubic and quartic graphs. You might want to look at symmetry and at where the graphs cross the axes.

CHAPTER SUMMARY

Equations of graphs of straight lines

$y = mx + c$ is one form for the equation of a straight line.
The value of m is the **gradient** of the graph.
The value of c tells you where the graph crosses the y-axis.

$y = 2x + 4$

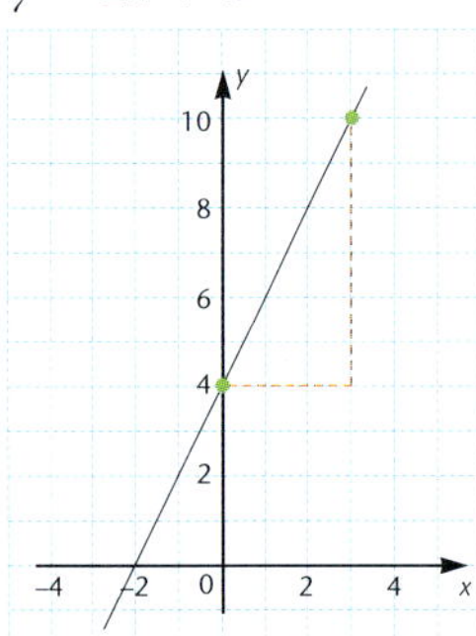

$$\text{Gradient} = \frac{\text{distance up}}{\text{distance across}} = \frac{6}{3} = 2$$

$y = -3x + 5$

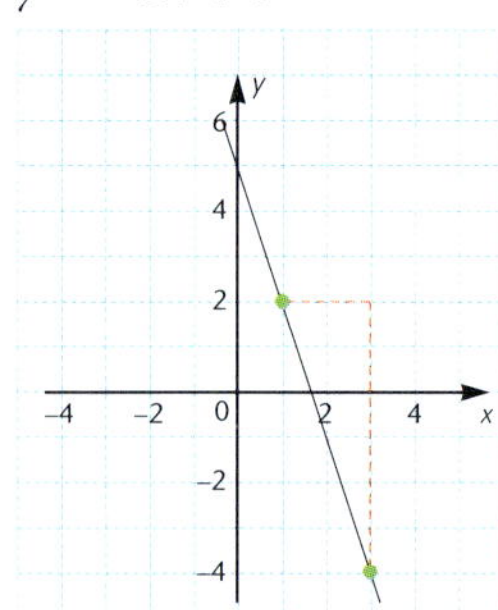

$$\text{Gradient} = \frac{\text{distance up}}{\text{distance across}} = \frac{-6}{2} = -3$$

Another common form for the equation of a straight line is $ax + by = c$. This is most easily sketched by finding where the line crosses each axis.

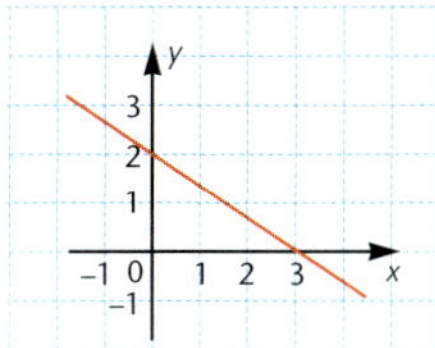

$2x + 3y = 6$ crosses the x-axis ($y = 0$) at the point (3, 0) and the y-axis ($x = 0$) at the point (0, 2)

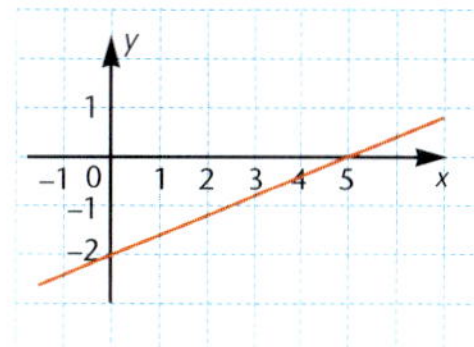

$2x - 5y = 10$ crosses the axes at (5, 0) and (0, −2)

Graphs involving x^2

All these graphs are the same shape. This shape is called a **parabola**. It has one line of symmetry (parallel to the y-axis).

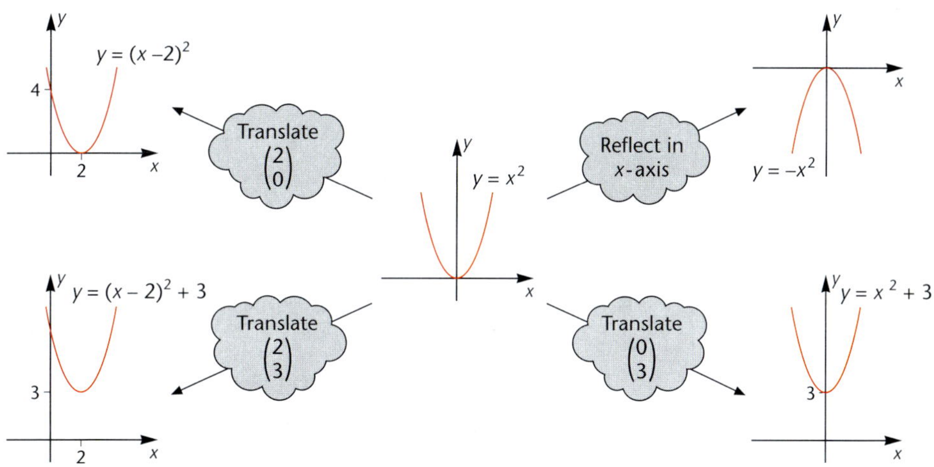

Graphs involving x^3

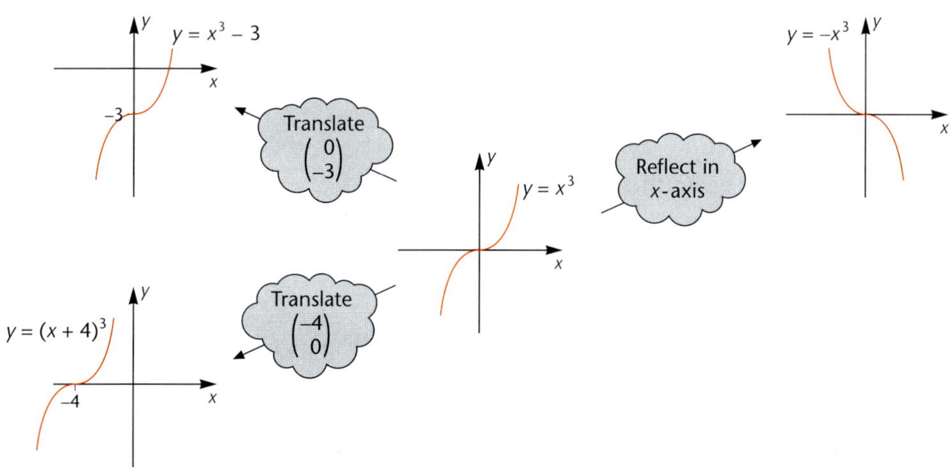

Graphs of equations involving x^2 or x as well as x^3 can have a range of different shapes:

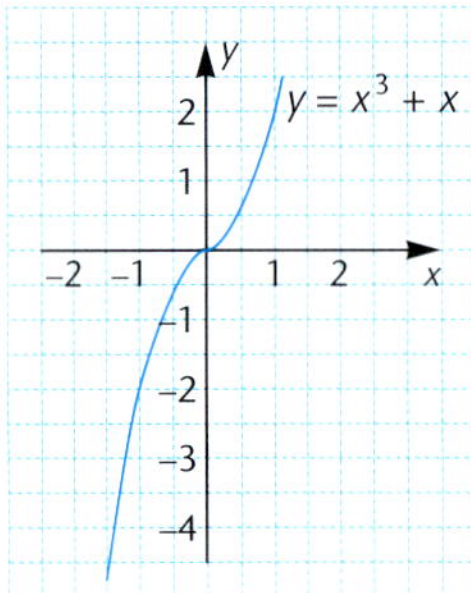

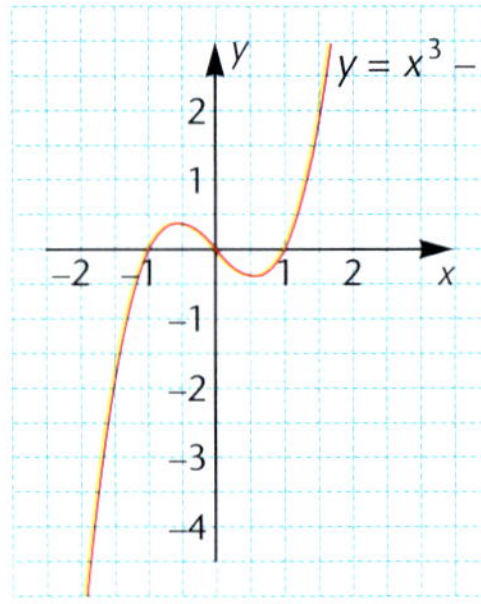

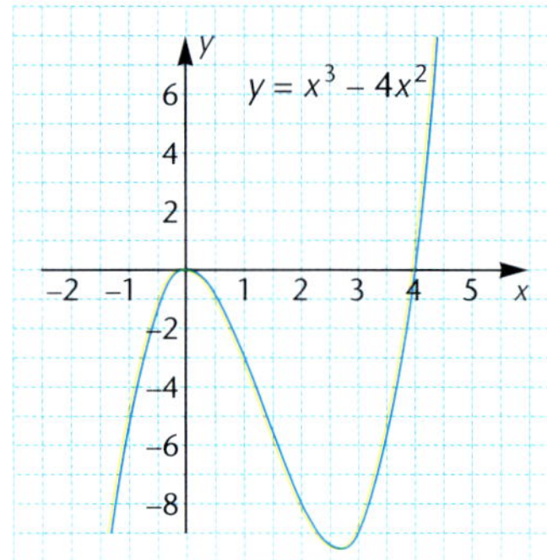

All of these graphs have half-turn rotational symmetry.

Graphs involving $\frac{1}{x}$

These graphs all have the same shape, which is called a **rectangular hyperbola**. This has two lines of symmetry (parallel to $y = \pm x$) and rotational symmetry of order 2.

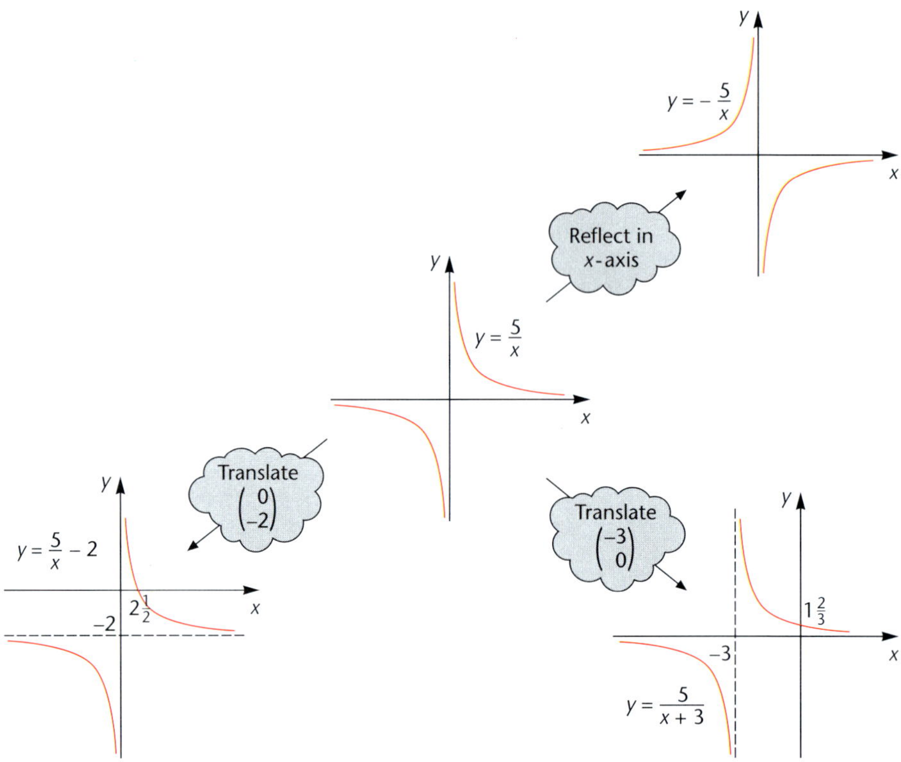

CHAPTER

12 MEASURES

This chapter is about:

- metric and Imperial units of measure
- the relationships between different units of measure
- using upper and lower bounds of measures
- areas of sectors and segments of a circle
- volume and surface area of prisms, including cylinders
- volume and surface area of pyramids, cones and spheres
- relationships between similar solids
- distinguishing formulae.

Metric and Imperial measures

The most common units used in Great Britain today are the **metric units**. These are the ones commonly used.

Length
1 km = 1000 m
1 m = 100 cm = 1000 mm
1 cm = 10 mm

Capacity
1 litre = 1000 ml
1 m^3 = 1000 litres
1 cm^3 = 1 ml

Mass or weight
1 tonne = 1000 kg
1 kg = 1000 g
1 g = 1000 mg

Area
1 hectare = 10000 m^2

However, you might need to use some of the older **Imperial units** which still occur in practice.

Length
1 mile = 1760 yards
1 yard = 3 feet
1 foot = 12 inches

Capacity
1 gallon = 8 pints

Mass or weight
1 ton = 20 hundredweight (cwt)
1 cwt = 8 stone
1 stone = 14 pounds (lb)
1 pound = 16 ounces (oz)

Area
1 acre = 4840 square yards

These are approximate equivalents between the two types of units: metric and Imperial.

Length
5 miles is about 8km
1 foot is about 30cm
1 yard is just a bit less than 1 metre
1 inch is about $2\frac{1}{2}$ cm

Capacity
1 gallon is about 4.5 litres
$1\frac{3}{4}$ pints is about 1 litre

Mass or weight
1 ton is about 1 tonne
2.2lb is about 1kg
1oz is about 30g

Area
$2\frac{1}{2}$ acres is about 1 hectare

The questions in Exercise 1 are taken from an actual homework exercise set for 11-year-old students in 1969.

EXERCISE 1

1 5 yards 2ft 7in + 2 yards 1ft 9in

2 8lb 12oz + 5lb 10oz

3 3 tons 14cwt + 9cwt

4 2 gallons 6 pints + 3 gallons + 3 gallons 5 pints

5 2 yards 10in + 2ft 6in + 6 yards 2ft 8in

6 1 yard – 2ft 7in

7 3 yards 1ft 2in – 1 yard 2ft 3in

8 3 gallons 2 pints – 1 gallon 6 pints

9 2 stones 10lb 4oz – 12lb 8oz

10 1 stone – 7lb 11oz

DISCUSSION POINT

Exercise 1 would have been easy for some 11-year-old pupils in 1969.
How did you find it?
How do calculations with metric units compare to these calculations?
When were metric measures introduced in the UK?
How often do *you* still use Imperial measures?

EXERCISE 2

1 Here are three recipes from an old cookery book which uses Imperial units. Re-write the recipes using metric units.

French onion soup

$\frac{3}{4}$ lb onions
$1\frac{1}{2}$ oz butter
$1\frac{1}{2}$ pints beef stock
Salt and pepper to taste
2 teaspoons dry sherry
4 slices French bread, each 1 inch thick
2oz grated Cheddar cheese

Parkin

6oz plain flour
$\frac{1}{2}$ level teaspoon salt
1 level teaspoon each of mixed spice, cinnamon, ground ginger and bicarbonate of soda
10oz medium oatmeal
6oz black treacle
5oz butter
4oz soft brown sugar
$\frac{1}{4}$ pint milk
1 standard egg, beaten

Beef stroganoff

$1\frac{1}{4}$ to $1\frac{1}{2}$ lb rump steak
1 small onion, grated
3oz butter
$\frac{1}{2}$ lb sliced button mushrooms
Salt and pepper
3 tablespoons white wine
$\frac{1}{4}$ pint fresh double cream

2 While working in an old house, a plumber needs to replace pipes with 1 inch and $\frac{1}{2}$ inch diameters.

Now it is only possible to buy new pipes in the metric sizes of 10mm, 15mm, 20mm or 25mm. Which pipes should the plumber buy?

1 metre is about 1.094 yards.

3 A shop sells material at £10.50 per metre. It claims this is the same as paying £9.50 per yard. Is this a fair claim?

4 One driver describes his speed as 45 m.p.h., while another describes his speed as 70 k.p.h. Which driver is travelling faster?

5 The petrol tank on an old car is said to hold $8\frac{1}{2}$ gallons. If petrol is sold at 65p per litre, how much would it cost to fill the petrol tank?

One litre of water weighs 1 kg.

6 How much does 1 gallon of water weigh, in pounds?

7 You may see these road signs while travelling in France.
Change the speeds, given in kilometres per hour, to miles per hour.

A B C

8 Milk is usually bought in pints from the milkman who delivers to the door, and sometimes in litres from the supermarket.
Which is the best buy: 1 pint of milk at 36p, or 2 litres of milk at £1.12?

Areas of plane shapes, including sectors and segments of circles

You may need to use Pythagoras' theorem for some questions in this exercise.

EXERCISE 3

1 Find the areas of each of these shapes.

A

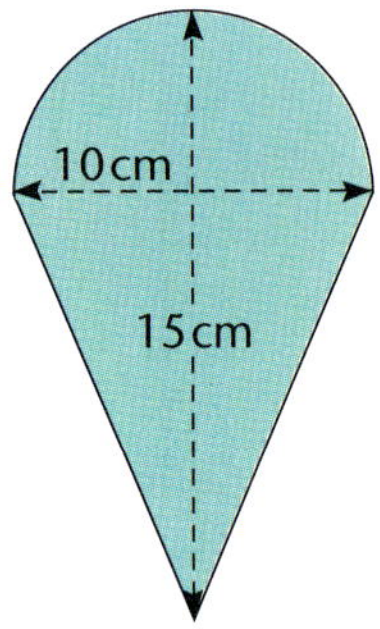

Isosceles triangle with semicircle

B

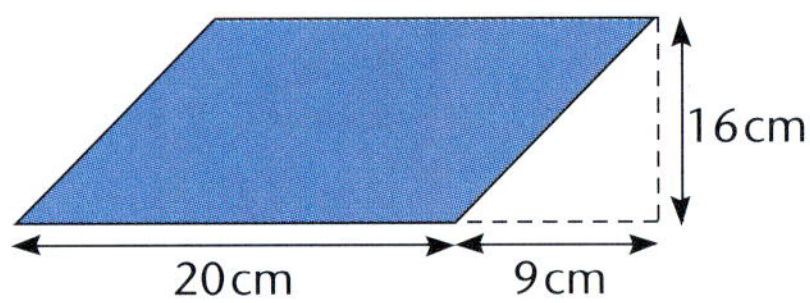

Parallelogram

C

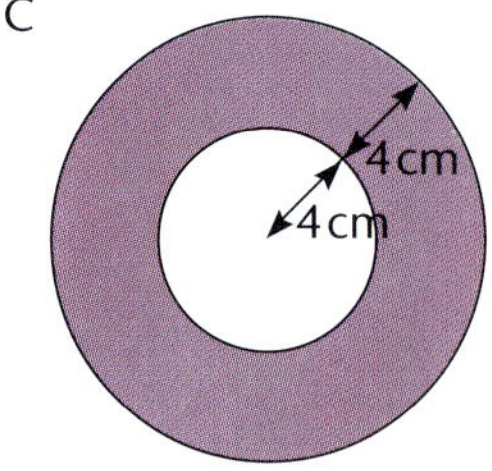

Concentric circles

D

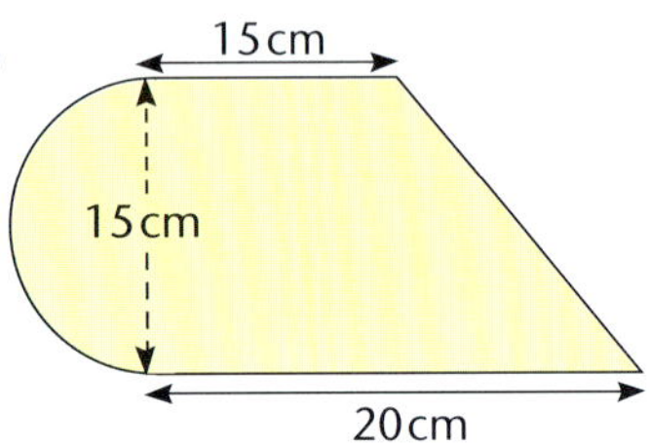

Semicircle and right-angled trapezium

E

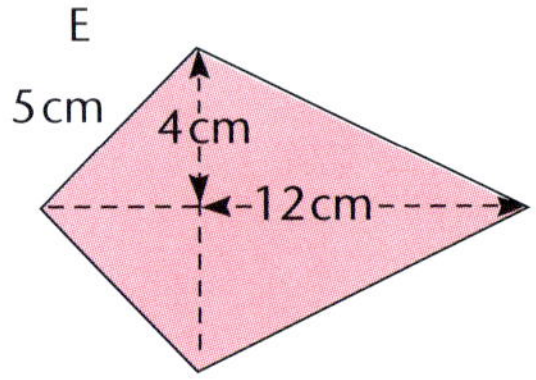

Kite

F

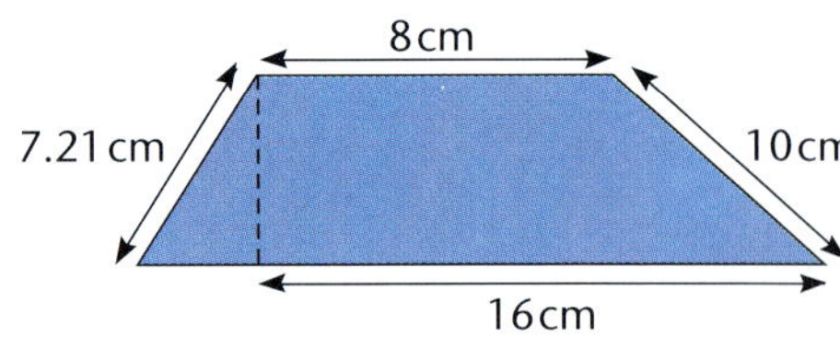

Trapezium

2 This jug shape is made from four arcs of circles, the centres of which are at the corners of the dotted square.
This square has sides of length 26 cm.
Calculate the shaded area.

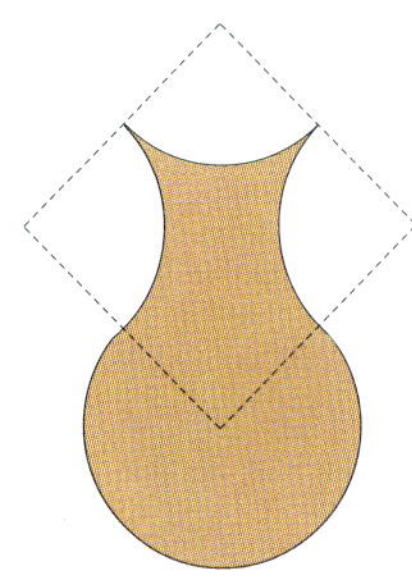

3 You have some string, tied into a loop of length 1 metre. Find, in square centimetres, the areas of these shapes made with the loop of string.

(**a**) A square (**b**) A rectangle in which one side is 15 cm

(**c**) A circle (**d**) A rectangle in which one side is $1\frac{1}{2}$ times the other

(**e**) A semicircle

DISCUSSION POINT

How can you find the length of the **chord** AB in this circle?

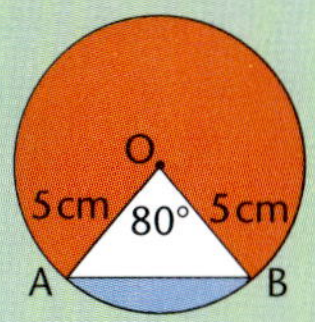

How can you find the length of the minor **arc** AB? (The minor arc is the shorter arc between A and B.)

How can you find the area of the major **sector** between the radii OA and OB, coloured red?

How can you find the area of the minor **segment** defined by the chord AB, coloured blue?

EXERCISE 4

1 The material needed to make a skirt is cut out in the shape of a sector of a circle, from a piece of cloth 1 m wide and 1.6 m long.

(**a**) What area of material will be wasted?

(**b**) Frilly ribbon is to be attached to the bottom edge of the skirt. What length of ribbon will be needed?

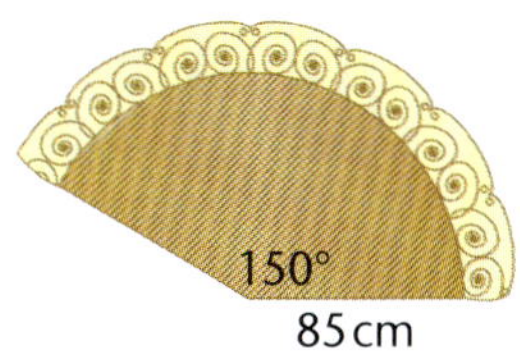

2 Calculate the area of each of these sectors.

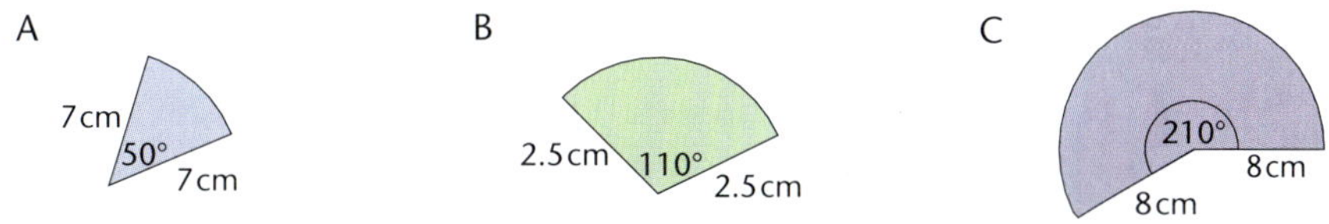

3 Calculate the perimeter for each of the sectors in Question 2.

4 Calculate the area of the red segment.

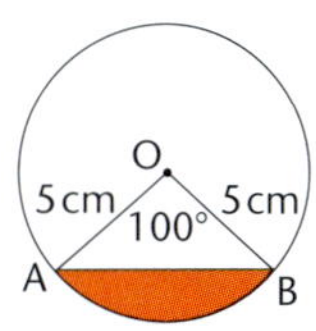

5 Calculate the coloured areas in each of these circles.

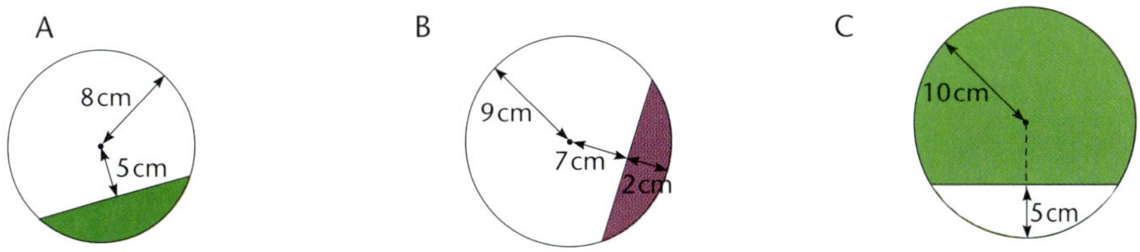

6 The area of the red sector is $124 cm^2$.
Calculate ∠AOB.

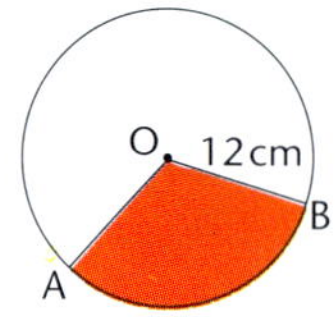

7 The area of the blue sector is $56 cm^2$.
What is the radius of the circle?

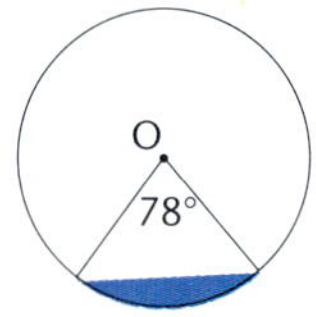

Upper and lower bounds of measures

DISCUSSION POINT

Whenever times and distances are measured, the measurements are approximate.

- Using the second hand on a watch, times can be given to the nearest second.
- Using a mechanical stop watch, times can be given to the nearest tenth of a second.
- Using the latest electronic device, times could be given to the nearest thousandth of a second, or even more accurately.

A runner finishes a 400-metre race in 46.9 seconds.

The track was measured to the nearest 0.5m and the stopwatch could be read to the nearest tenth of a second. The runner's average speed is $\frac{400\,\text{m}}{46.9\,\text{sec}} = 8.529\,\text{ms}^{-1}$

- Can the answer be given to this level of accuracy?
- What are the upper and lower bounds for the runner's speed?
- How accurately can the runner's speed be given?
- Find the lower and upper bounds for the average speed if the track had been measured more accurately (how accurate is realistic?) and the timing device gave the time of 46.900s to the nearest thousandth of a second.

Exercise 5

1 What is the difference in meaning between 2cm and 2.0cm?

2 In a swimming gala, the winner of the 100-m breaststroke finished in 95 seconds to the nearest second.

(a) What are the lower and upper bounds of the finishing time?

(b) The pool measured 50m to the nearest 5cm.
What are the lower and upper bounds for the distance of 100m?

(c) Find a sensible approximation for the average speed.

3 The world record for a swimming race was announced as 67.69 seconds to the nearest $\frac{1}{100}$ of a second.

A boy swam the same distance, using the same stroke in 68 seconds measured to the nearest second.

Did he beat the world record?

4 The radius of a circle is 1.5 cm to the nearest millimetre.
State the range of possible values for its

(**a**) radius (**b**) diameter (**c**) circumference (**d**) area

5 The lengths of the sides of this rectangle are given to the nearest centimetre.

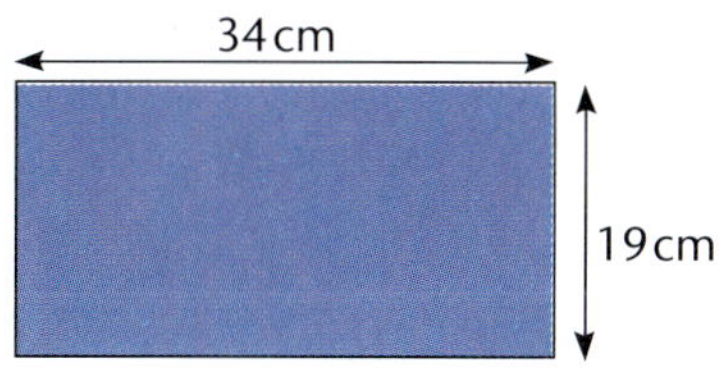

Work out the range of possible values for

(**a**) its perimeter

(**b**) its area

6 A full jar of coffee weighs 745 g. The empty jar weighs 530 g.

Both weights are accurate to the nearest 5 g.

Calculate the maximum and minimum possible values of the weight of coffee in the jar.

7 This diagram shows a rectangular room with a rug placed on the floor.

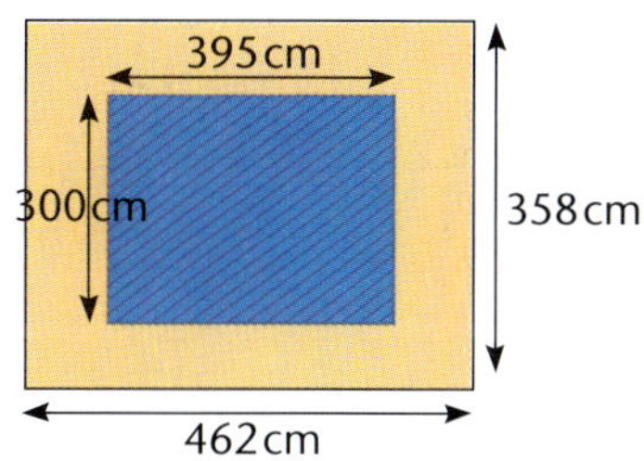

Find the maximum and minimum values for the area of

(**a**) the room

(**b**) the rug

(**c**) the floor left uncovered

8 All measurements on this open box are given correct to the nearest millimetre. The sides and the base of the box are 3 mm thick.

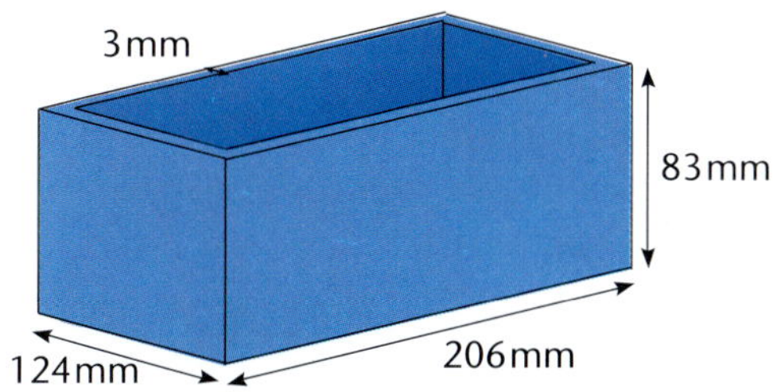

What is the range of values for the capacity of the box?

9 A square has an area of $20 cm^2$ to the nearest cm^2.
What is the range of possible values for the perimeter of the square?

10 A driver estimates that it has just taken her four hours to drive a distance of 250 miles.
If the time is given to the nearest half hour and the distance is given to the nearest 10 miles, find

(**a**) the maximum average speed for the journey

(**b**) the minimum average speed

11 Two model boats are timed over different distances.
Boat A covers 112 cm (measured to the nearest centimetre) in 1.5 seconds (to 1 decimal place).
Boat B covers 12 m (measured to the nearest metre) in 16 seconds (to the nearest second).
Which boat has the faster constant speed?

12 (**a**) A police speed trap in France measures the time a driver covers a distance of 100 m as 6 seconds.
If the distance has been measured to the nearest $\frac{1}{2}$ m, and the time is accurate to the nearest second, find the range of possible values for the speed of the driver, in k.p.h.

(**b**) This incident occurred in a 50 k.p.h. area.
Do you think the policemen charged the driver for speeding?

13 A train is travelling at a steady speed of $65 ms^{-1}$ (to the nearest $5 ms^{-1}$).
It takes four minutes (to the nearest 10 seconds) to travel between two stations.
What is the least distance, in kilometres, that the stations could be apart?

14 In 1992, Sebastian Coe's times of 1 minute 41.73 seconds for the 800 m and 2 min 12.18 sec for the 1000 m races were both world records.
What was the maximum difference between his average speeds in these two races, if both times were given to the nearest hundredth of one second and the distances are accurate to the nearest metre?

1 inch = 2.540 cm
[4 s.f.]

15 A photograph measures 8.0 inches by 6.0 inches.
It is to be placed in a frame measuring 22.0 cm by 17.0 cm.
What is the range of values for the area of space in square centimetres left uncovered by the photograph?

Volume and surface area of prisms

DISCUSSION POINT

How would you find the area of the label on this tin?
How would you find the surface area of the tin?

Volumes of prisms

Prisms are shapes which have a constant cross-section.

Volume of a prism = area of cross-section × length

Exercise 6

1 A salt container is in the shape of a cylinder.
The base of the cylinder has a radius of 3 cm.
The volume of the cylinder is 568 cm^3.

Calculate the height of the container.

2 This oil tank is a cuboid. The gauge on the tank is used to measure the volume of the oil remaining in the tank.

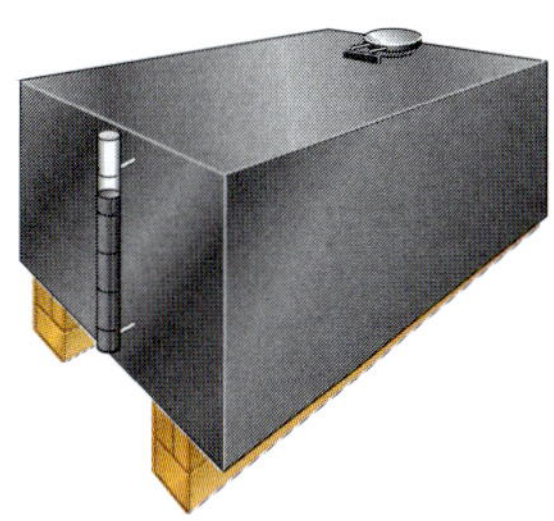

When the tank is full the height of oil in the gauge is 230 cm.

When 600 gallons are delivered the oil in the gauge rises by 50 cm.

(**a**) Write down the volume of oil delivered in litres.

(**b**) Calculate the volume of oil in the tank when it is full.

3 Find the surface areas of each of these solid shapes.

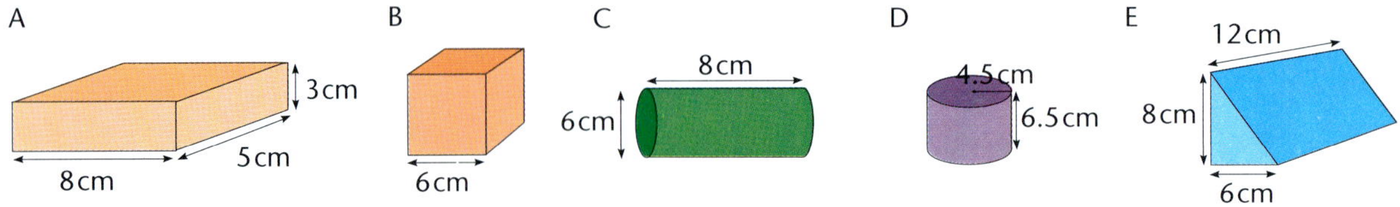

4 A 2.5-litre tin of paint is supposed to cover $32.5\,m^2$ of wall.
How thick would the layer of paint be?

5 Guttering with semi-circular cross-section is sold in 2-m lengths.

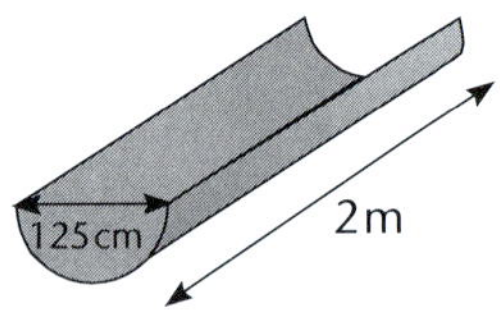

Calculate the capacity of 2m of this guttering.

6 A box of cheese contains six portions.

(**a**) Calculate the volume of cheese in one portion.

(**b**) Calculate the surface area of the cheese portion.

7 This picture shows the dimensions of a label taken from a cylindrical tin.

(**a**) Calculate the volume of the tin.

(**b**) A different cylindrical tin has a label of the same area.
Will it have the same volume?

8 This carton is made in the shape of a square-based cuboid, and contains 1.5 litres of fruit juice.
An alternative package is in the form of a plastic cylinder.
If the cylinder and the carton are the same height, what is the radius of the cylinder?

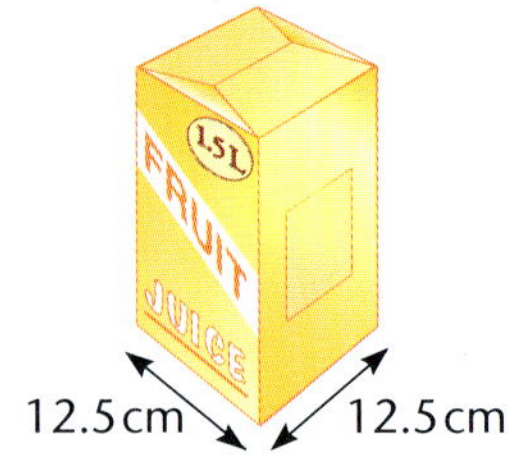

9 The length of a solid cylinder is equal to its diameter.
The cylinder has the same volume as a cube.
Find the ratio of the surface areas of the cylinder and the cube.

10 A large storage tank is in the shape of a cylinder.

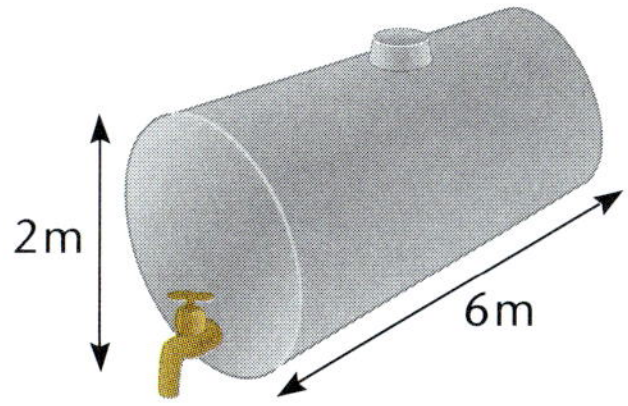

The liquid can be drawn off from the top so the depth varies from time to time, and the depth of the liquid can be checked by putting a dipstick into the tank.

Here is the cross-section at the point where the dipstick is put into the tank.

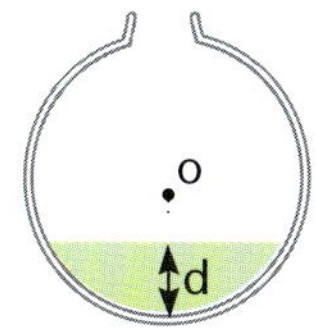

(**a**) Calculate the volume of liquid in the tank if the depth, d, is measured as 0.6m.

(**b**) What is the volume of liquid in the tank if the depth, d, is measured as 1.2m?

Pyramids, cones and spheres

▶ Resource Sheet R: *Net of a symmetrical square-based pyramid*
▶ Resource Sheet S: *Net of a skew square-based pyramid*

DISCUSSION POINT

These pictures show several pyramids.

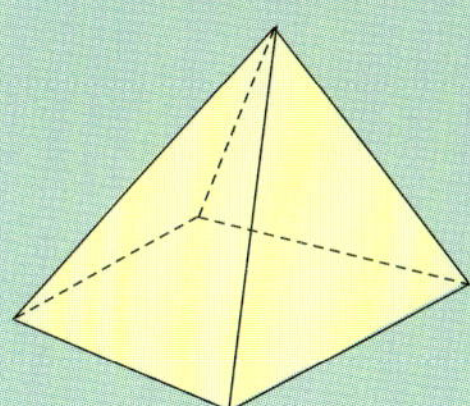

Square-based pyramid

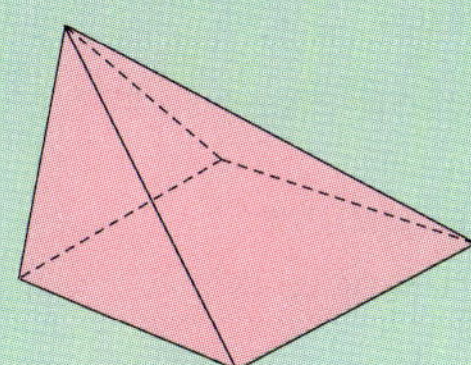

Skew square-based pyramid

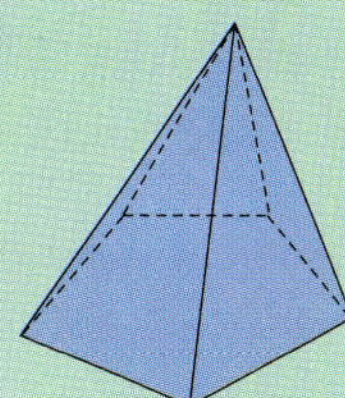

Pentagonal-based pyramid

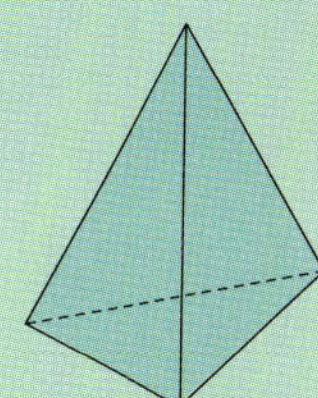

Triangular-based pyramid or tetrahedron

It may not be immediately obvious how to find their volumes, but it is clear that

volume of a pyramid < area of base × height

Make six identical models using the net on Resource Sheet R: *Net of a symmetrical square-based pyramid.*

Each model is a square-based pyramid. Fit your six models together to make a cube.

You wiill need more than one copy of each Resource Sheet.

Explain why this statement is true for the square-based pyramid you have made.

Volume of this pyramid = $\frac{1}{3}$ **× area of square base × height**

In fact, this formula holds for the volume of *any* pyramid.

Using a copy of Resource Sheet S: *Net of a skew square-based pyramid*, make the three pyramids. Fit them together to make a cube.

Use this to verify once again the formula for the volume of a pyramid.

Volume of pyramids and cones

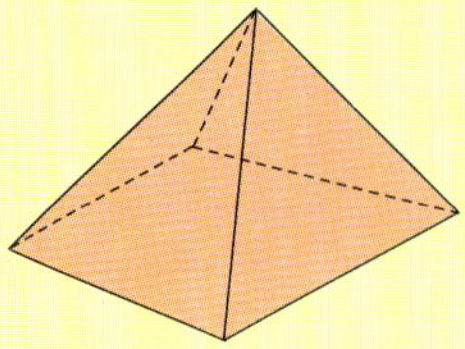

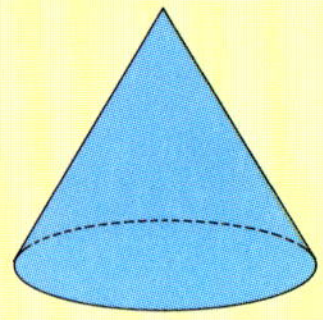

Volume = $\frac{1}{3} \times$ area of base $\times$ height

Volume of a sphere

The sphere and the cylinder shown have the same radius and height.

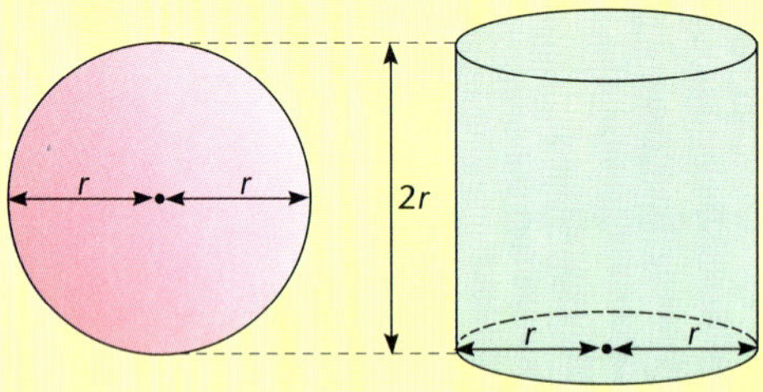

It is clear that the volume of the sphere is less than the volume of the cylinder.

Volume of sphere < $2\pi r^3$

In fact, volume of sphere = $\frac{4}{3}\pi r^3$

Surface area of a sphere

Surface area of sphere = $4\pi r^2$

- Resource Sheet T: *Tetrahedron nets*
- Scissors
- Glue or adhesive tape
- Card

Exercise 7

1 A ball has a radius of 14cm to the nearest centimetre.

(**a**) What is the volume of a sphere with radius 14cm?

(**b**) What is the range of values within which the volume of the ball must lie?

2 A tourist guide describes the Great Pyramid of Khufu/Cheops at El Giza, near Cairo, as a pyramid 147m, high based on a square with sides approximately 230m long.
Give a suitable range of values for the volume of the pyramid.
State your assumptions about the accuracy of the measurements given.

3 This lead weight, used for fishing, is moulded in the shape of a hemisphere and a cone joined together.

The hemisphere has a diameter of 22 mm.

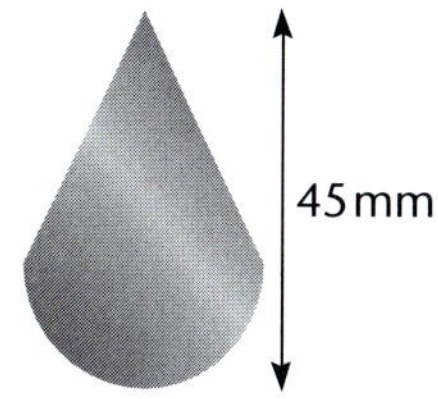

(**a**) What is the volume of the lead used in the weight?

(**b**) The lead weight is melted down and reshaped in the form of a sphere.
What is the radius of the sphere?

4 A solid ball has a mass of 540 g and a diameter of 105 mm.

(**a**) Find the density of the ball.

(**b**) A cube with edge length 75 mm is made from the same material.
What is the mass of this cube?

5 (**a**) The radius of a sphere is 6 cm.
The radius of a cylinder is 6 cm and its height is 12 cm (in other words, its height is the same as the height of the sphere).
Find the surface area of the sphere and the curved surface area of the cylinder. What do you notice?

(**b**) The radius of a sphere is x and the radius of a cylinder is x.
The height of the cylinder is the same as the height of the sphere.
Find the surface areas of the sphere and the cylinder.

6 This wine glass is in the shape of a hollow cone on a solid stem.
The tumbler is in the shape of a hollow cylinder.

The two glasses have the same capacity.
What is the radius of the tumbler?

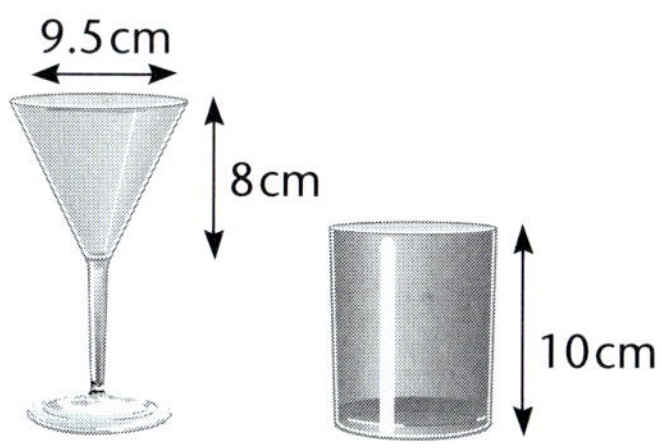

7 A traffic cone is made from plastic in the shape of a cone and a cuboid.
The cone has a radius OA = 22 cm
and the length of AB is 85 cm.
The cuboid has a square base, centre O,
of side 44 cm and height 9 cm.

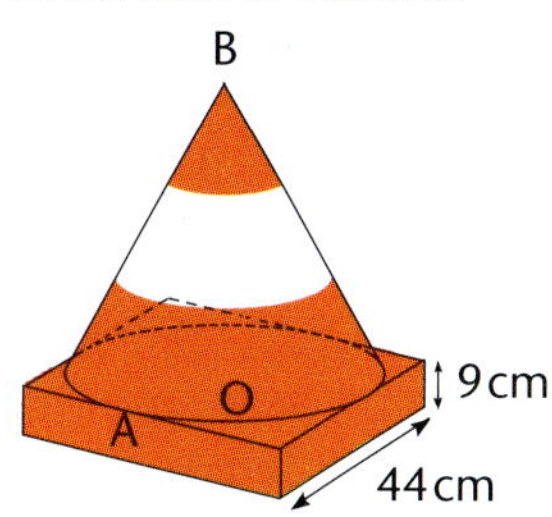

(**a**) Calculate the volume of the cone.

(**b**) Calculate the volume of the traffic cone.

8 This test tube is in the shape of a hollow cylinder and a hollow hemisphere.

(**a**) Calculate the capacity of the test tube.

(**b**) If 20 ml of water is poured into the test tube, how far from the *top* of the tube will the water level be?

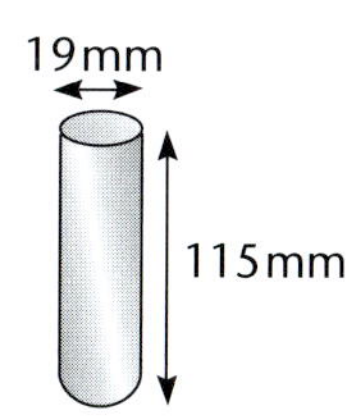

9 A solid lead ball-bearing of radius 12 mm is dropped into a cylinder partly filled with enough water to cover the ball-bearing.
If the cylinder has a diameter of 28 mm, how much does the water rise in level when the ball-bearing is dropped into it?

10 Container A consists of a cylinder of radius of r with a hemisphere of radius r at the base. Container B is a cone. The height of this cone is $10r$ and the top of the cone is a circle with radius $10r$.

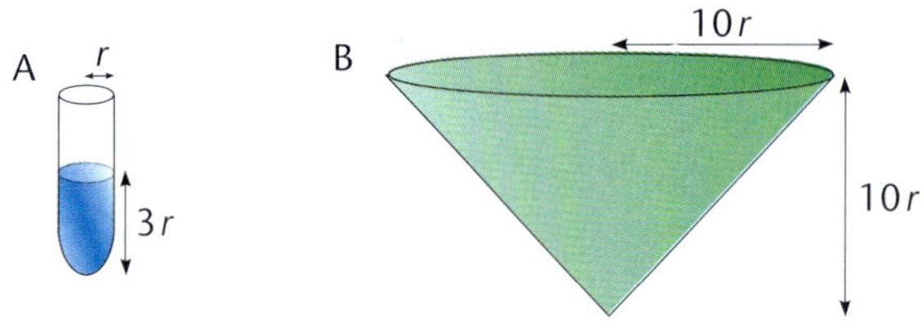

Container B is empty, and there is water in container A to a depth of $3r$.
This water is then poured into the container B.
What is the depth of the water in container B?

You will need two copies of Resource Sheet T.

11 Using a copy of Resource Sheet T: *Tetrahedron nets*, make up the five solids from the nets (4 of the upper shape and 1 of the lower shape). Fit them together to form a cube.

(**a**) If one edge of the cube is x, what is the volume of one of the four identical tetrahedra?

(**b**) What is the volume of the regular tetrahedron?

(**c**) What is the area of one face of the regular tetrahedron?

(**d**) What is the height of the regular tetrahedron?

12 A solid is obtained by slicing each of the vertices off a cube by a plane which passes through the mid-points of the three edges of the cube which meet at that vertex.

What fraction of the volume of the cube is the volume of the solid?

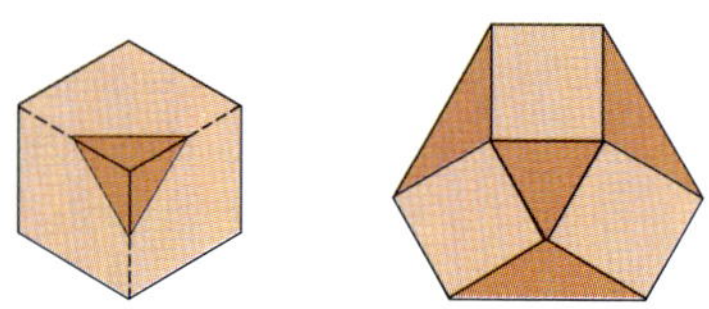

13 A regular octahedron has eight identical equilateral triangle faces.

The length of one edge of the octahedron is x.
Find the volume of the octahedron in terms of x.

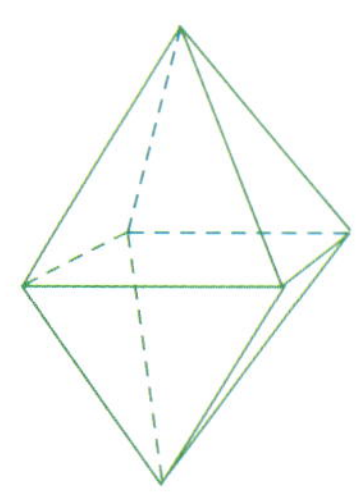

14 The shape of this ice-cream container is a *truncated* cone, a cone with the pointed end sliced off.

(**a**) Use similar triangles to find the height of the whole cone.

(**b**) What is the volume of the whole cone?

(**c**) Calculate the capacity of the ice-cream container.

(**d**) The container holds 525 g of ice-cream. What is the density of ice-cream?

(**e**) Ice-cream is scooped out of the container in a shape which is approximately spherical. The diameter of each sphere is 65 mm. What is the mass of one scoop of ice-cream?

(**f**) Approximately how many scoops can be obtained from the container?

15 Three solid shapes, a hemisphere, a cylinder and a cone, all have the same radius, and they all have the same volume.
Find the ratio of their surface areas.

DISCUSSION POINT

Here is a way of understanding the connection between the formulae for the volume of a cone, the surface area of a sphere and the volume of a sphere.

Imagine a sphere of radius r split up into a large number of 'cones', all having their apexes at the centre of the sphere. They won't be exact cones, but if the number of them is large they will be closer and closer to being exact cones.

The sum of the bases of all these cones is the surface area of the sphere, $4\pi r^2$.

The height of each of these cones is r.

How does this lead to the volume of the sphere, $\frac{4}{3}\pi r^3$?

This exercise is about how cones can be made from sectors of circles.

EXERCISE 8

1 A paper cone is made by rolling a sector of a circle, shown in the diagram.

(**a**) Find the length of the arc of the sector.

(**b**) Find the radius of the cone.

(**c**) What is the height of the cone?

(**d**) What is the volume of the cone?

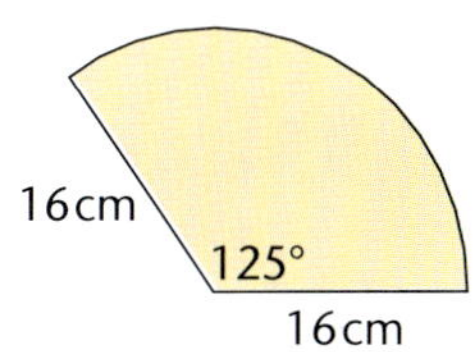

2 The wrapper on an ice-cream is made by rolling the sector of a circle.

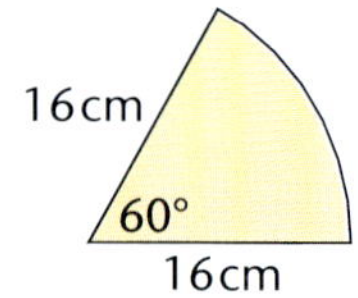

(**a**) Calculate the surface area of the wrapper.

(**b**) What is the radius and height of the cone?

(**c**) What is the capacity of the cone?

3 A wizard's hat is made from a circular piece of card. The card is cut along OA and then the cut edges are overlapped.

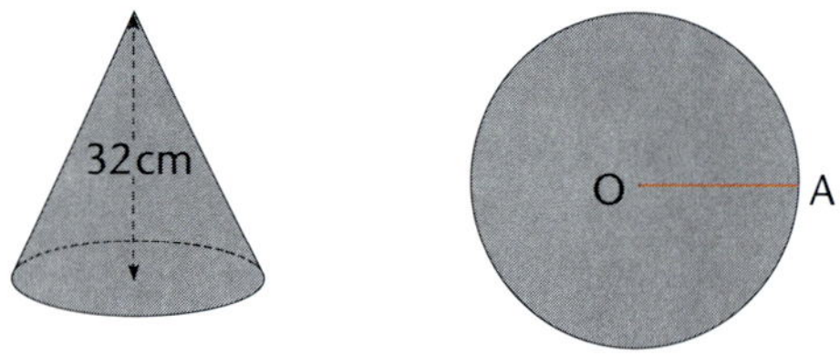

The circumference of the hat needs to be 60cm and the height of the hat must be 32cm.

(**a**) Calculate the radius of the circle of card needed to make the hat.

(**b**) What fraction of the circle is overlapped?

(**c**) What is the surface area of the outside of the hat?

4 The volume of this solid cone is 78cm³.
What is the curved surface area of the cone?

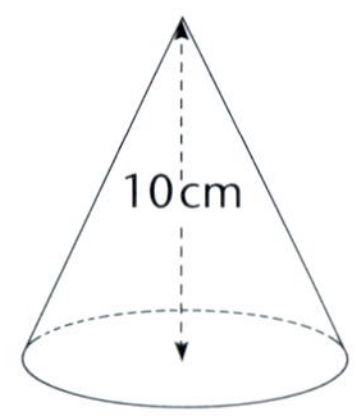

5 Individual apple pies are packed in foil cases like this.

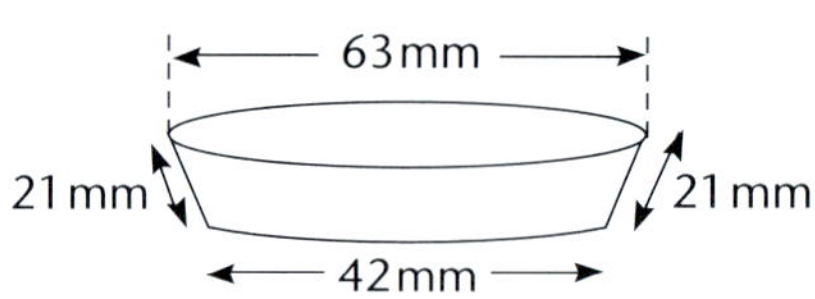

(**a**) What is the capacity of the case?

(**b**) The case is lined with a thin layer of pastry.
What is the area of pastry needed to line the case?

COURSEWORK OPPORTUNITY

Packaging candles

Candles for fragrance burners and nightlights are made in the shape of cylinders like this.

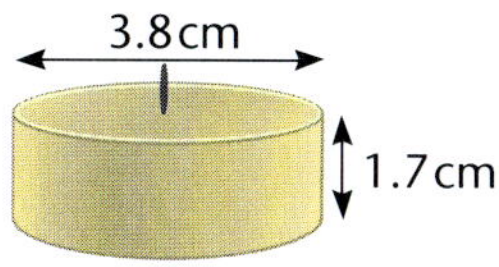

The candles are sold in packs of three in rectangular and triangular containers like these.

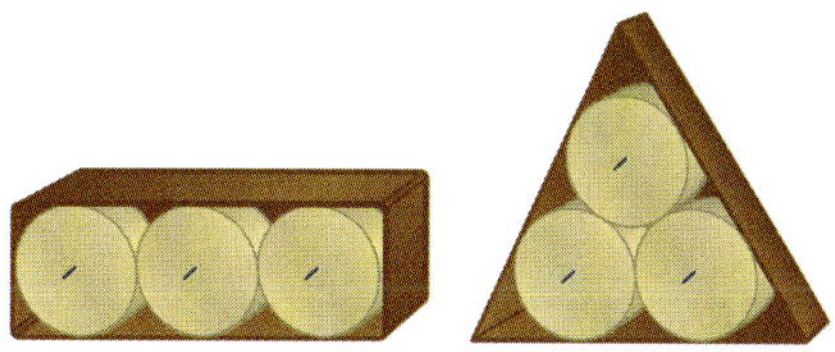

- Which of these packages are the most efficient?
  Consider the amount of wasted space within each container.
- Can you find a more efficient way of packing three candles?
- Consider containers for more than three candles.
- Consider containers for a large number of candles.
  Here are two different ways of packing 45 candles.

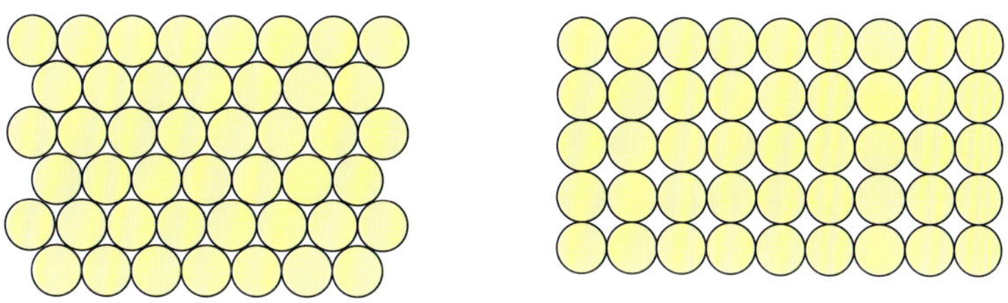

Similar solids

If the ratio of corresponding lengths on two similar solids are in the ratio k:1, corresponding areas will be in the ratio k^2:1 and their volumes will be in the ratio k^3:1. (See Chapter 7.)

EXERCISE 9

1 (**a**) Find the volume and surface area of this box.

(**b**) Another box is designed, similar in shape, but $\frac{1}{4}$ of the length of the box shown.

Find the volume and surface area of the new box.

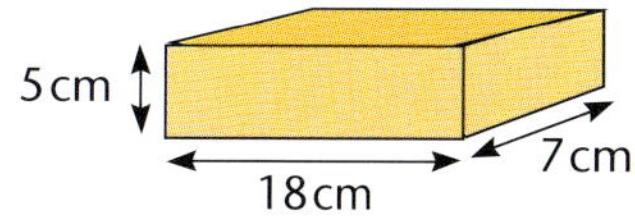

2 Cylinders are made in two sizes which are similar in shape, with the large cylinder being twice as long as the smaller one.
The contents of some small cylinders are emptied into a large cylinder.
How many small cylinders will be needed to fill the large cylinder?

3 These two buckets are similar in shape.

(**a**) What is the ratio of the heights of the smaller bucket and the larger bucket?

(**b**) What is the ratio of the diameters of the bottoms of the two buckets?

(**c**) If the circular base of the smaller bucket has a radius of 6cm, what is the area of its base?

(**d**) What is the area of the base of the larger bucket?

(**e**) The capacity of the larger bucket is 8.4 litres. What is the capacity of the smaller bucket?

4 Two cans of baked beans are similar in shape.
One has a height of 10cm and holds 400g of baked beans.
The other holds 500g of baked beans. What is its height?

5 Toothpaste is normally sold in a 50-ml tube which is 16cm long.
In a special offer, a new tube states that it contains an extra 50% free.
This tube is similar in shape to the smaller tube.

(**a**) How much toothpaste is in this new sized tube?

(**b**) Express the ratio of toothpaste contained in the two tubes in its simplest terms.

(**c**) Calculate the length of the larger tube.

6 Two spherical water melons of diameters 20cm and 30cm are sold for £1.25 and £2.50 respectively. Which appears to be the better buy?

7 These two bricks are similar in shape.

If the density of the bricks is $6.25 g/cm^3$, what is the mass of the small brick?

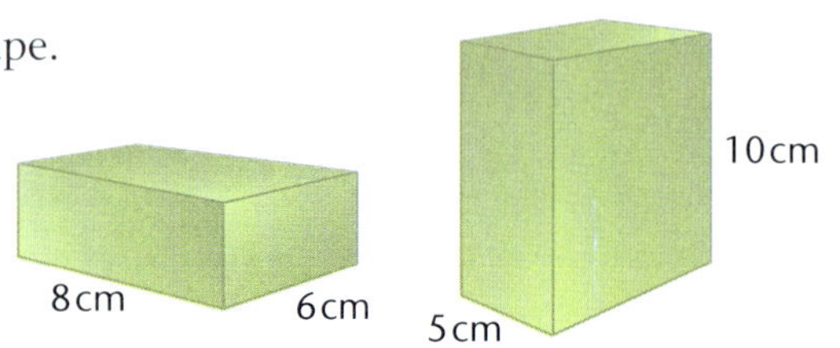

8 A box is in the shape of a cuboid. A new box is made by increasing the edge lengths of the original box by 50%.

(**a**) What is the percentage increase in surface area?

(**b**) What is the percentage increase in volume?

9 This conical flask has a capacity of 480ml.
How tall is the flask?

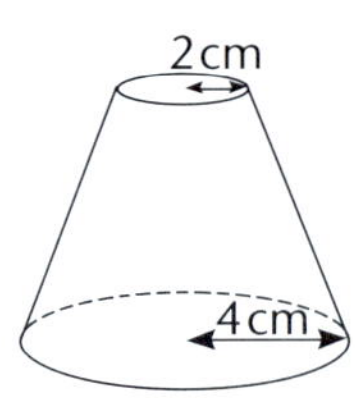

10 An ice-cream cone has the bottom quarter of its length completely full of chocolate. The rest of the cone is filled with ice-cream, level with the top of the cone.

(**a**) Show that the volume of the cone is $\frac{\pi d^2 h}{12}$.

(**b**) Write down an expression for the volume of chocolate at the bottom of the cone.

(**c**) Show that the volume of ice-cream can be written as $\frac{21\pi d^2 h}{256}$.

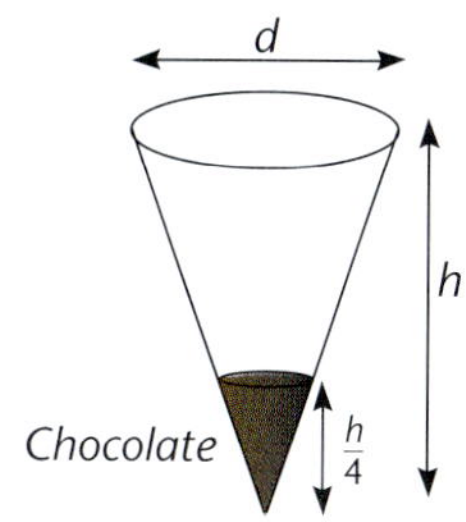

Distinguishing formulae

DISCUSSION POINT

Which of these formulae are likely to represent length, which area and which volume?

$\frac{(a+b)h}{2}$ $\quad 2(l+w) \quad \pi r^2 h \quad \frac{1}{2}ab\sin C$

What about the formula $x^2 + y$?

EXERCISE 10

1 x, y and z are all measures of length. Which of these formulae could represent a length, which an area, which a volume and which none of these?

$xyz \quad x^2 + \frac{y}{z} \quad \frac{xy}{z} \quad xy^2 \quad 2(xy + yz + xz) \quad \frac{x+y}{z} \quad x + \frac{y^2}{z} \quad \pi x^2 y$

2 If r and h are length measurements on a solid shape, which of these formulae could represent the volume of the shape?

$\pi^2 rh - \pi r^2 h \quad \pi r^2 h + 2\pi rh \quad \pi r^2 h - r^2 h \quad \pi r^2 h - r^2 h^2$

3 These are a collection of formulae: you may recognise some of them. Say whether each formula is for length, area or volume. If you recognise the shape to which the formula refers, write this down too.

$\frac{1}{2}ab\sin C \quad \pi r^2 \quad \frac{1}{2}(a+b)h \quad \pi r^2 + 2\pi r \quad \frac{1}{3}\pi r^2 h \quad 2\pi r^2 + 2\pi rh \quad 2l + 2w \quad \pi rl$

4 V is a volume, A is an area and h is a length.
For each of these formulae, say whether it is a length, an area or a volume.

$\frac{V}{h} \quad \frac{A^2}{V + h^3} \quad \frac{A^2}{3h} \quad \sqrt{(3Vh)} \quad \frac{h(V + 2Ah)}{A} \quad \frac{2V}{h^2}$

5 These formulae were found in *Machinery's Handbook*, published in 1939. All the letters used are measures of length.
Say whether each formula is for length, for area or for volume.

(a) $\frac{1.93d^2}{t} + d$

(b) $\frac{L(T + t)}{2} + Tn + a(S + n)$

(c) $R - \sqrt{R^2 - (\frac{1}{2}B)^2}$

(d) $\frac{D - \sqrt{D^2 - B^2}}{2}$

(e) $\frac{3(R^4 - r^4)}{8(R^3 - r^3)}$

(f) $\frac{3d^2 \tan 30°}{2}$

(g) $\frac{h}{2} + \frac{r^2(\tan\alpha)^2}{8h}$

(h) $W\sqrt{\frac{D^2 - W^2 - T^2}{W^2 + T^2}} - T$

CHAPTER SUMMARY

Relationship between metric and Imperial units

Metric measures

Length
1km = 1000m
1m = 100cm = 1000mm
1cm = 10mm

Mass or weight
1 tonne = 1000kg
1kg = 1000g
1g = 1000mg

Capacity
1 litre = 1000ml
$1m^3$ = 1000 litres
$1cm^3$ = 1ml

Area
1 hectare = $10000m^2$

Length

5 miles is about 8km
1 inch is about $2\frac{1}{2}$cm
1 foot is about 30cm
1 yard is just a bit less than 1 metre

Mass or weight

1 ton is about 1 tonne
2.2lb is about 1kg
1oz is about 30g

Capacity

1 gallon is about 4.5 litres
$1\frac{3}{4}$ pints is about 1 litre

Area

$2\frac{1}{2}$ acres is about 1 hectare

Imperial measures

Length
1 mile = 1760 yards
1 yard = 3 feet
1 foot = 12 inches

Mass or weight
1 ton = 20 hundredweight (cwt)
1cwt = 8 stone
1 stone = 14 pounds (lb)
1 pound = 16 ounces (oz)

Capacity
1 gallon = 8 pints

Area
1 acre = 4840 square yards

Areas of plane shapes

Area of **triangle** = $\frac{1}{2}$ × base × height

Area of **parallelogram** = base × height

Area of **trapezium** = $\frac{1}{2}$ × sum of parallel sides × distance between them

Area of **circle** = πr^2

Sectors and segments

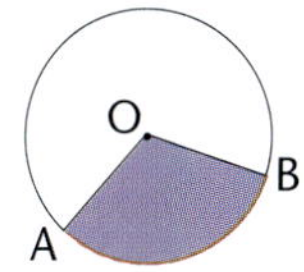

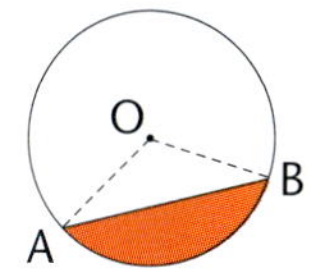

The length of the **arc** AB can be found by finding the appropriate fraction of the circumference of the circle. The area of the **sector** OAB (shaded blue) can be found by finding the appropriate fraction of the area of the circle. The area of the **segment** (shaded red) can be found by finding the area of the sector OAB and subtracting the area of the isosceles triangle OAB.

Upper and lower bounds of measures

Measurements are always given to a certain degree of accuracy.
Example: A measurement given as 7 mm to the nearest millimetre lies between 6.5 mm (**the lower bound**) and 7.5 mm (the **upper bound**).
A time given as 57.38 seconds lies between 57.375 and 57.385 seconds.

Solid shapes

Cylinder

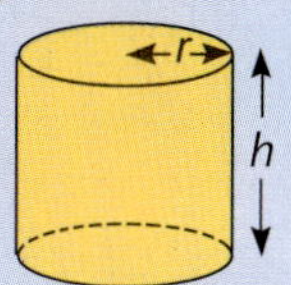

Cone

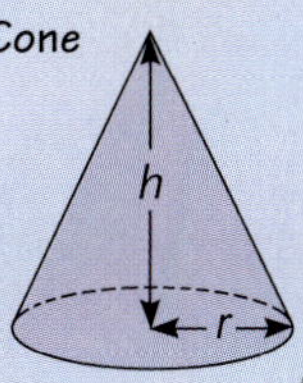

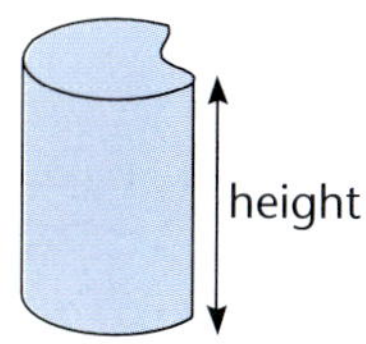

A solid shape which has a constant cross-section is called a **prism**.

Volume of a prism = area of cross-section × height

Volume of cylinder = $\pi r^2 h$

Area of the curved surface of a cylinder = $2\pi rh$

Volume of a pyramid = $\frac{1}{3}$ × area of base × height

Volume of a cone = $\frac{1}{3}\pi r^2 h$

Volume of a sphere = $\frac{4}{3}\pi r^3$

Surface area of a sphere = $4\pi r^2$

Similar solids

If corresponding lengths on two similar solids are in the ratio k:1, corresponding areas will be in the ratio k^2:1. Their volumes will be in the ratio k^3:1

Distinguishing formulae

r = radius
h = height
l = length
w = width
A = area
V = volume

In formulae for **length**, each term consists of just one length.

- Circumference of a circle = $2\pi r$
- Perimeter of a rectangle = $2(l + w)$
- Base of a triangle = $\frac{2A}{h}$

In formulae for **area**, each term consists of two lengths multiplied together.

- Area of a circle = πr^2
- Surface area of a cylinder = $2\pi rh + 2\pi r^2$
- Cross-section of a prism = $\frac{V}{h}$
- Surface area of a cone = $\pi r\sqrt{(r^2 + h^2)} + \pi r^2$

In formulae for **volume**, each term consists of three lengths multiplied together.

- Volume of a sphere = $\frac{4}{3}\pi r^3$
- Volume of a cylinder = $\pi r^2 h$
- Volume of a prism = Ah
- Volume of a cube = $(\sqrt{\frac{A}{6}})^3$

CHAPTER

13 EQUATIONS

This chapter is about:

- solving linear equations
- solving trigonometric equations graphically
- solving simultaneous linear equations algebraically and graphically
- solving quadratic equations by factorising and by trial and improvement
- solving quadratic equations by drawing graphs
- solving other equations by trial and improvement.

Linear equations

DISCUSSION POINT

An equation is a rule that a number must obey.
Equations are usually written with a letter standing for the number.
To solve the equation means to find a number which obeys the rule.
There may be only one number which does, or there may be many numbers which do.
It may be impossible to find a number which obeys the rule.

Can you solve these equations?

$3x + 5 = 56$ $\quad$ $7 - 3x = 13$ $\quad$ $\frac{x}{5} - 4 = 3$

$5x + 2 = 3x + 16$ $\quad$ $3x + 5(x + 1) = 7(5 - x)$ $\quad$ $6 + \frac{8}{x} = 22$

$\frac{x+3}{5} - 1 = \frac{x-4}{3}$

EXERCISE 1

1 Solve these equations.

(a) $5a - 7 = 23$ $\quad$ (b) $6b + 16 = 70$ $\quad$ (c) $12 + 2c = 4$

(d) $11 = 60 + 7d$ $\quad$ (e) $4e - 10 = 0$ $\quad$ (f) $24 + 5f = 6$

2 Solve these equations.

(a) $24 - 3a = 9$

(b) $7 = 29 - 2b$

(c) $5 - 2c = 19$

(d) $-3d + 13 = 19$

(e) $17 = 25 - 5e$

(f) $8 - 5f = 58$

3 Solve these equations.

(a) $\frac{a}{3} + 4 = 11$

(b) $\frac{b}{9} - 6 = 0$

(c) $10 + \frac{2c}{3} = 2$

(d) $\frac{17 + d}{3} = 5$

(e) $\frac{12 - e}{4} = 5$

(f) $27 - \frac{2f}{3} = 22$

4 Solve these equations.

(a) $40 + 5a = 24 + 3a$

(b) $7b - 3 = 6b + 3$

(c) $10c + 60 = 5c + 35$

(d) $4d - 10 = 2d - 3$

(e) $8e + 2 = 3e - 6$

(f) $10f - 7 = 6f - 4$

5 Solve these equations.

(a) $3a - 42 = 22 - a$

(b) $5b - 8 = 13 - 2b$

(c) $4c + 18 = 2c - 30$

(d) $2d + 47 = 17 - 4d$

(e) $e - 5 = 11 - 4e$

(f) $20 + 3f = 8 - 5f$

6 Solve these equations.

(a) $3(a + 2) - 14 = 13$

(b) $2(2b - 15) = 6 + b$

(c) $2(c + 20) = 3(5 - c)$

(d) $5(d + 2) = 2(d - 4)$

(e) $5(e - 2) = 2(e - 3)$

(f) $5(2f + 3) = 2(15 - f)$

7 Solve these equations.

(a) $5 + \frac{10}{a} = 7$

(b) $\frac{12}{b} + 17 = 23$

(c) $11 + \frac{12}{c} = 27$

(d) $\frac{6}{d} - 3 = 0$

(e) $5 - \frac{12}{e} = 1$

(f) $\frac{7}{f} - \frac{16}{f} = 3$

8 Solve these equations.

(a) $\frac{a + 6}{3} - 6 = \frac{2 - a}{2}$

(b) $\frac{2(b + 2)}{3} - 9 = \frac{5 - b}{5}$

(c) $\frac{c + 4}{3} = 1 + \frac{c - 1}{6}$

(d) $\frac{2d + 21}{4} = 2 + \frac{d + 2}{8}$

(e) $\frac{4e + 3}{2} + \frac{16e + 7}{4} = 7$

(f) $\frac{3(f + 3)}{2} - 3f = 6 + \frac{2 - f}{2}$

Using graphs to solve equations

DISCUSSION POINT

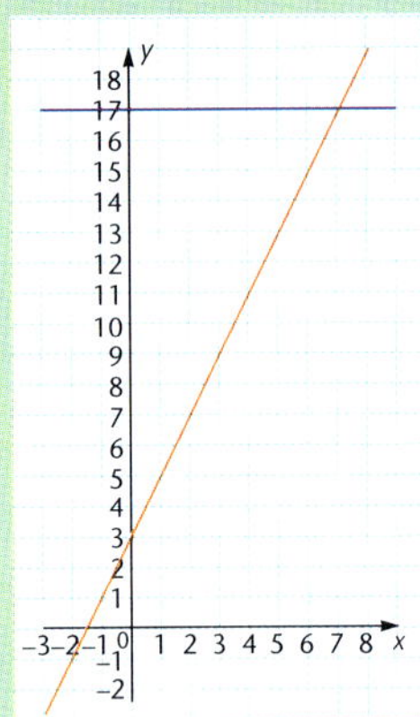

The graph of $y = 2x + 3$ can be used to solve $2x + 3 = 17$.

Use the graph to solve $2x + 3 = 0$, $2x + 3 = -1$, $2x + 3 = 6$ and $2x + 3 = 10.6$

This is only part of the graph $y = 2x + 3$.

How do you know there are no other solutions on another part of the graph?

▶ Graph paper

You will not usually draw graphs to solve linear equations like these in Exercise 2, but graphs might be useful on occasions.

EXERCISE 2

1 This is the graph of $y = 3x - 5$.
Use it to solve these equations.

(a) $3x - 5 = 0$

(b) $3x - 5 = 7$

(c) $3x - 5 = -6$

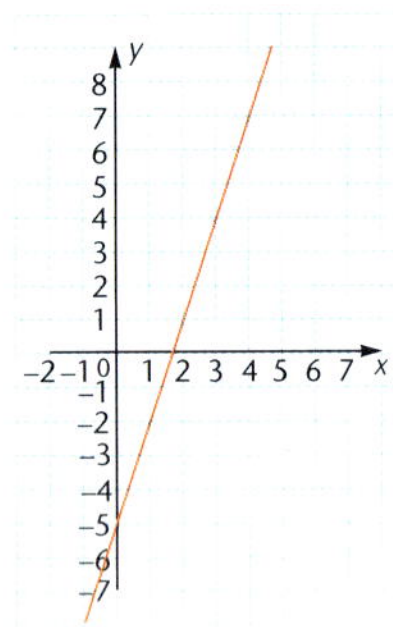

2 This is the graph of $y = 5 - 2x$.
Use it to solve these equations.

(a) $5 - 2x = 0$

(b) $5 - 2x = 10$

(c) $5 - 2x = -3$

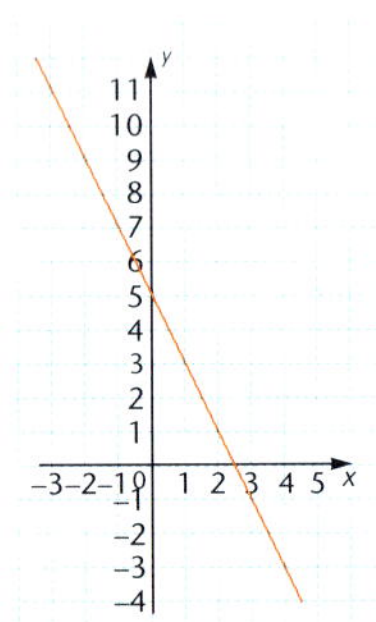

3 Draw the graph of $y = \frac{1}{2}x - 2$ for values of x from –6 to 10.
Use it to solve these equations.

(a) $\frac{1}{2}x - 2 = 0$ **(b)** $\frac{1}{2}x - 2 = 1.6$ **(c)** $\frac{1}{2}x - 2 = -3.4$

DISCUSSION POINT

This is the graph of $y = x^2 - 4x - 3$.
It can be used to solve equations like $x^2 - 4x - 3 = 2$.

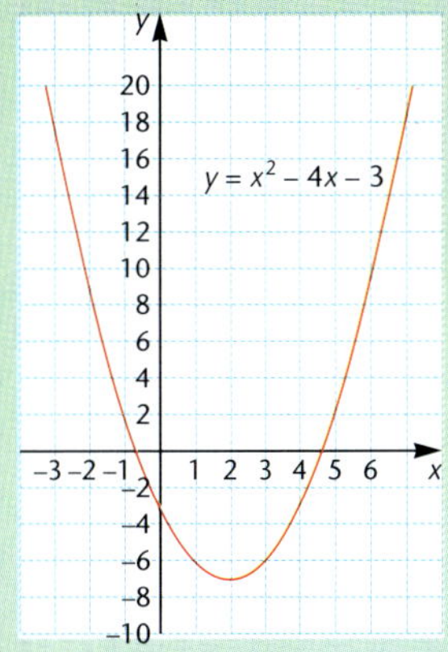

- There are two solutions.
  Use the graph to find what they are.
- Use your calculator to check that your solutions do satisfy the equation $x^2 - 4x - 3 = 2$.
- Would there be any more solutions if the graph were extended? Why?
- How many solutions are there for these equations?
  $x^2 - 4x - 3 = 9$ $\quad$ $x^2 - 4x - 3 = -6$
  $x^2 - 4x - 3 = -7$ $\quad$ $x^2 - 4x - 3 = -10$
  Check that you can use the graph to find the solutions of these equations.
- What are the solutions of $x^2 - 4x - 3 = 0$?

DISCUSSION POINT

This is the graph of $y = \sin x$.

It can be used to solve equations like $\sin x = 0.5$

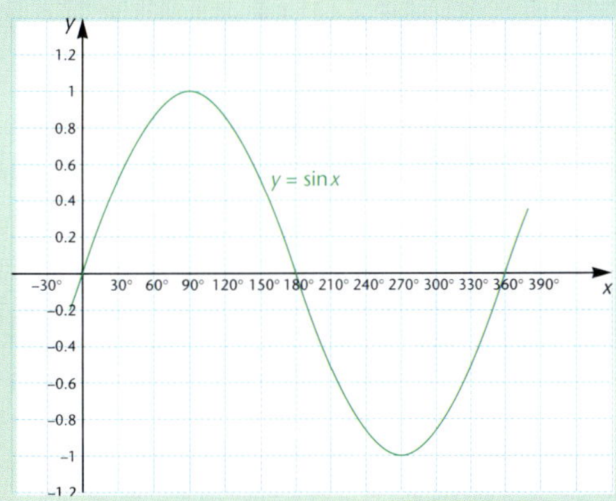

- How many solutions does the graph give to this equation?
- What are these solutions?
- Would there be any more solutions if the graph were extended?
- What are they?
- Use the graph to solve these equations.
  $\sin x = -0.5$
  $\sin x = 0$
  $\sin x = 2$

EXERCISE 3

1 (a) For $-4 \le x \le 4$, draw the graph of $y = x^2$ as accurately as possible.

(b) For each of these equations, say how many solutions there are and find them.

(i) $x^2 = 10$ (ii) $x^2 = -5$ (iii) $x^2 = 0$ (iv) $x^2 = 3$

2 **(a)** For $-4 \leq x \leq 4$, draw the graph of $y = x^2 - 3$ as accurately as possible.

(b) For each of these equations, say how many solutions there are and find them.

(i) $x^2 - 3 = 7$ **(ii)** $x^2 - 3 = -8$ **(iii)** $x^2 - 3 = 0$ **(iv)** $x^2 - 3 = 4$

3 **(a)** For $0 \leq x \leq 420°$, draw the graph of $y = \cos x$ as accurately as possible.

(b) For each of these equations, say how many solutions there are and find them.

(i) $\cos x = 1$ **(ii)** $\cos x = 0.8$ **(iii)** $\cos x = -0.5$ **(iv)** $\cos x = -1$

Using graphs to solve simultaneous equations

DISCUSSION POINT

Two numbers add up to 7 and the second is 2 more than the first.

What is this pair of numbers?

If the pair of numbers are called x and y, then the rule 'they add up to 7' can be written in algebra as $x + y = 7$.

The rule 'the second is 2 more than the first' can be written as $y - x = 2$ or $y = x + 2$.

This diagram shows the graphs of $x + y = 7$ and $y = x + 2$.

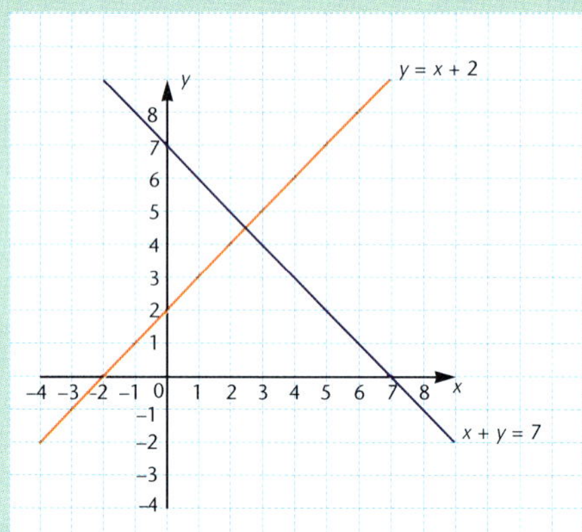

There is one point which is on both lines and so obeys both rules.

- What is it?
- Check that the coordinates of this point do add up to 7 and that the second is 2 more than the first.
- How do you know there is no other pair of numbers which obeys both rules?

Exercise 4

1 Draw the graphs of $x + y = 5$ and $y = x + 4$. Use your graphs to find this pair of numbers.

They add up to 5 and the second is 4 more than the first.

2 Draw the graphs of $x + y = 2$ and $y = x + 5$. Use your graphs to find this pair of numbers.

They add up to 2 and the second is 5 more than the first.

3 (a) Write down equations for these two rules about a pair of numbers, x and y.

They add up to 8, and the second is 3 more than the first.

(b) Draw the graphs of the equations and find the pair of numbers.

4 (a) Write down equations for these two rules about a pair of numbers, x and y.

They add up to 2, and the difference between them is 7.

(b) Draw the graphs of the equations and find the pair of numbers.

5 Draw graphs to find this pair of numbers.

They add up to 3, and the difference between them is 8.

6 For each of these, draw graphs to find a pair of numbers, x and y which obey both rules.

(a) $y = x + 2$ and $y = 2x - 3$

(b) $x + y = 4$ and $y = 3x - 2$

(c) $y = x + 1$ and $y = 2x + 3$

(d) $y = \frac{1}{2}x + 1$ and $y = 3x - 3$

7 For each of these, draw graphs to find a pair of numbers, x and y which obey both rules. Explain what happens and what it means.

(a) $y = 4 - x$ and $x + y = 6$

(b) $y = 2x - 3$ and $\frac{1}{2}y = x + 1$

For Question 8, you may want to rearrange each equation first.

8 Solve these simultaneous equations by drawing graphs.

(a) $2x - y = 1$
$x + 2y = 5$

(b) $x + y = 4$
$3x - y = 1$

(c) $-x + y = 2$
$3x - y = 5$

(d) $-x + y = 2$
$3x - 3y = -6$

Solving simultaneous equations algebraically

Here are two examples of how to find a pair of numbers which obey two rules at the same time, i.e. *simultaneously*.

Example 1

$x + y = 7 \Rightarrow x + y = 7$

$x + 3y = 11 \Rightarrow x + y + y + y = 11$

Compare these equations.
There are two extra 'y's in the second one and there is an extra 4 on the 'total'.

So, $2y = 4$ and y must be 2.

If $y = 2$, then x must be 5 for $x + y = 7$ to be true.

Check that when $x = 5$ and $y = 2$, the second rule $x + 3y = 11$ is true too.

Example 2

$x + y = 8 \Rightarrow x + y = 8$

$x + 5y = 0 \Rightarrow x + y + y + y + y + y = 0$

The four extra 'y's in the second equation have made the 'total' go down by 8.

So, $4y = -8$ and y must be -2.
If $y = -2$, then x must be 10 so that $x + y = 8$.

Check that these values make the second equation true, too.

DISCUSSION POINT

This pair is harder to solve.

$x + y = 5 \Rightarrow x + y = 5$

$3x + 2y = 18 \Rightarrow x + x + x + y + y = 18$

There are extra of both x and y in the second equation, which have added 13 to the total. So, $2x + y = 13$.
This does not give one of the values, so another step is needed.

If $x + y = 5$, can you see that $2x + 2y = 10$, $3x + 3y = 15$, ..., $10x + 10y = 50$?
There are many equations like this that are also true.
Choose the $2x + 2y = 10$ version.

$2x + 2y = 10 \Rightarrow x + x + y + y = 10$

$3x + 2y = 18 \Rightarrow x + x + x + y + y = 18$

The extra x has added 8 to the total, so $x = 8$. If $x + y = 5$, then $y = -3$.
Check that these values of x and y make the second equation true, too.

- What would happen if you worked from the $3x + 3y = 15$ version?
- Why is it not sensible to choose the $7x + 7y = 35$ version?

To keep track of how you've solved the equations, it is a good idea to label the equations and record each step, like this.

$x + y = 5$ ①
$3x + 2y = 18$ ②

①× 2 $\quad 2x + 2y = 10$ ③
$\quad 3x + 2y = 18$ ②
② − ③ $\quad x = 8$

In ① $\quad 8 + y = 5 \Rightarrow y = -3$
Check in ② $\quad 3x + 2y = 3 \times 8 + 2 \times -3 = 18$ ✓

So $x = 8$ and $y = -3$

Exercise 5

1 For each pair of simultaneous equations, find the values which make both equations true.

(a) $a + b = 7$
$a + 3b = 11$

(b) $2c + d = 10$
$c + d = 7$

(c) $e + f = 6$
$e + 4f = 9$

(d) $g + h = 13$
$3g + h = 25$

(e) $4j + k = 43$
$j + k = 13$

(f) $3m + n = 18$
$7m + n = 10$

2 For each pair of equations, find the values which make both equations true.

(a) $a + b = 10$
$2a + 3b = 23$

(b) $2c + 5d = 29$
$c + d = 7$

(c) $e + f = 10$
$3e + 4f = 39$

(d) $g + h = 13$
$3g + 2h = 34$

(e) $4j + 2k = 24$
$j + k = 9$

(f) $5m + 3n = 4$
$m + n = -2$

Making the coefficients the same

$6a + b = 15$
$3a + 2b = 12$

In equation $6a + b = 15$, the **coefficient** of a is 6 and the coefficient of b is 1.

The first step is to plan which coefficients to make the same.

You could make the coefficients of a the same:

$$\begin{array}{l} 6a + b = 15 \\ 3a + 2b = 12 \end{array} \Rightarrow \begin{array}{l} 6a + b = 15 \\ 6a + 4b = 24 \end{array} \Rightarrow 3b = 9 \Rightarrow b = 3 \text{ and } a = 2$$

Or you could make the coefficients of b the same:

$$\begin{array}{l} 6a + b = 15 \\ 3a + 2b = 12 \end{array} \Rightarrow \begin{array}{l} 12a + 2b = 30 \\ 3a + 2b = 12 \end{array} \Rightarrow 9a = 18 \Rightarrow a = 2 \text{ and } b = 3$$

Exercise 6

1 For each pair of equations, find the values which make both equations true.

(a) $2a + b = 12$
$3a + 2b = 19$

(b) $2c + d = 13$
$4c + 3d = 23$

(c) $2e + f = 26$
$3e + 2f = 42$

In Question 2, you will have to multiply both equations to make the coefficients of one letter the same.

2 For each pair of equations, find the values which make both equations true.

(a) $4a + 3b = 32$
$5a + 2b = 26$

(b) $2c + 3d = 53$
$3c + 2d = 47$

(c) $3e + 5f = -1$
$4e + 3f = 39$

What happens when the coefficients have different signs?
Here are two examples. In Example 1, if you add the two equations together, the terms in y cancel. The coefficients must both be the same number, one positive and the other negative, *before* you add the equations. In Example 2, you need to multiply $2x - y = -8$ by 3 to make the y terms cancel.

Example 1

$2x + y = 12$ ①
$x - y = 3$ ②

①+② $3x = 15$
$x = 5$

In ① $2x + y = 12 \Rightarrow y = 2$

Example 2

$x + 3y = 10$ ①
$2x - y = -8$ ②

② × 3 $6x - 3y = -24$ ③
①+③ $7x = -14$
$x = -2$

In ① $x + 3y = 10 \Rightarrow y = 4$

Exercise 7

1 Add these pairs of equations to find the values which make them both true.

(a) $a + b = 13$, $a - b = 7$
(b) $2c + d = 20$, $c - d = 4$
(c) $e + f = -11$, $3e - f = 27$

2 For each of these pairs of equations, find the values which make them both true.

(a) $2c + d = 22$, $c - 2d = 1$
(b) $4j - k = 75$, $j + 3k = 35$
(c) $2e - 3f = -19$, $5e + 6f = 101$

3 For each of these pairs of equations, find the values which make both equations true.

(a) $2a - b = 9$, $3a + 2b = 31$
(b) $2c - d = 3$, $4c + 3d = 31$
(c) $2e + f = 21$, $3e - 2f = 14$
(d) $4g + 2h = 32$, $3g - h = 34$
(e) $4j - 3k = 11$, $5j + 2k = 8$
(f) $4m + 7n = -5$, $5m - 6n = -21$

The pairs of equations in Question 4 are different, because there are two minus signs.

4 For each of these pairs of equations, find the values which make both equations true.

(a) $2a - b = 18$, $3a - b = 28$
(b) $3c - d = 13$, $c - d = 3$
(c) $5e - f = 24$, $2e - f = 3$
(d) $3g - h = 21$, $5g - 2h = 34$
(e) $2j - k = 22$, $j - 3k = 21$
(f) $-4m + 3n = 5$, $-5m + 2n = -13$

This exercise contains a variety of simultaneous equations of different types.

EXERCISE 8

1 Solve these simultaneous equations.

(a) $l + m = 23$, $l + 3m = 39$ (b) $l + m = 3$, $4l + 3m = 14$ (c) $5l + 2m = 19$, $3l + 4m = 3$

(d) $l - m = 2$, $3l + m = 18$ (e) $3l - 4m = 10$, $2l + 3m = 1$ (f) $7l + 2m = 75$, $3l - 4m = 3$

You may want to rearrange the equations in Question 2 before solving them.

2 Solve these simultaneous equations.

(a) $p - 2n = -14$, $n - 4p = 21$ (b) $5n + p - 13 = 0$, $n + p = 7$ (c) $5n + 2p - 6 = 0$, $n + p = 6$

(d) $3n + 4p = 12$, $p + 2n = 8$ (e) $5n - p - 1 = 0$, $n + p = 5$ (f) $5n = 73 + p$, $n + 3p = 5$

3 Solve these simultaneous equations.

(a) $2a + 3b = 53$, $a = b + 9$ (b) $3c + 5d = 97$, $d = 2c - 4$ (c) $4e - 5f = 19$, $e = 3f - 4$

(d) $-5g + 3h = -11$, $h = 23 - g$ (e) $-6j - 5k = 60$, $j = 1 - k$ (f) $3m - 7n = -28$, $n = 3m - 5$

4 Solve these simultaneous equations.

(a) $-3s - 2t = -2$, $2s + 5t = 16$ (b) $7s + 2t - 22 = 0$, $s + t = 1$ (c) $3s = t + 26$, $s + t = 2$

(d) $t = 3s - 53$, $s + 4t = 9$ (e) $3s = 19 + 4t$, $t = 9 - 2s$ (f) $3s - 4t + 19 = 0$, $t - 2s + 4 = 0$

5 Solve these simultaneous equations.

(a) $v + w = 5$, $3v + w = 2.6$ (b) $v = 5 - w$, $3v + 5w = 22$ (c) $v - w - 2 = 0$, $w + 3v - 11 = 0$

(d) $v = 5w$, $3v + w = 24$ (e) $10v + 3w = 24$, $5w = 3v - 19$ (f) $5v + 3w = 14$, $-3v - 2w = -7$

Using simultaneous equations to solve problems

DISCUSSION POINT

How much are fish and chips?

- The first person leaving a chip shop had bought 3 fish and 2 portions of chips. The order cost £7.40.
- The second had bought 4 fish and 3 portions of chips, costing £10.15.

Using f for the cost of the fish in pence and c for the cost of chips, the first person's order can be written as this equation: $3f + 2c = 740$.
Write an equation for the second person's order and solve the simultaneous equations to find the cost of a fish and the cost of a portion of chips.

In this exercise, from the information given, you will need to form two equations which are simultaneously true and then solve them.

Exercise 9

1 Two customers came into a shop. The first customer ordered a hamburger and a packet of fries. The cost was £1.55.
The second customer bought 3 hamburgers and 2 packets of fries which cost £4.05.
How much does a hamburger cost? How much does a packet of fries cost?

2 The sum of a pair of numbers is 59. The difference between them is 17. What are the numbers?

3 In a right-angled triangle, one of the smaller angles is 24° more than the other one. What size are the two angles?

4 A party of 10 adults and 4 children book some tickets to visit a pleasure park. The cost is £176. On the day of the visit, two of the children cannot go, but 3 more adults join the party. The extra to be paid at the gate is £24. What are the entrance fees for adults, and for children?

5 The perimeter of an isosceles triangle is 30cm.
Two of the sides are each 2cm longer than the shortest side.
What are the measurements of the sides of the triangle?

6 In six years' time, a mother will be three times as old as her daughter. Two years ago, she was seven times as old. How old are they now?

Using factorisation to solve quadratic equations

A quadratic equation is one involving x^2.

Examples: $x^2 = 16$ $\quad 3x^2 + 2x = 0$ $\quad x^2 + 2x - 5 = 0$

On page 225 and in Exercise 3 you found that quadratic equations may have two, one or no solutions.

DISCUSSION POINT

Can you find two solutions for each of these equations?

$x^2 = 16$ $\quad 5x^2 = 20$ $\quad 3x^2 - 75 = 0$

$x^2 = 3x$ $\quad x^2 + 2x = 0$ $\quad 4x^2 - x = 0$

Exercise 10

1 Solve these equations.

(a) $2a^2 - 15 = 17$ (b) $3(b^2 - 14) = 66$ (c) $32c^2 - 5 = 13$

(d) $10(d^2 - 2) = 28 - 17d^2$

2 Solve these equations.

(a) $x(x + 1) = 0$ (b) $x(x - 3) = 0$ (c) $x(x + 2) = 0$

(d) $x(4 + x) = 0$ (e) $x(5 - x) = 0$ (f) $x(2x - 1) = 0$

(g) $2x(x - 3) = 0$

3 Solve these equations by first factorising them.

(a) $x^2 + 7x = 0$ (b) $x^2 - 2x = 0$ (c) $x^2 + 3x = 0$

(d) $x^2 + 5x = 0$ (e) $6x - x^2 = 0$ (f) $2x^2 + x = 0$

(g) $2x^2 + 4x = 0$

4 First, rearrange these equations so they are written in the form $ax^2 + bx = 0$. Then, solve them by factorising.

(a) $x^2 = 5x$ (b) $-x^2 = 2x$ (c) $3x^2 = 9x$

(d) $4x^2 = 5x$ (e) $4x = 6x^2$ (f) $2x^2 = x$

(g) $4x^2 = -2x$

5 Why are there always two solutions for equations in the form $ax^2 + bx = 0$?

DISCUSSION POINT

What are the solutions to $(x + 4)(x - 3) = 0$?

How does this help you to solve the equation $x^2 + x - 12 = 0$?

Can you find two solutions to each of these equations?

$x^2 - 4x - 21 = 0$ $x^2 - 8x + 15 = 0$ $x^2 + 3x + 1 = 0$

Here is another example.

Solve $2x^2 + 5x - 3 = 0$

Factorise: $(2x - 1)(x + 3) = 0$

To make zero, one of the factors must be zero.

Either $2x - 1 = 0$ or $x + 3 = 0$.

$\Rightarrow$ $x = \frac{1}{2}$ or $x = -3$

EXERCISE 11

1 Solve these equations.

(a) $(x + 1)(x + 5) = 0$ (b) $(x + 2)(x + 3) = 0$ (c) $(x + 1)(x + 4) = 0$

(d) $(x + 1)(x + 3) = 0$ (e) $(x + 4)(x - 3) = 0$ (f) $(x - 3)(x + 3) = 0$

(g) $(x - 1)(x + 1) = 0$ (h) $(x + 2)(x - 5) = 0$ (i) $(x - 4)(x - 5) = 0$

2 Solve these equations.

(a) $(2x + 1)(x - 2) = 0$ (b) $(x + 1)(3x + 2) = 0$ (c) $(2x - 1)(x + 4) = 0$

(d) $(x + 1)(2x + 3) = 0$ (e) $(3x + 1)(x - 2) = 0$ (f) $(5x + 1)(x + 3) = 0$

(g) $(x + 1)(4x - 1) = 0$ (h) $(3x + 1)^2 = 0$ (i) $(x + 4)(5 - x) = 0$

3 In the factorised form there are generally two solutions.
What is the special case, when there is only one solution?

4 Factorise these equations to solve them.

(a) $x^2 + 2x + 1 = 0$ (b) $x^2 + 4x + 3 = 0$ (c) $x^2 + 6x + 8 = 0$

(d) $x^2 + 6x + 5 = 0$ (e) $x^2 + 8x + 12 = 0$ (f) $x^2 + 7x + 12 = 0$

(g) $x^2 + 8x + 15 = 0$ (h) $x^2 + 6x + 9 = 0$ (i) $x^2 + 4x + 4 = 0$

5 Factorise these equations to solve them.

(a) $x^2 + x - 2 = 0$ (b) $x^2 - x - 6 = 0$ (c) $x^2 + 3x - 4 = 0$

(d) $x^2 + 4x - 5 = 0$ (e) $x^2 - x - 12 = 0$ (f) $x^2 + 4x - 12 = 0$

(g) $x^2 - 2x - 8 = 0$ (h) $x^2 + 2x - 15 = 0$ (i) $x^2 - 4x - 12 = 0$

6 Factorise these equations to solve them.

(a) $x^2 - 2x + 1 = 0$ (b) $x^2 - 4x + 3 = 0$ (c) $x^2 - 6x + 8 = 0$

(d) $x^2 - 6x + 5 = 0$ (e) $x^2 - 8x + 16 = 0$ (f) $x^2 - 7x + 10 = 0$

(g) $x^2 - 6x + 9 = 0$ (h) $x^2 - 9x + 20 = 0$ (i) $x^2 - 4x + 4 = 0$

7 Rearrange these equations in the form $x^2 + bx + c = 0$ to solve them.

(a) $x^2 - 2x = 15$ (b) $x^2 + 6x = 7$ (c) $x^2 + 15 = 8x$

(d) $x^2 = 8x - 12$ (e) $4x + 5 = x^2$ (f) $x = 2 - x^2$

(g) $10 - x^2 = 3x$ (h) $x^2 = 2x + 8$ (i) $5x - x^2 = 6$

8 Factorise these equations to solve them.

(a) $2x^2 + 3x + 1 = 0$ (b) $3x^2 - 7x + 2 = 0$ (c) $3x^2 + 11x + 6 = 0$

(d) $2x^2 + x - 1 = 0$ (e) $6x^2 - x - 2 = 0$ (f) $6x^2 - 13x - 5 = 0$

(g) $5x^2 - 9x - 2 = 0$ (h) $4x^2 + 5x - 6 = 0$ (i) $2x^2 + 3x - 20 = 0$

(j) $10x^2 + 3x = 4$ (k) $6x^2 - 5x = 6$ (l) $7x^2 = 3 - 20x$

Not all quadratic equations can be solved by factorising, because some quadratics do not have obvious factors. These equations can be solved using graphs (see the next two sections). They can also be solved by algebraic methods, which are explained in *Book 2*.

Quadratic equations and graphs

DISCUSSION POINT

The line $y = 12$ crosses the quadratic graph $y = x^2$ at two points.

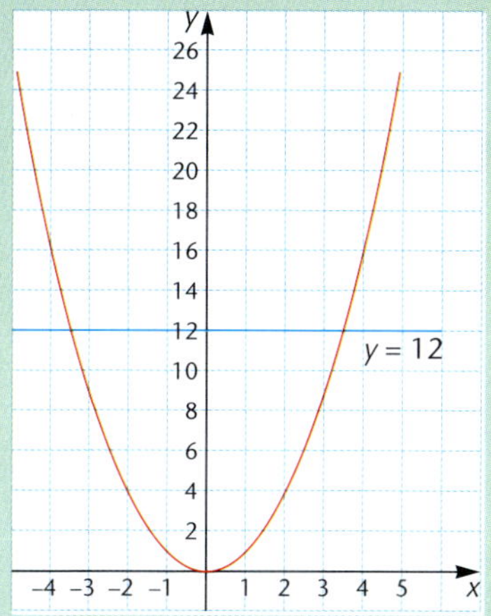

The x coordinates of these two points are the solutions of the equation $x^2 = 12$. What are the approximate solutions?

This diagram shows the graph of $y = x^2$ and the line $y = 4x + 3$.

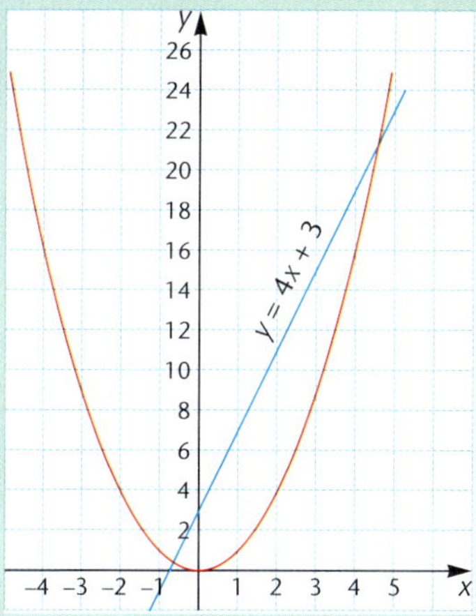

What are the solutions of $x^2 = 4x + 3$? Can you see they are also solutions of $x^2 - 4x - 3 = 0$?

Resource Sheet M: $y = x^2$

EXERCISE 12

1 Draw the line $y = 20$ on the graph of $y = x^2$ to solve $x^2 = 20$.

2 Draw a line on the graph of $y = x^2$ to solve $x^2 = 15$.

3 Draw a line on the graph of $y = x^2$ to solve $x^2 - 8 = 0$.

4 Explain how the graph shows you there are no solutions of $x^2 + 4 = 0$.

5 (a) Draw the line $y = 2x + 3$ on the graph of $y = x^2$.

(b) What are the x coordinates of the points where the two graphs cross? (These are the solutions of $x^2 = 2x + 3$.)

(c) What are the solutions to $x^2 - 2x - 3 = 0$?

6 (a) Draw the line $y = 4x - 3$ on the graph of $y = x^2$ to find values of x so that $x^2 = 4x - 3$.

(b) What are the solutions to $x^2 - 4x + 3 = 0$?

7 (a) Draw a line on the graph of $y = x^2$ to find values of x so that $x^2 = 10 - x$.

(b) Solve the equation $x^2 + x - 10 = 0$.

8 (a) Which line must be drawn on the graph of $y = x^2$ to solve $x^2 + x - 6 = 0$?

(b) Draw the line and solve it.

9 (a) Which line must be drawn on the graph of $y = x^2$ to solve $x^2 - 2x - 12 = 0$?

(b) Draw the line and solve it.

10 (a) Which line must be drawn on the graph of $y = x^2$ to solve $x^2 - 3x + 1 = 0$?

(b) Draw the line and solve it.

11 (a) Which line must be drawn on the graph of $y = x^2$ to solve $2x^2 + 3x - 12 = 0$?

(b) Draw the line and solve it.

DISCUSSION POINT

This is the graph of $y = x^2 + 2x - 3$.
Use the graph to solve $x^2 + 2x - 3 = 0$ and $x^2 + 2x - 3 = 5$.
Can you see how to solve $x^2 + 2x = 0$ on the same graph?
What about $x^2 + 2x - 5 = 0$ and $x^2 + 2x - 2 = 0$?

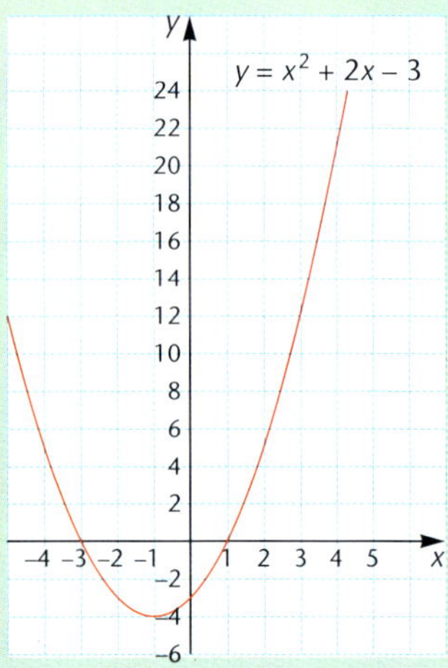

▶ Graph paper

You will need to keep the graphs you draw in this exercise for use in Exercise 14.

EXERCISE 13

1 For $-4 \leq x \leq 3$, draw the graph of $y = x^2 + 2x$.
Use your graph to solve these equations.

(a) $x^2 + 2x = 0$ (b) $x^2 + 2x = 8$ (c) $x^2 + 2x = 3$

(d) $x^2 + 2x - 7 = 0$ (e) $x^2 + 2x + 2 = 0$ (f) $x^2 + 2x + 1 = 0$

2 For $-5 \leq x \leq 4$, draw the graph of $y = x^2 + 3x - 2$.
Use it to solve these equations.

(a) $x^2 + 3x - 2 = 0$ (b) $x^2 + 3x - 2 = -2$ (c) $x^2 + 3x - 2 = 8$

(d) $x^2 + 3x + 1 = 0$ (e) $x^2 + 3x + 2 = 0$ (f) $x^2 + 3x - 1 = 0$

3 For $-2 \leq x \leq 5$, draw the graph of $y = x^2 - 3x - 1$.
Use it to solve these equations.

(a) $x^2 - 3x - 1 = 0$ (b) $x^2 - 3x = 0$ (c) $x^2 - 3x = 5$

DISCUSSION POINT

This is the graph of $y = x^2 - 4x - 3$.

How can it be used to solve these equations?

$x^2 - 4x - 3 = x$

$x^2 - 4x - 3 = 6 - 2x$

$x^2 - 4x - 1 = 0$

$x^2 - 3x - 3 = 0$

$x^2 - 6x + 2 = 0$

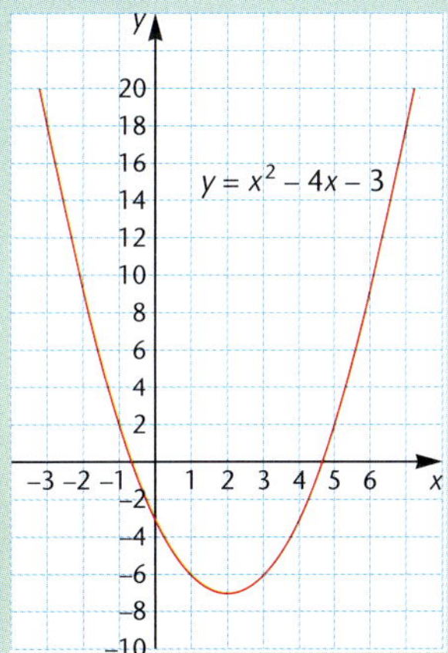

▶ Graph paper

EXERCISE 14

1 Use your graph of $y = x^2 + 2x$ from Question 1 in Exercise 13 to solve these equations.

(a) $x^2 + 2x = x$ (b) $x^2 + 2x = 2 - x$

(c) $x^2 - 3x - 3 = 0$ (d) $x^2 + 3x - 1 = 0$

2 Use your graph of $y = x^2 + 3x - 2$ from Question 2 in Exercise 13 to solve these equations.

(a) $x^2 + 3x - 2 = x$ (b) $x^2 + 3x - 2 = 3 + x$

(c) $x^2 + 4x - 2 = 0$ (d) $x^2 + x = 1$

3 For $-2 \le x \le 3$, draw the graph of $y = 2x^2 - x - 2$.
Then, use it to solve these equations.

(a) $2x^2 - x - 3 = 0$ (b) $2x^2 - x = 0$

(c) $2x^2 - 3x - 2 = 0$ (d) $2x^2 = 5$

4 Draw one graph to solve these equations.

(a) $x^2 - 3x + 1 = 0$ (b) $x^2 - 3x + 3 = 0$

(c) $x^2 - 4x = 6$ (d) $x^2 + x - 4 = 0$

Solving equations by trial and improvement

DISCUSSION POINT

Most equations are not solvable by neat methods, like factorising.
The trial-and-improvement method works for *any* equation, but it can be laborious.
A computer or programmable calculator could make light work of the process.
To solve $x^3 + 5x^2 = 10$, look at the graph of $y = x^3 + 5x^2$ and the line $y = 10$.

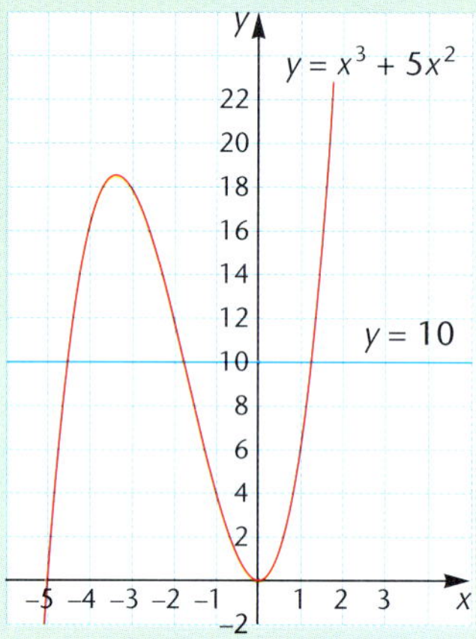

This shows there are three solutions.
One of them is close to –2.
What whole numbers are the other two solutions close to?
These provide the first guesses.
More accurate solutions can then be found by trial and improvement.
Use trial and improvement to find the three solutions of this equation, correct to 2 decimal places.

If you want a solution correct to 2 decimal places, you need to check whether 5 in the third decimal place gives an answer which is too big or too small.

Exercise 15

1 The solution of the equation $x^3 - 3x^2 = 5$ is close to 3.
Use the method of trial and improvement to find the solution, correct to 2 decimal places.

2 Use the method of trial and improvement to find both solutions of each of these quadratic equations, correct to 2 decimal places.

(a) $x^2 - 3x + 1 = 0$ (b) $x^2 + 6x = 1$ (c) $x^2 + x = 5$ (d) $x^2 + 7x + 5 = 0$

3 One solution of $3\sin x + 4\cos x = 4$ is close to 70°.
Use the method of trial and improvement to find this solution, correct to 1 decimal place.

4 Use the method of trial and improvement to find the solution of $5^x = 20$, correct to 2 decimal places.

5 Use the method of trial and improvement to find the fifth root of 70000, correct to 2 decimal places.

6 A cylindrical tin can is being designed to be 15cm high.
Its surface area is to be 500cm². What will the radius have to be?

7 A right-angled triangle with one side 7cm, must have a perimeter of 20cm.
What will the shortest side have to be?

COURSEWORK OPPORTUNITY

No solutions

The equation $x^2 + x + 3 = 0$ has no solutions.
Several different graphs can be drawn to show this. Here is one.

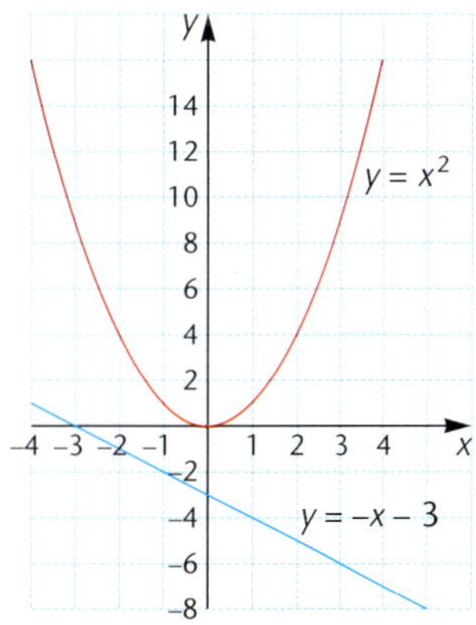

- Find some values for c so that $x^2 + x + c = 0$ will have some solutions.
- What about $x^2 - x + c = 0$, $x^2 + 2x + c = 0$, $x^2 - 2x + c = 0$, ...?
- Investigate the number of solutions of equations of the form $x^2 + bx + c = 0$.

CHAPTER SUMMARY

Solving simultaneous equations by drawing graphs

Find where the graphs of these equations intersect.

$x + y = 5$

$y = 2x + 1$

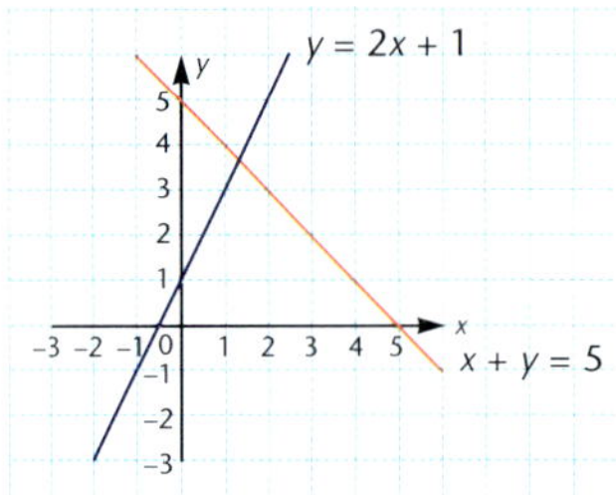

The lines appear to cross at $(1\frac{1}{3}, 3\frac{2}{3})$ so the solution is $x = 1\frac{1}{3}$, $y = 3\frac{2}{3}$.

This is the exact solution, which can be checked by substitution.

Solving simultaneous linear equations by eliminating one of the variables.

Example 1

	$3x - 4y = 10$	①
	$2x + 3y = 1$	②
① × 3	$9x - 12y = 30$	③
② × 4	$8x + 12y = 4$	④
③ + ④	$17x = 34$	
	$x = 2$	
In ①	$6 - 4y = 10$	
	$y = -1$	
Check in ②	$2x + 3y = 4 - 3 = 1$ ✓	

So, $x = 2$ and $y = -1$

Example 2

$4x - 5y = 19$ ①

$x = 3y - 4$ ②

Substitute ② in ①

$4(3y - 4) - 5y = 19$

$12y - 16 - 5y = 19$

$7y = 35$

$y = 5$

In ② $x = 15 - 4 = 11$

Check in ① $4x - 5y = 44 - 25 = 19$ ✓

So, $x = 11$ and $y = 5$.

Solving quadratic equations by factorisation

To solve $x^2 - 3x - 4 = 0$, first factorise.

$x^2 - 3x - 4 = (x - 4)(x + 1)$

$(x - 4)(x + 1) = 0$

To make zero, one of the factors must be zero.

Either $x - 4 = 0$ or $x + 1 = 0$.

$\Rightarrow$ $x = 4$ or $x = -1$

Solving quadratic equations by drawing graphs

To solve $x^2 - 3x - 1 = 0$, draw the graph of $y = x^2 - 3x - 1$ and see where it crosses the x-axis.

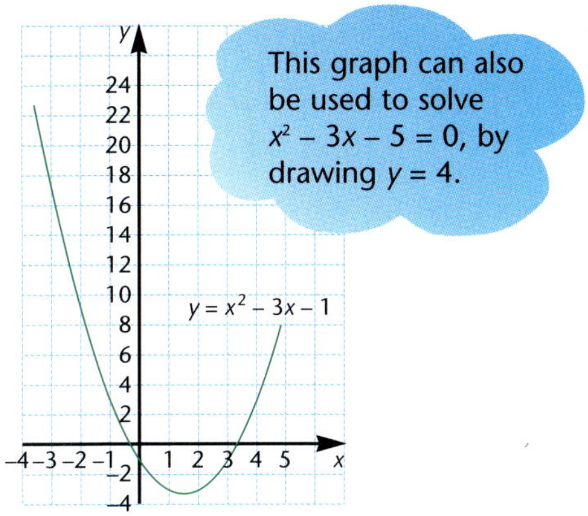

Notice that $x^2 - 3x - 1 = 0$ when $x = -0.3$ and when $x = 3.3$.

Another way of solving $x^2 - 3x - 1 = 0$ is to draw the graphs of $y = 3x + 1$ and $y = x^2$, and to see where they intersect.

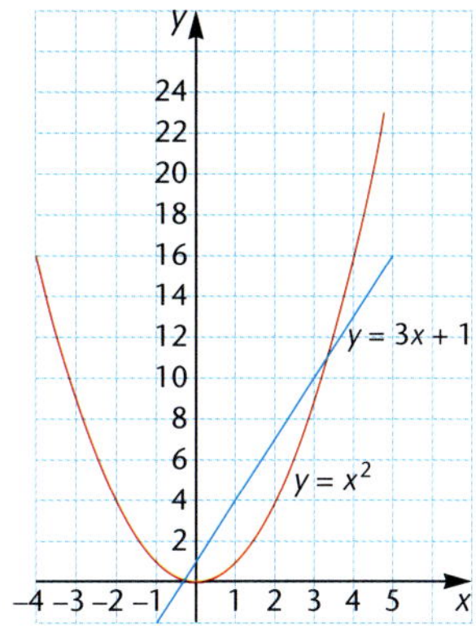

Notice that $x^2 = 3x + 1$ when $x = -0.3$ and when $x = 3.3$.

There are many other pairs of graphs whose intersection solves this quadratic, for example $y = x^2 - 4x$ and $y = 1 - x$.

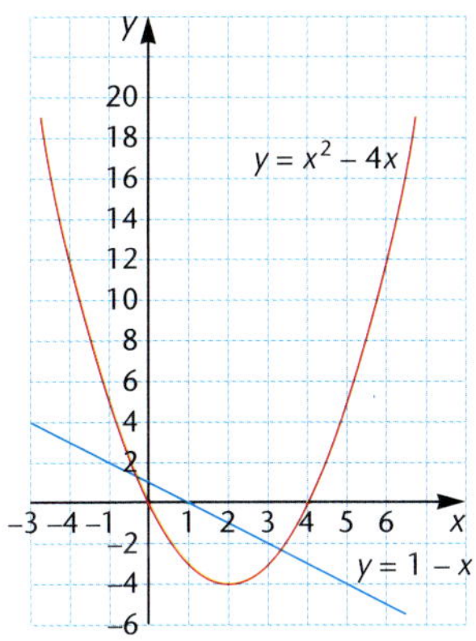

Notice that $x^2 - 4x = 1 - x$ when $x = -0.3$ and when $x = 3.3$.

Solving equations by the method of trial and improvement

To solve: $p^5 = 144$

Try $p = 2$: $2^5 = 32$, which is too small

Try $p = 3$: $3^5 = 243$, which is too large

Try $p = 2.5$ which is halfway between 2 and 3: $2.5^5 = 97.65625$, which is too small

Continue, trying values of p until the result is close enough, for the accuracy you require.

The solution is $p = 2.70$ (2 d.p.). To be sure that it is 2.70 and not 2.71, you need to check 2.705.

CHAPTER 14

GEOMETRY

This chapter is about:

- solid shapes and nets, including symmetry
- triangles, including the exterior angle theorem
- congruence
- locus
- ruler and compass constructions
- circle theorems.

Solid shapes and nets

Solid shapes can be made from nets.
Here are two possible nets of a cube.

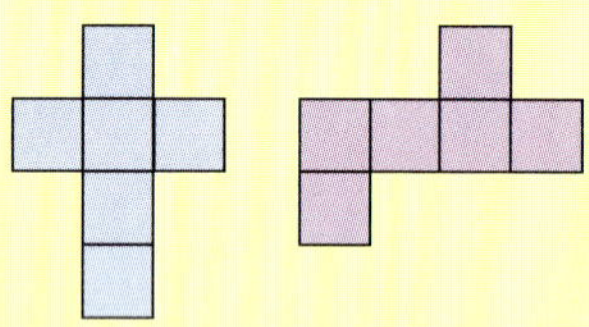

This is *not* the net of a cube.

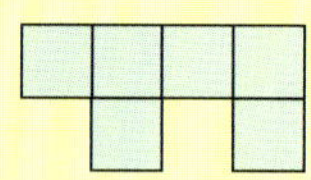

▶ Resource Sheet A: *Isometric dot*

A shape made of squares joined exactly edge to edge is called a **polyomino**.

A polyomino made of five squares is called a **pentomino**.

EXERCISE 1

1 Here are two different pentominoes.

(**a**) Draw all the different pentominoes (including the ones shown in the picture). Be sure that you have found them all.

(**b**) Describe the symmetry of each of your pentominoes.

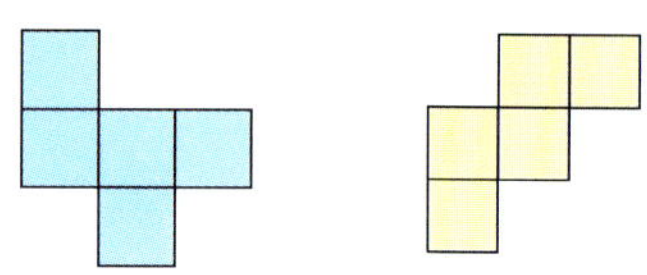

2 Which pentominoes are nets of a square box (a cube with one of its faces removed)?

Justifying a solution

3 Which of these hexominoes is a net of a cube?

A polyomino made of six squares is called a **hexomino**.

4 (a) Draw *all* the hexominoes which are nets of a cube.
Explain how you know you have found them all.

(b) Describe the symmetry of each of your nets.

A shape made of equilateral triangles joined exactly edge to edge is called a **polyiamond**.

5 Here is one tetriamond.

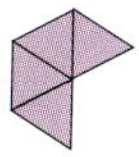

A polyiamond made of four triangles is called a **tetriamond**.

(a) Draw all the different tetriamonds.

(b) Which tetriamonds are nets of a regular tetrahedron?

6 Which of these statements are possible for a cuboid?

A: None of its faces is a square.

B: One of its faces is a square.

C: Two of its faces are squares.

D: Three of its faces are squares.

E: Four of its faces are squares.

F: Five of its faces are squares.

G: Six of its faces are squares.

7 Some of the faces of a cuboid are squares with area $1\,cm^2$.
Some of the faces are rectangles with area $2\,cm^2$.

(a) Draw a rough sketch of the cuboid.

(b) Draw two different nets of this cuboid.

(c) What different types of symmetry are possible for nets of this cuboid?
Draw a net to show each possible type of symmetry.

8 Which of these is a net of a cuboid?

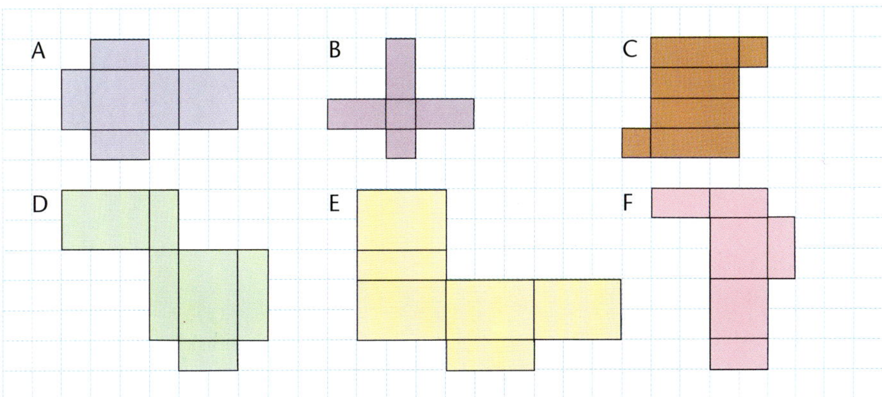

An **octiamond** is a polyiamond made from eight triangles.

9 Draw all the octiamonds which are nets of a regular octahedron.

A regular octahedron

These pictures show a net and an isometric drawing of a cube model made from five cubes.

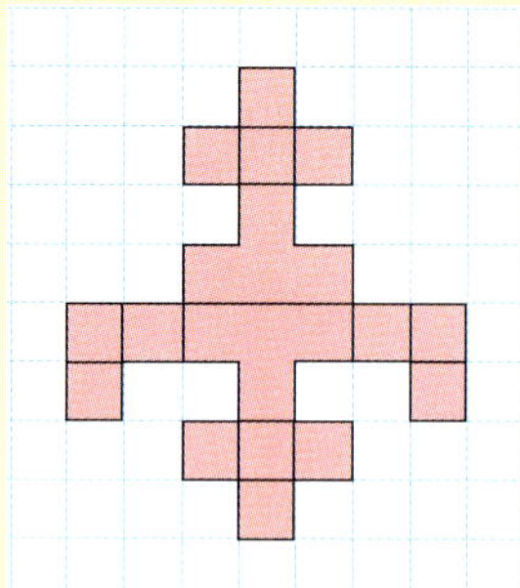

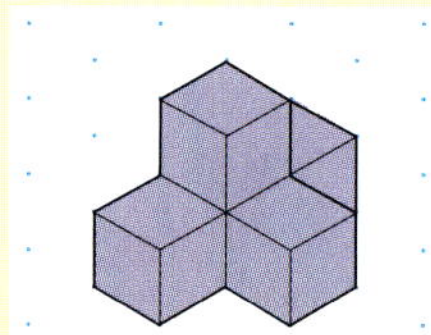

Some cube models have **mirror symmetry**.

The blue half of this model is the mirror image of the red half.

Some cube models have **rotational symmetry** about an **axis of symmetry**.

The **order** of rotational symmetry is the number of positions in which the solid looks the same when you rotate it.

This model has rotational symmetry of order 4.

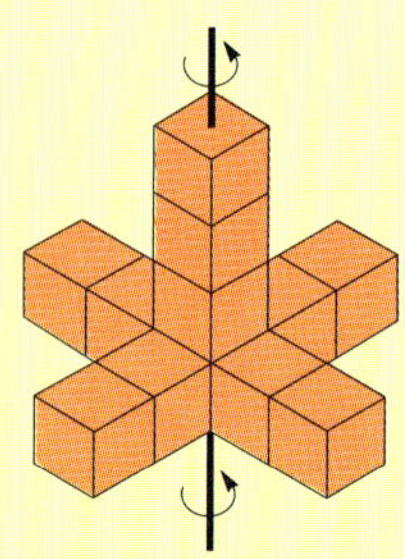

DISCUSSION POINT

Discuss what a **triangular prism** is.

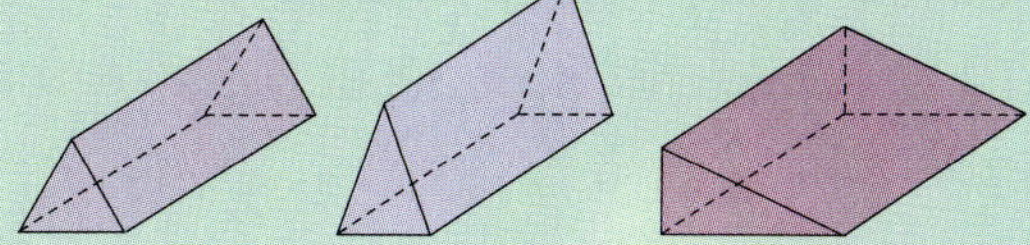

- How many faces, edges and vertices could it have?
- How many planes of symmetry could it have?
- What rotational symmetry could it have?

What symmetries could a **hexagonal prism** have?

What is a regular hexagonal pyramid?

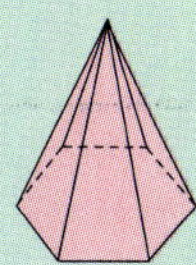

- How many faces, edges and vertices does it have?
- How many planes of symmetry does it have?
- What rotational symmetry does it have?

None of the faces of this cuboid is square.

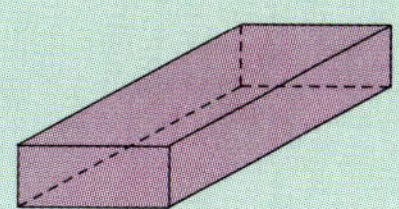

- How many planes of symmetry does it have?
- What rotational symmetry does it have?

What is a **truncated pyramid**?

- Resource Sheet A: *Isometric dot*
- Cubes
- Scissors

EXERCISE 2

1 Here is an isometric drawing of a cube model.

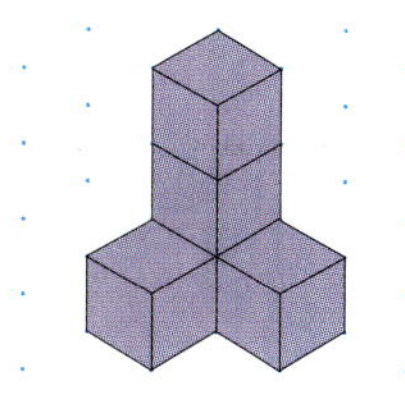

(a) Make the model from cubes.

(b) Describe the symmetry of the model.

(c) Draw a net for the model.

2 (a) Make a model (not a cuboid) from four cubes.

(b) Describe the symmetry of your model.

(c) Draw a rough sketch of your model.

(d) Make an isometric drawing of your model.

(e) Draw a net for your model.

3 Here is an isometric drawing of a cube model.

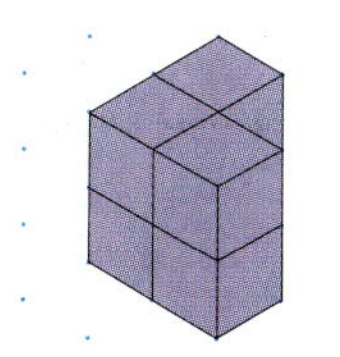

(a) What is the smallest number of cubes the model could have?

(b) What is the largest number of cubes the model could have?

(c) Make the model with the smallest number of cubes.

(d) Draw a net of the model you have made.

4 Here is the net of a cube model.

(**a**) Make the model from cubes.

(**b**) Describe the symmetry of the model.

(**c**) Make an isometric drawing of the model.

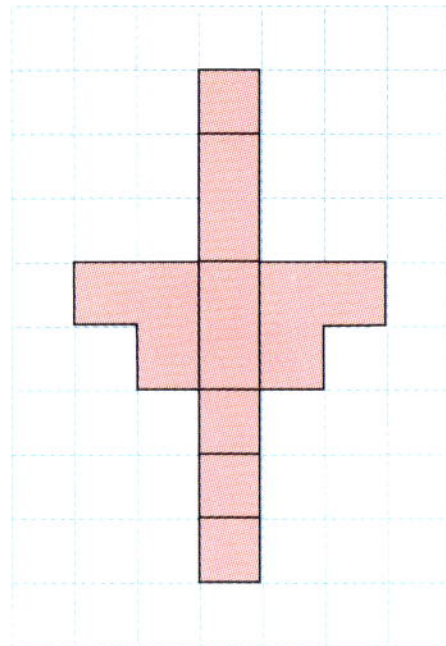

5 This is a picture of a regular tetrahedron with two of its nets.

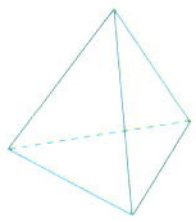

Regular tetrahedron

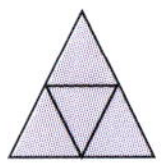

Net A

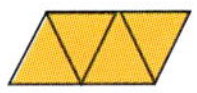

Net B

For each net, copy the picture of the tetrahedron and show which edges of the tetrahedron you would cut so that the tetrahedron could then be unfolded to give the net.

6 This is a picture of a cube with three of its nets.

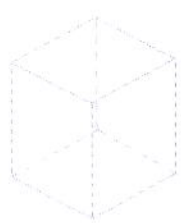

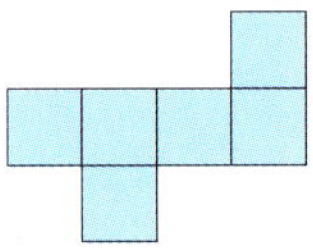

Net A

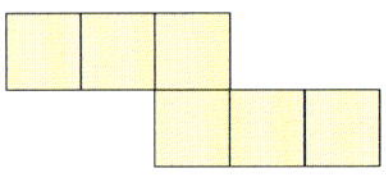

Net B

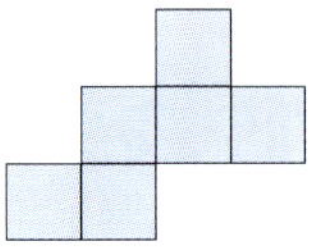

Net C

For each net, copy the picture of the cube and show which edges of the cube you would cut so that the cube could then be unfolded to give the net.

7 Which of these statements are possible for a tetrahedron?
Where it is possible, draw a net of a tetrahedron which satisfies the condition.

A: All its faces are congruent.

B: Exactly three of its faces are congruent.

C: It has two pairs of congruent faces.

D: It has one pair of congruent faces.

E: No two of its faces are congruent.

8 This is the net of a tetrahedron consisting of congruent isosceles triangles.

(**a**) Draw all the other arrangements of the four triangles which are also nets of the tetrahedron.

(**b**) Describe the symmetry of this tetrahedron.

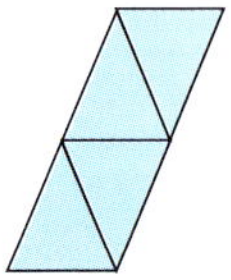

9 Describe the symmetry of a regular tetrahedron.

10 This is a picture of a regular octahedron with three of its nets.

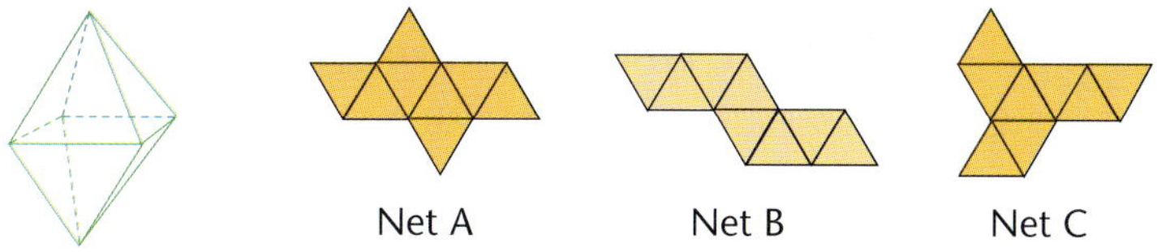

For each net, copy the picture of the octahedron and show which edges of the octahedron you would cut so that the octahedron could then be unfolded to give the net.

11 A solid has six faces made of rectangles and trapeziums.
Draw a rough sketch of what this solid might look like if four of the faces are

(**a**) rectangles (**b**) trapeziums

12 Describe a solid which has six faces if

(**a**) five of the faces are identical and one is different

(**b**) four of the faces are identical and the other two are different, but identical to each other

(**c**) all the faces are regular polygons, but it is *not* a cube

13 Describe a solid which has seven faces if

(**a**) six of the faces are identical and one is different

(**b**) all the faces are regular polygons, four of them are identical and the other three are different but identical to each other

14 Describe a solid which has eight faces if

(**a**) seven of the faces are identical and one is different

(**b**) six of the faces are identical and the other two are different and different from each other

(**c**) all the faces are identical

An *n*-gon is a polygon with *n* sides.

15 The base of a pyramid is an *n*-gon.

(**a**) How many vertices does the pyramid have?

(**b**) How many edges does it have?

(**c**) How many faces does it have?

16 The cross-section of a prism is an *n*-gon.

(**a**) How many vertices does the prism have?

(**b**) How many edges does the prism have?

(**c**) How many faces does the prism have?

17 Describe a solid which has

(**a**) 6 faces, 8 vertices and 12 edges

(**b**) 4 faces, 4 vertices and 6 edges

(**c**) 11 faces, 11 vertices and 20 edges

(**d**) 18 faces, 32 vertices and 48 edges

(**e**) 10 faces, 7 vertices and 15 edges

18 Look at these solids.

A

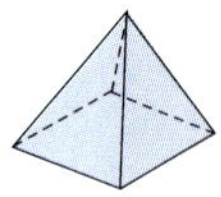

Square-based pyramid

B

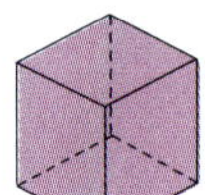

Cube

C

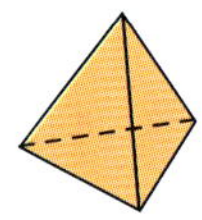

Regular tetrahedron

D

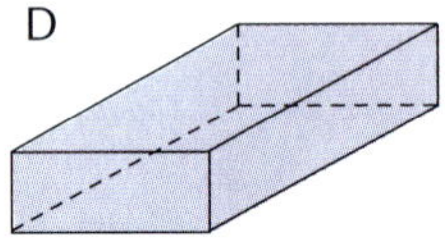

Cuboid

E

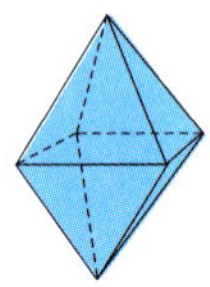

Regular octahedron

F

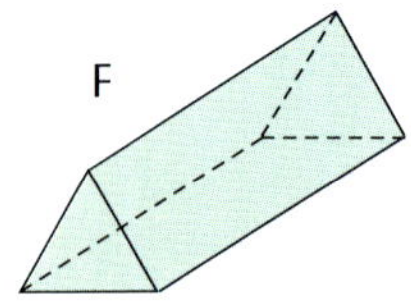

Equilateral triangular prism

> When a solid is cut into two pieces by a plane, the new face created on each piece is called a **cross-section** of the solid.

(**a**) Which of the solids have a cross-section which is an equilateral triangle? Explain how to cut the solids to get this cross-section.

(**b**) Which of the solids have a cross-section which is a square? Explain how to cut the solids to get this cross-section.

(**c**) Which of the solids have a cross-section which is a right-angled triangle?

19 Each of these pictures shows a way of cutting a solid in half. All the edges of the original solids are 4 cm long.

A

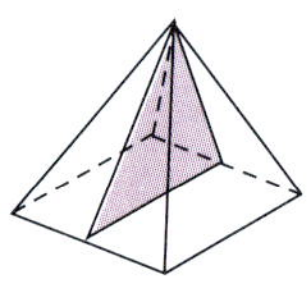

Regular square-based pyramid

B

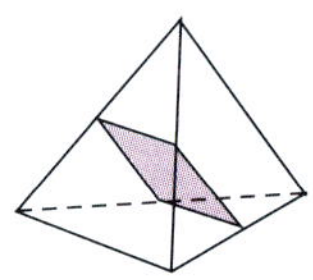

Regular tetrahedron

C

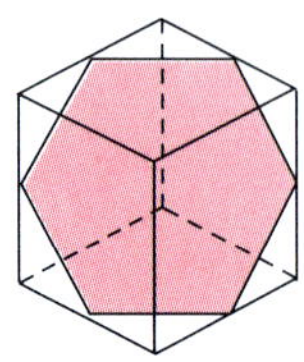

Cube

Draw accurately a net for one of the halves of each of these solids.

20 (**a**) A cuboid has two of its faces square.

(**i**) How many planes of symmetry does it have?

(**ii**) How many axes of symmetry does it have, and what is the order of rotational symmetry about each axis?

(**b**) (**i**) How many planes of symmetry does a cube have?

(**ii**) How many axes of symmetry does a cube have, and what is the order of rotational symmetry about each axis?

Triangles, including the exterior angle theorem

An exterior angle of a triangle is an angle made outside a triangle by extending one of its sides.

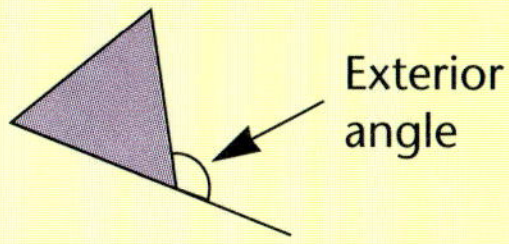

In this tessellation of triangles, all the red angles are equal, all the blue angles are equal, and all the green angles are equal.

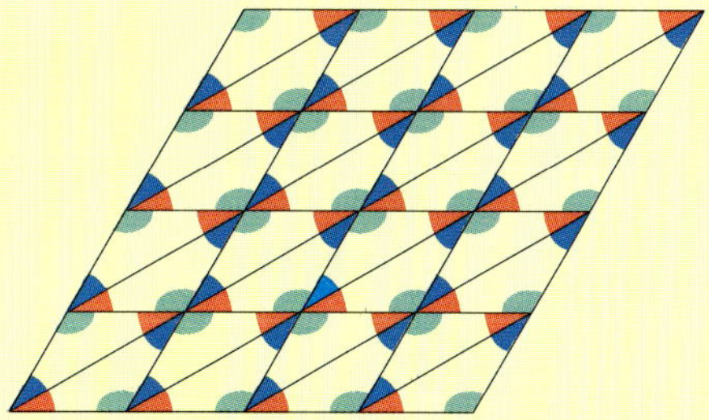

Here is a small part of this tessellation.

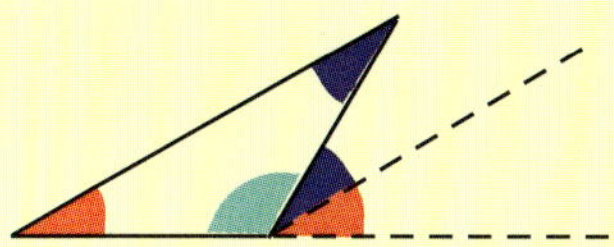

From this, you can see that the exterior angle at one vertex of a triangle is equal to the sum of the interior angles at the other two vertices.
This is called the **exterior angle theorem**.

EXERCISE 3

1 Sketch each of these drawings and find the size of the angle labelled *x*.

A

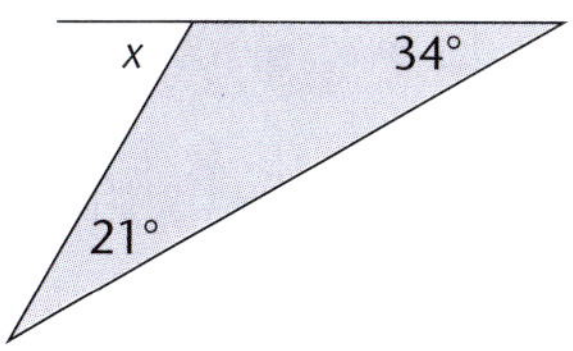

B

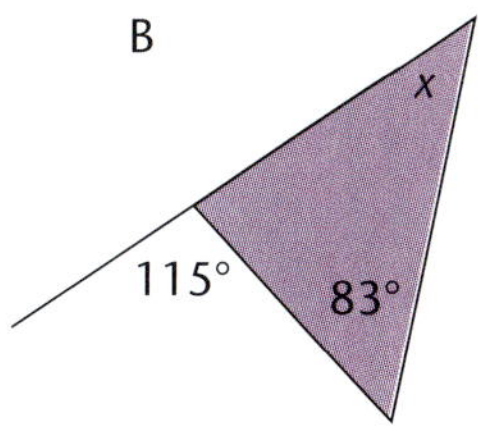

C

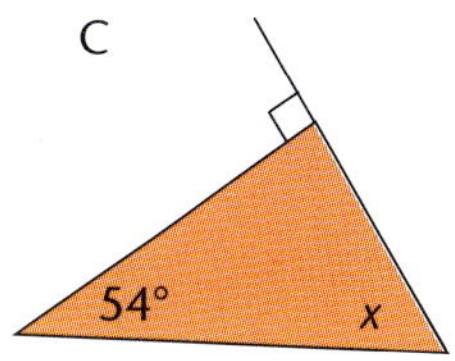

D

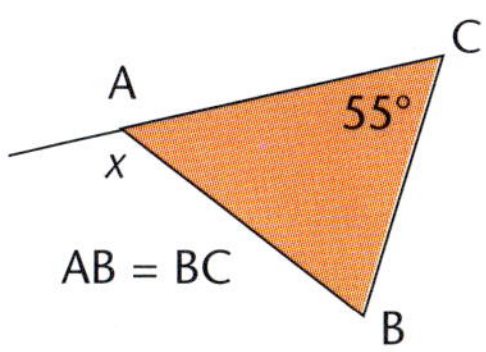

E

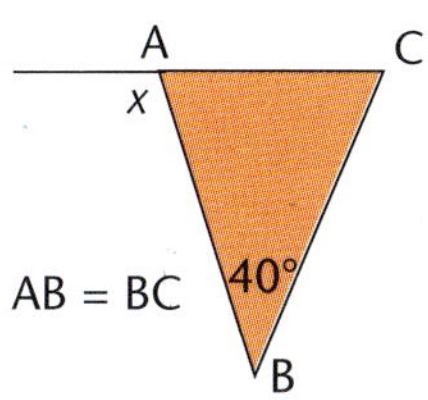

F

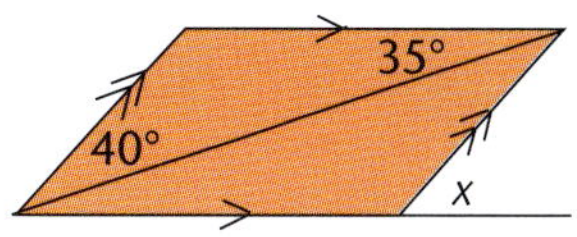

2 A right-angled triangle has an exterior angle of 125°.
What is the size of the smallest angle of the triangle?

3 The exterior angles at two vertices of a triangle are 120° and 140°.
Find the interior angle at the other vertex.

4 (a) An isosceles triangle has an exterior angle of 70°.
Find the equal interior angles of the triangle.
Is there only one answer?

(b) An isosceles triangle has an exterior angle of 140°.
Find the equal interior angles of the triangle.
Is there only one answer?

EXERCISE 4

1 Triangle ABC has been divided by the line BD. ∠ABD = 80° and AB = BD.

(a) Find the angles of triangle ABD.

(b) If triangle BDC is isosceles, find the three angles of triangle ABC.

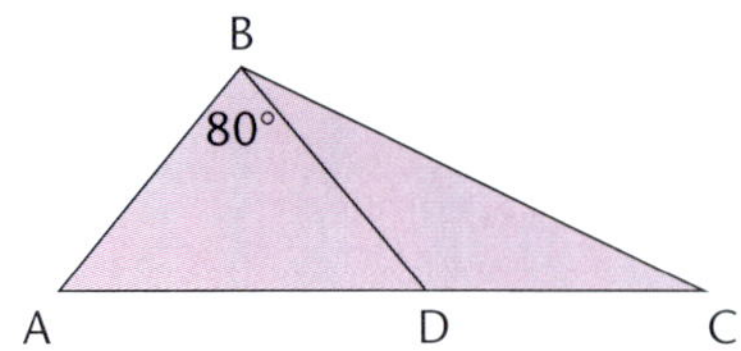

2 Triangle EFG has been divided by the line HG.
The lines EH, HG and FG are all the same length.

(a) Copy the diagram and mark which angles are equal to x and which are equal to y.

(b) What is the relationship between x and y?

(c) Find, in terms of x, the size of angle HGF.

(d) If triangle EFG is isosceles, find the values of x and y, and hence the angles of triangle EFG.

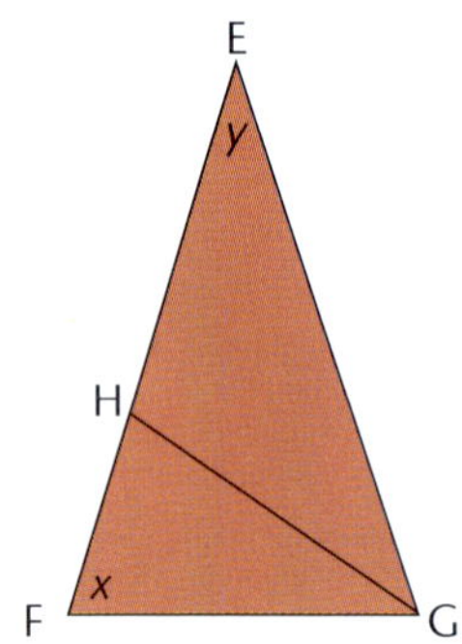

3 Triangle ABC has been divided into two isosceles triangles by the line CD.
The lines DA, DB and DC are all the same length.

(a) Copy the diagram. Use the letters x and y to mark equal angles.

(b) What is the relationship between x and y?

(c) Find the three angles of triangle ABC in terms of x.

(d) If triangle ABC is isosceles what are its three angles?

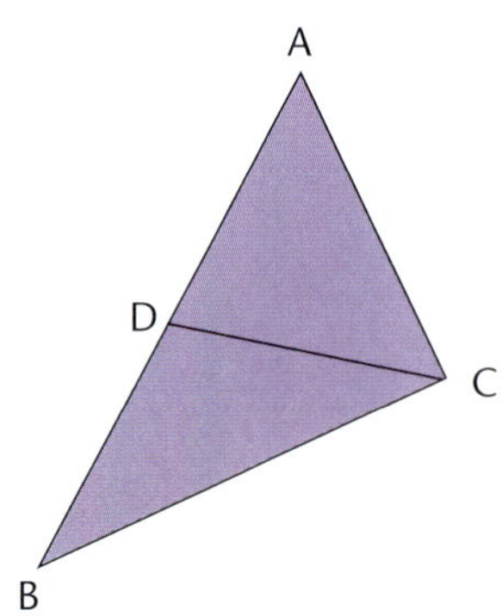

For Question 4, part (b), there are two possible answers.

4 Triangle ABC has been divided into two triangles by the line BD.
Lines BC and DC are equal in length,
and lines DB and AD are equal in length.

(**a**) Find the relationship between x and y.

(**b**) If triangle ABC is isosceles find its three angles.

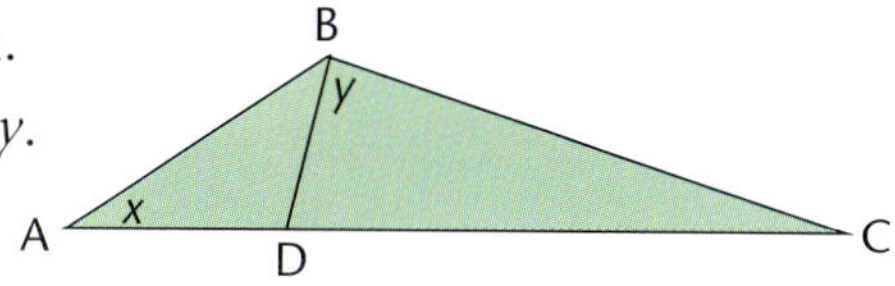

Congruence

▶ Resource Sheet A: *Isometric dot*
▶ Resource Sheet N: *Mystic hexagons*

This picture shows a right-angled isosceles triangle, cut into two congruent pieces.

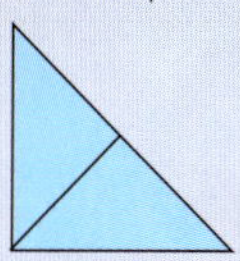

EXERCISE 5

1 Which of these triangles can be cut into two congruent pieces?

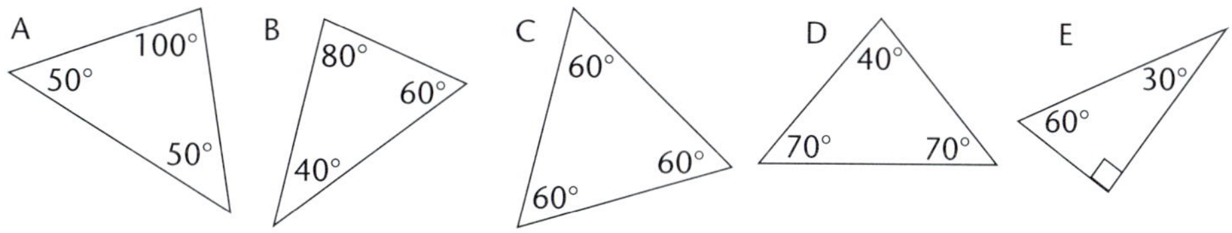

2 Which triangles in Question 1 can be cut into *three* congruent pieces?

3 Which triangles in Question 1 can be cut into *four* congruent pieces?

4 Which of these shapes can be cut into two congruent pieces?
If so, explain how.

A: Parallelogram
B: Kite
C: Isosceles trapezium
D: Right-angled trapezium

5 Which of the shapes in Question 4 can be cut into *three* congruent pieces?

6 Which of the shapes in Question 4 can be cut into *four* congruent pieces?

7 Which of the shapes in Question 4 can be cut into *eight* congruent pieces?

8 Which of these statements are true?

A: Any shape with line symmetry can be cut into two congruent pieces.
B: Any shape with rotational symmetry of order 2 can be cut into two congruent pieces.
C: Any shape with rotational symmetry can be cut into two congruent pieces.
D: Any shape with rotational symmetry of order 3 can be cut into three congruent pieces.
E: Any shape with two lines of symmetry can be cut into four congruent pieces.
F: Any shape with two lines of symmetry can be cut into eight congruent pieces.

Making and justifying generalisations

If a statement is true, explain how you know where to cut the shape.
If it is not true, give one example to disprove it.

A **mystic hexagon** is a regular hexagon with all its diagonals drawn.

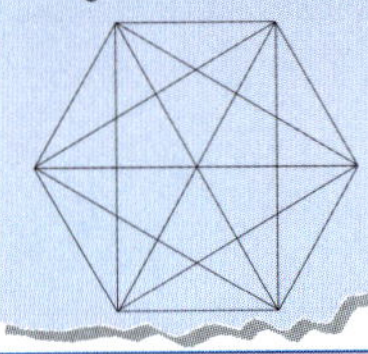

For Question 9, parts (e) and (f), leave your answer in surd form

9 Look at Resource Sheet N: *Mystic hexagons*.

(a) Into how many pieces is the mystic hexagon divided?

(b) The pieces are three different shapes. *Without* using a protractor, find all the angles of each of these three different shapes.

(c) What fraction of the hexagon is each of the three different shapes?

(d) What fraction of the mystic hexagon is the hexagon in the middle (the one coloured red in this diagram)?

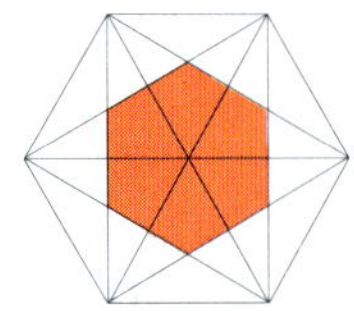

(e) Assume that the length of *one* side of the mystic hexagon is 6 units. Find the length of one of the sides of the red hexagon.

(f) Find the lengths of the sides of each of the three different shapes, you found the angles of, in part (b).

10 **(a)** Draw a regular hexagon on isometric dot paper. Divide it into *two* congruent pieces. In how many different ways can you do this?

(b) Draw a regular hexagon on isometric dot paper. Divide it into *three* congruent pieces. In how many different ways can you do this?

(c) Draw a regular hexagon on isometric dot paper. Divide it into *four* congruent pieces. In how many different ways can you do this?

(d) Can you divide a regular hexagon into five congruent pieces?
Into six? Seven? Eight? Nine?
In how many different ways can you do each?

Making and justifying generalisations

(e) Investigate ways of dividing a regular hexagon into n congruent pieces. For which values of n is this possible?

Loci

Exercise 6

▶ Compasses
▶ Resource Sheet O: *Loci*

For Questions 1 to 8, you need a copy of Resource Sheet O: *Loci*.

1 **(a)** On your copy of Resource Sheet O: *Loci*, mark two points which are the same distance from point A as from point B.

(b) Draw a line to show *all* the points which are the same distance from A as from B.

The line, drawn in part (b) of Question 1, is called the **locus** of points which are the same distance from A as from B.

2 Draw the locus of points which are 4 cm from C on the resource sheet.

3 Draw the locus of points which are 2 cm from the line *d*.

4 Draw the locus of points which are 1 cm from the circumference of circle E.

5 Draw the locus of points which are 1 cm from the perimeter of square F.

6 (a) Draw the points which are 4 cm from point G and 5 cm from point H.

(b) Draw the points which are 4 cm from point J and 5 cm from point K.

(c) Draw the points which are 4 cm from point L and 5 cm from point M.

7 Draw the locus of points which are the same distance from line *p* and line *q*.

8 Draw the locus of points which are the same distance from

(a) line *s* and line *t* (b) point U and point V

9 (a) Copy this design and shade all the points in the square which are nearer to A than to B.

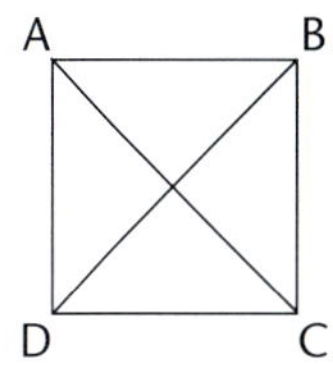

(b) Copy the design again and shade all the points in the square which are nearer to D than to B.

(c) Copy the design again and shade all the points in the square which are nearer to line AB than to line BC.

(d) Copy the design again and shade all the points in the square which are nearer to line AC than to line BD.

(e) Copy the design again and shade all the points in the square which are nearer to line AB than to line BD.

(f) Copy the design again and shade all the points in the square which are nearer to the perimeter of the square than to line BD.

Ruler and compass constructions

DISCUSSION POINT

It is often possible to **construct** lines, points and shapes accurately, *without* doing any measuring with a ruler or a protractor.

- You are given two points. Imagine a point which is the same distance from each of these points. Now imagine another.
  Discuss how to use a ruler and compasses to construct the locus of all points which are the same distance from each of these points.
  What is the angle between the locus and the line joining the two points?
- You are given two lines which intersect.
  Imagine a point which is the same distance from each of these two lines.
  Now imagine another.

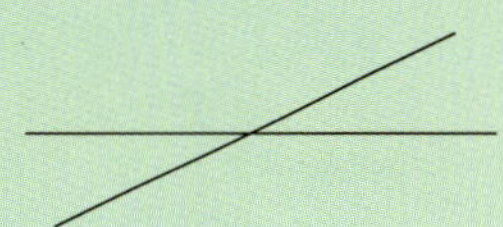

  Discuss how to use a ruler and compasses to construct the locus of all points which are the same distance from each of these lines.
  What does this locus do to the angles between the two lines?
- How can you use a ruler and compasses, but no protractor, to draw an angle of 60°?
- How can you use a ruler and compasses, but no protractor, to draw an angle of 90°?

Compasses

Do not use a protractor for this exercise, except for Question 7.
Use only a ruler and compasses.

Justifying a solution

EXERCISE 7

1 Draw two points, P and Q, 8 cm apart.
Construct the locus of points which are equidistant from P and Q.

2 (a) Draw any pair of intersecting lines.
(b) Construct the line which bisects the acute angles.
(c) Construct the line which bisects the obtuse angles.
(d) Prove that the two bisecting lines are at right angles.

3 Construct each of these angles.
(a) 30° (b) 45° (c) 75°

4 These sketches of triangles have *not* been drawn accurately.

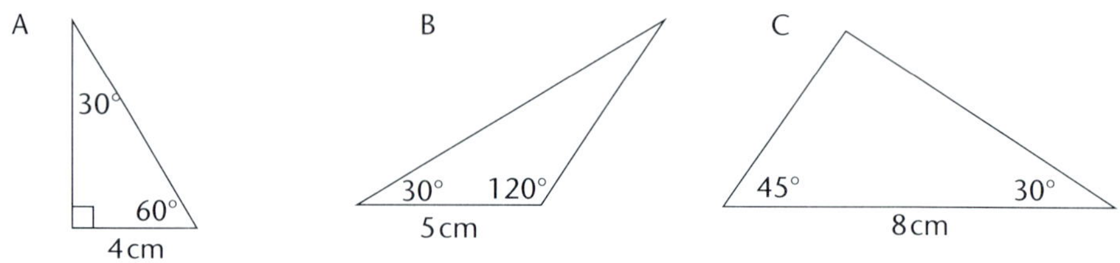

(a) Construct each of the triangles accurately.
(b) Measure the lengths of all the sides of the triangles and mark them on your drawings.

For Question 5, you may find it helpful to start by drawing a circle.

5 (a) Construct a regular hexagon.
(b) Construct a regular octagon.

6 (a) Construct this triangle.

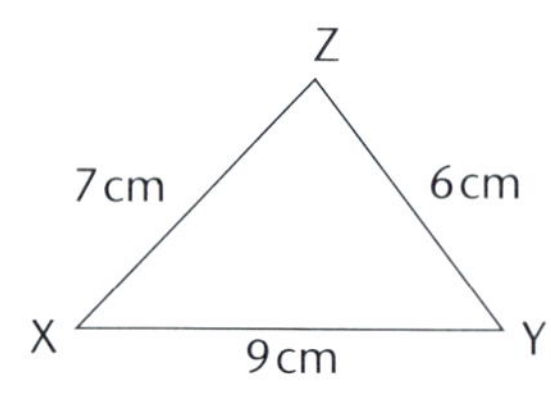

(i) Construct the locus of points which are the same distance from X as from Y.
(ii) Construct the locus of points which are the same distance from X as from Z.
(iii) Draw a circle which passes through the points X, Y and Z.

(b) Construct the triangle XYZ again.
(i) Construct the locus of points which are inside triangle XYZ and the same distance from side XY and from side XZ.
(ii) Construct the locus of points which are inside triangle XYZ and the same distance from side XZ and from side YZ.
(iii) Construct a circle which touches (but does not cross) each of the sides of triangle XYZ.

You will need a protractor for Question 7.

7 (a) Calculate the size of angles x and y in this diagram.

(b) Hence, or otherwise, draw accurately a triangle with perimeter 15 cm and angles of 50°, 60° and 70°.

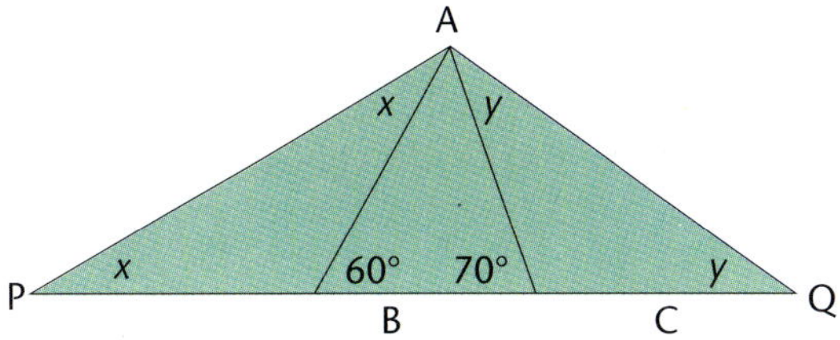

Circle theorems

▷ Card
▷ Scissors

EXERCISE 8

1 For this question, use a set square, or a piece of paper or card with an angle of 90°.

(a) Draw two points A and B, 6 cm apart.

(b) Place your card so that the points A and B lie on the edges of the card, as shown below.
Mark the position of the point P at the 90° angle.

Do this for several possible positions of the card.

(c) What is the locus of point P?

2 For this question, use a set square, or a piece of paper or card, with an angle of 60°.

(a) Draw two points A and B, 6 cm apart.

(b) Place your card so that the points A and B lie on the edges of the card, as shown below. Mark the position of the point P at the 60° angle.

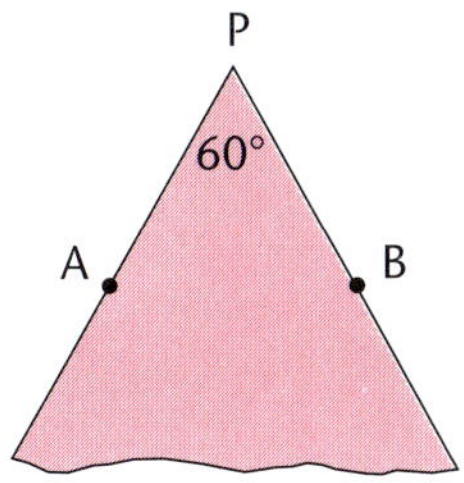

Do this for several possible positions of the card.

(c) What is the locus of point P?

3 A semicircle has AB as its diameter. P is a point lying on the semicircle. O is the centre of the semicircle.

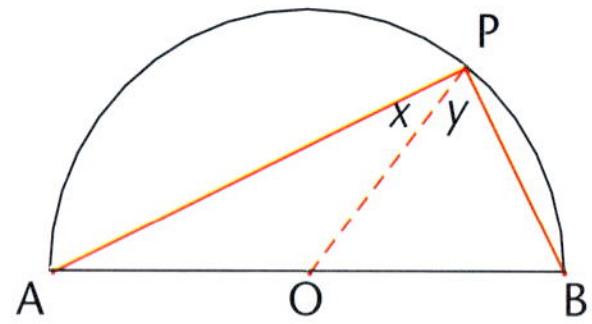

Justifying a generalisation

(a) Prove that the triangle APB is divided into two isosceles triangles by the line OP.

(b) The angles at P are labelled x and y, as shown in the diagram. Find the sum of the angles of the triangle APB in terms of x and y.

(c) What does this tell you about $x + y$?

(d) What does this tell you about the angle APB?

(e) What happens to angle APB as P moves round the semicircle?

4 O is the centre of a circle. A, B and P are points on the circle.

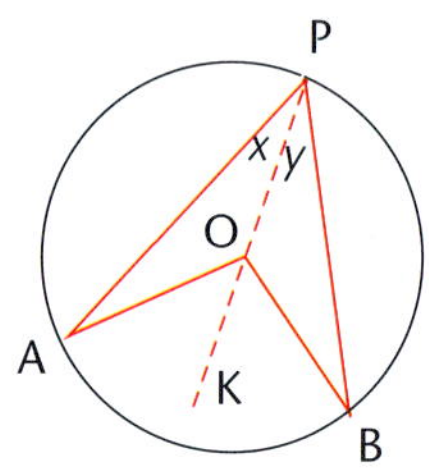

Justifying a generalisation

(a) Prove that the two triangles, PAO and PBO, are isosceles triangles.

(b) The angles at P are labelled x and y, as shown in the diagram. Find the angles AOK and BOK in terms of x and y.

(c) What is the relationship between angle AOB and angle APB?

(d) If A and B stay fixed and P moves round the circle on the major arc between A and B, what happens to the size of angle APB?

5 APBQ is a quadrilateral inscribed in a circle.

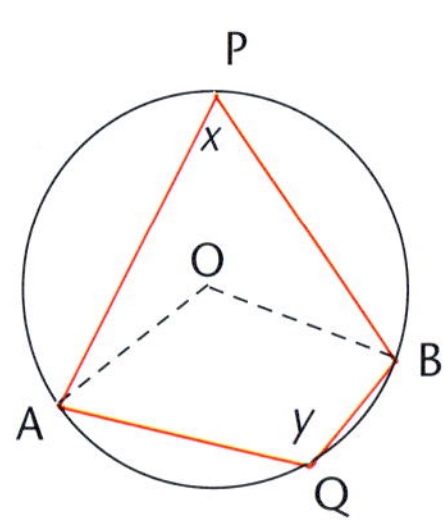

A quadrilateral which can be inscribed in a circle is called a **cyclic quadrilateral**.

Justifying a generalisation

(a) What is the size of the angle AOB in terms of x?

(b) What is the size of the reflex angle AOB in terms of y?

(c) What is the relationship between the angle P and the angle Q?

Dynamic geometry

The questions in Exercise 8 are about proving these four theorems.

The angle in a semicircle is 90°.

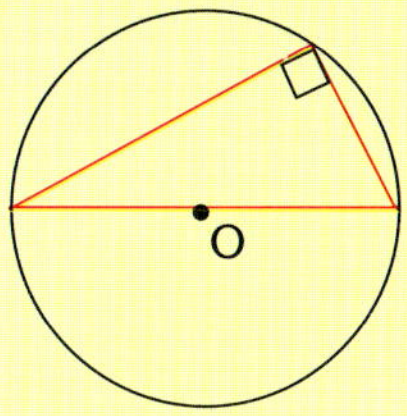

The angle at the centre is twice the angle at the circumference.

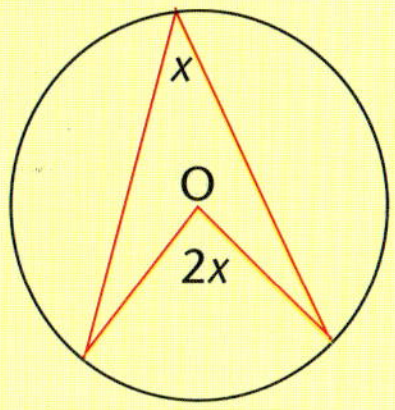

Angles in the same segment are equal.

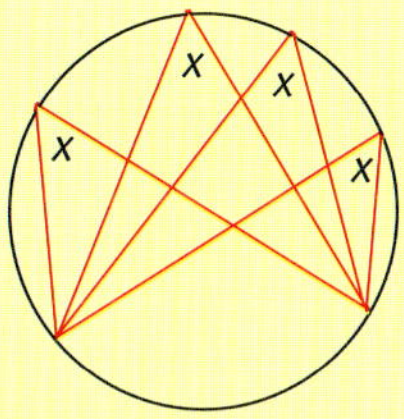

Opposite angles of a cyclic quadrilateral add up to 180°.

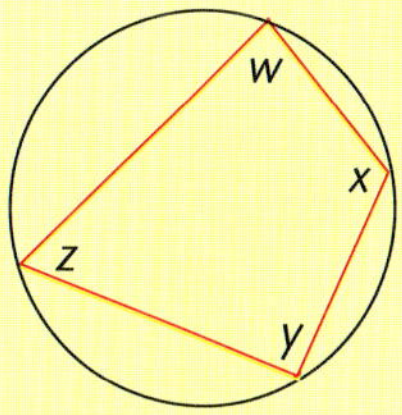

$x + z = 180°$
$w + y = 180°$

EXERCISE 9

1 In each of these diagrams, O is the centre of the circle.
Find the size of each angle marked x.

A

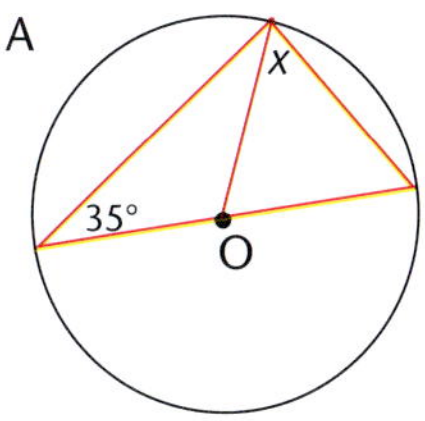

B

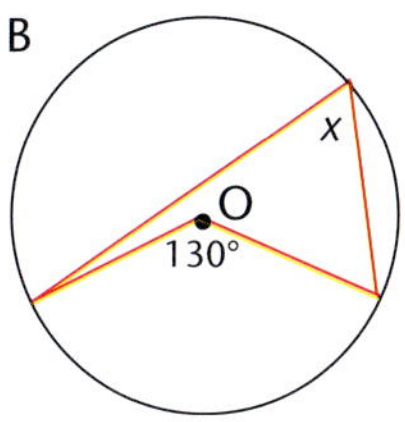

C

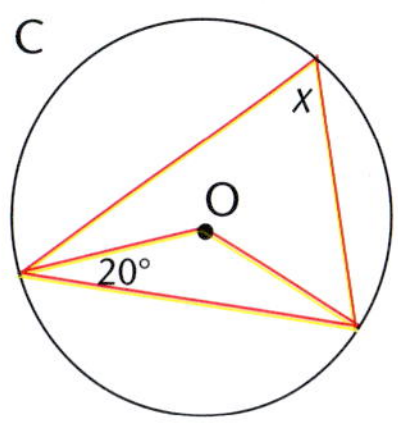

D

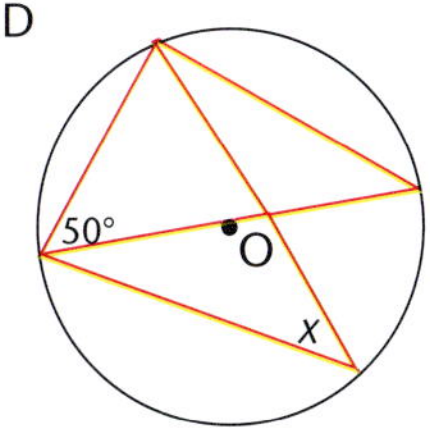

E

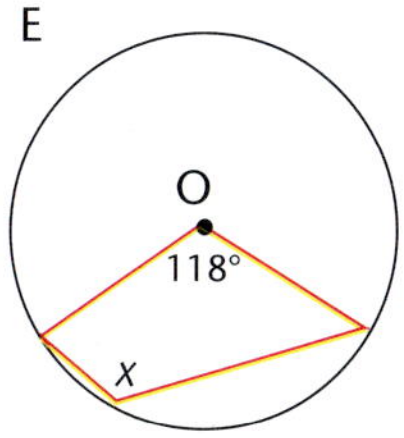

F

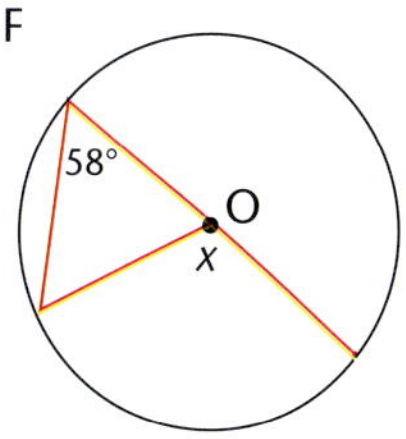

2 In each of these diagrams, O is the centre of the circle.
Find the size of each angle marked *x*.

A

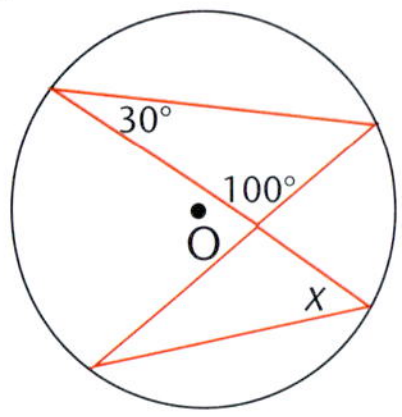

B

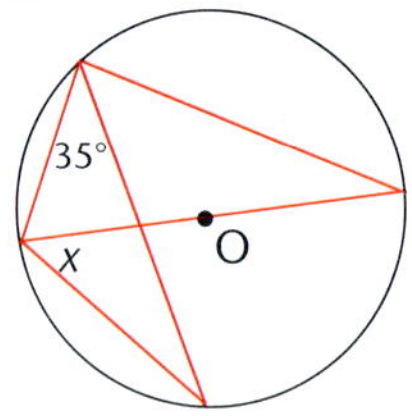

C

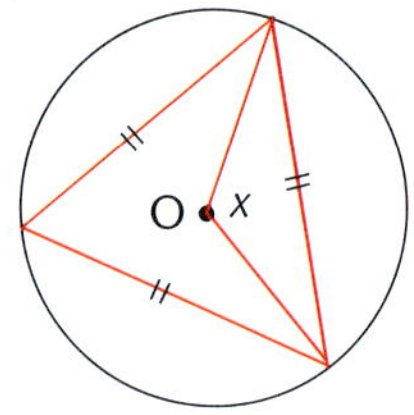

D

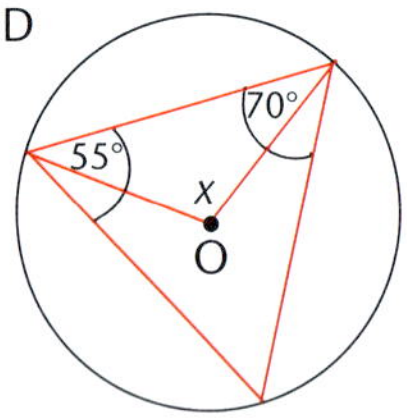

E

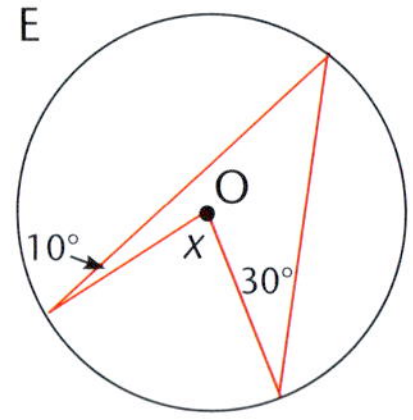

F

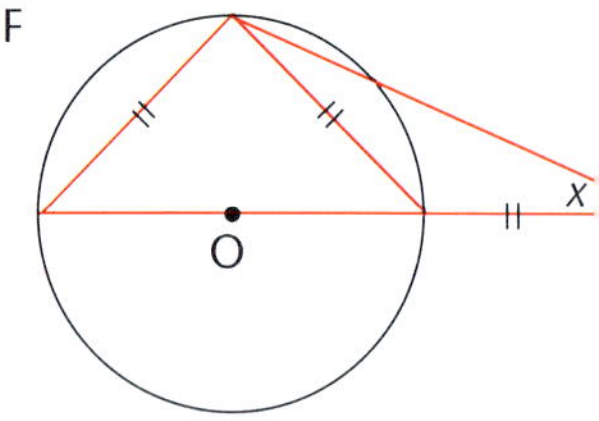

3 Find the angles marked *x* in these diagrams. (In diagram F, ABC and ADE are straight lines.)

A

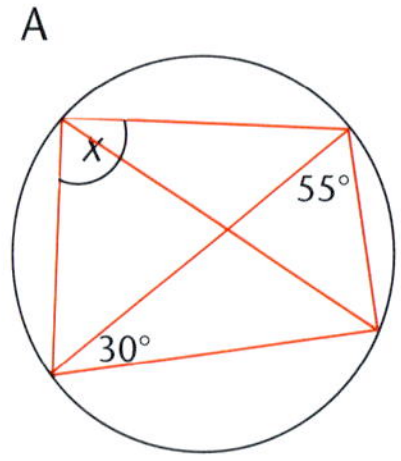

B

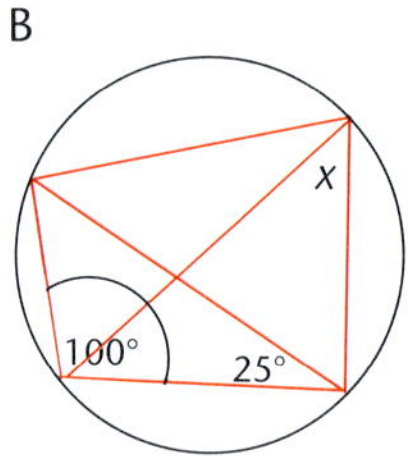

C

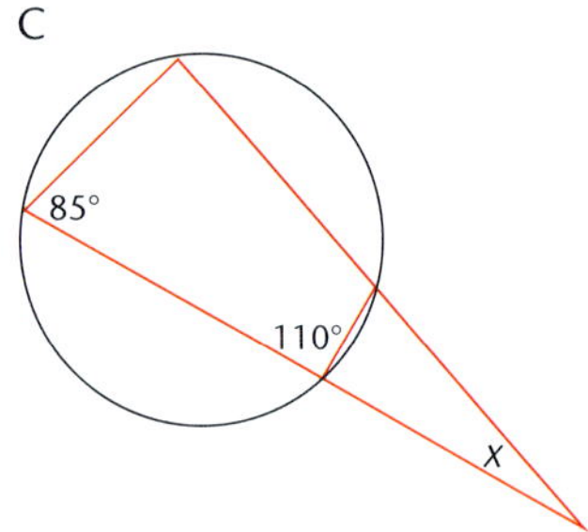

D

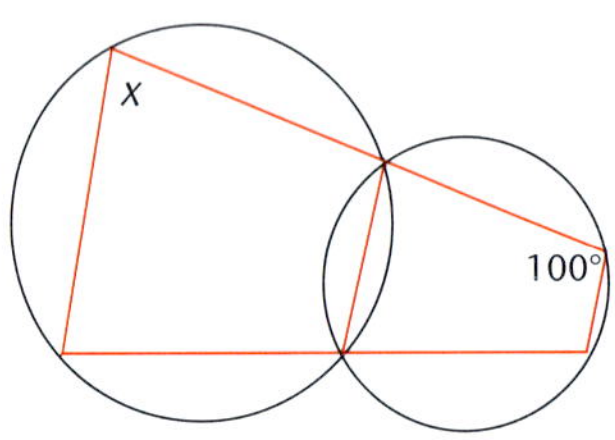

E

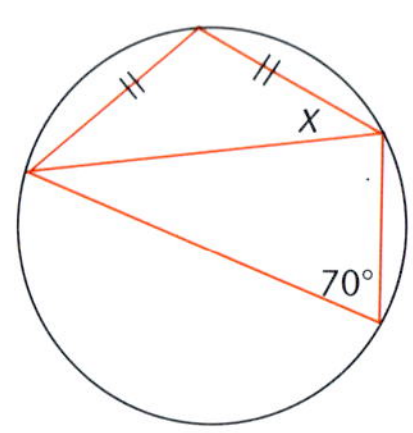

F

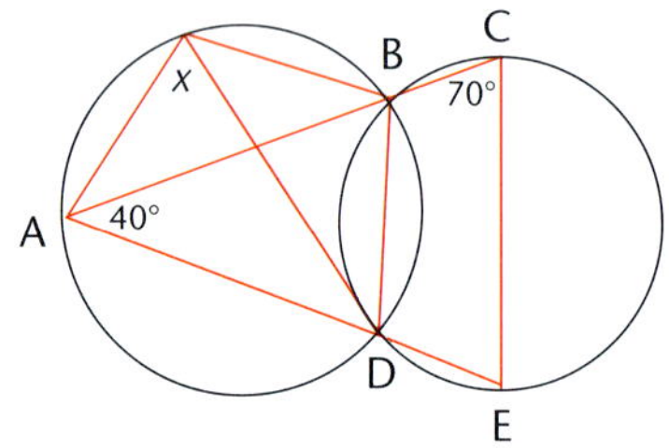

4 For each of these shapes, say whether it is *always* a cyclic quadrilateral, *sometimes* a cyclic quadrilateral or *never* a cyclic quadrilateral.

A: Square	B: Rhombus	C: Rectangle
D: Parallelogram	E: Trapezium	F: Kite

Justifying a generalisation

If it is *always*, explain why.

If it is *sometimes*, draw pictures to show one that is and one that isn't.

If it is *never*, explain why not.

5 ABCD is a fixed square.

A second square PQRS is to be drawn so that A lies on PQ and B lies on QR.

Draw a sketch showing several different possible positions of the square PQRS.

What is the locus of the vertex Q?

Explain your answer.

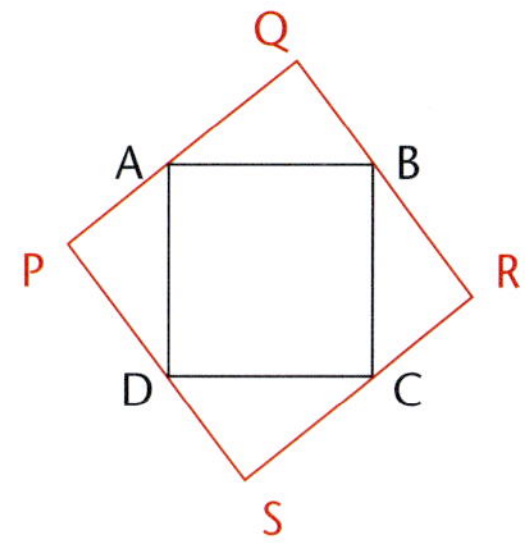

6 ABCD is a kite.

The diagonals of the kite meet at E.

The vertices A and B are fixed.

The vertices C and D can be anywhere, so long as ABCD is a kite.

Find the locus of E.

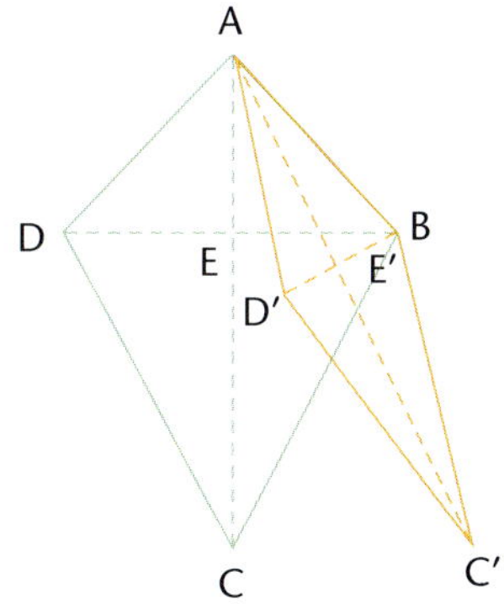

7 ABC is an equilateral triangle inscribed in a circle. The rectangle ABDE is also inscribed in the same circle.

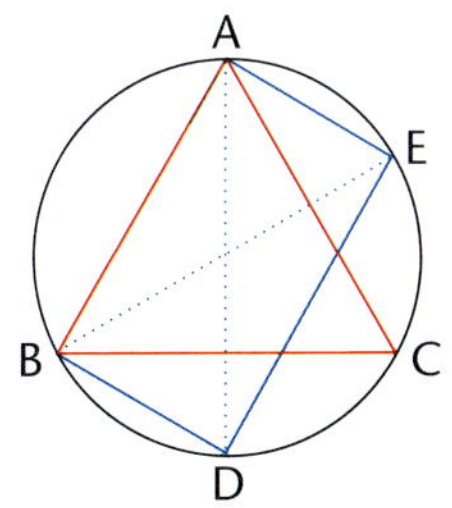

Find the angle between the diagonals of the rectangle.

8 ABCDE is an regular pentagon inscribed in a circle. The rectangle ABFG is also inscribed in the same circle.

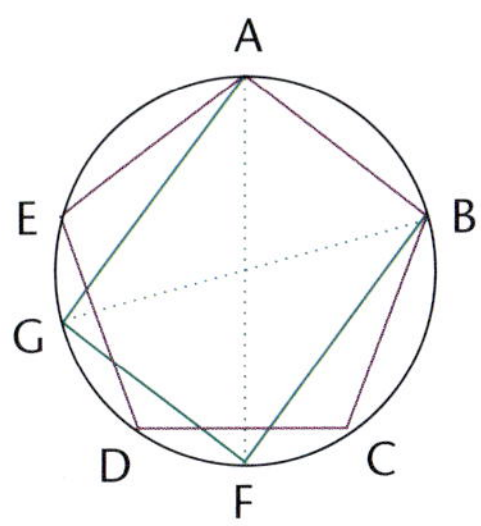

Find the angle between the diagonals of the rectangle.

9 In this circle, chords AB and EF are the same length and EC is the same length as CF.

What is the size of angle EFC?

Explain your answer.

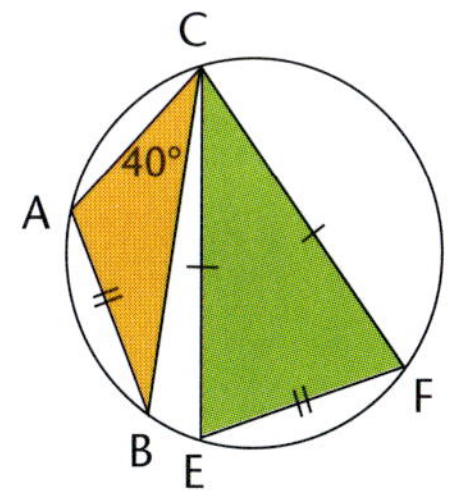

A **mystic pentagon** is a regular pentagon with all its diagonals drawn.

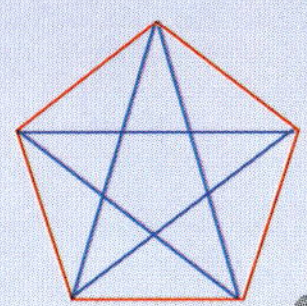

10 (**a**) In a mystic pentagon, there are three angles meeting at each vertex. What can you say about the size of these three angles? Explain your answer.

(**b**) Here is a mystic octagon.

What can you say about the angles meeting at each vertex of the red octagon?

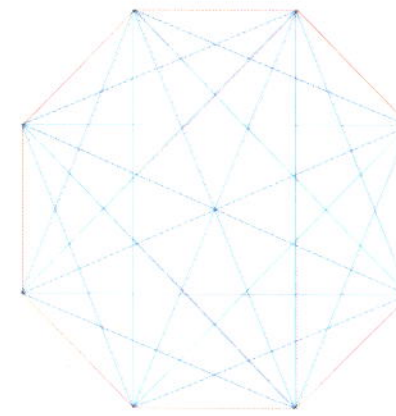

Making and justifying a generalisation

(**c**) What can you say about all the angles meeting at a vertex of any mystic rose?

A **mystic rose** is a regular polygon with any number of sides with all its diagonals drawn.

11 Draw accurately a triangle with angles 40°, 50° and 90°, whose vertices lie on a circle of radius 4cm.

12 Draw accurately a triangle with angles of 50°, 60° and 70°, whose vertices lie on a circle of radius 6cm.

13 (**a**) O is the centre of this circle. Calculate the size of angles OAB and ABO.

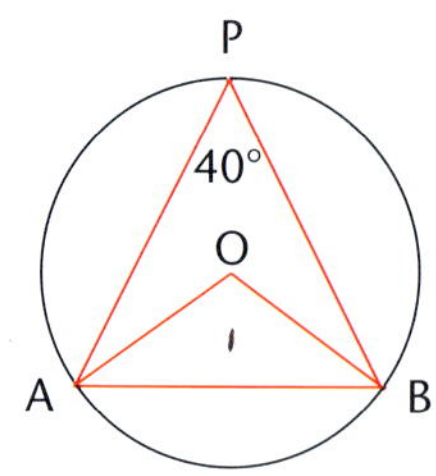

(**b**) A and B are two fixed points a distance of 6cm apart. Construct accurately the locus of P where P moves so that ∠APB = 40°.

14 A and B are two landmarks on a coast, 6 miles apart. The landmarks are both visible from a ship.

(**a**) Someone on the ship measures the angle between the two landmarks A and B as 60°. Draw a scale diagram and construct the locus of the positions where the ship might be.

(**b**) Another landmark C is spotted. C is 5 miles from B and ABC is a straight line. The angle between the landmarks B and C is measured as 45°. Draw another locus and hence find the position of the ship.

(**c**) Measure your scale drawing to find the distance of the ship from A.

15 ABC is a triangle in which the length of AB is 5cm and ∠C = 30°. Draw all possible triangles ABC accurately

(**a**) if the length of AC is 8cm

(**b**) if triangle ABC is isosceles

(**c**) if the area of triangle ABC is 15cm

COURSEWORK OPPORTUNITY

Triangle facts:
- The lengths of one or more of its sides
- The size of one or more of its angles
- Its area
- Its perimeter
- The number of lines of symmetry

and so on…

Fixing shapes

There are many different facts you can know about a triangle.

Suppose you know these three facts:

One side has length 6 cm. One side has length 7 cm. One side has length 8 cm.

Then this **fixes** the triangle.

A shape is **fixed** if, when several people draw the shape accurately, all the shapes drawn are congruent.

- How many facts do you need to fix a triangle?
- Can you sometimes manage with less than three?
- Do you sometimes need more than three?

Experiment with different combinations of three facts (for example you might know two sides and its area).

- When do three facts fix a triangle?
- Where three facts *do* fix a triangle describe, if possible, a method for drawing this triangle accurately.

Now do the same for quadrilaterals. You might want to divide these into types.

- How many facts are needed to fix a square? What kind of facts can these be?
- How many facts are needed to fix a parallelogram? What kind of facts can these be?

And so on.

CHAPTER SUMMARY

Solid shapes

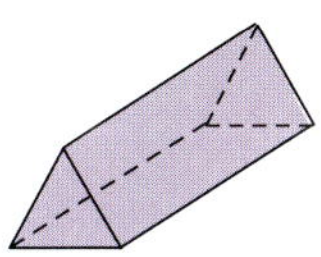

Triangular prism

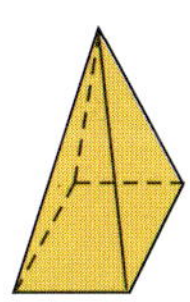

A square-based pyramid has 5 **faces**, 8 **edges** and 5 **vertices.**

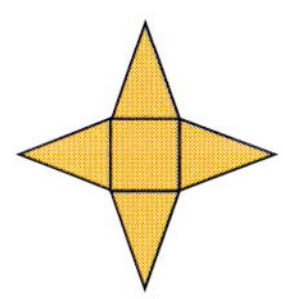

Net of a square-based pyramid

A square-based pyramid has **four planes of symmetry** (through the vertex and each of the four lines of symmetry of the base) and **one axis of rotational symmetry of order 4** (through the vertex and the centre of the base).

Exterior angle property of a triangle

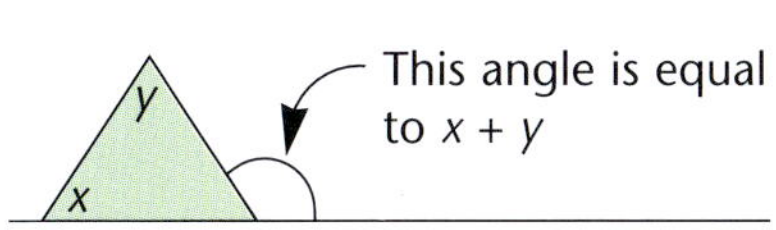

Congruence

Two shapes are **congruent** if one fits exactly onto the other (after turning over if necessary).

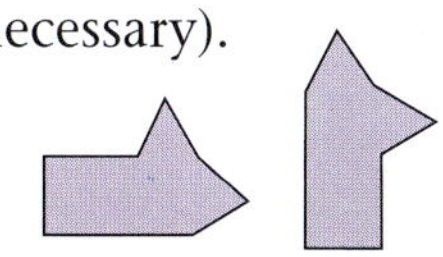

Loci

The **locus** of a point that is always a constant distance away from a fixed point is a **circle**.

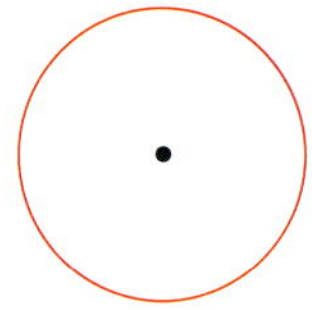

This is the locus of a point that is always a constant distance from a line of fixed length.

The locus of a point which is equidistant from two fixed points A and B is the **perpendicular bisector** of the line joining A and B.

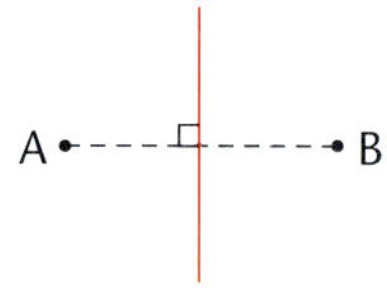

The locus of a point which is equidistant from two fixed lines is made up of both **angle bisectors** of the two lines.

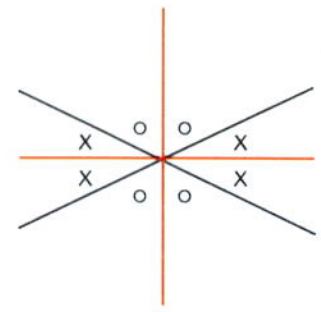

Circle theorems

The angle in a semicircle is 90°.

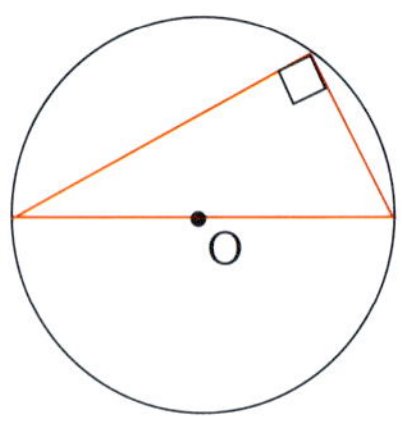

The angle at the centre is twice the angle at the circumference.

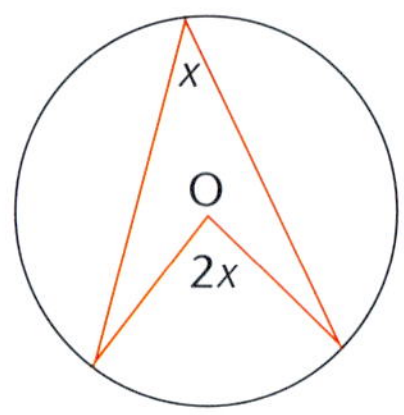

Angles in the same segment are equal.

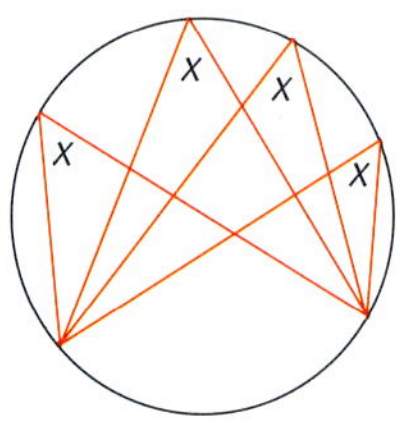

Opposite angles of a cyclic quadrilateral add up to 180°.

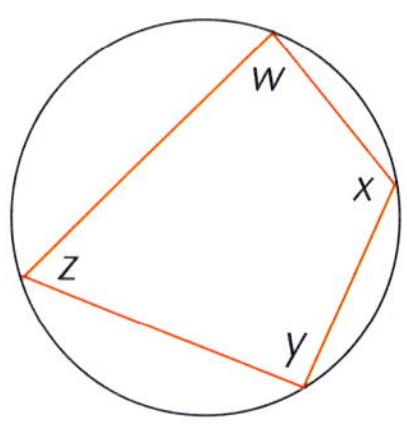

$x + z = 180°$

$w + y = 180°$

REVISION EXERCISES

1: NUMBERS AND ALGEBRA

Do not use a calculator for Questions 1 to 8.

1 (a) Express each of these numbers as the product of prime factors.
(i) 28 (ii) 63
(iii) 4900 (iv) 882
(b) Use your answers to part (a) to do these calculations.
(i) $4900 \div 28$ (ii) $882 \div 63$

2 $N = 2^5 \times 3^2 \times 7^6$.
(a) Write $140N$ as the product of prime factors.
(b) What is the largest number which is a factor of both N and 162?

3 Work out these.
(a) 40×0.5 (b) 64×0.75 (c) 0.8×0.4
(d) 40×0.05 (e) 12.5×0.04 (f) $20 \div 2.5$
(g) $0.8 \div 40$ (b) $4.9 \div 0.007$ (i) $11 \div 0.125$

4 Calculate these.
(a) $\frac{1}{9} + \frac{1}{12}$ (b) $2\frac{1}{3} + 3\frac{1}{4} + 4\frac{1}{6}$
(c) $\frac{13}{18} - \frac{2}{9}$ (d) $3\frac{1}{4} - 2\frac{1}{3}$
(e) $\frac{5}{6} \times \frac{9}{10}$ (f) $(1\frac{1}{3})^2$
(g) $\frac{5}{8} \div \frac{5}{6}$ (h) $3\frac{3}{5} \div 2\frac{2}{5}$

5 Simplify these.
(a) $\frac{a}{2} + \frac{a}{3}$ (b) $\frac{a-1}{2} + \frac{a+2}{4}$
(c) $\frac{3a+1}{5} - \frac{a-3}{10}$ (d) $\frac{a}{b} \times \frac{b}{c}$
(e) $\frac{ab}{c} \times \frac{bc}{d}$ (f) $\frac{ab}{c} \div \frac{bc}{d}$

6 (a) Convert these numbers to decimals.
(i) $\frac{3}{5}$ (ii) $\frac{1}{16}$ (iii) 63%
(iv) $\frac{2}{3}$ (v) $13\frac{1}{4}$% (vi) $\frac{2}{7}$
(b) Convert these numbers to fractions.
(i) 80% (ii) 0.85 (iii) 0.625
(iv) 1.5% (v) 236% (vi) $42\frac{6}{7}$%

7 (a) Evaluate these, writing them as whole numbers or decimals.
(i) 4^3 (ii) $3^{25} \div 3^{21}$ (iii) $11^{100} \div 11^{97}$
(iv) 7×2^{-3} (v) $(0.4)^{-3}$
(b) Simplify these.
(i) $4a^4 \times 3a^2$ (ii) $2ab^3 \times 3bc^3 \times 5c^2d$
(iii) $12a^5 \div 4a^5$ (iv) $8a^3b^2c \div 16ab^2c^3$

8 Copy and complete this table.

Number	Standard form
4631	4.631×10^3
	7.293×10^2
536000	
23000000	
	2.3×10^{-1}
0.0045	
Twenty thousand	
Five millionths	

9 (a) Estimate an answer for each of these calculations, *without* using a calculator.
(i) $\frac{5.67 + 4.36}{1.96}$ (ii) $7.94^2 - 23.7$
(iii) $(16.38 - 9.41)^2$ (iv) $\frac{18.14}{12.34 - 10.82}$
(v) $\sqrt{4.96^2 + 12.12^2}$ (vi) $\left(\frac{1}{2.04} - \frac{1}{5.97}\right)^2$
(b) Use a calculator to find answers to each of the calculations in part (a), correct to 3 significant figures.

10 A cereal packet says that the recommended daily intake of iron is 14mg.
The population of the Europe is 680 million.
Assuming that everyone takes this daily requirement, how much vitamin iron is consumed in Europe in a year?
Give your answer in kilograms, in standard form.

2: GEOMETRICAL PATTERNS

1 Find the size of an interior angle of a regular polygon with 12 sides.

2 Each interior angle of a regular polygon is 160°. How many sides does it have?

3 What is the angle sum of a decagon?

4 Which of these are possible? If it is possible, draw a sketch.
A: A triangle with one line of symmetry
B: A triangle with two lines of symmetry
C: A quadrilateral with rotational symmetry of order 4
D: A quadrilateral with rotational symmetry of order 2 and no line of symmetry
E: A hexagon with two lines of symmetry

5 (a) The diagonals of a rectangle intersect at an angle of 36°. Draw a sketch of the rectangle and its diagonals, and mark the sizes of all the angles in your sketch.
(b) One of the interior angles of an isosceles trapezium is 55°. Its diagonals intersect at an angle of 60°. Draw a sketch of the trapezium and its diagonals, and mark the sizes of all the angles in your sketch.

6 This is a tessellation of scalene triangles.

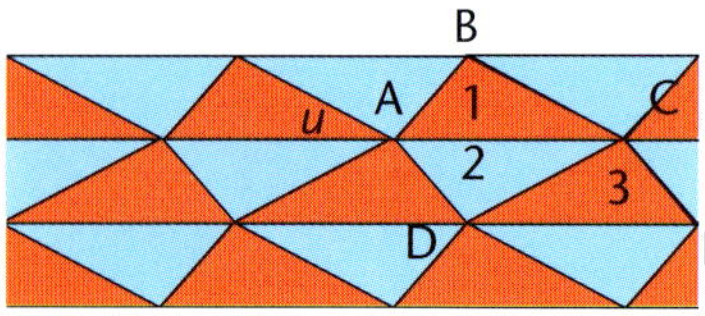

(a) Describe exactly the transformation which maps
(i) triangle 1 on to triangle 2
(ii) triangle 2 on to triangle 3
(b) State with reasons which angle in each of triangles 1, 2 and 3 is equal to u.

7 (a) Draw axes with x from 0 to 7 and y from –4 to 7.
Plot the points P(1, 2), Q(1, 4) and R(2, 4).
These are the vertices of triangle T_1.
Draw triangle T_1.
(b) Triangle T_2 is obtained by reflecting triangle T_1 in the line $y = 4$.
Draw triangle T_2.
(c) Triangle T_3 is obtained by reflecting triangle T_2 in the line $y = 1$.
Draw triangle T_3.
(d) Triangle T_4 is obtained by reflecting triangle T_2 in the line $y = x$.
Draw triangle T_4.
(e) Find the single transformation which transforms triangle T_1 to triangle T_3.
(f) Find the single transformation which transforms triangle T_1 to triangle T_4.

8 Triangle ABC is a scalene triangle.
D is the midpoint of BC, E is the midpoint of AC, and F is the midpoint of AB.
(a) Triangle ABC is an enlargement of triangle EDC.
What is the centre of enlargement?
What is the scale factor?
(b) What scale factor is needed to transform triangle ABC to triangle FBD?
Where is the centre of enlargement?
(c) Triangle T has its vertices at the midpoints of the sides of triangle DEF.
What is the scale factor of the enlargement which transforms triangle T to triangle ABC?

9 A polygon has 20 sides. Some of its angles are 170°, and the rest of the angles are 150°.
How many 150° angles does it have?

10

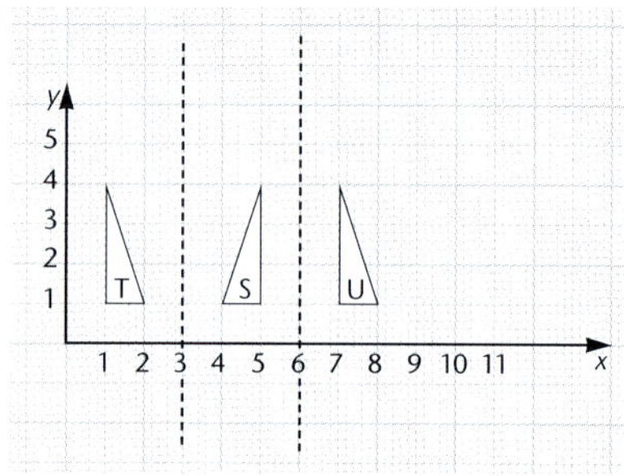

The diagram shows triangles T, S and U.
S is the image of T under a reflection in the line $x = 3$. U is the image of S under reflection in the line $x = 6$.
A reflection in the line $x = 3n$ where n is an integer, is denoted by R_n.
So S is the image of T under R_2 and U is the image of T under R_1 followed by R_2.
V is the image of T under the successive transformations R_1 followed by R_2 followed by R_3.
(a) Copy the diagram and draw V on it.
(b) Describe fully the single transformation that will map T to V.
W is the image of T under the successive transformations R_1 followed by R_2, followed by R_3 and so on to R_n.
(c) Describe fully the single transformation that will map T to W
(i) when n is even,
(ii) when n is odd.

ULEAC 1996

3: ALGEBRAIC MANIPULATION

Do not use a calculator for this exercise.

1 Factorise these.
(a) $4x - 8y$ (b) $6a^2 + 9a$
(c) $4ab - 10b^3$ (d) $2\pi r^2 + 2\pi rh$
(e) $14a^2b^3c^2 - 49a^3bc^3 + 70a^4b^2c$

2 Multiply out the brackets in each of these expressions.
(a) $(m + 3)(m + 5)$ (b) $(p - 1)(p - 6)$
(c) $(x - 4)(x + 3)$ (d) $(x - 3y)(x + 2y)$
(e) $(3x - 1)(x - 3)$ (f) $(m + n)(m - n)$
(g) $(2a - 5b)(2a + 5b)$ (h) $m(2m - 5n)(3m - 2n)$
(i) $(2p + q - 5)(5p - q + 2)$
(j) $(2a + 3b - 4c)(4a - 3b + 2c)$

3 Factorise these.
(a) $pq + p + q + 1$ (b) $ab - a - b + 1$
(c) $xy + 3x + 4y + 12$ (d) $mn - pq - mq + np$
(e) $6ab + 8cd - 16bc - 3ad$

4 Factorise these.
(a) $a^2 + 4a + 3$ (b) $x^2 + 7x + 10$
(c) $m^2 - 6m + 8$ (d) $a^2 + 4ab + 4b^2$
(e) $p^2 + 9pq + 18q^2$

5 Factorise these.
(a) $4m^2 + 5m + 1$ (b) $6p^2 - 5p + 1$
(c) $2a^2 + 5a + 2$ (d) $3m^2 - 8mn + 4n^2$
(e) $4x^2 + 12xy + 9y^2$

6 Factorise these.
(a) $a^2 - 2a - 3$ (b) $c^2 - c - 12$
(c) $x^2 + 2x - 8$ (d) $m^2 - 3mn - 4n^2$
(e) $p^2 - 7pq - 18q^2$

7 Factorise these.
(a) $2a^2 - 3a - 2$ (b) $3b^2 - b - 2$
(c) $6x^2 + 7x - 5$ (d) $3a^2 - 11ab - 4b^2$
(e) $18m^2 - 37mn - 20n^2$

8 Factorise these.
(a) $p^2 - q^2$ (b) $a^2 - 16$
(c) $x^2 - 25y^2$ (d) $100a^2 - b^2$
(e) $36p^2 - 81q^2$ (f) $3m^2 - 12$
(g) $50a^2 - 72b^2$ (h) $9m^3 - 16mn^2$
(i) $28a^2 - 63b^2$ (j) $4a^4 - 9b^2$

9 Factorise these.
(a) $3x^2 - 12x + 9$ (b) $25a^2 - 75a - 100$
(c) $14m^2 - 35mn + 14n^2$ (d) $x^2y + 5xyz + 6yz^2$
(e) $4pq^2 - 8pqr - 60pr^2$ (f) $x^2 - 4$
(g) $x^2 - 4x$ (h) $x^2 - 4x + 4$
(i) $x^2 - 4x - 5$ (j) $x^2 - 4x - 96$

10 Do these multiplications mentally in whatever way you want.
(a) 14×7 (b) 28×7
(c) 60×70 (d) 39×41
(e) 65^2 (f) 160×370
(g) 58×62 (h) 89^2
(i) 4367×8 (j) 123456789×9

4: WORKING WITH DATA

1 Find the median and interquartile range for this set of data.
12 19 22 8 23 15 31 27
22 19 18 24 34 7 26

2 This table shows the results of a survey into the number of chocolates in a box.

Number of chocolates	26	27	28	29	30	31	32
Number of boxes	2	6	13	14	3	1	1

(a) What is the modal number of chocolates in a box?
(b) Find the median number of chocolates in a box.
(c) Calculate the mean number of chocolates in a box.

3 A student records her last ten homework marks in Science and French. Here are the results.

Science	5	7	10	10	2	7	4	9	5	4
French	7	8	8	10	8	7	9	7	8	9

Compare these two sets of results using the mean and standard deviation.

4 A PE teacher timed a class of students as they ran a cross-country course.
This table shows the results.

Time taken (minutes)	Frequency
15–	3
17–	12
20–	12
25–	10
30–40	7

(a) Draw a histogram to represent these results.
(b) Write down the modal group of times.

5 The weights of 80 new-born babies are recorded in this table.

Weight (w kg)	Frequency
$0 \le w < 1.5$	2
$1.5 \le w < 2.5$	7
$2.5 \le w < 3.0$	19
$3.0 \le w < 3.5$	28
$3.5 \le w < 4.5$	16
$4.5 \le w < 6.5$	8

(a) Draw a histogram to represent this data.
(b) What is the modal group for this data?
(c) Estimate the mean weight of these babies.

6 Calculate the mean and standard deviation of these numbers.

9 11 14 12 8 8 14 12 10 12

7 A number of school children were asked about the amount of pocket money they received each week.
The results are shown in this table.

Pocket money (£ p)	Frequency	Cumulative frequency
$0 < p \le 1$	10	
$1 < p \le 2$	0	
$2 < p \le 3$	0	
$3 < p \le 4$	0	
$4 < p \le 5$	8	
$5 < p \le 6$	13	
$6 < p \le 7$	26	
$7 < p \le 8$	33	
$8 < p \le 9$	17	
$9 < p \le 10$	9	

(a) (i) Copy and complete the table.
(ii) Draw a cumulative frequency graph to represent the data.
(b) Use your graph to find
(i) the median amount of pocket money
(ii) the interquartile range
(c) Estimate the mean amount of pocket money.
(d) Is the mean or median the better average to use for this data?
Explain your answer.

8 The lateness of 60 buses arriving at a station was recorded to the nearest minute.

Minutes late	0–	2–	4–	6–	8–	10–	12–	14–16
Frequency	13	12	10	8	8	5	3	1

(a) Copy and complete this cumulative frequency table.

Minutes late	<2	<4	<6	<8	<10	<12	<14	<16
Cumulative frequency								

(b) Draw a cumulative frequency graph, and estimate the median and interquartile range of the lateness of the buses.
(c) Passengers on the slowest twelve buses were given a refund.
How late must a bus be before a refund is given?

9 The unfinished histogram and table show information about the salaries, in pounds, of the teachers at Mathstown High School.

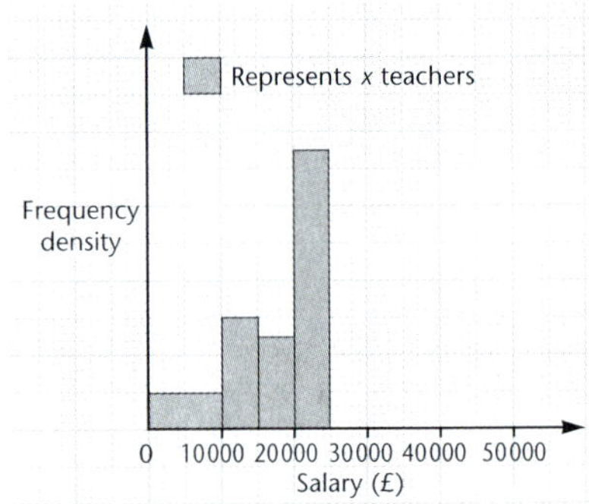

Salary (s) in pounds	Frequency
$0 \le s < 10000$	4
$10000 \le s < 15000$	6
$15000 \le s < 20000$	5
$20000 \le s < 25000$	.....
$25000 \le s < 30000$	8
$30000 \le s < 50000$	4

(a) Calculate the value of x.
(b) Use the information in the histogram to complete the table.
(c) Use the information in the table to copy and complete the histogram.

ULEAC 1995

10 A school reviewed the efficiency of its school bus service. For five weeks the school recorded the number of minutes, x, that the bus was late.
The results are summarised.

Minutes late	Frequency
$0 \le x < 2$	6
$2 \le x < 5$	12
$5 \le x < 10$	5
$10 \le x < 20$	2

(a) Draw a histogram to illustrate these data.
The actual results are given.
0, 0, 0, 1, 1, 1, 2, 2, 2, 2, 3, 3, 3, 3, 3, 4, 4, 4, 5, 6, 7, 7, 9, 12, 16.
(b) The mean of these numbers is 4. What is the standard deviation?
A year ago, the corresponding figures for lateness were
mean value = 2.5, standard deviation = 3.5.
(c) What do you conclude about the efficiency of the bus service, and why?

SEG 1997

5: PYTHAGORAS' THEOREM AND SIMILAR SHAPES

1 Use Pythagoras' theorem to help you to find the area of this isosceles triangle.

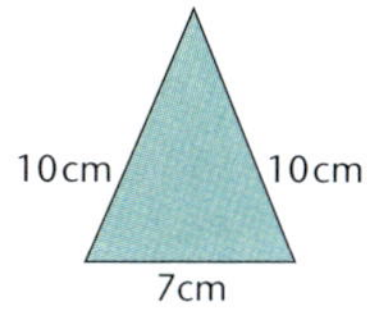

2 For these three triangles, the lengths of the three sides are given.

A: 12.8cm, 15.6cm and 21.5cm
B: 6.3m, 16.3m and 16.9m
C: 3.5 inches, 12.0 inches and 12.5 inches

Say whether each triangle is acute-angled, obtuse-angled or right-angled.

3 The diagonals of a rectangle are of length 17cm. Two of the sides of the rectangle are of length 15cm. Find the perimeter of the rectangle.

4 Two sides of a right-angled triangle have lengths of 20cm and 25cm. Find the two possible values for the perimeter of this triangle.

5 (**a**) Explain why $\sqrt{45} = 3\sqrt{5}$.
(**b**) Simplify this expression.

$$\frac{8\sqrt{5}}{\sqrt{45} + \sqrt{5}}$$

6 (**a**) Explain why triangle ABC is similar to triangle ADE.

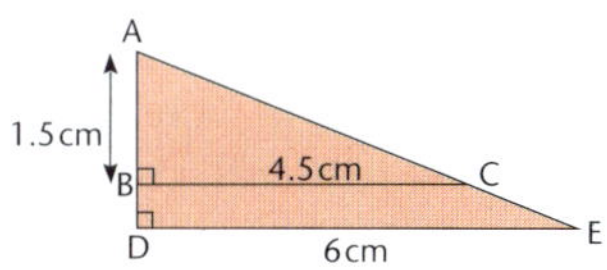

(**b**) Find the length of BD.
(**c**) Find the perimeter of triangle ADE.

7 (**a**) Explain why the triangles ABX and DCX are similar.

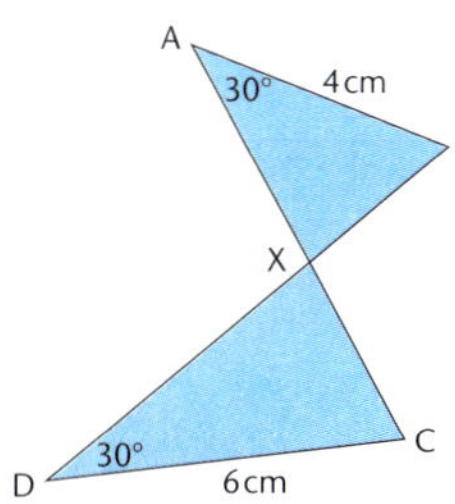

(**b**) The area of triangle CDX is 144cm^2. Find the area of triangle ABX.

8 Triangle ABC is similar to triangle DEF.

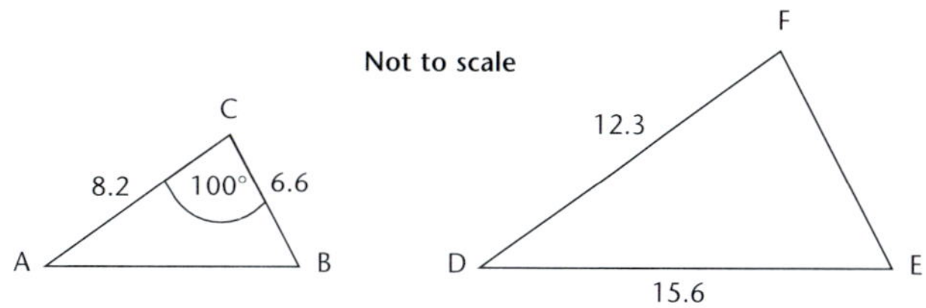

Find
(**a**) the length of FE,
(**b**) the length of AB,
(**c**) the size of angle DFE.

SEG 1996

9 The Mario Brothers produce large frozen pizzas of diameter 12 inches.

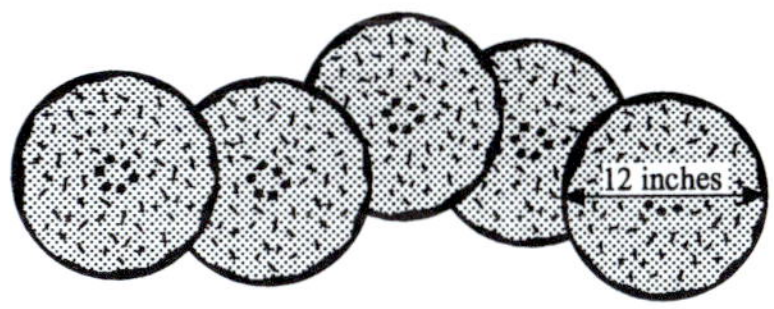

Paper discs are used in the packaging.
Each paper disc fits the base of a pizza exactly.
The paper discs are cut from sheets of paper, 40 inches wide and 1200 inches long.

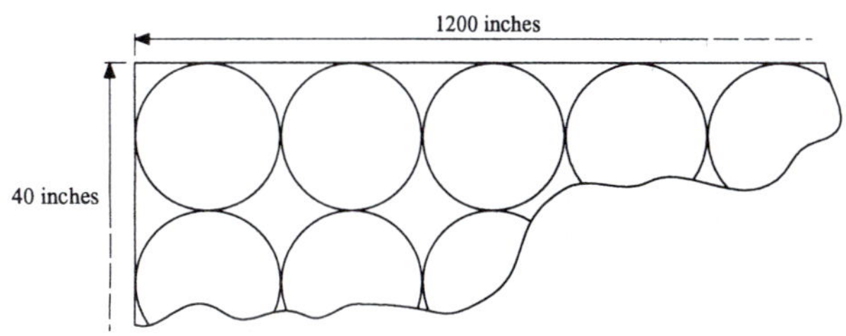

(**a**) (**i**) How many paper discs can be cut from the sheet?
(**ii**) What area of the sheet is wasted?

(**b**) To reduce the amount of wasted paper, the Mario Brothers try a new cutting arrangement from a different sized sheet for the paper discs as shown.

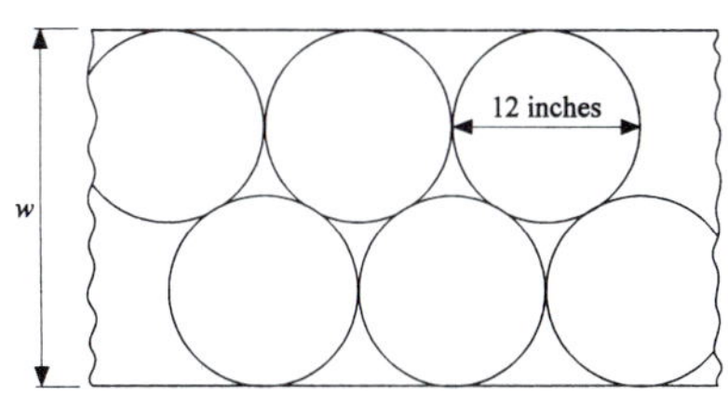

Calculate the width, w, of this sheet.

SEG 1996

10

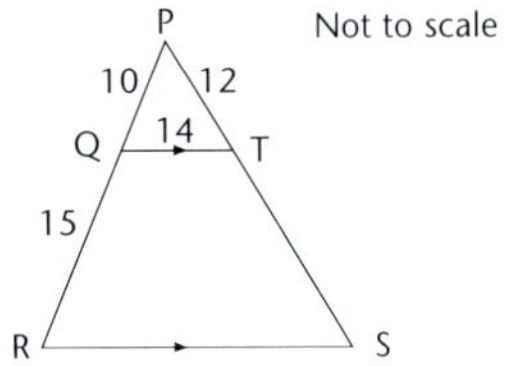

QT is parallel to RS;
PQ = 10cm;
QR = 15cm;
QT = 14cm;
PT = 12cm.

(a) Calculate the length of TS.
(b) Calculate the length of RS.
(c) A shape "L" has these lengths.

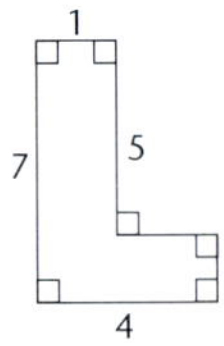

List any of the shapes *A*, *B*, *C*, *D* or *E* which are mathematically similar to the shape "L".

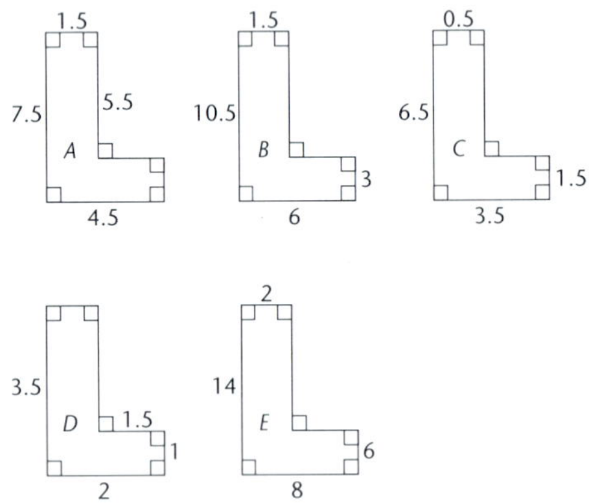

Not to scale

SEG 1996

11 This Z is to be painted onto a large poster.

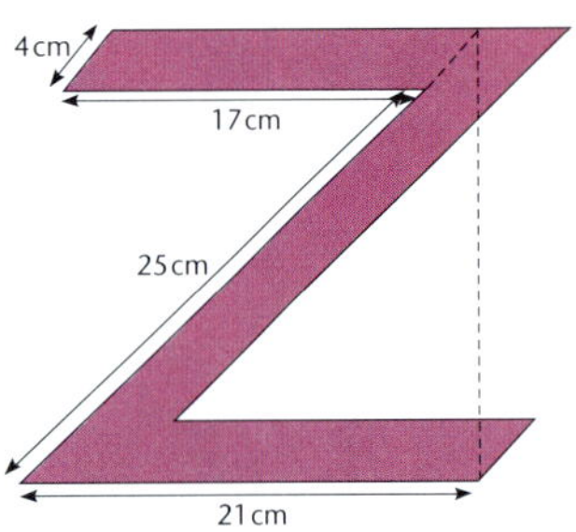

The outline of the Z consists of two sets of four parallel lines. The Z has rotational symmetry of order 2. Some of its dimensions are marked and the dotted lines help to describe the shape of the Z. Find the area of the Z.

6: PERCENTAGES

1 A settee which cost £499 last year is now priced at £525. What is the percentage increase in price?

2 £650 is invested in a savings account which pays 7.2% interest per year.
If no money is withdrawn, how much is in the account after five years?

3 A freezer costs £485.
A discount of 12% is offered to customers who pay cash.
(a) How much is the cash price?
(b) The freezer has risen in price by 4% since last year. What was the price of the freezer last year?

4 After one year, a car has depreciated in value by 45%. It is now worth £5800.
What was its value a year ago?

5 A builder charged £4350 to modernise a bathroom. This price included the VAT at 17.5%.
How much VAT was paid?

6 At Christmas, a hair dryer was priced at £37.
After Christmas, the price was reduced by 20%.
In August, after the shop was taken over, its price was increased by 25%.
What was the percentage change in price over the year?

7 It is estimated that a seal population in the North Sea has been decreasing by 20% a year. In May 1998, there were approximately 7300 seals.
(a) How many seals were there in May 1999?
(b) At this rate, how many seals will there be in May 2002?
(c) Estimate in which year the number of seals was over 15000.

8 A loan of £25000 is charged interest at the rate of 8% a year. At the end of each year, a repayment of £4000 is made.
(a) Complete the rows in this table to calculate how much is still owed after four years.

Year	Amount owing	With interest added	Less repayment
1	25000	27000	23000
2	23000		
3			
4			

(b) Estimate how many years it will take to pay off the loan.

9 Photographic prints come in two sizes: standard and jumbo.
The standard size measures 6 inches by 4 inches and the jumbo size is longer and wider by 25%.
(a) What are the measurements of the jumbo-sized prints?
(b) What is the percentage increase in area from standard size to jumbo?
(c) A giant size is being offered which will have twice the area of the standard size.
What will be the percentage increase in length and width measurements, from the standard size to the giant size?

10 It is estimated that 52% of the population of the UK is female, and that 20% of the females are aged 16 years or younger.
There are approximately 5990000 girls aged 16 years or younger.
(a) How many females are there in the UK?
(b) What is the population of the UK?

7: CUBES AND SEQUENCES

1 What are the next two terms, and the nth term, of each of these linear sequences?
(a) 3, 5, 7, 9, 11, ...
(b) 21, 26, 31, 36, 41, ...
(c) 100, 97, 94, 91, 88, ...

2 These formulae give the nth term of a sequence. For each one, write down the first six terms and the difference pattern.
(a) $8n + 17$
(b) $30 + 17n - 2n^2$
(c) $n(n - 1)(n + 2)$

3 What are the next two terms, and the nth term, of each of these quadratic sequences?
(a) 2, 8, 18, 32, 50, ...
(b) 1, 3, 6, 10, 15, ...
(c) 100, 98, 94, 88, 80, ...

4 What are the next two terms, and the nth term, of each of these geometric sequences?
(a) 14, 28, 56, 112, 224, ...
(b) 324, 108, 36, 12, 4, ...
(c) 96, 144, 216, 324, 486, ...

5 Look at this sequence of cube models.

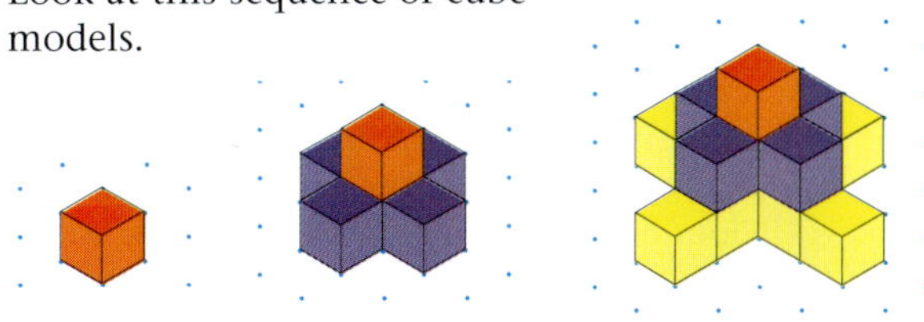

(a) Write down the numbers of cubes in the first six models.
(b) Find the nth term of the sequence of numbers of cubes.
(c) By considering the nth model, explain how you know that your formula is correct.

6 (a) Find the surface area of a cube with a volume of
(i) 27cm^3 (ii) 64000m^3 (iii) 50cm^3
(b) Find the volume of a cube with a surface area of
(i) 150m^2 (ii) 294cm^2 (iii) 80cm^2

7 Three solid cubes have edges of lengths 3cm, 4cm, and 5cm.
(a) (i) Find the total volume of the three cubes.
(ii) Calculate the length of the edge of a single cube which has the same volume as the total volume of the three cubes.
(b) The three original cubes are glued together and fixed to a table.
The external faces of the shape made from the cubes are painted.
What is the total surface area that is painted?

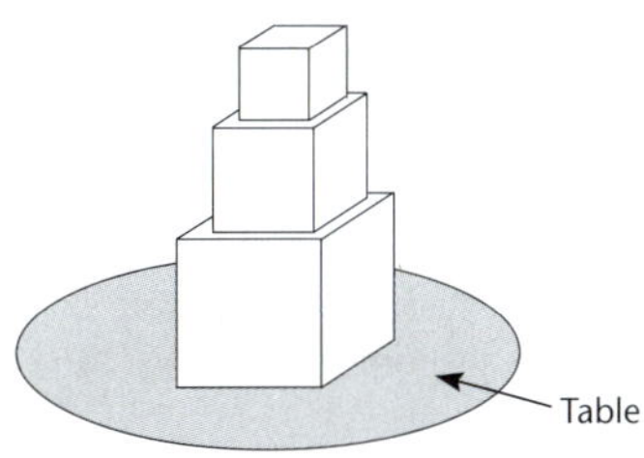

NEAB 1995

8 Cuboids A and B are similar. The surface area of cuboid A is 15cm^2, and its volume is 20cm^3.
The volume of cuboid B is 540cm^3.
What is its surface area?

9 A cuboid has sides of lengths 4cm, 7cm and 9cm.
(a) What is the distance between two vertices of the cuboid which are closest?
(b) What is the distance between two vertices of the cuboid which are furthest apart?

10 (a) Two of the dimensions of a cuboid are 3 units and 8 units. The volume of this cuboid is numerically equal to its surface area. What is the volume of this cuboid?
(b) The volume of a cuboid is 1372 cubic units. Four of its faces have the same area, and the total area of these four faces is half the surface area of the cuboid.
Find the dimensions of the cuboid.

8: RATIO, RATE AND PROPORTION

Do not use a calculator for Questions 1 to 5.

1 The distance between two points on a map is 56cm. The actual distance is 14km.
What is the scale of the map? Write your answer in the form 1:n, where n is a whole number.

2 A student on a holiday job earns £4.40 per hour. Her working week is 35 hours. She works a full week, and then 6 hours 20 minutes overtime at time and a half. How much does she earn?

3 A is directly proportional to B, and $A = 270$ when $B = 1000$. What is B when $A = 324$?

4 Someone is given a jigsaw puzzle, no longer in its original box but in a carrier bag. He wonders how many pieces there are. He takes out 80 of the pieces and sticks labels on the back of them.
He then puts the pieces back, shakes the bag well and takes out 80 pieces without looking.
Six of them have labels on. Estimate the number of pieces in the jigsaw puzzle.

5 M is inversely proportional to N, and $M = 0.5$ when $N = 1.6$. What is M when $N = 2$?

6 A top-class athlete ran 100m in 9.8 seconds.
What is his average speed, in miles per hour?

7 Two cubes, A and B, have the same mass of 80g, but the cubes are made of different materials. Cube A has edge length 6cm, and cube B has edge length 4cm.
(a) Find the ratio of the densities of cube A and cube B.
(b) Cube C is made of the same material as cube B and is the same size as cube A.
What is its mass?

8 $Y \propto X^3$
(a) What happens to the value of Y, if the value of X is multiplied by 5?
(b) What is the percentage increase in the value of Y, if the value of X is increased by 20%?
(c) What is the percentage decrease in the value of Y, if the value of X is decreased by 20%?

9 A motorist keeps a note of the times and distances of the stages of his journey.

	Clock	Odometer (miles)
Local roads	09.00 a.m.	0
Motorway	09.20 a.m.	12.5
Across country	11.40 a.m.	165
Destination	12.15 p.m.	188

(a) What is his average speed on each stage of the journey?
(b) What is his average speed for the whole journey?
(c) How much time would he save if he could average 70 m.p.h. on the motorway and 50 m.p.h. across country?

10 $Y \propto \frac{1}{X}$
(a) What happens to the value of Y when the value of X is multiplied by 7?
(b) What happens to the value of X when the value of Y is multiplied by 7?
(c) The value of Y is increased by 25%.
What happens to the value of X?

9: TRIGONOMETRY

1 For each of these triangles, find the length of the side marked a, correct to two significant figures

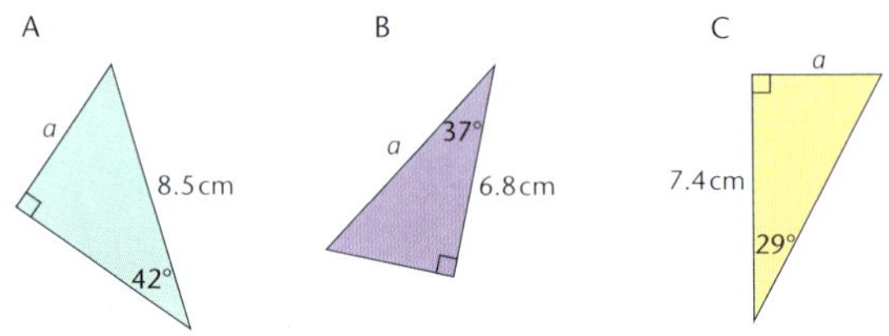

2 For each of these triangles, find the angle marked x, correct to the nearest degree.

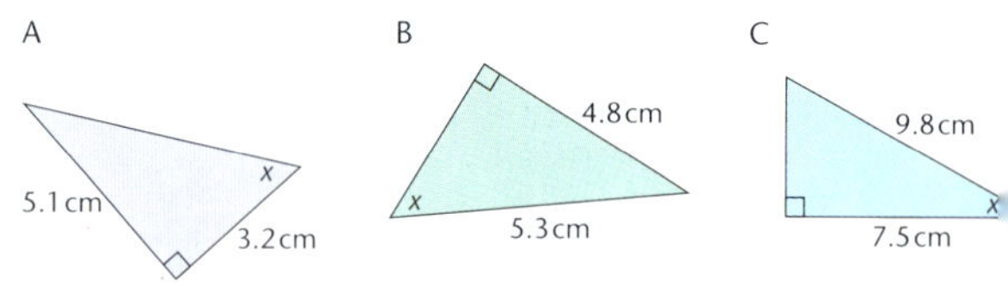

3 An isosceles triangle has a side of length 5cm and a side of length 8cm.
Find the angles of the triangle. (There are two possible answers.)

4 Find the area of this triangle, correct to 3 significant figures.

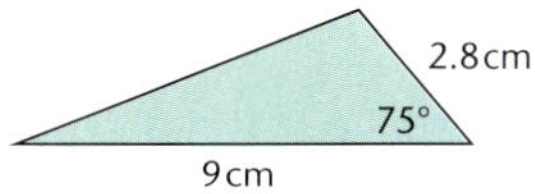

5 Find the lengths p and q, and the angle R in this diagram.

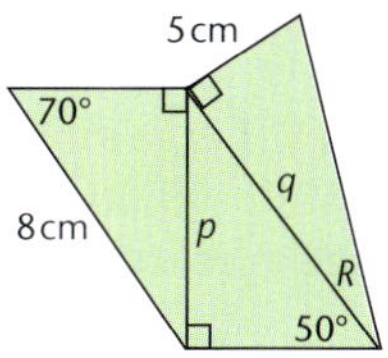

6 A ship, S, is 5 nautical miles from a harbour, H, on a bearing of 290°. A lighthouse, L, is due West of the harbour and due South of the ship.
The ship steers a straight course to the harbour.
What is its closest distance to the lighthouse?

7 A roof has a symmetrical frame, with dimensions as shown.

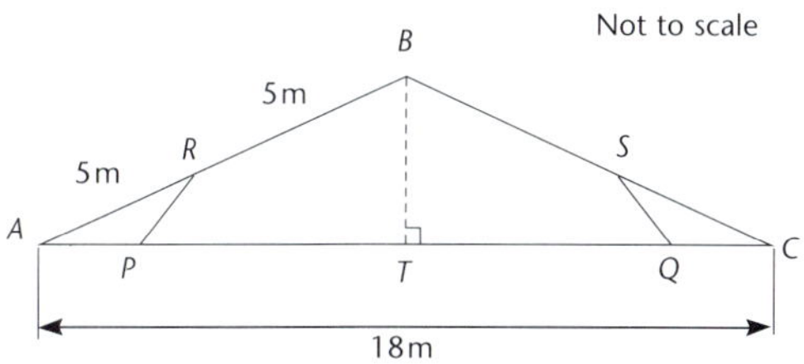

$AB = BC$, $PR = AP$, Angle $ATB = 90°$

(**a**) (**i**) Write down a triangle which is similar to triangle ABC.
(**ii**) Calculate the length PR.
(**b**) Calculate the value of angle BAT.

SEG, 5, Jun 95, No 17

8 $\cos x = \sin 36°$
(**a**) What acute angle x satisfies this equation?
(**b**) What other angle between 0° and 360° satisfies this equation?

9 A pilot is flying a light aircraft. At a particular time, she notes a landmark directly beneath the plane's horizontal flight path which has an angle of depression of 40°. Having travelled a further 200m, at the same height, she then notes the angle of depression is 45°.
What is the aircraft's height above the ground?

SEG 1996

10 A walker on the top of a hill notices four villages on the flat plain beneath. Village A is due South at an angle of depression of 13°. Village B is due East at an angle of depression of 17°. Village C is due North at an angle of depression of 11°. Village D is due West at angle of depression of 22°. The walker knows that villages C and D are 4.5km apart.
What is the distance between villages A and B?

10: PROBABILITY

1 Two tetrahedral dice, each numbered 1 to 4, are rolled. What is the probability that they both land on a 3?

2 Two cubes are taken in succession without replacement from a bag containing 3 white and 4 black cubes.
What is the probability that they are both black?

3 (**a**) Copy and complete this table about a group of students.

	Have their own car	Do not have their own car	Total
Have passed driving test	5		16
Have not passed			
Total		13	30

(**b**) A student is selected at random. Find the probability that
(**i**) the student has his/her own car and has not yet passed the driving test
(**ii**) if the student has his/her own car, he/she has not yet passed the test

4 A fair dice is thrown 30 times and the scores recorded.

Score	1	2	3	4	5	6
Frequency	5	4	4	9	4	4

(**a**) What is the relative frequency of a score of 4?
(**b**) The same dice is thrown a large number of times. What would you expect to happen to the value of this relative frequency?

5 In a bag, there are five red cubes and three green cubes. Two are taken out in succession, with replacement. What is the probability that
(**a**) both are red?
(**b**) they are the same colour?
(**c**) at least one of the cubes is green?

6 In a bag, there are five yellow counters and three green counters.

(a) Three counters are taken in succession, with replacement. What is the probability that at least two are yellow?

(b) Two counters are taken, *without* replacement. What is the probability that

(i) both are yellow?

(ii) they are the same colour?

(iii) there is at least one green counter?

7 In a game, you can 'start' when you throw a six on an ordinary dice. What is the probability of starting on

(a) the first throw?

(b) the second throw?

(c) the fifth throw?

8 A group of 30 students were asked about their work experience placements. Of the 24 who were given tasks for which they were responsible, 8 were not doing office work. Altogether 20 were doing office work. On the basis of this sample, estimate the probability that

(a) a work experience student does office work and is given responsibility for tasks

(b) a work experience student who does office work is given responsibility for tasks

9 Jane's mother says she will let her choose a pudding on her birthday and on the next day. The probability that Jane will choose ice-cream on her birthday is $\frac{7}{10}$.

If Jane chooses ice-cream on her birthday, there is a probability of $\frac{2}{5}$ that she will choose it on the next day.

If Jane does not choose ice-cream on her birthday, there is a probability of $\frac{9}{10}$ that she will choose it on the next day.

(a) Copy and complete the tree diagram to show all the probabilities for each day.

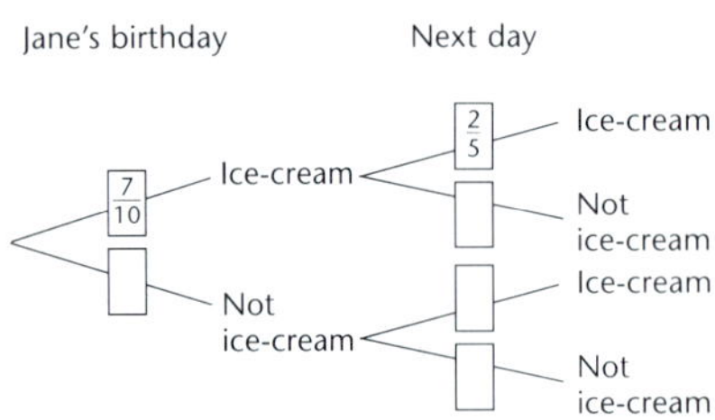

(b) What is the probability that Jane will choose ice-cream on the next day and not on her birthday?

(c) What is the probability that Jane will choose ice-cream on at least one of these two days?

MEG 1996

10 A bag contains two black discs and three white discs.

Three children play a game in which each draws a disc from the bag.

Parveen goes first, then Seema, and Jane is last.

Each time a disc is withdrawn it is not replaced.

The first child to draw a white disc wins the game.

(a) In a game, calculate the probability that

(i) Parveen wins,

(ii) Seema wins.

They replace the discs and play the game a second time.

(b) Calculate the probability that

(i) Parveen wins neither the first nor the second game.

(ii) Jane wins both games.

NEAB 1995

11: GRAPHS

1 Find an equation for the straight line that these points belong to.

(a)

x	−1	2	4
y	−6	12	24

(b)

x	−1	2	4	7
y	3	6	8	11

(c)

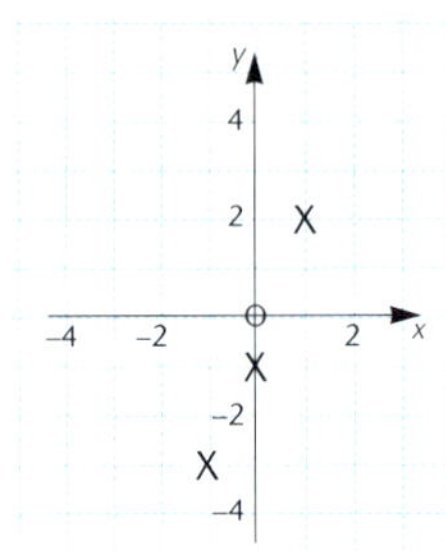

(d)

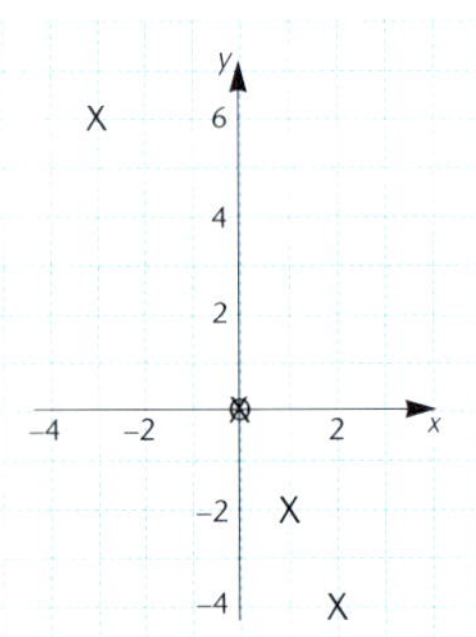

2 (a) Write down the gradient of each of these lines.
   (i) $y = 2x + 4$
   (ii) $y = -3x + 2$
 (b) Write down the coordinates of the points where each of these lines crosses the y-axis.
   (i) $y = 2x + 3$
   (ii) $y = -4x - 6$

3 Draw the graph of $y = 3x + 8$ for x between -3 and 3.

4 (a) Write the equation $2x + y = 5$ in the form $y = \ldots$.
 (b) Write down the gradient of this line.
 (c) What are the coordinates of the point where this line meets the y-axis?

5 Peter left home at 8 a.m. to cycle to his friend's home eight miles away. There was very little traffic so he managed to keep up an average speed of 12 m.p.h. all the way. He stayed for two hours and then set off home, arriving there at 12 noon. Draw a graph of the journey, and find the average speed of his return journey.

6 Rhombus PQRS has the x- and y-axes as lines of symmetry, and the points (0, 6) and (3, 0) as two vertices. Show that the equation for the side through these points is $2x + y = 6$.
Find equations for the other three sides of the rhombus.

7 This sketch shows the graphs of $y = x^2$, $y = x^2 + 4$ and $y = 3 - x^2$.

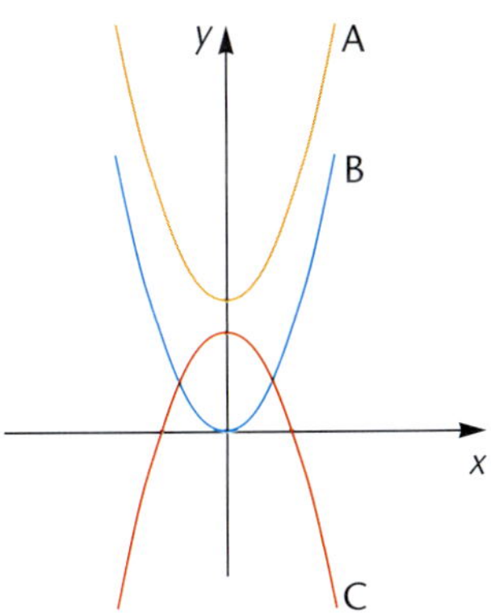

Say which graph is which.

8 Say which graph fits this container:

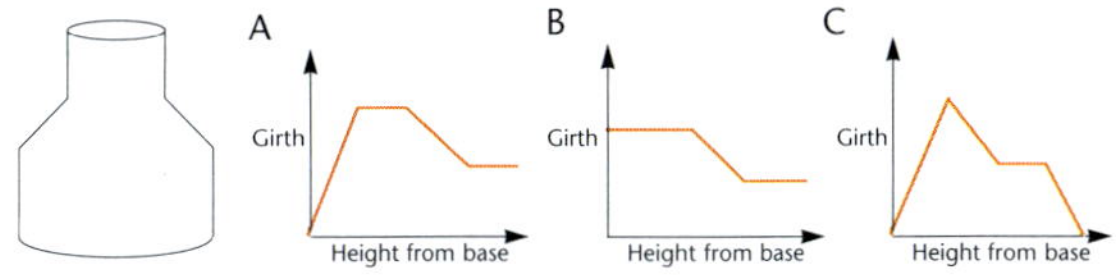

9 (a) Draw the graphs of $y = 2x - 4$ and $y = -x^2$ for values of x from -4 to 4.

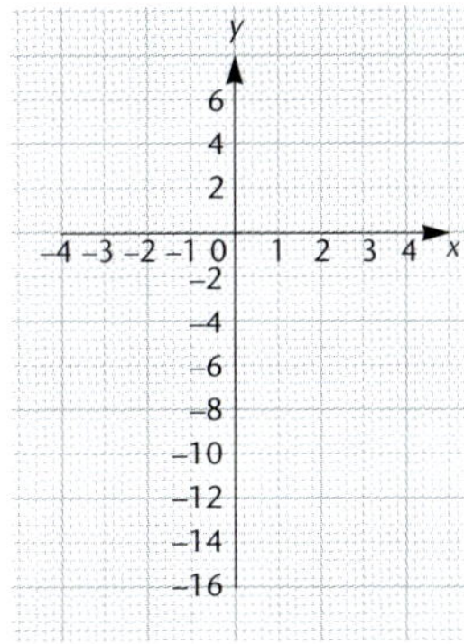

 (b) Use the graphs to find the smallest value of x which gives the same value of y in both equations.

SEG 1996

10 (a) Draw the graph of $y = x^3 - 3x$, for values of x between -3 and 3.
 (b) Use your graph to find the values of x for which $x^3 - 3x$ is negative.

12: MEASURES

1 Which would you expect to cost more?
 (a) 1 litre of car oil, or 1 pint of car oil?
 (b) 2lb onions, or 1kg onions?
 (c) 1oz dried parsley, or 20g dried parsley?
 (d) 1kg bananas, or 2 bananas?
 (e) 250g butter, or half a pound of butter?
 (f) Half a litre of wine, or 75cl of wine?

2 This diagram shows the shape of a flower bed formed from four quarter circles, each of radius 3m.

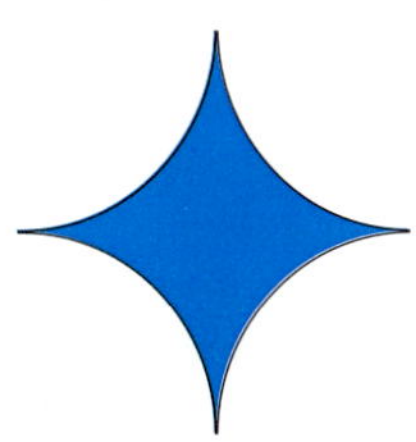

 (a) Calculate the perimeter of the flower bed.
 (b) Calculate the area of the flower bed.

3 This diagram shows the shape and dimensions of a box designed to store computer disks.
What is the volume of the box?

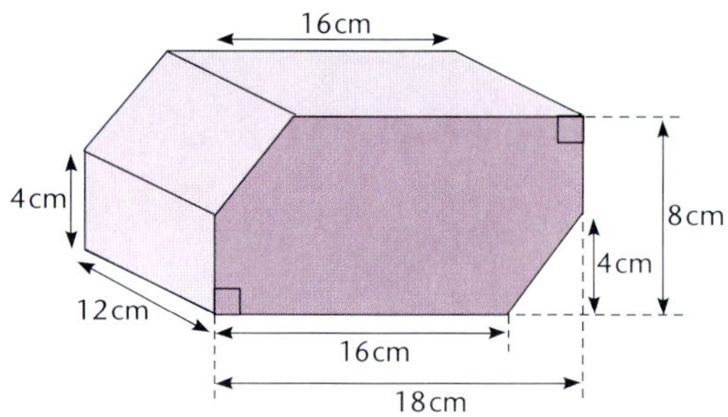

4 The radius of a circle with centre O is 6cm.
A chord AB of length 8cm is drawn in the circle.

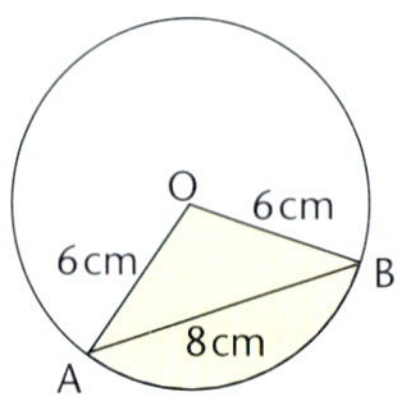

Calculate the area of sector OAB.

5 A runner runs 100m in 12.6 seconds.
The distance is measured correct to the nearest 10cm.
The time is measured correct to the nearest 0.1 seconds.
What are the upper and lower bounds for the speed of the runner?

6 A pyramid has a square base with edges of length 4cm, and its other four edges are each of length 6cm.

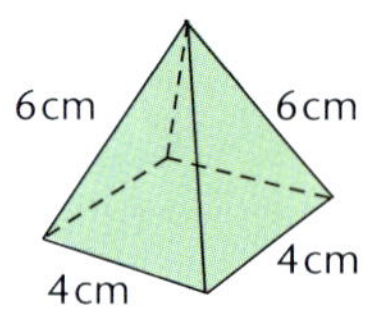

Find the volume of the pyramid.

7 Two containers of washing-up liquid are similar.
The smaller container holds 250g of liquid and the larger one 500g of liquid.
The height of the smaller container is 14cm.
Calculate the height of the larger container.

8 The volume of a square-based block is given by $V = a^2h$.

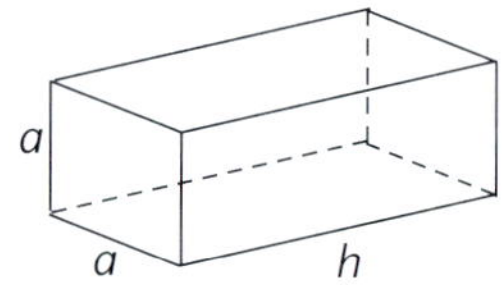

Not to scale

(a) In an experiment, the length, a, and height, h, are measured as 4cm and 11cm respectively, each measured to the nearest cm.
What are the maximum and minimum possible values of V in cm^3?

(b) In another experiment, the volume of the block is found to be 350cm^3, measured to the nearest 50cm^3, and its height is measured as 13.5cm, to the nearest 0.5cm.
(i) What are the maximum and minimum possible values of the length, a, in centimetres?
(ii) How many significant figures should be used to give a reliable answer for the value of a?

SEG 1996

9 In these formulae, r and h represent lengths, A represents an area and V represents a volume. State whether each formula represents a length, an area or a volume.

(a) $\frac{1}{3}Ah$ (b) $A - 2\pi rh$ (c) $\frac{V}{\pi R^2}$

(d) $\pi r\sqrt{(h^2 + r^2)}$ (e) $\sqrt[3]{\left(\frac{3V}{4\pi}\right)}$

10 A home-made lampshade is made from a circle of heat-resistant parchment. The radius of the circle is 30cm. A sector of angle 60° is cut away as shown, then the edges OA, OB are joined.

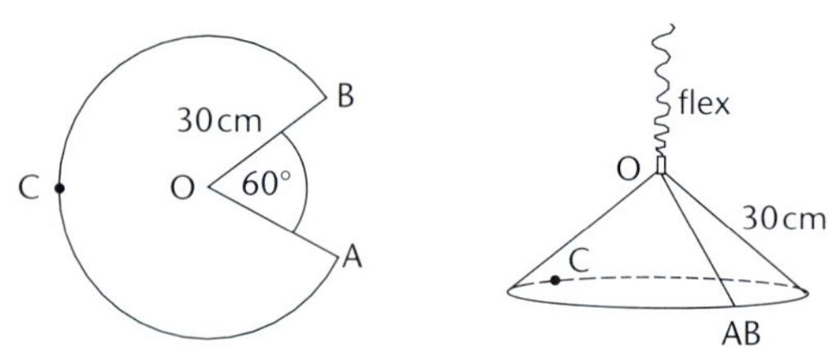

(a) Calculate the length of the arc ACB of the parchment.
(b) Show by calculation that the radius of the circular base of the lampshade is 25cm.
(c) Calculate the distance of the circular base below the vertex O.

MEG 1996

13: EQUATIONS

1 Solve these equations.
(a) $3(3x + 2) - 2(x - 3) = x + 6$
(b) $4(2x - 7) - 3(3x - 5) = 5x - 9$

2 Solve these equations.

(a) $\frac{2(x + 2)}{5} - 1 = \frac{x - 3}{2}$

(b) $\frac{2x - 3}{5} + \frac{2x + 3}{5} = \frac{3x - 2}{3}$

3 Solve these equations.
(a) $5x - y = 7$, $x + y = 2$
(b) $2a + 3b = 23$, $3a + 2b = 27$

4 I sold 50 tickets for a school concert and collected £233. Some tickets cost £5, and some cost £4. Use simultaneous equations to find how many of each were sold.

5 Solve these equations.
(a) $x^2 - x - 12 = 0$
(b) $x^2 + x - 12 = 0$
(c) $x^2 - 4x - 12 = 0$
(d) $12 = 11x + x^2$

6 Solve these equations.
(a) $x^2 + 3x = 10$
(b) $x^2 - 4x + 8 = 2x + 3$

7 (a) Draw the graph of $y = x^3 - 3x + 1$ for $-3 \le x \le 3$.
(b) Use it to solve the equation $x^3 - 3x = 2$.
(c) Draw the graph of $y = x + 1$, on the same axes, to solve the equation $x^3 - 4x = 0$.
(d) Use the method of trial and improvement to solve the equation $x^3 - 3x + 1 = 10$, correct to 2 decimal places.

8 Use the method of trial and improvement to find the positive solution of the equation $x^2 + 4x - 3 = 0$, correct to 2 decimal places.

9 This is the graph of $y = x^3 - 5x - 2$.

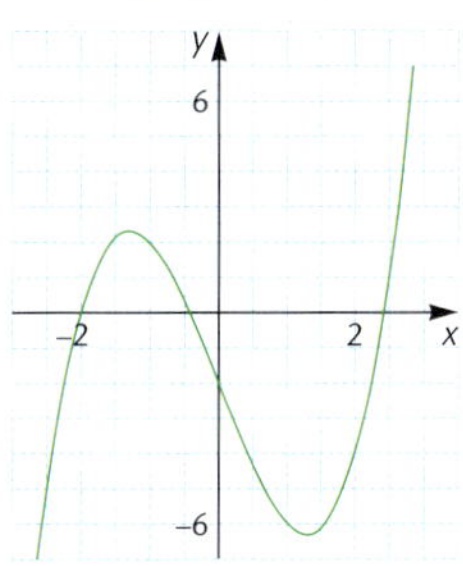

(a) Use it to solve the equation $x^3 - 5x - 2 = 0$.
(b) How many solutions are there to $x^3 - 5x = 4$?
(c) Use the graph to estimate the positive solution to $x^3 - 5x = 4$.
Then use trial and improvement to find this solution, correct to 2 decimal places.

10 x is a number such that $x(x + 1)(x - 1) = 20$.
(a) Find the two consecutive numbers between which x must lie.
(b) Use the method of trial and improvement to find the solution correct to 3 significant figures.

NEAB 1995

14: GEOMETRY

1 Which of these are nets of a triangular prism?

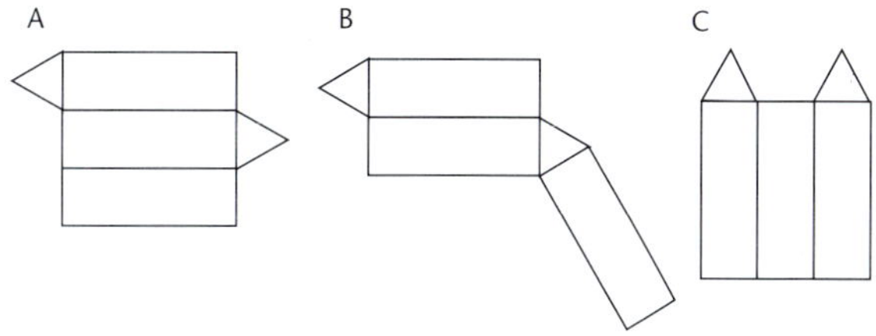

2 Describe a solid which has five faces if
(a) four of the faces are identical and one is different
(b) three of the faces are identical and the other two are different, but identical to each other
(c) three of the faces are identical, and the other two are different and different from each other
(d) two pairs of faces are identical and the fifth face is different

3 ABCD is a kite, with AB = AD and CB = CD. ∠BAD = 50° and ∠BCD = 100°.

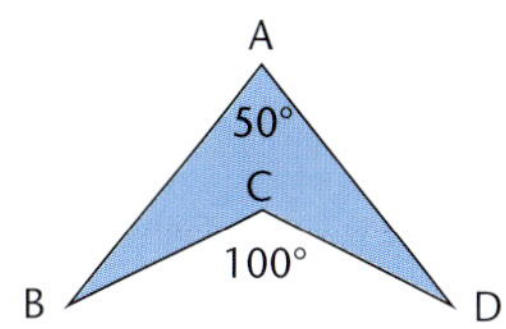

(a) Make a sketch of the kite and draw its line of symmetry, extending it outside the kite.
(b) Find ∠ABC and ∠ADC, in the kite.
(c) Prove that the length of the internal diagonal of the kite is equal to the length of two of the sides of the kite.

4 (a) Draw accurately a triangle ABC in which BC is 8 cm, AC is 4 cm and AB is 7 cm.
(b) On your triangle
(i) draw the locus of a point which is the same distance from A as it is from B
(ii) draw the locus of a point which is 4.5 cm from C
(c) There are two points that are both 4.5 cm from C and the same distance from A as from B. Mark these two points.

5 For each part of this question, you will need to copy this picture.

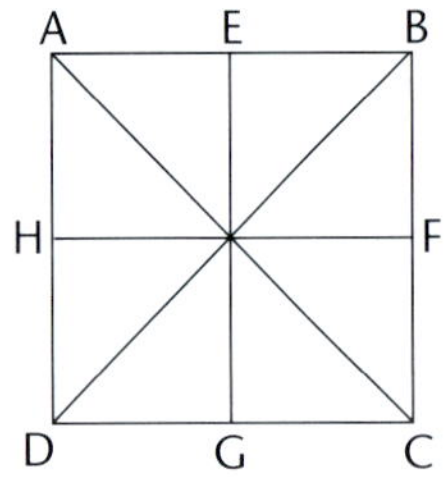

(**a**) P is a point in the square which is closer to H than F. Shade the region in which P must lie.

(**b**) P is a point in the square which is closer to H than F and closer to D than B.
Shade the region in which P must lie.

(**c**) P is a point in the square which is closer to line DB than it is to line AC.
Shade the region in which P must lie.

(**d**) P is a point in the square which is closer to B than it is to D, and closer to E than it is to G.
Shade the region in which P must lie.

6 Imagine this rectangle being toppled along a line, so that it rotates about each vertex in turn.

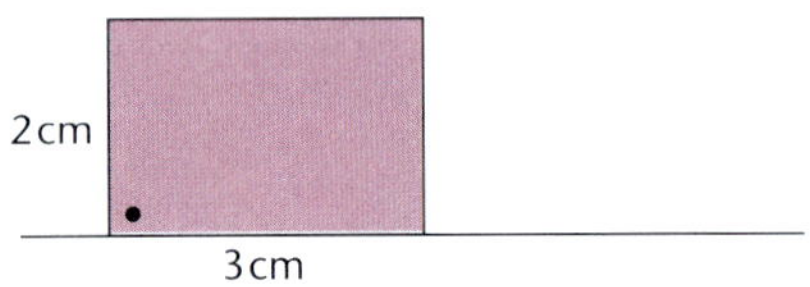

(**a**) Draw accurately each position of the rectangle in which one of its sides lies along the line.
Do this until the corner marked with a dot again becomes the bottom left-hand corner of the rectangle.

(**b**) Draw accurately the locus of the corner marked with a dot.

7 O is the centre of this circle.

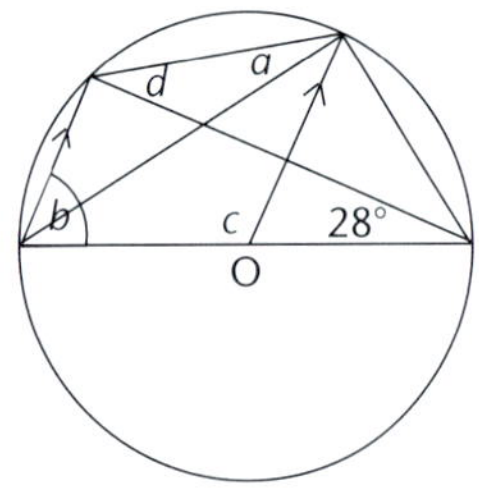

Find the angles marked *a*, *b*, *c* and *d*.

8 Draw accurately a triangle with angles of 55°, 60° and 65°, whose vertices lie on a circle of radius 5cm.

9

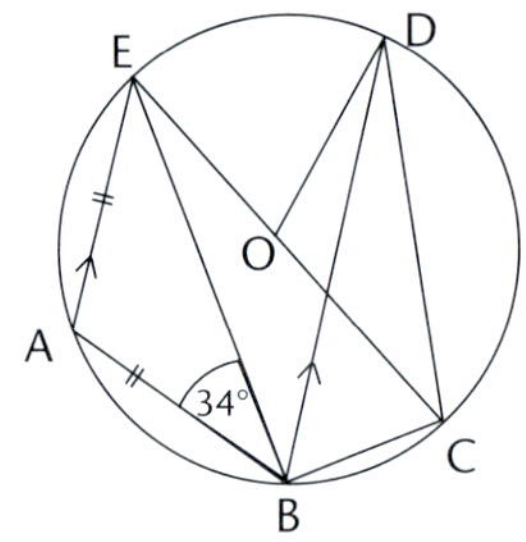

This diagram is not accurate

O is the centre and EC is a diameter of the circle.
AB = AE and AE is parallel to BD.
Angle ABE = 34°.
Calculate the size of

(**a**) angle BAE, (**b**) angle BCE,
(**c**) angle BEC, (**d**) angle DBE,
(**e**) angle EOD, (**f**) angle ODB.

CCEA 1996

10 You may use graph paper for this question.
A region of land, 50km square, has a radio transmitter, *T*, at one corner.
Transmitters send out radio signals which can be received within a circle of radius 30km.
With this arrangement some of the square does not receive radio signals.

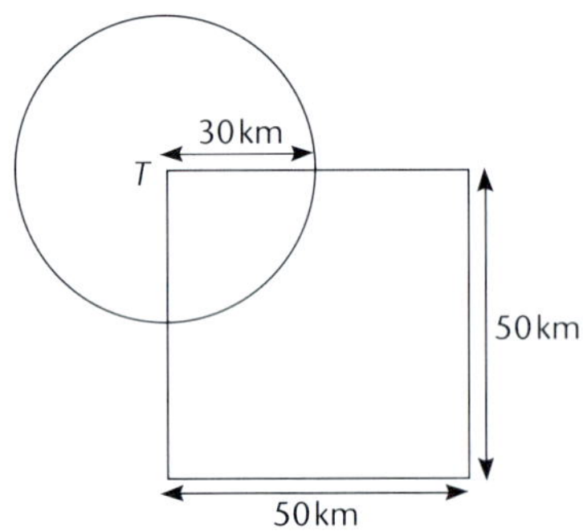

NOT TO SCALE

(**a**) It is possible for each part of the square to receive radio signals when **two** transmitters are used.
Draw a scale diagram of the square.
Label a possible position for each of the two transmitters, T_1 and T_2 and show the region covered by the radio signals from the two transmitters.

(**b**) The area of a square, with side 50km, is 2500km^2.
The area of a circle, radius 30km, is 2827km^2.
Explain why it is not possible for one transmitter alone to transmit to all parts of the square.

MEG 1996

SELECTED ANSWERS

4: WORKING WITH DATA

Exercise 4 Page 60

1 (a) 13.9
(b) On this evidence, the boy is more consistent

2 (a) A: Mean = 14.8, SD = 2.3
B: Mean = 115, SD = 47
C: Mean = 75.6, SD = 3.7
(b) Because the means are substantially different

3 Mean 2.63, SD = 2.2

4 (a) Mean = 14.25, SD = 1.56
(b) (i) Mean = 24.25, SD = 1.56 (ii) Mean = 4.25, SD = 1.56
(iii) Mean = 264.25, SD = 1.56 (iv) Mean = 28.5, SD = 3.34
(v) Mean = 1425, SD = 1.56 (vi) Mean = 3.56, SD = 0.39

5 (a) Mean = 4.4, SD = 2.1 (b) Mean = 4.1, SD = 1.5
(c) On this evidence, the first sentence

6 (a) E.g. 0, 0, 0, 10, 10, 10 with standard deviation 5
(b) E.g. 0, 5, 5, 5, 5, 10 with standard deviation 2.9

Exercise 5 page 62

2

	Mean	SD
First run (£million)	119.92	76.5
Adjusted figures 1996	437.7	303.8

The mean is much higher for the predicted 1996 figures because they have taken inflation into account.

Exercise 7 page 67

1 The mean height of beech trees is 6.5m
The mean height of oak trees is 7.6m

2 £98.05

3 50 marks

6 (a) Missing numbers are 8, 21, 76, 39 (b) 104 minutes

7 (a)

Distance travelled (d metres)	Frequency
$0 \le d < 100$	8
$100 \le d < 500$	28
$500 \le d < 1500$	35
$1500 \le d < 3000$	9

(b) 800m

8 (a) Frequency densities for histogram: 6.8, 23.6, 20.3, 11.6, 3.7, 2, 1.3, 0.4, 0.1
(b) Mean is about £29
(c) Median is about £20
(d) The mean is higher because a few customers spent substantially more than the rest. The mean gives a good estimate of how much the supermarket can take from a given number of customers. The median gives a good estimate of how much a 'typical' customer spends.
(e) The IRQ is about £30

9 (a) The number of pins in boxes which have fewer than 100 pins
(c) Actual mean = 99.64, actual SD = 9.1
(d) The mean becomes 99.94, and the SD = 8.4
Little change to the mean because of the large number of results

10 (a) Type A: median is a little over 2 hours; IQR is a little over 1 hour
Type B: median is about 2 hours; IQR is under 1 hour
(b) The medians are not very different, given the size of the IQRs. Type A varies a little more than Type B.
(c) Type A mean is about 2 hours 13 minutes
Type B mean is about 2 hours 4 minutes
The means are perhaps not significantly different, given the size of the IQRs
Means and medians are similar

5: PYTHAGORAS' THEOREM AND SIMILAR SHAPES

Exercise 2 page 76

1 5.6m

2 23cm

3 (a) 13.2cm (b) 33.3cm

4 (a) 41m and 70m (b) 228m

Exercise 3 page 77

1 9.85cm

2 A: 5.66cm B: 11.4cm C: 12.2cm D: 8.12cm

3 42.4cm

4 $\sqrt{7}$cm = 2.65cm

5 13.6cm^2

6 A: Height is 6.2cm; area is 13cm^2
B: 19.5cm^2
C: 5.12cm^2

7 (a) 39.8cm^2 (b) 25.7cm

8 7.3cm or 7.4cm

6: PERCENTAGES

Exercise 2 page 95

1 Using VAT at 17.5%
Garage: £18.38, £123.38
Plumber: £13.65, £91.65
Builder: £46.38, £311.38

2 (a) 6.25% (b) 25% (c) 40% (d) $6\frac{2}{3}$%
(e) $6\frac{2}{3}$% (f) $116\frac{2}{3}$%

3 A: 20.8% B: 13.9% C: –20%

4 Television: 22.6% reduction
Freezer: 23.6% reduction
Cooker: 24.2% reduction

5 26.9% profit

6 48%

Exercise 4 page 98

1 (a) £25 (b) £75 (c) £37.50 (d) £87
(e) £263.89 (f) 9p

2 (a) £50 (b) £80 (c) £210 (d) £9
(e) £5 (f) 20p

3 480ml

4 442ml

5 50% would be an increase on 189ml. This is close to 184ml, and so the offer is not misleading. Also, any inaccuracy is in the customer's favour.

6 (a)

RDA	Thiamin (mg)	Riboflavin (mg)	Niacin (mg)	Folacin (μg)
From 100g data	1.4	1.6	18	200
From 37.5g data	1.3	1.5	17.8	199.4

(b) Results not consistent because working with rounded off data

Exercise 5 page 99

1 17.4% reduction

2 $2000 \times 1.18^5 = 4575$
So, during fifth year, the population doubles

3 (a) £1228.40 (b) £1508.96

4 £14800

5 £16600

6 $500000 \times 1.07^n > 1000000$ when $n = 11$ so it takes 11 years

7 (a) £3544.68 (b) 18.2%

8: RATIO, RATE AND PROPORTION

Exercise 2 page 120

1 (a) £1.80 per hour (b) £5.40

2 (a) £24 (b) 320 hems

3 27 minutes

4 40m^2

5 (a) \$271.50 (b) £0.55 (c) The UK student

6 (a) 5g (b) 2.58kg

7 60 m.p.h.

8 75 miles

9 (a) 8 minutes 20 secs to walk; 16 minutes 40 secs to swim
(b) Walk 3.6km; swim 1.8km

10 1kg

11 2.63cm^3

12 7.8gcm^{-3}

13 550g

14 (a) 227.5 miles in town, 297.5 miles on motorway
(b) 94.1 litres (3 tanks full)

15 (a) 69.7 m.p.h., 42.6 m.p.h., 60 m.p.h., 17.1 m.p.h.
(b) 54m.p.h.

16 (a) 1.6km
(b) 0.625 miles
(c) 48 k.p.h, 80 k.p.h and 112 k.p.h.
(d) 75 m.p.h.
(e) 13.3ms^{-1}
(f) 10ms^{-1} = 22.5 m.p.h.

17 8 minutes 20 seconds

18 (a) Volume of Earth: 1.082×10^{24} m^3
Volume of Moon: 2.20×10^{24} m^3
(b) 1:49

9: TRIGONOMETRY

Exercise 4 page 141

1 A: a = 2.65cm B: a = 4.28cm C: a = 5.89cm
D: a = 1.55cm E: a = 5.28cm F: a = 66.3mm
G: a = 582mm H: a = 59.9mm I: a = 7.80cm
J: a = 64.9mm

2 A: 19.7cm B: 15.5cm C: 42.4cm D: 21.4cm

3 (a) 25.2cm and 45.4cm (b) 35.2cm and 75.5cm

Exercise 5 page 143

1 A: x = 26° B: x = 50° C: x = 44° D: x = 19°
E: x = 65° F: x = 45° G: x = 36° H: x = 21°

2 A: 84°, 48°, 48°
B: 78°, 78°, 23°
C: 122°, 29°, 29°

3 (a) 73.7°, 106.3°, 73.7°, 106.3°
(b) 66.4°, 66.4°, 113.6°, 113.6°

Exercise 6 page 144

1 23m

2 36m

3 1.4m

4 142°

5 13m

6 13°

7 8.3m

8 (a) 1140m (b) 2340m

9 (a) 760m (b) 690m

10 (a) 91cm (b) 65.2cm (c) 88.0cm (d) 37.5cm

11 (a) 18.4 miles (b) 336° (c) 5.37 miles

12 27°, 22°, 15°, 15°

13 6700m (2 s.f.)

14 81m

Exercise 7 page 146

1 51.3°, 51.3°, 77.4° and 66.4°, 66.4°, 47.2°

2 118.8°, 52.8°, 118.8°, 69.7°

3 (a) 128.57°
(b) 128.57° (four), 25.71° (four), 51.43° (four), 77.14°
(c) 7.21 cm, 7.21 cm, 8.99 cm
(d) 6.25 cm² (two), 25.4 cm²
(e) 20.3 cm²
(f) 58.3 cm²

4 (a) 140°
(b) 18.8 cm (two), 28.8 cm (two)
(c) 32.1 cm² (two), 173.9 cm², 141.8 cm²
(d) 618 cm²

5 (a) 38.8 cm; 991 cm² (b) 115 cm

6 (a) $x\sin 50°$ cm and $x\cos 50°$ cm
(b) 8.3 cm, 5.3 cm, 6.4 cm
(c) 17.0 cm²

7 107 cm² and 118 cm²

8 9.08 cm, 9.08 cm, 14.3 cm

9 (a) (i) 26.6 cm (ii) Impossible
(b) 20.569 cm; isosceles triangle

10: PROBABILITY

Exercise 4 page 165

1 (a) $\frac{4}{16}$ (b) $\frac{8}{16}$ (c) $\frac{8}{16}$ (d) $\frac{4}{16}$

2 (b) (i) $\frac{15}{36}$ (ii) $\frac{8}{36}$ (iii) $\frac{4}{36}$ (iv) $\frac{4}{8}$
(v) $\frac{4}{15}$ (vi) $\frac{19}{36}$
(c) $\frac{1}{3}$

3 (b) (i) $\frac{5}{9}$ (ii) $\frac{3}{9}$ (iii) $\frac{1}{9}$ (iv) $\frac{7}{9}$
(v) $\frac{1}{5}$ (vi) $\frac{1}{3}$ (vii) $\frac{1}{3}$ (viii) $\frac{3}{3}$ or 1

4 (a) $\frac{6}{20}$ (b) $\frac{12}{20}$

5 (a) $\frac{1}{16}$ (b) $\frac{1}{4}$ (c) $\frac{7}{16}$

6 (a) $\frac{4}{16}$ (b) $\frac{8}{16}$ (c) $\frac{8}{16}$ (d) $\frac{4}{8}$
(e) $\frac{4}{8}$ (f) $\frac{4}{16}$ (g) $\frac{12}{16}$ (h) $\frac{8}{16}$

7 (a) $\frac{9}{25}$ (b) $\frac{15}{25}$ (c) $\frac{15}{25}$ (d) $\frac{9}{15}$
(e) $\frac{6}{15}$ (f) $\frac{6}{25}$ (g) $\frac{19}{25}$ (h) $\frac{13}{25}$

Exercise 5 page 168

1 (a) $\frac{4}{25}$ (b) $\frac{16}{25}$

2 (a) $\frac{3}{16}$ (b) $\frac{3}{128}$

3 (a) (i) $\frac{7}{50}$ (ii) $\frac{1}{5}$
(b) (i) $\frac{7}{200}$ (ii) $\frac{21}{100}$

4 (a) $\frac{1}{8}$ (b) $\frac{1}{4}$ (c) $\frac{6}{169}$

Exercise 6 page 170

1 (a) $\frac{17}{25}$ (b) $\frac{8}{25}$

2 (a) $\frac{3}{25}$ (b) $\frac{31}{50}$ (c) $\frac{3}{4}$

3 (a) $\frac{1}{2}$ (b) $\frac{1}{4}$ (c) $\frac{100}{169}$ (d) $\frac{7}{16}$

4 (a) (i) 0.36 (ii) 0.48
(b) 0.28

5 (a) 0.54 (b) 0.46
A is more likely to win

Exercise 7 page 171

1 (b) (i) $\frac{29}{49}$ (ii) $\frac{20}{49}$

2 (a) $\frac{1}{8}$ (b) $\frac{3}{8}$ (c) $\frac{1}{2}$

3 (a) $\frac{6}{25}$ (b) $\frac{17}{25}$

4 (a) $\frac{9}{169}$ (b) $\frac{69}{169}$

5 (b) $\frac{36}{169}$ (c) $\frac{61}{169}$ (d) $\frac{57}{169}$

6 $\frac{7}{36}$

7 (b) (i) 0.216 (ii) 0.28 (iii) 0.936 (iv) 0.288

8 (a) $\frac{1}{216}$ (b) $\frac{125}{216}$ (c) $\frac{91}{216}$ (d) $\frac{15}{216}$

9 (a) $4 \times \left(\frac{1}{6}\right)^3 \times \frac{5}{6} = \frac{5}{324}$
(b) $5 \times \left(\frac{1}{6}\right)^4 \times \frac{5}{6} = \frac{25}{7776}$

10 (a) $\frac{25}{64}$ (b) $\frac{30}{64}$ (c) $\frac{27}{512}$ (d) $3 \times \left(\frac{5}{8}\right)^2 \times \frac{3}{8} = \frac{215}{512}$
(e) $n \times \left(\frac{5}{8}\right)^{n-1} \times \frac{3}{8}$

Exercise 8 page 174

1 (a)

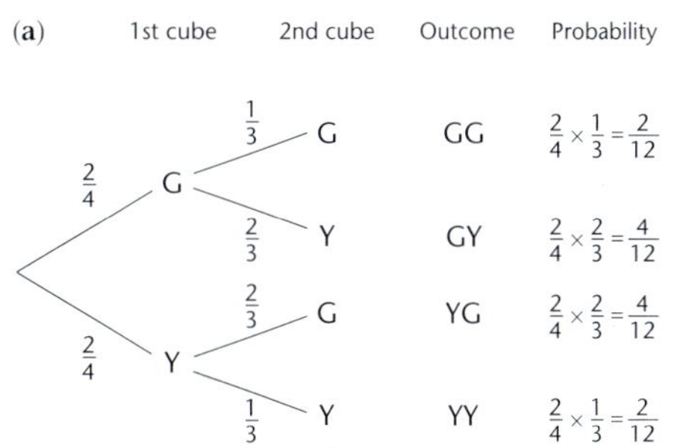

(b) (i) $\frac{1}{6}$ (ii) $\frac{1}{3}$ (iii) $\frac{1}{3}$ (iv) $\frac{2}{3}$

2 (b) (i) $\frac{1}{3}$ (ii) $\frac{7}{15}$ (iii) $\frac{39}{45}$ (iv) $\frac{39}{45}$
(v) $\frac{2}{15}$

3 P(same colour) = $\frac{26}{56}$.
P(one of each colour) = $\frac{30}{56}$ and is larger

4 (a) (i) $\frac{m(m-1)}{(m+n)(m+n-1)}$ (ii) $\frac{m(m-1)+n(n-1)}{(m+n)(m+n-1)}$

(iii) $\frac{2mn}{(m+n)(m+n-1)}$

(b) No, it is not possible. For example $m = 4$, $n = 5$ gives a greater probability of drawing different colours; $m = 6$, $n = 3$ gives equal probabilities; $m = 8$, $n = 2$ gives greater probability of drawing the same colour. (In fact, equal probabilities occur if m and n are consecutive triangular numbers.)

5 (a) $\frac{5}{468}$ (b) $\frac{5}{468}$

6 (a) $\frac{1}{840} = 0.0012$ (b) $\frac{1}{151200} = 6.6 \times 10^{-6}$

7 (a) $\frac{25}{102}$ (b) $\frac{1}{221}$ (c) $\frac{4}{17}$

8 (a) $\frac{11}{850}$ (b) $\frac{117}{850}$ (c) $\frac{169}{425}$

9 $\frac{11}{42}$

10 (a) (i) 4.25×10^{-4} (ii) 9.05×10^{-6}
(iii) 8.5×10^{-4} (iv) 5.43×10^{-4}
(b) 7.15×10^{-8}

Exercise 9 Page 176

1 No, because it is likely that the events are not independent

2 (a) 10^{-12}
(b) No! If you take a bomb on a plane with you the probability of having one bomb on the plane is 1!

3 (a) 0.16 (b) 0.064 (c) 0.288 (d) 0.0768

4 (a) (i) 0.419 (ii) 0.815
(b) For 20 throws, these become 1.98×10^{-4} and almost 1

5 (a) (i) 4.54×10^{-8} (ii) 0.841 (iii) 0.148
(b) So unlikely that one would suspect the quality of the consignment

6 (a) $0.68 + (0.32 \times 0.35) = 0.792$
(b) (i) 0.0374 (ii) 0.829

7 (a) $\frac{1}{4}$
(b) (i) $\frac{9}{64}$ (ii) $\frac{37}{64}$

12: MEASURES

Exercise 3 Page 204

1 A: 89.3 cm² B: 320 cm² C: 151 cm² D: 351 cm²
E: 60 cm² F: 84 cm²

2 676 cm²

3 (a) 625 cm² (b) 525 cm² (c) 796 cm² (d) 600 cm²
(e) 594 cm²

Exercise 4 Page 205

1 (a) 9460 cm² (b) 223 cm

2 A: 21.4 cm² B: 6 cm² C: 117 cm²

3 A: 20.1 cm B: 9.80 cm C: 45.3 cm

4 9.5 cm²

5 A: 26.1 cm² B: 15.5 cm² C: 253 cm²

6 98.7°

7 17.1 cm

Exercise 5 Page 206

1 2 cm is measured to nearest centimetre; bounds are 1.5 cm and 2.5 cm; 2.0 cm is measured to the nearest 0.1 cm; bounds are 1.95 cm and 2.05 cm

2 (a) 94.5 s, 95.5 s (b) 99.95 m, 100.05 m
(c) $1.05\,\text{m s}^{-1}$ (bounds are $1.0466\,\text{m s}^{-1}$ and $1.0587\,\text{m s}^{-1}$)

3 67.69 s implies a world record of between 67.685 and 67.695 seconds; 68 s implies the boy's time is between 67.5 and 68.5 seconds; $67.5 < 67.685 < 67.695 < 68.5$; therefore it is possible that the boy beat the record but not certain

4 (a) 1.45 cm, 1.55 cm (b) 2.9 cm, 3.1 cm
(c) 9.11 cm, 9.74 cm (d) 6.61 cm², 7.55 cm²

5 (a) 104 cm, 108 cm (b) 619.75 cm², 672.75 cm²

6 210 g, 220 g

7 (a) 164 986.25 cm², 165 806.25 cm²
(b) 118 152.75, 118 847.75 cm²
(c) 46 138.5, 47 653.5 cm² (assuming all measurements are accurate to the nearest 1 cm!)

8 1827 cm³, 1950 cm³

9 17.66 cm, 18.11 cm

10 (a) 68 m.p.h. (b) 57.6 m.p.h.

11 Using the given data, the constant speed of both boats appears to be $75\,\text{cm s}^{-1}$
The constant speed for boat A is between $71.935\,\text{cm s}^{-1}$ and $77.586\,\text{cm s}^{-1}$, and for boat B, between $69.697\,\text{cm s}^{-1}$ and $80.645\,\text{cm s}^{-1}$

12 (a) 55 k.p.h., 66 k.p.h. (b) Speeding

13 14.7 km

14 1.11 k.p.h. (or $0.30788\,\text{m s}^{-1}$)

15 57.84 cm², 70.78 cm²

Exercise 6 Page 209

1 20 cm

2 (a) 2700 litres
(b) 2800 gallons or 12 000 litres

3 A: 158 cm² B: 216 cm² C: 207.35 cm² D: 311 cm²
E: 336 cm²

4 0.08 mm

5 12.27 litres

6 (a) 1.51 cm² (b) 8.2 cm²

7 (a) 980 cm³
(b) Not necessarily, because area of label is $A = 2\pi rh$ and volume is $\pi r^2 h = \frac{Ar}{2}$
Two tins can have the same area of label but a different radius

8 7 cm

9 (a) 4.75 m³ = 4750 litres (b) 11.8 m³ = 11 800 litres

10 $\pi:(\sqrt[3]{2\pi})^2$ or 0.923:1

Exercise 7 Page 212

1 (a) 11494cm^3 (b) 10300cm^3, 12800cm^3

2 2500000m^3, 2700000m^3

3 (a) 7.1cm^3 (b) 12mm

4 (a) 0.89gcm^{-3} (b) 375g

5 (a) Both equal to $144\pi\text{cm}^2$ or 452cm^2
(b) Both are $4\pi x^2$

6 2.5cm

7 (a) 41610cm^3 (b) 59000cm^3

8 (a) 31.7cm^3 or 31.7ml (b) 41mm

9 12mm

10 $2r$

11 (a) $\frac{1}{6}x^3$ (b) $\frac{1}{3}x^3$ (c) $\frac{\sqrt{3}}{2}x^2$
(d) $\frac{2x}{\sqrt{3}}$ or $1.16x$

12 $\frac{5}{6}$

13 $\frac{\sqrt{2}}{3}x^3$

14 (a) 477mm (b) 2110cm^3 (c) 1.15 litres
(d) 0.46gcm^{-3} (e) 66g (f) 8 scoops

15 Height of cylinder = $\frac{2}{3}r$
Height of cone = $2r$
S.A. of hemisphere = $3\pi r^2$
S.A. of cylinder = $\frac{10}{3}\pi r^2$
S.A. of cone = $(1 + \sqrt{5})\pi r^2$
Ratio is $3 : \frac{10}{3} : 1 + \sqrt{5}$

Exercise 8 Page 215

1 (a) 34.9cm (b) 5.6cm (c) 15.0cm (d) 492.6cm^3

2 (a) 134cm^2
(b) Radius = 2.67cm; height = 15.8cm
(c) 118.0cm^3

3 (a) 33.4cm (b) 71% (c) 1000cm^2

4 88.9cm^2

5 (a) 40cm^3 (b) 43.9cm^2

Exercise 9 Page 217

1 (a) 630cm^3, 502cm^2 (b) 9.84cm^3, 31.4cm^2

2 8 small cylinders

3 (a) 2:3 (b) 2:3 (c) 113.1cm^2 (d) 254.5cm^2
(e) 2.5 litres

4 10.8cm

5 (a) 75ml (b) 2:3 (c) 18.3cm

6 £1.25 melon is the better buy

7 1200g

8 (a) 125% (b) 237.5%

9 16.4cm

10 (b) $\frac{\pi d^2 h}{768}$ (c) $\frac{\pi d^2 h}{12} - \frac{\pi d^2 h}{768}$

13: EQUATIONS

Exercise 12 page 235

1 $x = \pm 4.47$

2 $y = 15$, $x = \pm 3.87$

3 $y = 8$, $x = \pm 2.83$

4 The line $y = -4$ does not cross $y = x^2$, so there are no solutions

5 (b) $x = -1$, $x = 3$ (c) $x = -1$, $x = 3$

6 (a) $x = 1$, $x = 3$ (b) $x = 1$, $x = 3$

7 (a) $x = -3.7$, $x = 2.7$
(b) $x = -3.7$, $x = 2.7$

8 (a) $y = 6 - x$ (b) $x = -3$, $x = 2$

9 (a) $y = 12 - 2x$ (b) $x = -2.6$, $x = 4.6$

10 (a) $y = 3x - 1$
(b) $x = 0.4$, $x = 2.6$

11 (a) $y = 6 - 1\frac{1}{2}x$ (b) $x = -3.3$, $x = 1.8$

Exercise 13 page 237

1 (a) $x = -2$, $x = 0$ (b) $x = -4$, $x = 2$ (c) $x = -3$, $x = 1$
(d) $x = -3.83$, $x = 1.83$ (e) No solutions (f) $x = -1$

2 (a) $x = -3.56$, $x = 0.56$ (b) $x = -3$, $x = 0$
(c) $x = -5$, $x = 2$ (d) $x = -2.62$, $x = -0.38$
(e) $x = -2$, $x = -1$ (f) $x = 0.3$, $x = -3.3$

3 (a) $x = -0.3$, $x = 3.3$ (b) $x = 0$, $x = 3$ (c) $x = -1.2$, $x = 4.2$

Exercise 14 page 237

1 (a) $x = 0$, $x = -1$ (b) $x = 3.6$, $x = 0.6$
(c) $x = -0.8$, $x = 3.8$ (d) $x = -3.3$, $x = 0.3$

2 (a) $x = 2.7$, $x = 0.7$ (b) $x = -3.4$, $x = 1.4$
(c) $x = -4.4$, $x = 0.4$ (d) $x = -1.6$, $x = 0.6$

3 (a) $x = -1$, $x = 1.5$ (b) $x = 0$, $x = 0.5$ (c) $x = -0.5$, $x = 2$

4 (a) $x = 0.4$, $x = 2.6$
(b) No solutions
(c) $x = -1.2$, $x = 5.2$
(d) $x = -2.6$, $x = -1.6$

INDEX